Jesus versus Yhwh

PETER GILLIES

versus Jesus
YHWH

A spirited and sometimes freewheeling commentary on
The Gospel of Jesus of Nazareth
& the Son of Man's singular mission
to free Israel from its tribal God

A·B·C·

abceditions

enjoy life *&* love others
be you have fun

The Gospel of Jesus of Nazareth, published separately as ISBN 978-2-9546352-3-1, is here reproduced for the purposes of commentary.

REVISED EDITION

A·B·C· EDITIONS ♦ FRANCE

Jesus versus YHWH
ISBN 978-2-9546352-7-9

PUBLISHED IN THE UNITED KINGDOM

♦ ♦ ♦ ♦ ♦ ♦ ♦ ♦ ♦ ♦

For my children…
who can now, at last, say, 'It's finished!'

Contents

Introduction

EVERYTHING IS A STORY.

From infancy, we are told stories. Our minds learn to apprehend the world through the paradigm of the story, and by the time we are adults, we seamlessly understand both ourselves and life itself in this way. In consequence, literally everything that humans assert or express – and I do mean everything – reflects this foundational paradigm. Everything becomes a story. More tellingly, for a vast majority of people *the story is everything*. The only thing. The story is felt to be sacred. The story is seen as the Truth. The story is why people die for their beliefs; the story is why they kill others for theirs.

The Biblical story told about Jesus of Nazareth has informed Western thought ever since the Christian era got firmly underway in the fourth century. But there has never been only just one story; no sooner did Jesus leave the earthly sphere than his followers separated into factions; competing narratives about the man vied for primacy as contenders for the shepherdship tried to win the flock. One group's revealed truth was another group's heresy. Many of those stories – and their devotees – were suppressed. In the end, the Council of Nicaea's story won out.

Yet who was Jesus, really? What was he trying to do? Why did he go to Jerusalem and get himself sacrificed on the cross? Christianity portrays Jesus as a divine, miracle-working Son of God who gave his life to redeem mankind from sin. Is that the story Jesus of Nazareth would have told about himself if he'd left a written testimony? I doubt it. My personal conviction is that most of Jesus' disciples misconstrued his aims, and that his own story was lost in that early first century shuffle.

It was to look for Jesus' story that I went back to the Gospels. If despite their Christian roots they contained seeds of truth about Jesus's life – and by truth I mean words he may have actually said, things that may have actually happened – then perhaps I could write a 'story' that would get closer to the mark than the one told by the Gospels.

The story I came up with is found in my book, *The Gospel of Jesus of Nazareth*.

•

Unfortunately, it is a difficult book. It is difficult for many reasons, but the principal reason is the way it uses scripture to develop its ideas: to follow my line of reasoning, the reader is called upon to look up the numerous Biblical verses that are cited in the margins…and that, for any reader, is not only a daunting task, but laborious to boot.

I didn't want to leave Jesus hanging like that, as it were, with no one to understand the story I'd come up with about him. So I decided to write the present book, to explain at least in part what I'd written in the other, and to facilitate a reader's grasp of the scriptural underpinnings of my take by providing quotations of the salient passages. At times, Biblical verses alone are the only 'commentary' that I have felt is needed – they either support what is said in direct fashion, or they stand in such stark contrast to it that one cannot help but see my intended point. There are of course numerous other verses to be found in the margins of *The Gospel of Jesus of Nazareth* that add depth and richness to the whole; readers who are interested in delving deeper will not go unrewarded.

In placing scripture at the heart of my work, I am taking my cue from the example Jesus set when he argued with the devil in the wilderness. As we know, it was for good reason that their battle of words took the form of a verse-for-verse slugfest – *You shall not add to the word which I command you, neither shall you take away from it* [...]. (De 4:2) Put differently, the Bible is a closed system...so when it comes to arguing about the meaning and significance of the Scriptures – as Jesus did with the devil, and as I am doing here – you have to keep within strict confines. This is why my examination of the Gospels and interpretation of Jesus' intent is so carefully wrought and so thoroughly tied to the Scriptures – it is the only method of argument that can bear scrutiny and, hopefully, carry the day.

For if a historical, human Jesus – irretrievable though he may be – is hidden within the folds of the Jesus portrayed in the Gospels, to uncover the man behind the myth we're going to have to come to terms with two distinct yet indissolubly linked realities: one is temporal, the other scriptural. In the temporal reality, Jesus was a man who truly lived. He was mortal; he was born of woman; he grew to be a man; he had ideas about God and life; he came to public notice and developed a following; he went to Jerusalem with the clear intent, it seems, of being tried by the Sanhedrin and condemned; and he was put to death. Concurrent with this temporal reality is a scriptural reality that ineluctably arises because – if the Gospels are to be believed – Jesus deliberately set out to link his life and death with the Hebrew Scriptures. In this scriptural reality, Jesus, a Jew, is a son of YHWH; in going up to Jerusalem, he, like Isaac, ascends Mount Moriah; he prays to his 'Abba' that this cup might pass him by; he is offered up in sacrifice to the God of Israel; and the sacrifice is accepted, since his death – unlike Isaac's – is not averted.

It is precisely the way in which one combines and accounts for these two realities that determines how one comprehends the man, who seems to be rooted in each. For example, if you embrace a spiritual reality that says Jesus is the divine Son of God, then it is not possible for you that his death could be a cut and dried, mortal affair in the temporal reality: he must be resurrected to eternal life. This is what the Scriptures are said to have 'promised', and so, you say, that is what must have happened on a temporal level. The trouble with this, of course, is that those of us who adhere to a vision of the world based on physical laws cannot accept that such a thing could be so. Some people profess that Jesus was conceived by the Holy Spirit and born of a virgin; that he walked on the sea and calmed a storm; that he changed water into wine; that he raised Lazarus from the dead; that he himself was resurrected from death and appeared to his followers; yet all that is a matter of faith. It is a hermetic spiritual reality that longs to be a believable, ironclad temporal reality; but wishing it so don't make it so…and it leaves us with a Jesus who is unrecognizable as a human being.

Yet if we assert that the temporal reality shows Jesus to have been a typical Jewish holy man or 'man of God', a charismatic healer, or an 'Eschatological Enthusiast' (as Geza Vermes so nicely puts it in *The Changing Faces of Jesus*), although we end up with a believable and recognizable human being, we create for ourselves a different problem: such a portrayal conflicts with the scriptural reality related in the Gospels. For example, no Jewish holy man would have ever told his followers, as Jesus apparently did, that they must eat his blood – the eating of blood is anathema to Jews. Likewise, no Jewish holy man would have proposed himself as a human sacrifice to YHWH – the God of Israel forbids human sacrifice. One must also downplay certain actions and teachings that are found in the Gospels: we see this for example when it is argued – with emphasis placed on his having said, *"Do not think that I came to destroy the law or the prophets. I did not come to destroy, but to fulfill."* (Mt 5:17) – that far from opposing the Law, Jesus was teaching his followers a purer, more 'spiritual' form of Judaism, a Judaism of the highest order. The temporal reality interpreted in this way seems to be wishful thinking, too…and it leaves us with a Jesus whose portrait fails to reflect numerous significant details that are found in the Gospels.

What to do? How might we account for the temporal reality of Jesus' life within the framework and context of the spiritual reality that he so deliberately established? If we could answer to the concerns of both, would we be a step closer to Jesus' own story?

In *The Gospel of Jesus of Nazareth*, I have sought to present the Gospel narrative in such a way as to reconcile these two realities. Such an undertaking necessarily begins with the question that bedevils every person who explores the Gospels: in all that is written, what might be a reliable report of what Jesus said and of what happened; and, just as important, what was added to the story later to underpin the doctrinal needs of the early Jesus-movements? To work with the Gospels, one is called upon to separate the wheat from the chaff. Having chosen what I feel to be the words that Jesus may have truly said and the events that may have truly happened, I have developed an interpretation of Jesus' life that hopes to plausibly account for why a Jewish man from Galilee would offer himself in sacrifice on a Roman cross.

♦

Still and all, I don't call this a 'sometimes freewheeling' commentary for nothing. *The Gospel of Jesus of Nazareth* may be decidedly serious in its interpretation, but since there's surely no reason why my elucidation of its ideas need hew to a staid, no-nonsense line, I have very happily given myself free rein to take neither myself nor the Bible too seriously. In these pages, when the Gospel narratives pique my imagination, or when there's an interesting historical detail to explore, you can be sure I'll be chatty…and on occasion, even naughty.

After all, I'm not trying to convince anyone, and it would be such a shame to miss out on all the fun to be had along the way.

With that as our covenant, shall we begin?

Jesus versus Yhwh

*YOU shall place these words of mine upon your heart
and your soul, you shall bind them as a sign upon
your hand, and as a frontlet between your eyes.*

Deuteronomy 11:18

*AND he causes all, the small and the great, the rich and
the poor, the free and the slaves, to receive a mark upon
their right hand, or upon their foreheads.*

Revelation 13:16

0
Before the word

EPIGRAPH

The juxtaposition of Deuteronomy 11:18 with Revelation 13:16 gives succinct expression to a central tenet: that in the Bible, YHWH and Satan are one and the same being.[1] Satan, if you like, is the personification of the Jewish god's dark side. YHWH is, of course, a god to Israel and the 'creator' of their covenant, but I do not see YHWH as being 'God' in the largest, overarching sense...although he routinely insists otherwise.

As for the 'mark upon their right hand', it may be objected that Jews traditionally wear their *shel yad* or arm-tefillin on the left arm; but those who are left-handed are allowed to wear them on the right. Since the prophet in his vision sees the mark on the right hand, this might lead us to wonder: was the author of Revelation left-handed?

1
The Beginning

1:1-14 PROLOGUE

The prologue is comprised of verses loosely drawn from a striking passage that appears in Ezekiel, chapter 28, wherein the prophet speaks of the prince or ruler of Tyre in terms that pointedly evoke the God of Israel, with unmistakable references to the breast-plate of judgment, the ark of the covenant, Mount Sinai, and the garden of Eden.

At the time it was written, Ezekiel's prophesy of impending downfall was likely directed against Ithobaal III, whom Josephus records as having reigned in Tyre from 591-573 BCE. It is our wont, though, to give prophesies wider currency once their specificity has played out. Many readers see this passage as foretelling the overthrow of Satan; to this I would add that the compelling references to the God of Israel indicate that it is also speaking implicitly of YHWH.

If Jesus read in this passage a prophesy of YHWH's downfall, he may have felt inspired to try to bring it about. Now, why would Jesus try to dethrone YHWH? For this reason: having come to the perception that the Jewish god had sinned against his own people, he determined to free his fellow Jews from the covenant that held them in bondage to their tribal god. The prologue develops these ideas and sets the stage for all that is to follow, so it's worth our while to tackle a bit of scripture here at the outset and gain a bird's eye view of where we're going. (But take heart – livelier fare awaits us just around the next corner...)

The Gospel of Jesus of Nazareth

THE beginning of the gospel of Jesus of Nazareth, the son of man.

2 As it is written in Ezekiel the prophet, "SON OF MAN, SAY TO THE PRINCE OF TYRE, 'THUS SAYS THE LORD GOD:[a]

3 YOUR HEART IS PROUD, AND YOU SAY, "I AM GOD,[b] SITTING ON A GOD'S THRONE[c] IN THE MIDST OF THE OPEN SEAS."[d]

4 "'BUT YOU ARE ONLY A MAN,[e] THOUGH YOU BOAST YOURSELF TO BE LIKE GOD.[f]

5 "'YOU ARE WISER THAN DANIEL, FOR THERE ARE NO SECRETS THAT YOU DO NOT KNOW,[g] AND YOU HAVE USED YOUR WISDOM AND YOUR UNDERSTANDING TO AMASS RICHES;[h] YOUR WISDOM HAS MADE YOU WEALTHY, AND PROUD.[i]

a Eze 28:2
b Isa 44:6
  Isa 45:11,12
  Isa 46:9
  Isa 47:10
  Isa 54:5
c Ex 25:17-22
  2Sa 6:2
  Ps 99:1
  Isa 6:1-3
  Eze 10:1
  Eze 43:7
d Eze 28:2
e Ge 32:24,28,30
  Eze 1:26
  Eze 43:6
f De 32:39
  Isa 41:4
  Isa 43:13
  Eze 28:2,9
g Job 38:1-41
  Job 39:1-30
  Job 40:6-24
  Job 41:1-34
  Eze 28:3
h Ex 25:1-9
  Ex 38:24-29
  Jos 6:19
  1Ch 29:2-9
  Hag 2:8
i 1Ch 29:11
  Eze 28:5
  Da 4:35

1:1 – The beginning of the gospel of Jesus of Nazareth, the son of man.

Jesus ever refers to himself as 'the son of man'. More about this in a moment, but in my view, Jesus' choice of words is not meant to be an oblique form of self-reference for the purposes of humility or to avoid speaking too plainly about himself when it came to the taboo subject of his own death,[2] but rather is meant in the first instance to point his followers to the prophecies of Ezekiel, whom Yhwh addresses as 'son of man'.[3]

1:3 – "' [...] you say, "I am God" [...] '"

This is something Yhwh is keen to stress.

Isa 44:6 – *"I am the first, and I am the last; and besides me there is no God."*

Yhwh clearly sees himself as being far more than a tribal god: he is the one and only 'God' – *"I am God, and there is no other."* (Isa 46:9)

1:4 – "'But you are only a man [...] '"

Ge 32:24,28,30 – *Jacob was left alone, and wrestled with a man there until the breaking of the day. | He said, "Your name will no longer be called Jacob, but Israel; for you have fought with God and with men, and have prevailed." | Jacob called the name of the place Peniel: for, he said, "I have seen God face to face, and my life is preserved."*

Jacob has wrestled with a man, and in doing so has not only prevailed, but has seen the Jewish god face to face. Yhwh may be a god, but he is here described as being a man.[4]

I think we might see in this a deeper signification of Jesus referring to himself as 'the son of man'. Jesus, as are all Jews, is a son of Yhwh, the Jewish tribal god – *'Israel is my son, my firstborn.'* (Ex 4:22) But if Jesus saw Yhwh as being the man spoken of by Ezekiel (*"yet you are a man, and not God"*), then he may have sought to draw attention to this by

4

plainly stating that he was the son of man.[5] At the same time, the definitive article 'the' elevates him to the rank of a universal son. In his death on the cross, therefore, Jesus is the quintessential Son of YHWH.

1:4 – "' [...] THOUGH YOU BOAST YOURSELF TO BE LIKE GOD.'"

Of course, when it comes to YHWH it's hard to make the charge of boasting stick, since we can't say in which spirit he was making his assertions, but he clearly sees himself as the one and only God.

De 32:39 – *"See now that I myself am he. There is no god with me. I kill and I make alive. I wound and I heal. There is no one who can deliver out of my hand."*

Isa 41:4 – *"Who has worked and done it, calling the generations from the beginning? I, Yahweh, the first, and with the last, I am he."*

Sounds like someone who's trying to pump himself up. Does YHWH maybe feel a wee bit insecure?

1:5 – "'[...] THERE ARE NO SECRETS THAT YOU DO NOT KNOW [...]'"

In a high and mighty discourse that runs to no less than four chapters in the book of Job, YHWH makes it clear that he knows everything and is not to be crossed. Poor Job's profoundly legitimate gripes are quite simply quashed by YHWH's tidal wave of divine self-justification.

1:5 – "' [...] YOU HAVE USED YOUR WISDOM AND YOUR UNDERSTANDING TO AMASS RICHES [...] '"

The sanctuary built for YHWH was duly sumptuous – see Exodus 25:1-9 and 28:24-29. Joshua instructed the Jews that *"all the silver, gold, and vessels of brass and iron, are holy to Yahweh. They shall come into Yahweh's treasury."* (Jos 6:19) Under David, riches were again amassed for building the house of God – see 1 Chronicles 29:2-9. In Haggai, the God of Israel himself spells things out: *'The silver is mine, and the gold is mine,' says Yahweh of Armies.* (Hag 2:8)

1

j Ex 25:8,9
   Eze 43:10
k Job 12:13
   Job 36:4
l Ps 50:2
   Ps 96:6
   Isa 33:17
   Eze 28:12
m Ge 3:8
n Ex 28:17-21
o Ex 28:13-15
   Ex 28:22-27
p Eze 28:13
q Ex 25:17-22
   Ex 30:25,26
   Ex 40:9
   Nu 7:89
   2Sa 6:2
   Ps 47:2
   Ps 99:1
   Isa 37:16
r Ex 3:1,5
   Ex 19:2,3
   Ex 19:18,20
   Ex 24:13
s Ex 24:10,17
   De 5:4
   Eze 1:26-28
   Eze 28:14
t Job 10:7
   Job 19:6,7
   Ps 55:20
   Eze 28:15
u Ps 148:13
   Isa 45:23
   Eze 36:22,32
   Eze 38:23
   Mal 1:6,11
v Ps 27:4
   Ps 50:2
   Ps 96:4,6
   Ps 104:1
   Pr 16:18
w Job 28:12-19
   Ps 104:1
   Eze 28:17

6 "'YOU WERE SEALING A PATTERN OF PERFECTION;[j] FULL OF WISDOM WERE YOU,[k] AND PERFECT IN BEAUTY.[l]

7 "'YOU WERE IN EDEN,[m] THE GARDEN OF GOD; EVERY PRECIOUS STONE WAS YOUR COVERING,[n] AND THE GOLD OF YOUR SETTINGS, FINE WORKMANSHIP, WAS IN YOU.[o] THE DAY YOU WERE CREATED, THEY WERE PREPARED.[p]

8 "'YOU WERE THE ANOINTED CHERUB WHO COVERS.[q] ON THE HOLY MOUNTAIN OF GOD,[r] YOU WALKED IN THE MIDST OF THE STONES OF FIRE.[s]

9 "'YOU WERE PERFECT IN YOUR WAYS FROM THE DAY YOU WERE CREATED, UNTIL WRONG WAS FOUND IN YOU.[t]

10 "'BUT YOUR HEART WAS FILLED WITH PRIDE[u] BECAUSE OF YOUR BEAUTY,[v] AND YOUR WISDOM WAS CORRUPTED FOR THE SAKE OF YOUR SPLENDOR.[w] YOUR RICHES FILLED YOU WITH VIOLENCE, AND YOU SINNED.[x]

11 "'THEREFORE, I WILL CAST YOU DOWN FROM THE MOUNTAIN OF GOD,[y]

12 AND I WILL DESTROY YOU, O COVERING CHERUB, FROM THE MIDST OF THE STONES OF FIRE.[z]

1:5 – "'[…] YOUR WISDOM HAS MADE YOU WEALTHY, AND PROUD.'"
No verse in the Bible actually accuses the God of Israel of being proud *per se*, but if we look once again at Job, chapters 38 through 43, YHWH certainly comes off as being full of his own importance. When David praises him in 1 Chronicles 29:11 – *"Yours, Yahweh, is the greatness, the power, the glory, the victory, and the majesty! For all that is in the heavens and in the earth is yours. Yours is the kingdom, Yahweh, and you are exalted as head above all."* – one can imagine YHWH's vainglorious, peacock pleasure.

1:6 – "' […] AND PERFECT IN BEAUTY.'"
Ps 50:2 – *Out of Zion, the perfection of beauty, God shines out.*
Ps 96:6 – *Honor and majesty are before him. Strength and beauty are in his sanctuary.*

1:7 – "'YOU WERE IN EDEN, THE GARDEN OF GOD; EVERY PRECIOUS STONE WAS YOUR COVERING […]'"
Who was in Eden? YHWH, the serpent, Adam and Eve. So I reckon we're talking about YHWH here.

As for precious stones, they adorned the breastplate of judgment:
Ex 28:17-21 – *You shall set in it settings of stones, four rows of stones: a row of ruby, topaz, and beryl shall be the first row; | and the second row a turquoise, a sapphire, and an emerald; | and the third row a jacinth, an agate, and an amethyst; | and the fourth row a chrysolite, an onyx, and a jasper […]*

1:7 – "' […] AND THE GOLD OF YOUR SETTINGS, FINE WORKMANSHIP, WAS IN YOU. […]'"
Ex 28:13-15 – *"You shall make settings of gold, | and two chains of pure gold; you shall make them like cords of braided work: and you shall put the braided chains on the settings. | You shall make a breastplate of judgment, the work of the skillful workman […]"*

7

1:8 – "'YOU WERE THE ANOINTED CHERUB WHO COVERS. [...] '"

There were two cherubim set at either end of the ark of the covenant, and YHWH – a 'great King' (and kings are anointed) – was above them:

Ex 25:17-22 – *"You shall make a mercy seat of pure gold. [...] | You shall make two cherubim of hammered gold. You shall make them at the two ends of the mercy seat. [...] | There I will meet with you, and I will tell you from above the mercy seat, from between the two cherubim which are on the ark of the testimony, all that I command you for the children of Israel.*

Nu 7:89 – *When Moses went into the Tent of Meeting to speak with Yahweh, he heard his voice speaking to him from above the mercy seat [...], from between the two cherubim: and he spoke to him.*

2Sa 6:2 – *David arose [...] to bring up from there God's ark, which is called by the Name, even the name of Yahweh of Armies who sits above the cherubim.*

Ps 47:2 – *For Yahweh [...] is a great King over all the earth.*

Ps 99:1 – *Yahweh reigns! [...] He sits enthroned among the cherubim. [...]*

Eze 28:14 – *"You were the anointed cherub who covers. [...]"*

1:8 – "'[...] ON THE HOLY MOUNTAIN OF GOD [...] '"

Ex 3:1,5 – *Now Moses [...] came to God's mountain, to Horeb. | [...]*

Ex 19:18,20 – *All of Mount Sinai smoked, because Yahweh descended on it in fire [...] | Yahweh came down on Mount Sinai, to the top of the mountain. [...]*

Ex 24:13 – *Moses rose up with Joshua, his servant, and Moses went up onto God's Mountain.*

1:8 – "'[...] YOU WALKED IN THE MIDST OF THE STONES OF FIRE.'"

Ex 24:10,17 – *They saw the God of Israel. Under his feet was like a paved work of sapphire stone [...] | The appearance of Yahweh's glory was like devouring fire on the top of the mountain in the eyes of the children of Israel.*

8

De 5:4 – *Yahweh spoke with you face to face on the mountain out of the middle of the fire.*

I think it's clear by now that Ezekiel's prophesy is speaking of YHWH.

1:9 – "'YOU WERE PERFECT IN YOUR WAYS [...] UNTIL WRONG WAS FOUND IN YOU.'"

Job 10:7 – *"Although you know that I am not wicked, there is no one who can deliver out of your hand."*

Job 19:6,7 – *"Know now that God has subverted me [...]."*

Ps 55:20 – *He raises his hands against his friends. He has violated his covenant.*

1:10 – "'BUT YOUR HEART WAS FILLED WITH PRIDE [...]'"

Eze 38:23 – *"I will magnify myself, and sanctify myself, and I will make myself known [...]; and they shall know that I am Yahweh."*

Mal 1:6,11 – *"A son honors his father, and a slave his master. If I am a father, then where is my honor? And if I am a master, where is the respect due me? says Yahweh of Armies to you, priests, who despise my name. [...] | For from the rising of the sun even to the going down of the same, my name is great [...], and in every place incense will be offered to my name, and a pure offering: for my name is great among the nations," says Yahweh of Armies.*

1:10 – "' [...] YOUR RICHES FILLED YOU WITH VIOLENCE, AND YOU SINNED.'"

This is the crux of the matter, the reason for why Jesus would seek to bring about the denouement of Ezekiel's prophesy by giving his own life in sacrifice: YHWH has sinned against his own people.

Ex 20:13 – *"You shall not murder."*

Ex 23:7 – *"Keep far from a false charge, and don't kill the innocent and righteous: for I will not justify the wicked."*

De 19:10 – *This is so that innocent blood will not be shed in the middle of your land which Yahweh your God gives you for an inheritance, leaving blood guilt on you.*

Ps 109:16 – *Because he didn't remember to show kindness, but persecuted the poor and needy man, the broken in heart, to kill them.*

Pr 28:17 – *A man who is tormented by life blood will be a fugitive until death; no one will support him.*

If YHWH transgresses his own Law by killing the innocent, then the blood guilt should be upon him. In consequence, no one should support him. So, let us consider:

La 2:20-22 – *Look, Yahweh, and see to whom you have done thus! Shall the women eat their offspring, the children that are dandled in the hands? Shall the priest and the prophet be killed in the sanctuary of the Lord? | The youth and the old man lie on the ground in the streets. My virgins and my young men have fallen by the sword. You have killed them in the day of your anger. You have slaughtered, and not pitied. | […] There was no one that escaped or remained in the day of Yahweh's anger. My enemy has consumed those whom I have dandled and brought up.*

La 4:4,9-11 – *The tongue of the nursing child clings to the roof of his mouth for thirst: the young children ask bread, and no man breaks it to them. | Those who are killed with the sword are better than those who are killed with hunger; for these pine away, stricken through, for want of the fruits of the field. | The hands of the pitiful women have boiled their own children; they were their food in the destruction of the daughter of my people. | Yahweh has accomplished his wrath, he has poured out his fierce anger; he has kindled a fire in Zion, which has devoured its foundations.*

Thought to have been inspired by the destruction of Jerusalem in 586 BCE, the Book of Lamentations is poignant in its grief. YHWH is seen as the perpetrator of the tragedy, and the poems lay responsibility for the deaths of Israel's innocent children and righteous priests and prophets squarely at his feet.

It is my feeling that Jesus, with his manifest love for children, would have been deeply affected by these accounts, which he may have seen as an unpardonable transgression by the God of Israel. If YHWH flouts his own Law, should this not lead to his own downfall? For if he is judged by his own standards, then he has sinned.

Mr 14:36 – *He said, "Abba, Father, all things are possible to you. Please remove this cup from me. However, not what I desire, but what you desire."*

Mr 15:34 – *At the ninth hour Jesus cried with a loud voice, saying, "Eloi, Eloi, lama sabachthani?" which is, being interpreted, "My God, my God, why have you forsaken me?"*

Jesus is portrayed in the Gospels as being wholly innocent and undeserving of death, so his death on the cross amounts to the shedding of innocent blood. By forsaking Jesus in his hour of need, YHWH shows that it was his wish that Jesus die. YHWH's silence is the silence of consent …a tacit nod to the sacrifice of his Jewish son.

1:11 – "'THEREFORE, I WILL CAST YOU DOWN FROM THE MOUNTAIN OF GOD,'"

Jn 12:31 – *"Now is the judgment of this world. Now the prince of this world will be cast out."*

1:13 – "'ONTO THE EARTH I WILL THROW YOU. […]'"

Isa 14:12 – *"How you have fallen from heaven, morning star, son of the dawn! How you are cut down to the ground, who laid the nations low!"*

1:14 – "'AND THEY THAT KNOW YOU WILL BE ASTONISHED, AND YOU WILL BE NO MORE.'"

Isa 14:16,17 – *Those who see you will stare at you. They will ponder you, saying, "Is this the man who made the earth to tremble, who shook kingdoms; | who made the world like a wilderness, and overthrew its cities; who didn't release his prisoners to their home?"*

Jer 10:11 – *"You shall say this to them: 'The gods that have not made the heavens and the earth, these shall perish from the earth, and from under the heavens.'"*

In the context that I have created here – in which Y<small>HWH</small>, though he boasts himself to be like God, is but a man, and not God – Jeremiah may be read as a prophecy that he and other tribal gods like him will perish.

1:15-24 THE ANGEL OF THE LORD COMES TO MARY

1:15 – Now the angel of *the* Lord came to a city of Galilee, whose name *was* Nazareth,

Ge 32:24,26,28 – *Jacob was left alone, and wrestled with a man there until the breaking of the day. | The man said, "Let me go, for the day breaks." Jacob said, "I won't let you go, unless you bless me." | He said, "Your name will no longer be called Jacob, but Israel; for you have fought with God and with men, and have prevailed."*

Ho 12:3,4 – *In […] his manhood he contended with God. | Indeed, he struggled with the angel, and prevailed. […]*

I think we can presume this angel is Y<small>HWH</small> himself. After all, when Hagar saw Y<small>HWH</small>'s 'angel', she had in fact seen Y<small>HWH</small> – cf. Ge 16:7-13.

1:16 – to a virgin *who was* betrothed to a man whose name was Joseph, of *the* house of David; and the name of the virgin *was* Mary.

'Marriage consists of two stages: *kiddushin*, or erusin, whereby the matrimonial bond is made, not to be broken without divorce; and *huppah*, or home taking, without which cohabitation is forbidden. A woman who has undergone the first ceremony is called an *arusah* (betrothed); after the second she is called a *nesu'ah* (married).'[6]

Mary was thus an *arusah*; having undergone *kiddushin*, she was betrothed to be married. Was she a virgin? Well, sure… for the time being. But not for much longer.

The angel of the Lord comes to Mary   1

13 "'ONTO THE EARTH I WILL THROW YOU.[a] I SHALL BRING FORTH A FIRE FROM THE MIDST OF YOU, IT SHALL DEVOUR YOU;[b] AND I WILL BRING YOU TO ASHES UPON THE EARTH, IN THE SIGHT OF ALL.[c]

14 "'AND THEY THAT KNOW YOU WILL BE ASTONISHED, AND YOU WILL BE NO MORE.'"[d]

15 Now the angel[e] of *the* Lord came to a city of Galilee, whose name *was* Nazareth,[f]

16 to a [1]virgin *who was* betrothed to a man whose name was [2]Joseph, of *the* house of David; and the name of the [1]virgin *was* [3]Mary.[g]

17 And having come to her, he said, "Rejoice, *you who are* favored with grace. The Lord *is* with you!"[h]

18 And at the word, she was greatly agitated, and was debating what kind of salutation this might be.[i]

19 And the angel said to her, "Fear not, Mary – you have indeed found favor with God.[j]

20 "And behold, you will conceive in your womb and will bring forth a son, and you will call his name [4]Jesus."[k]

x Ex 20:13
   Ex 23:7
   De 19:10
   Ps 109:16
   Pr 28:17
   La 2:11-13
   La 2:20-22
   La 4:4,9-11
   Eze 28:16
   Mr 14:36
   Mr 15:34
y Eze 28:16
   Jn 12:31
z Eze 28:16
a Isa 14:12
   Eze 28:17
b Jer 51:25
c Eze 28:18
d Isa 14:16,17
   Isa 47:11
   Jer 10:11
   Jer 51:26
   Eze 28:19
e Ge 32:24,26,28
   Ho 12:3,4
f *Lu 1:26*
g *Lu 1:27*
h Ge 32:29,30
   Lu 1:28
i La 3:38
   Lu 1:29
j *Lu 1:30*
k *Lu 1:31*

---

1 Or, *maiden*
2 Gr., *Ióséph,* for the Hebrew *Yosef*
3 Gr., *Maria,* for the Hebrew *Miriam*
4 Gr., *Iésous,* for the Hebrew *Yehoshua',* or Joshua

1   Joseph desires to divorce Mary secretly

l *Lu 1:34*
m De 22:23,24
   Isa 14:14
n Ps 2:7
   Ps 82:6
   Eze 28:2
   Lu 1:35
o Le 19:20
p Ps 51:5
   Lu 1:38
q *Lu 1:38*
r *Mt 1:18*
s De 22:13-21
t *Mt 1:19*
u *Mt 1:20*
v Job 4:12,13

21 But Mary said to the angel, "How will this be, since I know not a man?"[l]

22 And answering, the angel said to her, "Holy spirit will come upon you, and power of *the* highest will overshadow you,[m] wherefore the holy *spirit* being born will be called *a* son of God."[n]

23 But Mary said, "Behold, the female slave[o] of the Lord – be it done to me according to your word."[p]

24 And the angel departed from her.[q]

25 Now the birth of Jesus was thus – his mother Mary having been betrothed to Joseph, but before their coming together, was found to be pregnant.[r]

26 But Joseph, her husband, being righteous, and not wishing to make her an example,[s] desired [5]to send her away secretly.[t]

27 But he having considered this, *the* angel of *the* Lord appeared to him in a dream, saying, "Joseph, son of David, fear not to receive Mary as your wife, for the *child* in her, having been conceived from spirit, is holy."[u]

28 But Joseph, having been woken from sleep,[v] did as the angel of the Lord commanded him, and

---

5 Or, *to divorce*

1:17,18 – And having come to her, he said, "Rejoice, *you who are favored with grace. The Lord is with you!*" And at the word, she was greatly agitated, and was debating what kind of salutation this might be.

That's some pick up line – *"The Lord is with you!"* Flustered, Mary doesn't know what to think about this guy. What's he got in mind?

1:19,20 – And the angel said to her, "Fear not, Mary – you have indeed found favor with God. And behold, you will conceive in your womb and will bring forth a son, and you will call his name Jesus."

Smooth talker. Tells her how much he likes her, then sets the tone for what's about to follow.

1:21 – But Mary said to the angel, "How will this be, since I know not a man?"

'Don't you worry 'bout that, sweetie. We'll see that you learn.'

1:22 – And answering, the angel said to her, "Holy spirit will come upon you, and power of *the* highest will overshadow you […]"

Isa 14:14 – " […] *I will make myself like the Most High!*"

When a 'god' covers you, it's a pretty powerful experience. One imagines Leda could tell us a thing or two about that.

1:22 – "[…] wherefore the holy *spirit* being born will be called *a* son of God."

As for the issue of such a union, you naturally get a child of that god.

Ps 2:7 – *I will tell of the decree. Yahweh said to me, "You are my son. Today I have become your father."*

The conception story establishes Jesus as the symbolic firstborn son of YHWH in the context of the Gospels. For this reason, Jesus' sacrificial death on the cross amounts to YHWH sacrificing his own firstborn son.

1:23 – But Mary said, "Behold, the female slave of the Lord – be it done to me according to your word."

No doubt beguiled by the angel's seductive words, Mary decides then and there to go ahead and offer herself on the spot to YHWH's desire, a willing party to the sowing of his holy seed. What's more, by signifying herself a slave, she offers her lover – YHWH in spirit or disguise, or an angelic young man whom she may have fancied in passing – a symbolic protection from being stoned to death should they ever be caught:

Le 19:20 – *"If a man lies carnally sowing with a woman who is a slave girl, pledged to be married to another man, and not ransomed, or given her freedom; they shall be punished. But they shall not be put to death, because she was not free."*

On the other hand, if you prefer, since she's a bondservant of YHWH Mary's reply may simply reflect her submissive acquiescence to Middle Eastern mores, whereby masters were tacitly entitled to have their way with female slaves. For bibilical precedents on this score, we can look back to Hagar, Bilhah and Zilpah – see Genesis 16:1-6; 30:1-13. Some 600 years later, we find it in the Qur'an – see 23:5,6; 33:50.

1:24 – And the angel departed from her.

Whereupon Mary, more than likely, wasn't a virgin anymore. She would soon be expecting, in a wholly big way.

Now, for my part, and more prosaically, I think Mary found herself pregnant not by the Holy Spirit, but by someone else. Maybe a man with whom she was in love but could not marry for one reason or another. Or maybe she was seduced by an ephemeral inamorato.[7] More darkly, she may have been a victim of incest or rape. Or perhaps she had engaged in harlotry and played *'the prostitute in her father's house.'*

Regardless of who did the inseminating – whether YHWH himself or a more down-to-earth donor with a boner – the Gospels tell us that Mary was pregnant long before she consummated her marriage with Joseph.

1:25-30 JESUS IS BORN

1:25,26 – Now the birth of Jesus was thus – his mother Mary having been betrothed to Joseph, but before their coming together, was found to be pregnant. But Joseph, her husband, being righteous, and not wishing to make her an example, desired to send her away secretly.

For Joseph, the only alternative to divorcing Mary – be it done 'secretly' or otherwise – would have been to duly charge her with infidelity:

De 22:13-21 – *If any man takes a wife, and goes in to her, hates her, | accuses her of shameful things, and gives her a bad name, and says, "I took this woman, and when I came near to her, I didn't find in her the tokens of virginity"; | then the young lady's father and mother shall take and bring the tokens of the young lady's virginity to the elders of the city in the gate. | […] But if this thing is true, that the tokens of virginity were not found in the young lady; | then they shall bring out the young lady to the door of her father's house, and the men of her city shall stone her to death with stones, because she has done folly in Israel, to play the prostitute in her father's house. […]*

To his credit, though, Joseph has no desire to make Mary an example. Or maybe he just didn't want to air their dirty laundry in public.

1:27 – But he having considered this, *the* angel of *the* Lord appeared to him in a dream, saying, "Joseph, son of David, fear not to receive Mary as your wife, for the *child* in her, having been conceived from spirit, is holy."

To save her from being disgraced or stoned, did Mary's lover take it upon himself to sneak into Joseph's house and whisper a suggestion in his rival's ear? Or did Joseph dream this up himself, spurred on by his unconscious mind to go through with the marriage after all?

Considering that Joseph's initial impulse was to divorce Mary when he first learned she was pregnant, we might wonder if there were other reasons, on top of his dream, for why this good, upstanding, righteous fellow ultimately consented to keep a woman who'd gotten herself knocked up. Perhaps he was a man who was particularly anxious to be married and have children of his own. Perhaps he'd been unlucky in love; perhaps a first marriage had ended in divorce or with his wife's untimely death and left him without offspring; perhaps he was now in his mid- to late-twenties and, keenly aware that other men his age all had wives and had started families, felt that time was slipping by. Mary clearly wasn't chaste, but she was probably – or at least put on a good show of being – contrite about it; she was evidently fertile, and so fit for bearing children; to help things along, her father might have made the marriage terms more attractive by increasing the dowry. For any of these reasons, Joseph could have felt that, all things considered, he was better off going through with it.

1:28,29 – But Joseph, having been woken from sleep, did as the angel of the Lord commanded him, and received his wife, and knew her not until she had given birth to her firstborn son.

Still, according to Matthew, he refused to consummate the marriage until after his wife had given birth to her illegitimate child. (Mt 1:25)[8]

Of course, Joseph – and Mary's parents if they were involved – would have wanted to keep things hush-hush about her being already in the family way. Why, they may have even concocted a plan to scoot Mary out of town before her 'condition' started to show. Indeed, a timely reason to make a trip to Bethlehem in Judea, such as the census ordered by Publius Sulpicius Quirinius, legate of Syria, in 6 CE (cf. Luke 2:1-6), would have been more than a god-send, if only so that Mary could give birth far from the prying curiosity of onlookers. At any rate, Joseph and Mary would have likely wanted to keep things under wraps, in hopes that time would cover their tracks.

Jesus is born   1

received his wife,[w]

29 and knew her not until she had given birth to her firstborn son.[x]

30 And when *the* eight days were fulfilled for his circumcision,[y] his name was called Jesus, the *name he had* been called by the angel before his being conceived in the womb.[z]

31 And when the days of their purification[a] were fulfilled, they brought him to Jerusalem, to present *him* to the Lord,[b]

32 and to offer a sacrifice according to the law of the Lord – two young pigeons.[c]

33 And when they had accomplished everything according to the law of the Lord, they returned to Galilee, to their city, Nazareth.[d]

34 And the child grew and became strong, being filled with wisdom, and God's grace was upon him.[e]

35 And every year, his parents went to Jerusalem at the feast of the Passover.[f]

36 And when he was twelve years *old*, they had gone up, according to the custom of the feast.[g]

37 And having completed the days, as they were returning, the boy Jesus remained behind in

w *Mt 1:24*
x *Mt 1:25*
y Ge 17:10-14
   Ex 22:29,30
   Le 12:2,3
z *Lu 2:21*
a Le 12:4
b Ex 13:2,12-15
   Nu 3:13
   Lu 2:22
c Le 12:6-8
   Lu 2:24
d *Lu 2:39*
e *Lu 2:40*
f Ex 23:15
   De 16:1-6
   Lu 2:41
g *Lu 2:42*

But as Jesus himself observed, *"there is nothing hidden, except that it should be made known; neither was anything made secret, but that it should come to light."* (Mr 4:22) The good people of Nazareth must have eventually divined the truth, considering that Mark says Jesus was referred to as *'the son of Mary'* by the people in his hometown (Mr 6:3). Now, in the Gospels, men are routinely referred to as being the son of their father, so this epithet appearing in the earliest of the four canonical Gospels stands out. Recounting the same visit by Jesus and his disciples to Nazareth, Mark's fellow synoptic evangelists, writing later, present this differently: in Matthew 13:55 we read, *"Isn't this the carpenter's son? Isn't his mother called Mary* [...] *?"*, and in Luke 4:22, *"Isn't this Joseph's son?"* Since both evangelists maintain that Mary was a betrothed virgin when she was found to be pregnant, the change in wording insures that attention is not unnecessarily drawn to Jesus' questionable parentage.

Mark's wording invites us to speculate as to what sort of home life Jesus may have experienced while he was growing up. Would the converse of his being seen as *'the son of Mary'* be a certain distance between him and his step-father? Joseph may well have been a righteous man and, by the standards of the times, considered to be Jesus' father,[9] but nothing would have obliged him to actually *love* as a son his unchaste wife's first child by another man. Did Jesus grow up in home where Joseph's fatherly affections were markedly warmer towards his own offspring, Jesus' younger half-siblings?

1:30 – And when the eight days were fulfilled for his circumcision, his name was called Jesus, the name he had been called by the angel before his being conceived in the womb.

Iésous is Greek for *Yehoshua'*, or Joshua, which in Hebrew means 'YHWH is Salvation'. With Joseph having consented to keep her as a wife after all, we could wonder whether Mary may have chosen to name her illegitimate son *Yehoshua'* because she felt she had been saved from disgrace, despite her adulterous little slip-up with the LORD.

At any rate, since Jesus was a Jew, and since all Jewish men underwent circumcision at that time, it seems most probable that Jesus was circumcised,[10] as is strongly suggested, though not categorically stated, by Luke 2:21. Indeed, in this way, you could say he *'made'* himself a son of God – see John 19:7.

1:31-33 JESUS IS PRESENTED TO THE LORD

1:32 – and to offer a sacrifice according to the law of the Lord – two young pigeons.
    Le 12:6-8 – " [...] | *If she cannot afford a lamb, then she shall take two turtledoves, or two young pigeons.* [...]"
    Joseph and Mary were apparently of modest means.

1:34-45 JOSEPH AND MARY FIND JESUS IN THE TEMPLE

Talk about chutzpah! Jesus gives his parents the slip and stays behind in Jerusalem.

It's fun to give this some thought. Having dutifully attended the springtime feast of the Passover, Joseph and Mary are now set to travel home to Nazareth in the company of relatives and acquaintances. Given the numbers of Jews who made the pilgrimage each year to Jerusalem for the Passover, this was probably a sizeable group. Jesus' parents had no doubt checked that he was present and accounted for prior to the departure. As the company set off, friends and relatives were likely seeking each other out to gossip and swap stories about their Passover week; in the midst all that bustle and excitement, who would have noticed a determined young boy quietly slipping away before the city was left behind?

1 Joseph and Mary find Jesus in the temple

h *Lu 2:43*
i *Lu 2:44*
j *Lu 2:45*
k *Lu 2:46*
l *Lu 2:48*
m *De 18:5*
   Ps 26:8
   Ps 68:5
   Lu 2:49
n *Lu 2:50*
o *Ex 20:12*
   Le 19:3
   Le 20:9
   La 3:27
   Lu 2:51
p *Pr 4:7*
   Ec 1:13-18
q *Lu 2:52*

Jerusalem; and his parents did not know it.[h]

38 But having assumed him to be in their caravan, they went a day's journey; and they searched for him among the relatives and the acquaintances,[i]

39 and not having found *him*, they returned to Jerusalem, searching for him.[j]

40 And it came about, after three days, *that* they found him in the temple, sitting in the midst of the teachers, and hearing them and questioning them.[k]

41 And having seen him, they were thunderstruck, and his mother said to him, "Child! Why have you done this to us? Behold, your father and I too were deeply anguished, *and* were searching for you!"[l]

42 And he said to them, "Why were you searching for me? Did you not know that I should be among the *children* of my Father?"[m]

43 And they did not understand the statement that he spoke to them.[n]

44 And he went down with them and he came to Nazareth, and he was subject to them.[o]

45 And Jesus advanced in wisdom[p] and stature and [6]favor with God and men.[q]

---

6 Or, *grace*

Jesus was twelve at this time; a certain number of his four brothers and several sisters were probably part of the brood by now; his mother would have had her hands full all day long taking care of her younger children. Over the course of the day, it may have occurred to Joseph once or twice to look for the boy, but with the caravan having stretched out as it proceeded, not finding him nearby, he would have concluded quite logically that Jesus must be walking with other friends or relatives. I certainly find it easy enough to picture Mary and Joseph not realising that her son had gone missing until after a whole day's journey.

We can imagine their consternation. Not only would they have to go back to Jerusalem to look for him, but afterwards, they would have to find another group with whom to travel home. And what to do with the other children? Send some or all of them on with relatives? Bring them along on their return to Jerusalem for their urgent errand? Mary would have been beside herself with worry – had harm come to her twelve year old Jesus? Though equally worried, Joseph might also have been beside himself with rage – what in God's name was that boy up to, disappearing like that?

'Nothing but trouble, this foster son of mine!'

1:41 – And having seen him, they were thunderstruck, and his mother said to him, "Child! Why have you done this to us? Behold, your father and I too were deeply anguished, *and* were searching for you!"

Once they got back to Jerusalem, it took them three whole days of anxious searching before they found Jesus. And when they did find him, where was he? In the temple of all places, *'sitting in the midst of the teachers, both hearing them and questioning them.'* They were thunderstruck. *"Child! Why have you done this to us?"* There may have been no love lost between Jesus and his foster father, but that was surely no reason to inconvenience the whole family by running away from the caravan.

1:42,43 – And he said to them, "Why were you searching for me? Did you not know that I should be among the *children* of my Father?" And they did not understand the statement that he spoke to them.[11]

Is it any wonder that Mary and Joseph found this statement hard to understand? What kind of nonsense was that? 'And your "father", young man,' Mary might have added for good measure, 'is to all intents and purposes Joseph, until you're old enough to marry.'[12]

Ps 26:8 – *Yahweh, I love the habitation of your house, the place where your glory dwells.*

Ps 68:5 – *A father of the fatherless, and a defender of the widows, is God in his holy habitation.*

Yet if he suffered from ostracism as he grew up in his hometown of Nazareth, where the local population is said to have referred to him as 'the son of Mary', or from a dearth of fatherly love – I note that Joseph did not accompany his wife when she traveled to Capernaum in hopes of reasoning with her wayward son (Mr 3:21,31), and he is nowhere mentioned as being present at the crucifixion or lamenting his foster son's death – Jesus may have been acutely and even painfully aware that his illegitimate conception made him 'fatherless'.

While still a young boy, having gleaned that Joseph was not his true father, Jesus may have pestered his mother to tell him who his father was. We would understand if Mary found it easier to gloss over a painful or shameful memory with an ironic euphemism – 'Who was your father? Why, your father was the Lord himself, my son.' If he took comfort in the notion of his father being YHWH, whom the psalmist sings is *'a father of the fatherless'*, the youthful Jesus may have felt particularly drawn to the 'house' of his 'father'. Years later, he might have even joked about having had YHWH for an 'abba' as he grew up…

In the end, though, it all comes down to the same, and it gives you three good reasons for why Jesus is the son of YHWH – his being a Jew makes him a son of YHWH; his being the son of an unnamed father – and hence 'fatherless' – makes him a son of YHWH; and his being conceived by his tribal god's Holy Spirit makes him a son of YHWH.

1:44 – And he went down with them and he came to Nazareth, and he was subject to them.

Ex 20:12 – *"Honor your father and your mother [...]"*

La 3:27 – *It is good for a man that he bear the yoke in his youth.*

The reference verses aim to underscore what we are told by Luke, namely that Jesus was 'subject to' his parents' authority. He may have rebelled now and then and chafed at the bit, but he was forced by his youthful age to knuckle down and toe the line. The Gospels would have us believe that he learned his foster father's trade in the years that followed (*"Isn't this the carpenter?"* Mr 6:3; *"Isn't this the carpenter's son?"* Mt 13:55), and if he hewed to Jewish social standards, Jesus would have married in his early twenties at the latest and started raising a family of his own. Then again, if being 'the son of Mary' made it socially difficult for him to find a wife for himself in the parochial backwater of Nazareth, he may have preferred to see what lay beyond the horizons of Galilee. It's fun to think of Jesus exploring the eastern Mediterranean during his so-called 'silent years', increasing his exposure to the Greek mindset and possibly learning a thing or two about the secretive mystery religions of the time...but I think it more likely that he spent those lost years toiling as a *tektón* and mulling the Scriptures.

At any rate, a day came when Jesus decisively turned his back on life in Nazareth. Shaking his hometown's dust from the soles of his feet, he set off to find out what John the Baptist was doing on the banks of the Jordan River.

2

John the Baptist and the devil

2:1-22 THE PREACHING OF JOHN THE BAPTIST

John – teaching his followers a strict return to the codified values of Judaism and menacing the unworthy chaff with winnowing forks and unquenchable fire – is surely the antithesis of Jesus.

He must have been quite a charismatic figure, to have drawn not only crowds of common people coming down to the Jordan from Jerusalem and all of Judea, but scores of supercilious Pharisees and Sadducees as well. He got them all worked up with his preaching and baptising, until they were begging him to tell them what they should do to bear good fruit and save themselves from being axed and thrown into the fire.

2:11 – […] "He that has two tunics, let him share with him that has none; and he that has food, let him do likewise."

This is clearly implied in the Law of Moses.

De 15:7,8 – " […] *you shall not harden your heart, nor shut your hand from your poor brother; | but you shall surely open your hand to him […]."*

2:13 – […] "Collect nothing more than what you have been ordered to."

Pr 22:22,23 – *Don't exploit the poor, because he is poor; and don't crush the needy in court; | for Yahweh will plead their case, and plunder the life of those who plunder them.*

CHAPTER 2

Now in those days, John came baptising in the wilderness,[a] preaching a baptism of repentance for the forgiveness of sins,[b]

2   and saying, "Repent, for the kingdom of the heavens has drawn near."[c]

3   For this is the *one who was* spoken of through Isaiah the prophet, saying,

> "A VOICE OF ONE CRYING IN THE WILDERNESS,
> 'PREPARE THE WAY OF THE LORD,
> MAKE HIS PATHS STRAIGHT.'"[d]

4   Moreover, John was clothed in camel's hair, and about his waist *he wore* a leather belt, and he was eating locusts and wild honey.[e]

5   At that time, Jerusalem went out to him, and all Judea, and all the neighboring *areas* of Jordan,[f]

6   and were baptised by him in the Jordan River, confessing their sins.[g]

a Isa 40:3
   Mal 3:1
   Mt 3:1
b Mr 1:4
   Lu 3:3
c Isa 65:17
   Da 2:44
   Da 4:3
   Da 6:26
   Da 7:14,27
   Mt 3:2
d Ps 68:4
   Isa 35:8-10
   Isa 40:3
   Isa 57:14
   Isa 62:10
   Mt 3:3
   Mr 1:2
   Jn 1:23
e Mt 3:4
   Mr 1:6
f Mt 3:5
   Mr 1:5
g Nu 5:6,7
   Mt 3:6
   Mr 1:5

2   The preaching of John the Baptist

h De 28:15-68
   Jer 11:11
   Eze 7:2-9
   Mt 3:7
   Lu 3:7
i Ge 17:1-8
   Ge 26:3
   Ge 32:9
   Ex 3:6
   Isa 41:8,9
j Mt 3:8,9
   Lu 3:8
k Eze 21:31,32
   Mt 3:10
   Lu 3:9
l Lu 3:10
m De 15:7,8
   Lu 3:11
n Lu 3:12
o Pr 22:22,23
   Pr 28:20,22
   Lu 3:13
p Ex 20:16
   Ex 23:7
q Lu 3:14
r Isa 9:6,7
   Isa 11:1-5
   Jer 23:5
   Jer 30:8,9
   Jer 33:14-18
   Eze 37:24-28
   Mic 5:22-4
   Zec 6:12,13
   Zec 9:9
   Lu 3:15
   Jn 3:28

7   But having seen the many Pharisees and Sadducees coming to his baptism, he said to them, "Children of vipers, who warned you to flee from the coming wrath?"[h]

8   "Produce therefore fruit worthy of repentance, and do not think to say within yourselves, 'For father we have Abraham';[i] for I say to you, that God is able to raise up children to Abraham from these stones.[j]

9   "But the axe is already laid at the root of the trees. Therefore, every tree not bearing beautiful fruit is cut down with the axe and thrown into *the* fire."[k]

10   And the multitudes questioned him, saying, "What then shall we do?"[l]

11   And answering, he was saying to them, "He that has two tunics, let him share with him that has none; and he that has food, let him do likewise."[m]

12   And *some* tax collectors also came to him to be baptised, and they said to him, "Teacher, what shall we do?"[n]

13   And he said to them, "Collect nothing more than what you have been ordered to."[o]

14   And *some* soldiers were also questioning him, saying, "And what shall we do?" And he said to them,

2:14 – " [...] Coerce no one, nor accuse *anyone* falsely. [...] "

Ex 23:7 – *"Keep far from a false charge, and don't kill the innocent and righteous: for I will not justify the wicked."*

2:16 – " [...] He who is mightier than I is coming [...] "

Ps 98:9 – *Let them sing before Yahweh, for he comes to judge the earth. He will judge the world with righteousness, and the peoples with equity.*

In the Scriptures, it is not the messiah but Yhwh himself who comes, to judge his people.

2:16 – " [...] He will baptise you with holy spirit and fire;"

Some readers infer that John is speaking here about the coming messiah, whom they identify as being Jesus. This seems to me incorrect for two reasons. First, in the Scriptures it is Yhwh himself, and not the messiah, who is depicted as a blazing fire – cf. the reference verses given in the margins, notes *z* and *b*, for verses 2:19 and 2:20. Second, and notably unlike both John the Baptist and the God of Israel, Jesus is portrayed in the Gospels as being particularly tolerant and forgiving of those who transgress the Law.

2:17 – "whose winnowing fork is in His hand [...] "

Mic 4:12 – *But they don't know the thoughts of Yahweh, neither do they understand his counsel; for he has gathered them like the sheaves to the threshing floor.*

2:17 – " [...] but He will burn up the chaff with an unquenchable fire."

De 4:24 – *"For Yahweh your God is a devouring fire, a jealous God."*

Isa 5:24,25 – *Therefore as the tongue of fire devours the stubble, and as the dry grass sinks down in the flame, so their root shall be as rottenness, and their blossom shall go up as dust; because they have rejected the law of Yah-*

weh of Armies, and despised the word of the Holy One of Israel.| Therefore Yahweh's anger burns against his people, and he has stretched out his hand against them, and has struck them. [...] For all this, his anger is not turned away, but his hand is still stretched out.

Na 1:6 – Who can stand before his indignation? Who can endure the fierceness of his anger? His wrath is poured out like fire, and the rocks are broken apart by him.

Mal 4:1 – "For, behold, the day comes, it burns as a furnace; and all the proud, and all who work wickedness, will be stubble; and the day that comes will burn them up," says Yahweh of Armies, "that it shall leave them neither root nor branch."

In his preaching, John seems hell-bent on saving his fellow Jews from YHWH's terrible wrath.

2:21 – " [...] 'THE DAY OF THEIR DISASTER IS NEAR, AND THE EVENTS THAT AWAIT THEM ARE SOON TO COME.'"

De 32:35 – "Vengeance is mine, and recompense, at the time when their foot slides; for the day of their calamity is at hand. Their doom rushes at them."

Joe 1:15 – Alas for the day! For the day of Yahweh is at hand, and it will come as destruction from the Almighty.

Joe 2:1,11 – Blow the trumpet in Zion, and sound an alarm in my holy mountain! Let all the inhabitants of the land tremble, for the day of Yahweh comes, for it is close at hand | [...] for the day of Yahweh is great and very awesome, and who can endure it?

Verses 18 to 22 in the text are of course not found in the Gospels, but they nevertheless dovetail with John's theme on God's wrath and serve to highlight the dire threats made by YHWH in the books of Moses and reported by the prophets. Readers who take the time to look up the numerous reference verses that are given for these five verses will be confronted with the portrait of a vengeful god whose terrifying fury knows no bounds.

"Coerce no one, nor accuse *anyone* falsely;[p] and be content with your wages."[q]

15 Now the people were waiting for and were all reasoning in their hearts about John, *as to* whether or not he might be the [1]messiah.[r]

16 John answered, saying to *them* all, "Indeed, I baptise you *with* water, but He who is mightier than I is coming,[s] of whom I am not worthy to untie the thong of His sandals[t] – He will baptise you with holy spirit and fire;[u]

17 whose winnowing fork is in His hand[v] – He will thoroughly cleanse His threshing floor, and will gather the wheat into His barn, but He will burn up the chaff with an unquenchable fire.[w]

18 "'FOR THEY ARE A PERVERSE GENERATION, SONS IN WHOM THERE IS NO FAITHFULNESS.[x]

19 "'IN MY ANGER,[y] I HAVE IGNITED A FIRE,[z] AND IT WILL BURN DOWN TO THE DEPTHS OF SHEOL;[a]

20 MY ANGER WILL BLAZE AGAINST THEM, AND I WILL ANNIHILATE THEM.[b]

21 "'FOR VENGEANCE IS MINE,' SAYS THE LORD. 'THE DAY OF THEIR DISASTER IS NEAR, AND THE

---

1 Gr., *messias*, for the Hebrew *mashiach*; certain later mss. read, *christos*

s Ps 96:13
  Ps 98:9
  Zec 2:10
t Ps 60:8
  Ps 108:9
  Jn 1:27
u Isa 4:4
  Isa 33:10-14
  Isa 63:10
  Mt 3:11
  Mr 1:8
  Lu 3:16
v Mic 4:12
w De 4:24
  Pr 29:19
  Isa 5:24,25
  Na 1:6
  Mal 4:1
  Mt 3:12
  Lu 3:17
x De 32:20
  Pr 29:21
  Isa 1:2
  Isa 30:9
  Isa 44:21
y Ex 34:14
  Pr 6:34
  Pr 29:11
  Ec 7:9
  Jer 25:30-38
z De 4:24
  Ps 79:5
  Pr 27:4
  Ca 8:6
  Isa 30:27,30
  Jer 15:14
  Eze 22:20-22
a De 32:22
b Nu 11:1,3
  De 6:15
  De 7:4
  Isa 5:25
  Isa 29:6
  Isa 66:16
  Jer 23:29
  Eze 21:31,32
  Eze 22:31
  Na 1:2,6
  Mal 4:1

2   Jesus is baptised by John the Baptist

c De 32:35
   Isa 13:6,9
   Joe 1:15
   Joe 2:1,11
d Ps 50:4
   Eze 5:8
   Eze 7:3
   Eze 20:36,37
   Eze 33:20
   Mt 7:1,2
e Mt 3:13
   Mr 1:9
   Lu 3:21
f Jn 1:35
g Ge 22:8,13
   Isa 53:7,10
   Jn 1:36
h Jn 1:37
i Jn 1:38
j Jn 1:39
k Jn 1:40

EVENTS THAT AWAIT THEM ARE SOON TO COME.[c]

22 "'FOR THE LORD WILL JUDGE HIS PEOPLE.'"[d]

23 And it happened in those days, that Jesus came from Nazareth in Galilee, and was baptised in the Jordan by John.[e]

24 And again, on the following day, John was standing, and two of his disciples;[f]

25 and having looked on Jesus walking, he said, "Behold, the lamb of God."[g]

26 And the two disciples heard him speaking, and they followed Jesus.[h]

27 But having turned, and having seen them following *him*, he said to them, "What are you seeking?" And they said to him, "Rabbi, where are you staying?"[i]

28 And he said to them, "Come and see." So they went and saw where he was staying, and they stayed with him that day, about the [2]tenth hour.[j]

29 And Andrew, the brother of Simon, was one of the two having heard this from John, and having followed him.[k]

30 He found his own brother Simon first, and —

---

2 I.e., 4 p.m.

2:23-37 Jesus is baptised by John the Baptist; his first followers declare him to be the Messiah

2:23 – And it happened in those days, that Jesus came from Nazareth in Galilee, and was baptised in the Jordan by John.

Jesus may have left Nazareth for a Mediterranean walkabout during his 'silent years', but he's evidently returned home since. Tales of the Baptist must have piqued his curiosity. He traveled to Judea, and it is reasonable to imagine that he stayed with John, becoming a disciple and soaking up the Baptist's take on spiritual duties and the Scriptures. However, while he may have adopted John's way of thinking for a time, in the end Jesus distanced himself and went his own way: I see few if any parallels between the two men's teachings. John is all about repentance, and warns of God's wrath, whereas Jesus stresses love and forgiveness and tolerance.

That Jesus underwent John's baptismal rites in the Jordan River[13] seems to have inconvenienced the early Jesus-movement: the Gospels go to great lengths to ensure that John is portrayed as being secondary to Jesus.

2:25 – and having looked on Jesus walking, he said, "Behold, the lamb of God."

Ge 22:8,13 – *Abraham said, "God will provide himself the lamb for a burnt offering, my son." […] | Abraham went and took the ram, and offered him up for a burnt offering instead of his son.*

Isa 53:7,10 – *[…] As a lamb that is led to the slaughter, and as a sheep that before its shearers is silent, so he didn't open his mouth. | Yet it pleased Yahweh to bruise him. He has caused him to suffer. When you make his soul an offering for sin […]*

John identifies Jesus as being the lamb of God who will be offered in sacrifice. While this is certainly the role that Jesus seems to have set for himself, we may have reason to doubt that the Baptist said this about him there on the banks of the Jordan; after all, as the evangelist has John say, *"I didn't recognize him."* (Jn 1:33)

John the Baptist's many words on Jesus' behalf – *'a man who is preferred before me, for he was before me', 'for this reason I came baptising in water: that he would be revealed to Israel', 'I have seen the Spirit descending like a dove out of heaven, and it remained on him', 'the same is he who baptises in the Holy Spirit'* (Jn 1:30-33) – would seem to have been put in his mouth by the early Jesus-movement. They probably felt a need to underpin their own teacher's superiority so as to counter the Baptist's followers, who *'reasoned in their hearts concerning John, whether perhaps he was the Christ'* (Lu 3:15). What better way than to have the rival preacher John clearly state *"I am not the Christ"* and testify that Jesus *"is the Son of God."* (Jn 1:20,33)

2:24,26,29 – And […] John was standing, and two of his disciples; And the two disciples heard him speaking, and they followed Jesus. And Andrew, the brother of Simon, was one of the two having heard this from John, and having followed him.

During his time at the Jordan, Jesus met a few other Galileans who were likewise John's disciples. There must have been something about Jesus' spiritual outlook and approach, though, that appealed to them more than the Baptist's fire and brimstone; they quickly forgot about John and started following Jesus.

The evangelist plainly states that there was another disciple who heard John speaking and who followed Jesus. Why isn't that disciple named? This happens once again in the Gospel according to John, when he writes that *'Simon Peter followed Jesus, as did another disciple. Now that disciple was known to the high priest, and entered in with Jesus into the court of the high priest.'* (Jn 18:15) I think this can only have been Judas; he is the only disciple who is named as having met with the chief priests, so he must have therefore been known to them. Keeping Judas' name out of the record on such occasions may have been a way of insuring that he never be seen in a good light,[14] be it in Jerusalem on that fateful night, where as *the other disciple, who was known to the high priest* he would have done his fellow disciple Peter a good turn by having him brought into the courtyard (Jn 18:16), or here by the banks of the Jordan, where his having been among the very first disciples to have known Jesus – in point of fact, earlier in the chronology than Simon Peter – could have counted in his favour.

2:27 – […] he said to them, "What are you seeking?" And they said to him, "Rabbi, where are you staying?"

Meeting Jesus for the first time, the two disciples are said to address him as 'Rabbi', or teacher. This could suggest that although he was still in the area, Jesus had perhaps already distanced himself from John and was no longer counting himself among the Baptist's disciples. Certainly Andrew and the other disciple consider him a teacher in his own right when they meet him, and they are eager to know where he is staying, one supposes so that they can learn more about him.

2:30 – He found his own brother Simon first, and – saying to him, "We have found the messiah" – he led him to Jesus.[15]

Well, Jesus has certainly made an impression, indeed so much so that both Andrew and Nathanael declare him to be the messiah and the king of Israel. In hopes of seeing an earthly kingdom of God established in their lifetime, the Jews were awaiting a messiah who would bring an end to Roman occupation and restore Israel's fortunes in the world.

It is of course possible that Jesus himself toyed with the idea of being such a messiah – after all, this time around he doesn't tell Andrew and Nathanael to cool it with the messiah thing – but I would argue that by the end of his forty days in the wilderness, he'd come to have a very different view of himself. As we have seen in the prologue, the Scriptures themselves seem to foretell an end to YHWH's reign; as I read it, Isaiah's 'Suffering Servant' is the agent by whom this comes about. I think Jesus decided that his mission was to be not a messiah-king, but rather the agent by whom Israel would be freed of its covenant with YHWH.

Incidentally, in the chronologies presented by the four gospels, this is the earliest recorded instance of Jesus saying, *"Follow me!"* I like to think that he was convoking Philip to come join him and the others for some evening festivities.

'Hey, it's getting late. Do you want to join us for supper? Follow me!'

2:38-51 JESUS IS TEMPTED BY SATAN IN THE WILDERNESS

2:38 – But Jesus, full of holy spirit, returned from the Jordan, and was led by the spirit into the wilderness.

Luke's wording suggests that Jesus had already returned to Galilee, before the spirit led him off into the wilderness for a forty day fast, a symbolic reference to Israel's forty year trek in the desert. The margin notes link this spirit with YHWH:

Ex 13:21 – *Yahweh went before them by day in a pillar of cloud, to lead them on their way, and by night in a pillar of fire, to give them light, that they might go by day and by night.*

Ne 9:19-21 – *"yet you in your manifold mercies didn't forsake them in the wilderness. […] | You gave also your good Spirit to instruct them […] | Yes, forty years you sustained them in the wilderness. […]"*

2:39 – And he was in the wilderness for forty days, being tempted by Satan; […]

All right, when it comes to the Scriptures, who does the tempting or testing?

saying to him, "We have found the [3]messiah" — he led him to Jesus.[l]

31 On the following day, he was wanting to go forth into Galilee, and finding Philip, Jesus said to him, "Follow me!"[m]

32 Now Philip was from Bethsaida, the city of Andrew and Simon.[n]

33 Philip found Nathanael, and said to him, "We have found *him* of whom Moses wrote in the law, and the prophets, Jesus of Nazareth."[4][o]

34 And Nathanael said to him, "Can any good thing come out of Nazareth?" Philip said to him, "Come and see."[p]

35 Jesus saw Nathanael coming to him, and he said about him, "Behold, truly an Israelite, in whom *there* is no [5]deceit."[q]

36 Nathanael said to him, "From where do you know me?" Jesus answered and said to him, "Before Philip called *you*, being under the fig tree, I saw you."[r]

37 Nathanael answered him, "Rabbi, you are the son of God, you are the king of Israel."[s]

l Jn 1:41,42
m Jn 1:43
n Jn 1:44
o De 18:15
   Isa 11:1
   Zec 3:8
   Jn 1:45
p Jn 1:46
q Ge 27:30-35,40
   Jn 1:47
r 1Ki 4:25
   Mic 4:4
   Zec 3:10
   Jn 1:48
s De 17:15
   Ps 2:6-9
   Jer 23:5
   Jn 1:49

---

3 Gr., *messian*, for the Hebrew *mashiach*
4 Certain later mss. add, *the son of Joseph*
5 Or, *guile*

2   Jesus is tempted by Satan in the wilderness

t Ex 13:21
   Ne 9:19-21
   Ps 78:14
   Lu 4:1
u Ex 24:15,18
   De 2:7
v Ge 22:1
   Ex 20:20
   De 8:2
   Ps 26:2
w Mt 4:1
   Mr 1:13
   Lu 4:2
   Jn 20:12
x Ex 34:28
   De 9:9
y Ps 107:5
   Mt 4:2
   Lu 4:2
z Jn 8:44
a Ex 4:22
   De 14:1,2
b Ex 24:12
   De 9:11
c Ps 78:18
   Mt 4:3
   Mt 7:9
   Lu 4:3
d Ex 20:1-17
   Le 18:5
   De 4:1,2
   De 8:3
   De 32:45-47
   Jer 15:16
   Mt 4:4
   Lu 4:4
e Ps 82:6
f Mt 4:5,6
   Lu 4:9
g Ps 91:11
   Mt 4:6
   Lu 4:10
h Ps 91:12
   Mt 4:6
   Lu 4:11
i De 6:16
   Mt 4:7
   Lu 4:12
j Nu 27:12
   De 32:49

38 But Jesus, full of holy spirit, returned from the Jordan, and was led by the spirit into the wilderness.[t]

39 And he was in the wilderness for forty days,[u] being [6]tempted by Satan;[v] and he was with the wild beasts, and the angels were serving him.[w]

40 And having fasted forty days and forty nights,[x] afterwards he was hungry.[y]

41 Then the tempter,[z] having come near, said to him, "If you are *a* son of the god,[a] [7]ask, that these stones[b] might become loaves of bread."[c]

42 But answering, he said, "It has been written, IT IS NOT BY BREAD THAT MAN DOES LIVE, BUT BY EVERY WORD THAT PROCEEDS FROM THE MOUTH OF GOD."[d]

43 Then the devil led him to Jerusalem, and stood him upon the temple's [8]pinnacle, and said to him, "If you are *a* son of the god,[e] *then* cast yourself down from here,[f]

44 for it has been written, HE WILL COMMAND HIS ANGELS CONCERNING YOU,[g]

45 and IN THEIR HANDS THEY WILL RAISE YOU

---

6 Or, *tested*
7 According to the best ancient mss.; most later mss. read, *speak*
8 Or, *battlement*

Ge 22:1 – […] *God tested Abraham, and said to him, "Abraham!"*

Ex 20:20 – *Moses said to the people, "Don't be afraid, for God has come to test you, and that his fear may be before you, that you won't sin."*

De 8:2 – *You shall remember all the way which Yahweh your God has led you these forty years in the wilderness, that he might humble you, to prove you, to know what was in your heart, whether you would keep his commandments, or not.*

Ps 26:2 – *Examine me, Yahweh, and prove me. Try my heart and my mind.*

The Hebrew word *satan* means 'adversary'; it can also be understood as 'enemy' or 'accuser'. We find him marvelously portrayed in the book of Job, where his words prompt YHWH to put his blameless and upright servant to the test, with YHWH remarking to Satan, " […] *my servant Job* […] *still maintains his integrity, although you incited me against him, to ruin him without cause.*" (Job 2:3) If we compare the following, though, this Satan character seems to be YHWH himself:

2Sa 24:1 – *Again Yahweh's anger burned against Israel, and he moved David against them, saying, "Go, count Israel and Judah."*

1Ch 21:1 – *Satan stood up against Israel, and moved David to take a census of Israel.*

Or again, consider the telling words used in Lamentations to describe YHWH:

La 2:4,5 – *He has bent his bow like an enemy, he has stood with his right hand as an adversary* […]|| *The Lord has become as an enemy, he has swallowed up Israel* […]

La 4:11,12 – *Yahweh has accomplished his wrath,* […] *He has kindled a fire in Zion* […]|| *The kings of the earth didn't believe,* […] *That the adversary and the enemy would enter into the gates of Jerusalem.*

Basically, when YHWH gets angry, he acts like the devil.

2:41 – Then the tempter, having come near, said to him, "If you are *a* son of the god [...]"

Ex 4:22 – "[...] *'Yahweh says, Israel is my son, my firstborn.'*"

De 14:1,2 – *You are the sons of Yahweh your God.* [...] | [...]

All Jews are the sons of YHWH, so Jesus was a son of the Jewish tribal god. I make no distinction here between 'a' son or 'the' son, since there is no definitive article attached to 'son' in the original Greek; in contrast, the definitive article 'the' is attached to *theos*, 'god'.

2:41 – "[...] ask, that these stones [...]"

Ex 24:12 – *Yahweh said to Moses, "Come up to me on the mountain, and stay here, and I will give you the stone tablets with the law and the commands that I have written, that you may teach them."*

De 9:11 – *"It came to pass at the end of forty days and forty nights, that Yahweh gave me the two stone tablets, even the tablets of the covenant."*

2:41 – "[...] might become loaves of bread."

Ps 78:18 – *They tempted God in their heart by asking food according to their desire.*

Mt 7:9 – *"Or who is there among you, who, if his son asks him for bread, will give him a stone?"*

Thwarting temptation with a scriptural defense, Jesus counters that man does not live by bread alone.

2:46 – And answering, Jesus said to him, "Again, it is written, YOU SHALL NOT TEST THE LORD YOUR GOD."

The devil justifies his second temptation by quoting scripture. Jesus counters with the same. Naturally, since the Scriptures are hermetic, this is the only legitimate way of dealing with such matters. Since both points have scriptural support, it is not the verses that count, but rather how well they are wielded that determines who gains the upper hand.

Incidentally, I should like to point out here that Yʜᴡʜ has a double standard. He can test – in Hebrew *nasah*, variably translated *tempt, test, prove, assay* – his holy people all he likes, but they've got a different rule:

De 6:16 – *You shall not tempt* [nasah] *Yahweh your God* [...].

2:47 – And the devil, having led him up to a high mountain [...]

Nu 27:12 – *Yahweh said to Moses, "Go up into this mountain of Abarim, and see the land which I have given to the children of Israel."*

De 32:49 – *"Go up into this mountain of Abarim, to Mount Nebo, which is in the land of Moab, that is across from Jericho; and see the land of Canaan, which I give to the children of Israel for a possession."*

2:47 – [...] showed him all the kingdoms of the inhabited world, in a moment of time;

Ge 13:14,15 – *Yahweh said to Abram, after Lot was separated from him, "Now, lift up your eyes, and look from the place where you are, northward and southward and eastward and westward, | for all the land which you see, I will give to you, and to your offspring forever."*

De 34:1-4 – *Moses went up from the plains of Moab to Mount Nebo, to the top of Pisgah, that is over against Jericho. Yahweh showed him all the land of Gilead, to Dan, | and all Naphtali, and the land of Ephraim and Manasseh, and all the land of Judah, to the western sea, | and the south, and the Plain of the valley of Jericho the city of palm trees, to Zoar. | Yahweh said to him, "This is the land which I swore to Abraham, to Isaac, and to Jacob, saying, 'I will give it to your offspring.' [...]"*

2:48 – and the devil said to him, "I will give to you all this domain [...]"

Ge 26:3,4 – *"Live in this land, and I will be with you, and will bless you. For I will give to you, and to your offspring, all these lands, and I will establish the oath which I swore to Abraham your father. | I will multiply your offspring as the stars of the sky, and will give all these lands to your offspring."*

Ge 28:13,14 – *Behold, Yahweh stood above it, and said, "I am Yahweh, the God of Abraham your father, and the God of Isaac. The land whereon you lie, to you will I give it, and to your offspring.* | *[…] and you will spread abroad to the west, and to the east, and to the north, and to the south. […]"*

2:48 – " […] for it has been handed over to me […] "

Ex 19:5 – *" […] for all the earth is mine."*

De 10:14 – *Behold, to Yahweh your God belongs heaven and the heaven of heavens, the earth, with all that is therein.*

Ps 24:1 – *The earth is Yahweh's […]; the world, and those who dwell therein.*

2:48 – " […] and I give it to whomever I wish."

Je 27:5 – *"I have made the earth, the men and the animals that are on the surface of the earth, by my great power and by my outstretched arm; and I give it to whom it seems right to me."*

Da 4:17 – *" […] the Most High rules in the kingdom of men, and gives it to whomever he will […]. "*

2:49 – "If you will therefore fear and serve me […] "

De 10:12 – *Now, Israel, what does Yahweh your God require of you, but to fear Yahweh your God, to walk in all his ways, and to love him, and to serve Yahweh your God with all your heart and with all your soul.*

De 13:4 – *You shall walk after Yahweh your God, fear him, keep his commandments, and obey his voice, and you shall serve him, and cling to him.*

Ps 34:9,11 – *Oh fear Yahweh […]*| *Come, you children, listen to me. I will teach you the fear of Yahweh.*

2:49 – " […] and swear by my name […] "

De 6:13 – *You shall fear Yahweh your God; and you shall serve him, and shall swear by his name.*

UP, LEST EVER YOU SHOULD STRIKE YOUR FOOT AGAINST A STONE."[h]

46 And answering, Jesus said to him, "Again, it is written, YOU SHALL NOT TEST THE LORD YOUR GOD."[i]

47 And the devil, having led him up to a high mountain,[j] showed him all the kingdoms of the inhabited world, in a moment of time;[k]

48 and the devil said to him, "I will give to you all this domain,[l] and their glory, for it has been handed over to me,[m] and I give it to whomever I wish.[n]

49 "If you will therefore fear and serve me,[o] and swear by my name,[p] then I will give this all to you,[q] and EVERY PLACE ON WHICH THE SOLES OF YOUR FEET SHALL TREAD SHALL BE YOURS."[r]

50 And answering, Jesus said to him, "Depart, Satan! How shall it benefit a man if he gains the whole world, yet loses himself;[s] for what shall a man give in exchange for his soul,[t] once he has lost it [9]forever?"[u]

51 And having finished every temptation, the devil departed from him, until *an* opportune time.[v]

---

9 Lit., *to the age*

k Ge 13:14,15
   De 34:1-4
   Mt 4:8
   Lu 4:5
l Ge 13:14,15
   Ge 26:3,4
   Ge 28:13,14
m Ex 19:5
   De 10:14
   Ps 24:1
   Ps 89:11
   Nu 14:8
n Jer 27:5
   Da 4:17
   Lu 4:6
o De 5:29
   De 6:24
   De 10:12
   De 13:4
   De 28:58-63
   Ps 34:9,11
p De 6:13
   De 10:20
q Ge 17:7,8
   Ps 2:8
   Ps 37:22
   Isa 1:19
   Mt 4:9
   Lu 4:7
r De 11:22-24
   Jos 1:3
s Le 25:55
   Isa 44:21
   Mr 8:36
   Lu 9:25
t De 10:12
   Ps 49:8
   Eze 18:4
   Mt 16:26
   Mr 8:37
u Ge 17:7
   Job 41:4
   Ps 105:8
   Isa 44:21
   Jer 5:23
   Jer 31:31-33
   Jer 32:38-40
   Eze 11:19,20
   Eze 36:26,27
v Na 1:9
   Lu 4:13

2:49 – " […] then I will give this all to you […] "

Ge 17:7,8– *"I will establish my covenant between me and you and your offspring after you throughout their generations for an everlasting covenant, to be a God to you and to your offspring after you. | I will give to you, and to your offspring after you, the land where you are traveling, all the land of Canaan, for an everlasting possession. I will be their God."*

Ps 37:22– *For such as are blessed by him shall inherit the land. Those who are cursed by him shall be cut off.*

2:49 – " […] and EVERY PLACE ON WHICH THE SOLES OF YOUR FEET SHALL TREAD SHALL BE YOURS."

De 11:22-24 – *For if you shall diligently keep all these commandments which I command you, […] | then will Yahweh drive out all these nations from before you […]. | Every place whereon the sole of your foot treads shall be yours […].*

Jos 1:3 – *"I have given you every place that the sole of your foot will tread on, as I told Moses."*

2:50 – And answering, Jesus said to him, "Depart, Satan! How shall it benefit a man if he gains the whole world, yet loses himself; […] "

Le 25:55 – *"For to me the sons of Israel are slaves; they are my slaves whom I brought out of the land of Egypt. I am Yahweh your God."*

Lu 9:25– *For what does it profit a man if he gains the whole world, and loses or forfeits his own self?*

2:50 – " […] for what shall a man give in exchange for his soul […] "

De 10:12 – *Now, Israel, what does Yahweh your God require of you, but to […] serve Yahweh your God with all your heart and with all your soul.*

Ps 49:7,8 – *None of them can by any means redeem his brother, nor give God a ransom for him. | For the redemption of their life is costly, no payment is ever enough.*

2:50 – " […] once he has lost it forever?"

Ge 17:7 – *"I will establish my covenant between me and you and your offspring […] for an everlasting covenant […]."*

Job 41:4 – *"Will he make a covenant with you, that you should take him for a slave forever?"*

Isa 44:21 – *"Remember these things, Jacob and Israel; for you are my slave. I have formed you. You are my slave."*

Mt 16:21 – *"For what will it profit a man, if he gains the whole world, and forfeits his soul? Or what will a man give in exchange for his soul?"*

In this final exchange, I have sought to emphasize that it is YHWH who rules the kingdoms of the earth and bestows them on whom he wishes. All he requires is that his servants fear and worship him.

Jesus' reply here departs from the Gospel narrative, following instead what he says elsewhere in the Gospels of Matthew, Mark and Luke: *"For what does it profit a man, to gain the whole world, and forfeit his soul? | For what will a man give in exchange for his soul?"* (Mr 8:36,37) If we consider that the everlasting covenant established by YHWH and agreed to by Abraham was a deal in which the Jewish patriarch's offspring gained the whole world in exchange for their souls, this statement has far-reaching implications.

2:51 – And having finished every temptation, the devil departed from him, until an opportune time.

Na 1:9 – *What do you plot against Yahweh? He will make a full end. Affliction won't rise up the second time.*

This time around, Jesus beats YHWH at his game. But as we shall see, the devil had other ways to turn the tables on this upstart from Galilee.

3   Jesus settles in Capernaum   Four disciples are called

CHAPTER 3

a *Mt 14:3*
   Mr 6:17
   Lu 3:20
b *Mt 4:12*
   Mr 1:14
   Lu 4:14
c *Mr 2:1*
d *Mt 4:13*
e *Mt 4:18*
   Mr 1:16
f *Mt 4:19*
   Mr 1:17
g *Mt 4:20*
   Mr 1:18
h *Mt 4:21*
   Mr 1:19
i *Mt 4:21,22*
   Mr 1:20

NOW having heard that John had been handed over,[a] he withdrew into Galilee.[b]

2   And having left Nazareth, *and* having come, he settled in Capernaum,[c] which is by the sea.[d]

3   And as he was passing by the sea of Galilee, he saw Simon, and Andrew, the brother of Simon, casting a net into the sea; for they were fishermen.[e]

4   And he said to them, "Come, follow me!"[f] And immediately, they left their nets and followed him.[g]

5   And having gone on from there, he saw others, two brothers, James the *son* of Zebedee, and John, his brother, in the boat with Zebedee, their father, preparing their nets.[h]

6   And at that moment he called them; and having left their father Zebedee in the boat with the hired servants, they went away after him.[i]

7   And when he came to Capernaum, immediately

3

The new wine

3:1-6 JESUS SETTLES IN CAPERNAUM

Jesus' new friends were living in Capernaum, so following his encounters with the devil, he went to look up Andrew, Simon, James and John. It seems the boys were mighty glad he came round – they immediately dropped what they were doing and ran off to follow him.[16] Nevertheless, when the father of James and John saw his two sons jump ship to go gallivanting about with the interloper from Nazareth, one can imagine how he most likely reacted to being left behind with the hired servants. I like to think that Zebedee's vociferations may have inspired Jesus to nickname James and John the 'sons of thunder'.

3:7-14 JESUS TEACHES IN CAPERNAUM

3:8 – And they were thunderstruck by his teaching, for he was teaching them as *one* having authority, and not as the scribes.

Who is this guy? Where's he from? Who's his rabbi? Who gave him authority to teach and interpret the Scriptures in this way?

It appears that from the very start of his public career, Jesus was seen as preaching a new message. His wasn't the 'old wine' of the scribes or the Pharisees or the Sadducees; his was a 'new wine'. But from where did it come? Who had given it to him? Had Jesus come up with it all by himself?

I think it required many long years of gestation, and it may have only coalesced as a certitude in his mind during the final weeks of his wilderness fast, but by the time Jesus arrived in Capernaum he knew what his message was. More to the point, he knew what his mission would be.

3:9 – And at that moment in their synagogue there was a man with *an* unclean spirit [...]

On occasion, footnotes in *The Gospel of Jesus of Nazareth* inform us that *certain mss. read*, or *most later mss. add*, or that verses such-and-such *are not found in the best ancient mss.* This is of course fictive; there are no such manuscripts. My purpose is neither to covertly rewrite the scriptures nor to falsify the historical record, but rather to focus attention on certain incongruities that are found in the authentic Gospel manuscripts and to offer what I think are plausible suggestions for how we might clarify those passages, or account for the readings that have come down to us (see endnote, page 422). Here, for example, it seems to me that the episode of the man with the unclean spirit might have easily been added at a later date to attest to Jesus' special miraculous powers, for the passage reads just as well without it – the people in the synagogue are simply thunderstruck by Jesus' authority and teaching, and so news about him goes out *'immediately into all the surrounding area of Galilee.'*

3:15-17 JESUS HEALS SIMON'S MOTHER-IN-LAW [17]

Well, maybe. Or maybe she was the sort of conscientious woman who, when guests showed up, wasn't going to stay in bed with a fever. Rising to the occasion, Simon's mother-in-law hauls herself out of bed and serves all five of them: her son-in-law, his brother Andrew, their two fishermen friends, James and John, and this new fellow they met at the Jordan River who's just arrived in town. All five men are served by a woman who's been lying in bed with a fever. "A miracle!" you say? I'm

on the Sabbath, Jesus entered the synagogue and was teaching.[j]

8   And they were thunderstruck by his teaching, for he was teaching them as *one* having authority, and not as the scribes.[k]

9   [1][And at that moment in their synagogue there was a man with *an* unclean spirit, and he cried out,[l]

10   saying, "What do these people have to do with you, Jesus of Nazareth? Have you come to destroy us?[m] I know who you are – the holy *one* of God!"[n]

11   And Jesus rebuked him, saying, "Be quiet, and come forth out of him!"[o]

12   And the unclean spirit, having convulsed him, and having shouted with a great voice, came out of him.[p]]

13   And all were astonished, so as to question among themselves, saying, "What is this new teaching, with *such* authority? [1][He commands even the unclean spirits, and they obey him!"[q]]

14   And the news about him went out immediately into all the surrounding area of Galilee.[r]

15   And having left the synagogue, immediately

j   *Mr 1:21*
    Lu 4:31
k   *Mt 7:28,29*
    Mr 1:22
    Lu 4:32
l   *Mr 1:23*
    Lu 4:33
m   *De 13:1,3*
n   *Mr 1:24*
    Lu 4:34
o   *Mr 1:25*
    Lu 4:35
p   *Mr 1:26*
    Lu 4:35
q   *Mr 1:27*
    Lu 4:36
r   *Mr 1:28*
    Lu 4:37

---

1 Verses 9-12 and part of verse 13 are not found in the best ancient mss.

3

s *Mt 8:14*
   Mr 1:29
   Lu 4:38
t *Mt 8:14*
   Mr 1:30
   Lu 4:38
u *Mt 8:15*
   Mr 1:31
   Lu 4:39
v *Mr 1:32,34*
   Lu 4:40
w *Ps 19:2*
   Ps 119:15,147
   Ps 143:5
   Mr 1:35
   Lu 4:42
   Lu 5:16
x *Mr 1:36*
   Lu 4:42
y *Mr 1:37*
z *Mr 1:38*
   Lu 4:43
a *Mt 4:23*
   Mr 1:39
   Lu 4:44

they came into the house of Simon and Andrew, with James and John,[s]

16 for Simon's mother-in-law was lying ill with fever; and immediately they spoke to him about her.[t]

17 And having come to *her*, he raised her up, having taken her hand; and the fever left her, and she served them.[u]

18 But at the setting of the sun, all those who were ill with various sicknesses were brought to him, and having laid the hands on each one of them, he healed them.[v]

19 And in the very early morning, when it was still night, he arose and went out and departed *by himself* to a solitary place to pray.[w]

20 And Simon and those with him went searching for him;[x] and having found him, they reproached him, saying, "Everyone is looking for you!"[y]

21 But he said to them, "Let us go *by* another way, into the neighboring towns, that I might preach also there. It was for this that I left *the house*."[z]

22 And he was preaching in the synagogues of Galilee.[a]

23 And having returned again to Capernaum after

more inclined to vote for a woman with a strong sense of duty, catering to an indolent bunch of Middle Eastern men. (See also Luke 10:38-42.)

3:18 JESUS HEALS THOSE WHO ARE BROUGHT TO HIM

The laying on of hands was a gesture that accompanied the giving of one's blessing (Genesis 48:9-16, Mark 10:16) or praying for someone (Matthew 19:13-15 – though we should note that Jesus did not pray). Those who were ill would no doubt feel better, even possibly healed.

3:19-22 JESUS DEPARTS TO A LONELY PLACE

Some guest! The guy goes off without telling anyone. Jesus wasn't big on manners, it seems. Maybe he was one of those self-absorbed, other-worldly types. Still, his disappearance sparks a pre-dawn manhunt, and Simon is understandably peeved with his houseguest when they finally track him down: *"Everyone is looking for you!"* Neatly dodging the reproach, Jesus claims that he left the house to go into the neighboring towns, so that he can preach there, too. A laudable plan…or, realising that he'd just gaffed big time with his host, a clever dodge to disappear for a few days until things blew over. It would be a little while before his new friends got used to his impulsive ways.

3:23-29 THE PARALYTIC

Sickness and infirmities were seen to be the result of sin. According to Jewish tradition, though, children were not held accountable under the Law for their own acts;[18] so in the minds of the Jews, and no less the minds of the disciples (see John 9:2), if a child were sick it was because YHWH – hardly one to spare an innocent child, we might add – was likely making him pay for a fault committed by one of his ancestors:

Nu 14:18 – *'Yahweh* […] *will by no means clear the guilty, visiting the iniquity of the fathers on the children, on the third and on the fourth genera-tion.'*

"But that you might know that the son of man on the earth has authority to forgive sins," Jesus says to the boy, *"take up your mat and go away to your house."* On one level, these are words of comfort said to a child who suffers and who may wrongly imagine that he is to blame for his plight, so that the boy will feel blessed and forgiven. But there is of course more to it than that: just as Jesus will later assert that the son of man is master of the Sabbath, here he arrogates to himself YHWH's authority to forgive sins. It doesn't count for much, because the boy isn't actually guilty of sin, but still, the Pharisees have reason to grumble about this. I rather doubt though that the boy jumped up, all healed and well – after all, he's bearing the brunt of YHWH's hard-heartedness, and no one but YHWH can heal (cf. Exodus 15:26, Deuteronomy 32:39) – but he might have waddled out, bravely believing that his life would improve from that moment forward. Jesus gave him hope, and that in itself is no small miracle.

It is of note that in the Gospels, Jesus is only reported to have forgiven sin in two instances – here, with the paralytic, and on one other occasion found in Luke 7:36-50, where Jesus says *"Your sins are forgiven"* to the woman who has so lovingly attended to his feet. As such, 'forgiving sin' doesn't seem to count for much in his program. I think that's because he simply intended to do away with the Law altogether. After all, to sin is to transgress the Law, and if the Law is annulled, then so is sin.

3:30,31 LEVI IS CALLED [19]

"Follow me!" he says. But where do they go? To Levi's house, where they share a tremendous feast with *'a great crowd of tax collectors and others who were reclining with them.'* (Lu 5:29) Maybe 'Follow me!' is code for

some days, and it was heard that he was in a house.[b]

24   And behold, they brought to him a paralytic, lying on a mat; and seeing their faith, Jesus said to the paralytic, "Take heart, child – your sins have been forgiven."[c]

25   But some of the scribes said within themselves, "He blasphemes."[d]

26   But Jesus, having perceived their thoughts, said to them, "Why do you think evil in your hearts?[e]

27   "For which is easier – to say, 'Your sins have been forgiven you', or to say, 'Rise up and walk'?[f]

28   "But that you might know that the son of man on the earth has authority to forgive sins –" he said to the paralytic, "Take up your mat and go away to your house."[g]

29   And having gotten up, he went away to his house.[h]

30   And he went out again by the sea, and all the crowd came to him, and he taught them.[i]

31   And passing by, he saw Levi, the *son* of Alphaeus, sitting in the tax collector's booth, and he said, "Follow me!" And he rose and followed him.[j]

32   And it came about, that as he was reclining in

b Mr 2:1
c Ex 34:7
   Nu 14:18
   Jer 32:18
   Mt 9:2
   Mr 2:5
   Lu 5:20
d Mt 9:3
   Mr 2:6,7
   Lu 5:21
e Mt 9:4
   Mr 2:8
   Lu 5:22
f Mt 9:5
   Mr 2:9
   Lu 5:23
g Mt 9:6
   Mr 2:10,11
   Lu 5:24
h Mt 9:7
i Mr 2:13
j Mt 9:9
   Mr 2:14
   Lu 5:27,28

k Ec 5:18
   Ec 8:15
   Ec 9:7
   Mt 9:10
   Mt 11:19
   Lu 7:34
l Mr 2:15
   Lu 15:1
m Isa 22:13
   Jer 16:8
   Mt 9:11
   Mr 2:16
   Lu 5:30
   Lu 15:2
n De 28:58-61
   Isa 1:5,6
   Jer 15:18
   Jer 30:12-15
   Mt 9:12
   Mr 2:17
   Lu 5:31
o 1Ki 8:46
   Job 25:4-6
   Ps 143:2
   Pr 20:9
   Ec 7:20
p Mt 9:13
   Mr 2:17
   Lu 5:32
q Joe 2:12
   Lu 18:11,12
r Mt 9:14
   Mr 2:18
   Lu 5:33
   Lu 18:11,12
s Isa 22:12
t Isa 22:13
   Mt 9:15
   Mr 2:19
   Lu 5:34

the house, many tax collectors and sinners came, and they were reclining at table with Jesus and his disciples;[k] for there were many of them, and they were following him.[l]

33 And the scribes of the Pharisees, having seen him eating with the sinners and tax collectors, said to his disciples, "Why does he eat with tax collectors and sinners?"[m]

34 And hearing this, Jesus said to them, "It is not those who are healthy who need a physician, but those who are sick.[n]

35 "But rather, go and learn what *this* means, 'NO MAN IS RIGHTEOUS AND DOES NOT SIN.'[o] I did not come to call the righteous, but sinners."[p]

36 And John's disciples and the Pharisees were fasting; and they came to him, saying, "Why do John's disciples and the Pharisees' disciples fast,[q] yet you and your disciples do not fast?"[r]

37 And Jesus said to them, "Can the sons of the bridal chamber fast,[s] while the bridegroom is *there* with them? As long as they have the bridegroom with them, they cannot fast.[t]

38 "But the days will come when the bridegroom

'Let's go eat, drink, and be merry!' The last time he said it, he and his friends – after a quick detour to the synagogue along the way to drop in on the Sabbath service – ended up at Simon and Andrew's house, where they enjoyed a meal. (We recall that Simon's mother-in-law was lying sick in bed with a fever, but she still got up and served them.)

3:32-35 THE SCRIBES OF THE PHARISEES QUESTION JESUS

3:32 – And it came about, that as he was reclining in the house, many tax collectors and sinners came, and were reclining at table with Jesus and his disciples; [...] [20]

Ec 9:7 – *Go your way – eat your bread with joy, and drink your wine with a merry heart; for God has already accepted your works.*

It seems Jesus and his followers were keen to put this wisdom into daily practice, but the scribes of the Pharisees were not amused; they took him to task for eating with disreputable tax gatherers and sinners.

3:34 – And hearing this, Jesus said to them, "It is not those who are healthy who need a physician, but those who are sick."

De 28:58-61 – *If you will not observe to do all the words of this law that are written in this book, [...] | then Yahweh will make your plagues fearful, and the plagues of your offspring, even great plagues, and of long duration, and severe sicknesses, and of long duration. | He will bring on you again all the diseases of Egypt, which you were afraid of; and they will cling to you. | Also every sickness and every plague, which is not written in the book of this law, Yahweh will bring them on you, until you are destroyed.*

Jer 30:12-15 – *For Yahweh says, "Your hurt is incurable, and your wound grievous. | [...] I have wounded you with the wound of an enemy, with the chastisement of a cruel one [...] . | Why do you cry for your hurt? Your pain is incurable: for the greatness of your iniquity, because your sins were increased, I have done these things to you."*

By implication, the sick are those who, having displeased YHWH, are being punished by him for their sins. Yet as Jesus here reminds his listeners, 'NO MAN IS RIGHTEOUS AND DOES NOT SIN.'

Ec 7:20 – *Surely there is not a righteous man on earth, who does good and does not sin.*

The Pharisees openly disdained the sinners with whom he spent his time, but Jesus embraced them. Indeed, these were the Jews he hoped to save from YHWH's promised wrath…by redeeming them from the covenant that bound them to their tribal god, as we shall see.

3:36-38 FASTING

3:36 – […] "Why do John's disciples and the Pharisees' disciples fast, yet you and your disciples do not fast?"

Joe 2:12 – *"Yet even now," says Yahweh, "turn to me with all your heart, and with fasting, and with weeping, and with mourning."*

Since fasting was a common practice for 'righteous' men, people naturally wondered why Jesus did not fast – and probably all the more so, since they knew he had followed John and been baptised by him.

On this point as on so many others, Jesus strikes a new chord, one that is unfamiliar to Jews inculcated with an abiding fear of YHWH and an unswerving obedience to Judaism's precepts and traditions.

3:39-41 THE NEW WINE

I equate the 'new wine' with Jesus' teachings and the 'old wine' with the Judaism of his time. Just as you cannot put new wine into old wineskins, you cannot make Jesus' new teachings conform to the older religion.

"Yet no one who has drunk the old desires the new," he observes, *"for he says the old wine is good."* Jesus was well aware that his coreligionists would have a hard time giving up the faith of their fathers.

will have been taken away from them,[u] and then will
they fast.[v]

39 "No one sews a piece of new cloth on an old
garment, lest the patch pulls away from it, the new
from the old, and a worse tear occurs.[w]

40 "And no one puts new wine into old wineskins,[x]
lest the wine burst the wineskins, and the wine and
the wineskins are utterly destroyed; but new wine *is
put* into fresh wineskins, and both are preserved.[y]

41 "Yet no one who has drunk the old desires
new, for he says the old *wine* is good."[z]

42 And it came about that he was passing through
the grain fields on the Sabbath, and his disciples
began to make their way, picking the heads of grain.[a]

43 But some of the Pharisees said, "Why are you
doing what is not lawful on the Sabbath?"[b]

44 And he said to them, "Have you not read what
David did when he was in need and was hungry, he
and those who were with him;[c]

45 how he entered into the house of God in *the time
of* Abiathar, *who became* high priest,[d] and *he* ate the
consecrated bread,[e] which is not lawful *for anyone* to
eat, except for the priests,[f] and he even gave *it* to those

u Isa 22:14
   Isa 53:8
v Mt 9:15
   Mr 2:20
   Lu 5:35
w Mt 9:16
   Mr 2:21
   Lu 5:36
x Jer 51:26
y Mt 9:17
   Mr 2:22
   Lu 5:37,38
z Isa 25:6
   Lu 5:39
a De 23:25
   Mt 12:1
   Mr 2:23
   Lu 6:1
b Ex 20:8-11
   Ex 31:13-17
   Mt 12:2
   Mr 2:24
   Lu 6:2
c Mt 12:3
   Mr 2:25
   Lu 6:3
d 1Sa 21:1
e Ex 25:30
f Le 24:5-9

3   The Sabbath

g 1Sa 21:3-6
   Mt 12:4
   Mr 2:26
   Lu 6:4
h Le 1:7
   Le 6:12,13
   Nu 28:2,9,10
i Ex 31:14,15
   Ex 35:2,3
j Mt 12:5
k Ex 23:12
   De 5:14
l Mt 12:8
   Mr 2:27,28
   Lu 6:5
m Mt 12:9,10
   Mr 3:1
   Lu 6:6
n Mr 3:4
   Lu 12:57
   Lu 14:3,4
o Mt 12:13
   Mr 3:5
   Lu 14:4
p Mt 12:11
   Lu 14:5

who were with him?[g]

46 "Or, have you not read in the Law that the priests in the temple[h] break the Sabbath,[i] and *yet* are guiltless?"[j]

47 And he said to them, "The Sabbath was made for the sake of man,[k] and not man for the sake of the Sabbath. Therefore, the son of man is master also of the Sabbath."[l]

48 And it came to pass on another Sabbath, that he entered into the synagogue and was teaching, and there was a man there, whose right hand was withered.[m]

49 And he said to them, "Is it lawful on the Sabbath to do good, or to do evil? To save a life, or to kill?" But they were silent.[n]

50 And having looked around on them with seething anger, being grieved by the hardness of their heart, he said to the man, "Stretch out your hand." And having taken hold *of him*, he laid on the hands, and he healed him, and let *him* go.[o]

51 And he said to them, "Which one of you shall have a donkey or an ox fall into a pit, and will not immediately pull him out on the Sabbath day?[p]

52 "Then how much more valuable is a man than

3:42-53 THE SABBATH

Here again, Jesus bucks convention. He does what he likes on the Sabbath, be it plucking heads of wheat as he walks through a field, or performing an act of goodness by laying his hands on a man in need of comfort and healing.

3:47 – And he said to them, "The Sabbath was made for the sake of man, and not man for the sake of the Sabbath. [...]"

Ex 23:12 – *"Six days you shall do your work, and on the seventh day you shall rest, that your ox and your donkey may have rest, and the son of your servant, and the alien may be refreshed."*

The purpose of the Sabbath, clearly stated by Moses, is so that everyone can have a day off, get some rest, and be refreshed.

3:47 – "[...] Therefore, the son of man is master also of the Sabbath."

Laying claim to a surprising degree of self-determination, Jesus plainly states that the son of man is master of the Sabbath; moreover, he presents his assertion as a logical conclusion (Greek, *hóste*; 'therefore') to the foregoing, so he is speaking not only for himself, but for all Jews. Since his reasoning has no basis in the Torah, I personally read Jesus' stance as an outright rejection of the Law's – and by extension YHWH's – authority to decide what a man can or cannot do on the Sabbath.

3:52 – " [...] Therefore, it is lawful to good on the Sabbath."

Jesus is said to be seething with anger. His fellow Jews didn't hesitate to do good for their donkey or ox in a pinch on the Sabbath, but when it came to reacting with similar intelligence to situations that concerned their fellow man, they were so deeply in thrall to the precepts of Mosaic Law that they were paralysed. Looking around, he may have wondered to himself, *"Why don't you judge for yourselves what is right?"* (Lu 12:57)

4

The teaching

4:1-7 THE TWELVE DISCIPLES ARE NAMED

Jesus has spent enough time in Capernaum to have collected a group of close followers. Word about him has gone out into the surrounding area of Galilee; he's been to the neighboring towns and preached in their synagogues, and crowds of people had been coming to the seashore to listen to him teach. The man from Nazareth has been making a name for himself, I imagine as a freethinking nonconformist.

Jesus selected twelve devoted followers, that he might send them out to preach. He wanted to spread his message, and he needed some help.

Jesus chose twelve men. In the Synoptic Gospels, without exception, Simon tops the list. James and John and Andrew come next, followed by Philip, Bartholomew, Matthew, Thomas, James the son of Alphaeus, Thaddaeus, and Simon the Zealot. Likewise without exception, Judas the Iscariot is mentioned last. A margin note offers us Matthew 20:16 for consideration in this regard: *"So the last will be first, and the first last."*

As will be seen, I believe Judas was Jesus' closest friend and confidant, so perhaps we should see in this list a hidden ranking of the disciples based on their relative merits. Judas – to whom Jesus entrusted not only the group's money bag, but above all the critical and delicate task of arranging for his arrest – would have been Jesus' right-hand man; whereas Simon – slow to understand (*"Explain the parable to us"*), prone to mistaken conclusions (*"You are the messiah"*, *"Yes, my master*

a sheep! Therefore, it is lawful to do good on the Sabbath."[q]

53 And they were not able to reply to these *things*.[r]

q Mt 12:12
r Lu 14:6

CHAPTER 4

Now it came to pass in these days, that he went out to the mountain to pray, and he was spending the whole night in prayer to God.[a]

2   And when it became day, he called to *him* those he wanted, and they went to him.[b]

3   And he appointed twelve, that they might be with him, and that he might send them out to preach.[c]

4   And to Simon he was applying the name Cephas;[d]

5   and James, the *son* of Zebedee, and John, the brother of James,[e] and he was applying to them the name [1]Boanerges;[f]

a Lu 5:16
   Lu 6:12
   Lu 11:9
b Mr 3:13
   Lu 6:13
c Mr 3:14
d Mt 10:2
   Mr 3:16
   Lu 6:14
e Mt 10:2
   Lu 6:14
f Mr 3:17

1 Of Aramaic origin; possibly, *sons of thunder*

4   The Beatitudes

g *Mt 10:2,3*
   Mr 3:18
   Lu 6:14,15
h *Mt 10:4*
   Mt 19:30
   Mt 20:16
   Mr 3:18,19
   Lu 6:15,16
i *Mr 3:7*
   Lu 6:17
j *De 28:58-60*
k *Lu 6:18*
l *Lu 6:19*
m *Mr 3:9*
n *Mt 5:2*
o *La 1:7*
p *Mt 5:3*
   Lu 6:20

6   and Andrew; and Philip; and Bartholomew; and Matthew; and Thomas; and James, the *son* of Alphaeus; and Thaddaeus;[g]

7   and Simon, the Zealous; and [2]Judas, the [3]Iscariot.[h]

8   And having descended with them, he stood on a level place; and *there was* a large crowd of his disciples, and a great multitude of people from Galilee,[4][i]

9   who came to hear him and to be healed of their sicknesses;[j] and those *who were* troubled by unclean spirits were cared for.[k]

10   And all the crowd sought to touch him, for power went out from him and healed all.[l]

11   And he spoke to his disciples, that a boat might stand ready for him, on account of the crowd, that they might not press upon him.[m]

12   And having opened his mouth, he taught them, saying,[n]

13   "Blessed *are* the poor,[o] for yours is the kingdom of God.[p]

---

2 Gr., *Ioudas*, for the Hebrew *Yehudah*
3 Meaning uncertain; certain later mss. add, *who also handed him over*
4 Certain later mss. add, *and from all Judea and Jerusalem, and the sea coast of Tyre and Sidon*

pays the temple tax"), arrogant (*"Even if all will be made to stumble because of you, I will never be made to stumble!"*) and cowardly (*"I don't know this man of whom you speak!"*) – would have been Jesus' biggest headache.

4:8-11 JESUS TEACHES AT THE SEASHORE

Jesus probably attracted a certain following from the area surrounding Capernaum, but to say that *'a great number of the people from all Judea and Jerusalem, and the sea coast of Tyre and Sidon'* (Lu 6:17) were coming to hear him as well seems to me far-fetched.

4:12-15 THE BEATITUDES

4:13 – "Blessed *are* the poor, for yours is the kingdom of God."

La 1:7 – *Jerusalem remembers in the days of her affliction and of her miseries, all her pleasant things that were from the days of old: when her people fell into the hand of the adversary, and no one helped her, the adversaries saw her, they mocked at her desolations.*

The poor are those whom YHWH has repudiated. Yet to them, says Jesus, will be the kingdom of God.

4:14 – "Blessed *are* those who are hungering now, for you will be filled."

La 2:12,20 – *They ask their mothers, "Where is grain and wine?", when they swoon as the wounded in the streets of the city, when their soul is poured out into their mothers' bosom. | Look, Yahweh, and see to whom you have done thus! Shall the women eat their offspring, the children that are dandled in the hands? […]*

La 3:1,43 – *I am the man that has seen affliction by the rod of his wrath. | You have covered us with anger and pursued us. You have killed. You have not pitied.*

La 4:4,9 – *The tongue of the nursing child clings to the roof of his mouth for thirst: the young children ask bread, and no man breaks it to them. | Those who are killed with the sword are better than those who are killed with hunger; for these pine away, stricken through, for want of the fruits of the field.*

Those who are hungering are but suffering YHWH's wrath.

4:15 – "Blessed *are* those who are weeping now, for you will laugh."

Those who are weeping have YHWH to thank for that:

La 1:12 – *"Is it nothing to you, all you who pass by? Look, and see if there is any sorrow like my sorrow, which is brought on me, with which Yahweh has afflicted me in the day of his fierce anger."*

La 2:5,11 – *The Lord has become as an enemy, He has swallowed up Israel; He has swallowed up all her palaces, He has destroyed his strongholds; He has multiplied in the daughter of Judah mourning and lamentation. | My eyes fail with tears, my heart is troubled; my liver is poured on the earth, because of the destruction of the daughter of my people, because the young children and the infants swoon in the streets of the city.*

La 3:48,49 – *My eye runs down with streams of water, for the destruction of the daughter of my people. | My eye pours down, and doesn't cease […].*

To those who are poor, who are hungering or weeping, Jesus will bring liberation. To them will be the kingdom of God and fullness and laughter, once they are free.

4:16-26 LOVE YOUR ENEMIES

4:16 – "You have heard that it was said, YOU SHALL LOVE YOUR NEIGHBOR and HATE YOUR ENEMY."

That one should hate one's enemy and show him no mercy is clear from certain passages in the Scriptures, among which are these:

De 7:2,16,24 – *And when Yahweh your God delivers them up before you, and you strike them; then you shall utterly destroy them. You shall make* *no covenant with them, nor show mercy to them; | you shall consume all the peoples whom Yahweh your God shall deliver to you. Your eye shall not pity them* [...] | *He will deliver their kings into your hand, and you shall make their name perish from under the sky.*

Ps 139:22 – *I hate them with perfect hatred. They have become my enemies.*

4:17 – "But I say to you who hear, love your enemies [...] "

Jesus' instruction to *"love your enemies"* stands in stark contrast to YHWH's conduct:

Ex 23:22,23,27 – *"But if you* [...] *do all that I speak, then I will be an enemy to your enemies, and an adversary to your adversaries. | For my angel shall go before you, and bring you in to the Amorite, the Hittite, the Perizzite, the Canaanite, the Hivite, and the Jebusite; and I will cut them off. | I will send my terror before you* [...], *and I will make all your enemies turn their backs to you."*

4:17 – " [...] *and do well to those who hate you."*

Compare that to the Scriptures, wherein YHWH promises his wrath to those who hate him:

De 5:9 – *"* [...] *I, Yahweh, your God, am a jealous God, visiting the iniquity of the fathers on the children, and on the third and on the fourth generation of those who hate me."*

De 7:10 – *[Yahweh] repays those who hate him to their face, to destroy them. He will not be slack to him who hates him. He will repay him to his face.*

De 32:41 – *"* [...] *I will take vengeance on my adversaries, and will repay those who hate me."*

In this teaching alone, Jesus shows that he stands utterly apart from YHWH. Not only is the idea of loving one's enemies and doing well to those who hate you at odds with the Torah, it's contrary to basic human nature, and some of Jesus' own disciples had a hard time curbing their natural tendencies. James and John revealed that they were poor students of their teacher's 'do well to those who hate you' rule when they eagerly asked if they could toast the inhospitable Samaritan village: *"Lord, do you want us to command fire to come down from the sky, and destroy them, just as Elijah did?"* (Lu 9:54 ; cf. 2 Kings 1:10)

4:18 – "You have heard that it was said, AN EYE FOR AN EYE, AND A TOOTH FOR A TOOTH."

De 19:21 – *Your eyes shall not pity: life for life, eye for eye, tooth for tooth, hand for hand, foot for foot.*

4:19,20,21 – "But I say to you, to him who strikes you on the cheek, offer *him* also the other; and from him who takes away what is yours, do not ask for it back. To every one *who* asks you, give; and from him who takes away what is yours, do not ask *for it* back. And just as you desire that men should do to you, do to them in the same way."

Clearly, Jesus means it literally when he says do well to those who hate you or who do you an injustice, and he gives his hearers some concrete examples. Here again, his message is at variance with the Torah, where a tit-for-tat, even-steven equality aims to maintain order and keep things in check.

But as Jesus next points out, there is nothing special or meritorious in only doing well to those who treat you well.

4:22 – "And if you love *only* those who love you, what credit is that to you? [...] "

Ex 20:5,6 – *" [...] I, Yahweh your God, am a jealous God, visiting the iniquity of the fathers on the children, on the third and on the fourth generation of those who hate me, | and showing loving kindness to thousands of those who love me and keep my commandments."*

14 "Blessed *are* those who are hungering[q] now, for you will be filled.[r]

15 "Blessed *are* those *who are* weeping[s] now, for you will laugh.[t]

16 "You have heard that it was said, YOU SHALL LOVE YOUR NEIGHBOR[u] and HATE YOUR ENEMY.[v]

17 "But I say to you who hear, love your enemies,[w] *and* do well to those who hate you.[x]

18 "You have heard that it was said, AN EYE FOR AN EYE, AND A TOOTH FOR A TOOTH.[y]

19 "But I say to you, to him who strikes you on the cheek, offer *him* also the other; and from him who takes away your cloak, do not withhold the tunic.[z]

20 "To every one *who* asks you, give; and from him who takes away what *is* yours, do not ask *for it* back.[a]

21 "And just as you desire that men should do to you, do to them in the same way.[b]

22 "And if you love *only* those who love you, what credit is that to you?[c] For even sinners love those who love them.[d]

23 "And if you do good *only* to those who do good to you, what credit is that to you?[e] For even sinners do likewise.[f]

q La 2:12,20
La 3:1,43
La 4:4,9
r Mt 5:6
Lu 6:21
s La 1:12
La 2:5,11
La 3:48,49
La 5:7,8
t Lu 6:21
u Le 19:17,18
Le 19:33,34
v De 7:2,16,24
De 20:17
Ps 18:37,38,40
Ps 139:22
Mt 5:43
w Ex 23:22,23,27
x De 5:9
De 7:10
De 32:41
Mt 5:44
Lu 6:27
y Ex 21:24,25
Le 24:17-21
De 19:21
Mt 5:38
z Mt 5:39,40
Lu 6:29
a Mt 5:42
Lu 6:30
b Mt 7:12
Lu 6:31
c Ex 20:5,6
De 7:9
Ps 103:11
d Mt 5:46
Lu 6:32
e Nu 14:8
De 30:9,10
Ps 18:25
Isa 1:19
Jer 7:23
f Lu 6:33

De 7:9 – *Know therefore that Yahweh your God himself is God, the faithful God, who keeps covenant and loving kindness with them who love him and keep his commandments to a thousand generations.*

Y<small>HWH</small> loves those who love him, but so what? *"For even sinners love those who love them."*

4:23 – "And if you do good *only* to those who do good to you, what credit is that to you? […] "

Nu 14:8 – *If Yahweh delights in us, then he will bring us into this land, and give it to us; a land which flows with milk and honey.*

De 30:9,10 – *Yahweh your God will make you plenteous in all the work of your hand, in the fruit of your body, in the fruit of your livestock, and in the fruit of your ground, for good […] | if you will obey Yahweh your God's voice, to keep his commandments and his statutes which are written in this book of the law; if you turn to Yahweh your God with all your heart, and with all your soul.*

Isa 1:19 – *"If you are willing and obedient, you shall eat the good of the land."*

Y<small>HWH</small> generously promises to do good to those who obey his voice and keep his commandments. Let no one doubt, though, that he has a different lot in store for those who do not do him the good of being obedient, and of loving him with all their heart and soul.

4:24 – "And if you lend *to those* from whom you expect to receive, what credit is that to you? […] "

To whom does Y<small>HWH</small> lend?

Le 25:18-22 – " […] *The land shall yield its fruit, and you shall eat your fill, and dwell therein in safety. | If you said, "What shall we eat the seventh year? Behold, we shall not sow, nor gather in our increase"; | then I will command my blessing on you in the sixth year, and it shall bear fruit for the three* *years.* | *You shall sow the eighth year, and eat of the fruits, the old store; until the ninth year, until its fruits come in, you shall eat the old store."*

Since good husbandry requires that land must lie fallow once every seven years, YHWH says he'll advance his people food for three years running, to tide them over till the 'fruits come in' the ninth year. But he can easily afford to do that, in view of what he expects to receive from the harvest:

Ex 22:29 – *"You shall not delay to offer from your harvest and from the outflow of your presses."*

Ex 23:14-16 – *"You shall observe a feast to me three times a year. | You shall observe the feast of unleavened bread [...] and no one shall appear before me empty-handed. | And the feast of harvest, the first fruits of your labors, which you sow in the field; and the feast of ingathering, at the end of the year, when you gather in your labors out of the field."*

Le 23:15-21 – *" [...] you shall offer a new meal offering to Yahweh. | You shall bring out of your habitations two loaves of bread for a wave offering [...]. | You shall present with the bread seven lambs without defect a year old, one young bull, and two rams. They shall be a burnt offering to Yahweh, with their meal offering, and their drink offerings [...]. | You shall offer one male goat for a sin offering, and two male lambs a year old for a sacrifice of peace offerings. | [...] This is a statute forever in all your dwellings throughout your generations."*

4:25,26– "But love your enemies, and do good, and lend, expecting nothing in return; and be compassionate, just as your Father is compassionate – for He makes His sun rise on *both* evil and good, and sends rain on *both the* righteous and unrighteous."

As attested by the reference verses, Israel's father YHWH is not always compassionate towards his people:

Isa 27:11 – [...] *Therefore he who made them will not have compassion on them, and he who formed them will show them no favor.*

Jer 13:14 – *"I will dash them one against another, even the fathers and the sons together," says Yahweh: "I will not pity, nor spare, nor have compassion, that I should not destroy them."*

Eze 8:18 – *"Therefore will I also deal in wrath. My eye won't spare, neither will I have pity. Though they cry in my ears with a loud voice, yet I will not hear them."*

Hence, Jesus cannot be referring here to YHWH, but is rather using the word 'Father' to signify the indefinable 'God' of all. Of course, in the Bible and for the Jews, YHWH is seen as being both Israel's father *and* the God of all. But it is the premise of *The Gospel of Jesus of Nazareth* that Jesus came to see the two as being distinct: YHWH was a tribal god, from whom the Jews could free themselves; the other, God, was the one true god of all, who required neither sacrifice nor obedience nor fear, who simply was and is and ever will be. This is the compassionate Father who is in the heavens,[21] who makes His sun rise on both the evil and good and sends rain on both the righteous and unrighteous. In other words, it doesn't matter if you keep the commandments or not – you get what you get.

Ec 8:14 – *There is a vanity which is done on the earth, that there are righteous men to whom it happens according to the work of the wicked. Again, there are wicked men to whom it happens according to the work of the righteous.* [...]

Ec 9:2 – *All things come alike to all. There is one event to the righteous and to the wicked; to the good, to the clean, to the unclean, to him who sacrifices, and to him who doesn't sacrifice. As is the good, so is the sinner; he who takes an oath, as he who fears an oath.*

In my view, all of these teachings plainly contradict the instructions given by YHWH to Moses.

4:27-31 JUDGE NOT, THAT YOU NOT BE JUDGED

YHWH is the judge of Israel.

Ps 7:8-11 – *Yahweh administers judgment to the peoples.* [...] *God is a righteous judge, yes, a God who has indignation every day.*

Isa 33:22 – *Yahweh is our judge. Yahweh is our law-giver.*

Let's see where this might lead us...

4:27 – "Judge not, that you not be judged; and do not condemn [...]"

De 12:31 – [...] *every abomination to Yahweh, which he hates, have they done to their gods; for they even burn their sons and their daughters in the fire to their gods.*

Ps 94:21 – *They gather themselves together against the soul of the righteous, and condemn the innocent blood.*

Ps 106:37,38 – *Yes, they sacrificed their sons* [...]. | *They shed innocent blood, even the blood of their sons* [...]

Eze 16:20,21 – "[...] *you have taken your sons* [...], *and you have sacrificed these* [...] | *you have slain my children, and delivered them up* [...]"

YHWH condemns his people for delivering up their children to be sacrificed and for shedding innocent blood.

4:27 – " [...] that you not be condemned. [...] "

Ex 4:22 – [...] *Yahweh says, Israel is my son, my firstborn.*

Mr 14:36 – *He said, "Abba. Father, all things are possible to you. Please remove this cup from me. However, not what I desire, but what you desire."*

Mr 15:34 – *At the ninth hour Jesus cried with a loud voice, saying, "Eloi, Eloi, lama sabachthani?" which is, being interpreted, "My God, my God, why have you forsaken me?"*

Jesus is a son of YHWH. If YHWH accepts his sacrifice on the cross, then by his own standards of judgment, he may be condemned.

Do not judge others

g Ex 22:29
   Ex 23:14-16
   Le 23:15-21
   Le 25:18-22
h *Lu 6:34*
i Ps 37:3
   Pr 25:21
j *Lu 6:35*
k De 19:21
   Isa 27:11
   Jer 13:14
   Eze 8:18
   Eze 24:14
   Lu 6:36
l Ec 8:14
   Ec 9:2
   Mt 5:45
m *Mt 7:1*
n De 12:31
   Ps 94:21
   Ps 106:37,38
   Eze 16:20,21
o Ex 4:22
   Mr 14:36
   Mr 15:34
p Isa 50:1
q Le 17:10,14
   Mt 26:27,28
   Mr 10:45
   Mr 14:23,24
   Lu 6:37
r Ex 20:13
   Ex 23:7
   De 19:10
   Eze 7:3
   Eze 20:36,37
   Eze 33:20
s La 2:20-22
   Mt 7:2
t Le 10:2
   Nu 16:20,21,33
   De 6:15
   De 25:14
   Eze 24:14
u Isa 14:15
   Eze 28:8,18,19
   Mt 7:2
   Lu 6:38
   Re 12:9
v Jer 2:19
   Jer 5:7

24 "And if you lend *to those* from whom you expect to receive, what credit is that to you?[g] For even sinners lend to sinners, so that they might receive back the same.[h]

25 "But love your enemies, and do good,[i] and lend, expecting nothing in return;[j]

26 and be [5]compassionate, just as your Father is [6]compassionate[k] – for He makes His sun rise on *both* evil and good, and sends rain on *both the* righteous and unrighteous.[l]

27 "Judge not, that you not be judged;[m] and do not condemn,[n] that you not be condemned.[o] [6]Release,[p] and you will be [7]released.[q]

28 "For with the judgment that you judge,[r] you will be judged;[s] and with the measure that you measure,[t] it will be measured to you.[u]

29 "But why do you see the speck in your brother's eye,[v] and do not perceive the beam *that is* in your own eye?[w]

30 "How can you say to your brother, 'Let me take out the speck that *is* in your eye', when you yourself do

---

5 Or, *merciful*
6 Or, *set free; send away*
7 Or, *set free; sent away*

4:27 – " […] Release […] "

Luke 6:37 employs the word *apoluó*. Many translations render this as *forgive*. However, if 'forgive' were here the intended meaning, a different Greek word – *aphiémi* – would have served to better effect.[22]

As it is more customarily translated, *apoluó* means to *release, set free, send away*…and also, very specifically, *divorce*.

Isa 50:1 – *Yahweh says, "Where is the bill of your mother's divorce, with which I have put her away? Or to which of my creditors have I sold you? Behold, you were sold for your iniquities, and your mother was put away for your transgressions."*

It may be said that in his fury, YHWH has released, or divorced, Israel in the past.

4:27 – " […] and you will be released."

Le 17:10,14 – *"Any man of the house of Israel, or of the strangers who live as foreigners among them, who eats any kind of blood, I will set my face against that soul who eats blood, and will cut him off from among his people. | For as to the life of all flesh, its blood is with its life: therefore I said to the children of Israel, 'You shall not eat the blood of any kind of flesh; for the life of all flesh is its blood. Whoever eats it shall be cut off.'"*

Mr 10:45 – *"For the Son of Man also came not to be served, but to serve, and to give his life as a ransom for many."*

Mr 14:23,24 – *He took the cup, and when he had given thanks, he gave to them. They all drank of it. | He said to them, "This is my blood of the new covenant, which is poured out for many."*

By drinking the blood of sacrifice that Jesus proposes, his disciples will be releasing themselves – *apoluó* – from the covenant that binds them to YHWH. Put differently, they will divorce their god.

4:28 – "For with the judgment that you judge […] "

Ex 20:13 – *"You shall not murder."*

Ex 23:7 – *" […] do not kill the innocent and righteous […]"*

4:28 – " […] you will be judged; […] "

La 2:20-22 – *Look, Yahweh, and see to whom you have done thus! Shall the women eat their offspring, the children that are dandled in the hands? Shall the priest and the prophet be killed in the sanctuary of the Lord? | The youth and the old man lie on the ground in the streets. My virgins and my young men have fallen by the sword. You have killed them in the day of your anger. You have slaughtered, and not pitied. | […] There was no one that escaped or remained in the day of Yahweh's anger. My enemy has consumed those whom I have dandled and brought up.*

If YHWH's judgment is *'You shall not murder'* and *'do not kill the innocent and righteous'*, then by that judgment he himself should be judged.

4:28 – " […] and with the measure that you measure […] "

Le 10:2 – *Fire came out from before Yahweh, and devoured them, and they died before Yahweh.*

Nu 16:20,21,33 – *"Separate yourselves from among this congregation, that I may consume them in a moment!" | They fell on their faces, and said, "God, the God of the spirits of all flesh, shall one man sin, and will you be angry with all the congregation?" | So they, and all that belonged to them went down alive into Sheol. The earth closed on them, and they perished […].*

De 6:15 – *For Yahweh your God among you is a jealous God; lest the anger of Yahweh your God be kindled against you, and he destroy you from off the face of the earth.*

De 25:14 – *You shall not have in your house diverse measures, one large and one small.*

YHWH destroys his people with fire and casts them into Sheol, destroying them from off the face of the earth. If there must not be diverse measures, one large, one small, then the measure that YHWH has used against his people must be the same for himself.

4:28 – " […] it will be measured to you."
    Isa 14:15 – *Yet you shall be brought down to Sheol, to the depths of the pit.*
    Eze 28:8,18,19 – *"They shall bring you down to the pit […] | Therefore I have brought out a fire from the middle of you. It has devoured you. I have turned you to ashes on the earth in the sight of all those who see you. | All those who know you among the peoples will be astonished at you: you have become a terror, and you shall exist no more."*
    Just as YHWH has done to his people, so shall it be done to him when he is judged by his own measure and found to have sinned: he will be brought down to Sheol, to the pit; a fire will be kindled, and he will be turned to ashes in the sight of all.

4:29– "But why do you see the speck in your brother's eye […] "
    Jer 2:19 – *"[…] Know therefore and see that it is an evil and bitter thing, that you have forsaken Yahweh your God, and that my fear is not in you."*
    Jer 5:7 – *"How can I pardon you? Your children have forsaken me. […]"*
    YHWH accuses his people of having forsaken him.

4:29– " […] and do not perceive the beam *that is* in your own eye?"
    De 4:31 – *For Yahweh your God is a merciful God. He will not fail you, neither destroy you, nor forget the covenant of your fathers which he swore to them.*
    Ps 94:14 – *For Yahweh won't reject his people, neither will he forsake his inheritance.*
    Isa 49:15 – *"Can a woman forget her nursing child, that she should not have compassion on the son of her womb? Yes, these may forget, yet I will not forget you!"*

And yet, despite such promises...

Jer 12:7 – *"I have forsaken my house. I have cast off my heritage. I have given the dearly beloved of my soul into the hand of her enemies."*

Jer 23:39,40 – *"Therefore, behold, I will utterly forget you, and I will cast you off [...]. | I will bring an everlasting reproach on you, and a perpetual shame, which shall not be forgotten."*

La 5:20,22 – *Why do you forget us forever, and forsake us so long time? | But you have utterly rejected us; you are very angry against us.*

The God of Israel does not see that he has forsaken his people.

4:32-34 EACH TREE IS KNOWN BY ITS FRUIT

4:32 – "For there is no good tree producing bad fruit [...] "

Ge 1:12 – *The earth yielded grass, herbs yielding seed after their kind, and trees bearing fruit, with their seeds in it, after their kind; and God saw that it was good.*

Ge 2:8,9 – *Yahweh God planted a garden eastward, in Eden, and there he put the man whom he had formed. | Out of the ground Yahweh God made every tree to grow that is pleasant to the sight, and good for food, including the tree of life in the middle of the garden and the tree of the knowledge of good and evil.*

Ge 3:6,22 – *When the woman saw that the tree was good for food, and that it was a delight to the eyes, and that the tree was to be desired to make one wise, she took some of its fruit, and ate; and she gave some to her husband with her, and he ate it, too. | Yahweh God said, "Behold, the man has become like one of us, knowing good and evil. Now, lest he reach out his hand, and also take of the tree of life, and eat, and live forever."*

Among the trees in the garden of Eden that YHWH made to grow and that was good for food was the tree of the knowledge of good and evil. Its fruit, therefore, was not bad fruit.

not see the beam in your own eye?[x]

31 "Hypocrite! First pull out the beam from your own eye, and then you will see clearly the speck that is in your brother's eye.[y]

32 "For there is no good tree, producing bad fruit;[z] nor again a bad tree, producing good fruit.[a]

33 "For each tree is known by its own fruit.[b] For they do not gather figs from thorn bushes, nor do they gather a cluster of grapes from a bramble.[c]

34 "The good man, out of the good treasure of the heart, brings forth that which *is* good; and the bad *one*, out of the bad *treasure*, brings forth that which *is* bad. For his mouth speaks from that which fills his heart.[d]

35 "Again, you have heard that it was said to the ancients, YOU SHALL NOT SWEAR FALSELY,[e] BUT YOU SHALL KEEP YOUR VOWS TO THE LORD,[f] and YOU SHALL SWEAR BY HIS NAME.[g]

36 "But I say to you, do not swear at all – neither by the sky, because it is the throne of God,[h]

37 nor by the earth,[i] because it is a footstool for His feet;[j] nor by Jerusalem, because it is the city of the great King.[k]

w De 4:31
Ps 94:14
Isa 49:15
Jer 12:7
Jer 23:39,40
La 5:20,22
Mt 7:3
Mt 27:46
Mr 15:34
Lu 6:41
x Mt 7:4
Lu 6:42
y Mt 7:5
Lu 6:42
z Ge 1:12
Ge 2:8,9
Ge 3:6,22
a Mt 7:18
Lu 6:43
b Ex 3:13,14
Ex 4:22
De 14:1
Ps 78:36,37
Isa 1:2
Isa 30:9
Isa 63:10
Isa 64:8
c Mt 7:16
Lu 6:44
d De 28:15-68
Jer 9:11
Eze 7:2-9
Eze 7:25-27
Eze 21:3-5
Eze 22:19-22
Mt 12:34,35
Lu 6:45
e Le 19:12
f Nu 30:2
De 23:21,23
Ps 66:13
Ps 76:11
Mt 5:33
g De 6:13
De 10:20
h Isa 66:1
Mt 5:34
i Isa 65:16
j Isa 66:1
k Ps 48:2
Mt 5:35

4:33 – "For each tree is know by its own fruit. [...] "

De 14:1 – *You are the children of Yahweh your God. [...]*

Isa 1:2 – *Hear, heavens, and listen, earth; for Yahweh has spoken: "I have nourished and brought up children, and they have rebelled against me."*

Isa 30:9 – *For it is a rebellious people, lying children, children who will not hear Yahweh's law.*

Isa 64:8 – *But now, Yahweh, you are our Father. We are the clay, and you our potter. We all are the work of your hand.*

If each tree is know by its fruit, then we may know YHWH's nature by considering his fruit: his children. If they are rebellious, lying children who disregard his Law, as he fulminates, then what does that say about the father who begot them? That he disregards his own Law, too...?

4:34 – "The good man, out of the good treasure of the heart, brings forth that which *is* good; and the bad *one,* out of the bad *treasure,* brings forth that which *is* bad. For his mouth speaks from that which fills his heart."

In a long passage found in Deuteronomy 28:15-68, Moses details the treasure trove of curses that YHWH promises to heap upon Israel, if they do not observe his statutes. In like manner, if *'his mouth speaks from that which fills his heart'*, it is instructive to consider what YHWH says to the prophets Jeremiah and Ezekiel:

Jer 9:11 – *"I will make Jerusalem heaps, a dwelling place of jackals. I will make the cities of Judah a desolation, without inhabitant."*

Eze 7:2-9 – *"You, son of man, thus says the Lord Yahweh to the land of Israel, 'An end! [...] | Now is the end on you, and I will send my anger on you, and will judge you according to your ways. I will bring on you all your abominations. | [...] Your doom has come to you, inhabitant of the land! The time has come! The day is near, a day of tumult [...] | Now I will shortly pour out my wrath on you, and accomplish my anger against you, and will judge you according to your ways. [...] | My eye won't spare, neither will I have pity. [...] and you will know that I, Yahweh, strike."*

Eze 21:3-5 – *Tell the land of Israel, 'Yahweh says: "Behold, I am against you, and will draw my sword out of its sheath, and will cut off from you the righteous and the wicked. [...] | All flesh will know that I, Yahweh, have drawn my sword out of its sheath. It will not return any more."'*

4:35-39 DO NOT SWEAR AT ALL

4:36,39 – "But I say to you, do not swear at all [...]. But your word 'yes' *must* be 'yes', *and* 'no', 'no'; anything more *than* this comes from the bad *treasure.*"

Here again, Jesus' teaching is plainly contrary to the Law, where it is stipulated that *'You shall fear Yahweh your God [...] and shall swear by his name.'* (De 6:13)

In telling his listeners that anything more than simply saying 'yes' or 'no' comes from the bad – or, if you prefer, *"Whatever is more than these is of the evil one"*, as Matthew 5:37 is more commonly translated – Jesus may be construed as implying that YHWH is bad, or evil, for it is YHWH who instructs his people to swear by his name.

4:40-42 SALT IS GOOD

In *The Gospel of Jesus of Nazareth*, I end Jesus' seaside discourse with a freely concocted amalgam of his words dealing with salt. It seemed to me that this passage could be easily adapted to his pattern of starting with *'You have heard that it was said...'* The sources are: *"You are the salt of the earth, but if the salt has lost its flavor, with what will it be salted? It is then good for nothing, but to be cast out and trodden under the feet of men."* (Mt 5:13) and *"For everyone will be salted with fire, and every sacrifice will*

4   His own people come for him

l Mt 5:36
m Mt 5:37
n Le 2:1-3
   Le 2:9,13
o Le 2:13
   Mr 9:49
p Job 6:6,7
q Mr 9:50
r Mt 5:13
s Mr 9:50
t Lu 7:1
u Mr 3:20

38 "Nor shall you swear by your own head, for you cannot turn one hair white or black.[l]

39 "But your word 'yes' *must* be 'yes', *and* 'no', 'no'; anything more *than* this comes from the bad *treasure*.[m]

40 "You have heard that it was said, EVERY GRAIN OFFERING BY FIRE SHALL BE SALTED,[n] and EVERY SACRIFICE SHALL BE SALTED WITH SALT.[o]

41 "Therefore, salt is good. But if the salt becomes tasteless,[p] with what will you season it?[q] It is fit for nothing, except, having been cast out, to be trampled underfoot by men.[r]

42 "Have salt in yourselves, and be at peace with one another."[s]

43 And when he had fulfilled saying all of his words in the hearing of the people, he entered into Capernaum.[t]

44 And he came into a house, and again a crowd gathered, so that they were not able to eat even bread.[u]

45 And [8]his own people, having heard *of this*, went out to seize him; for they were saying, "He is out of

8 Lit., *those of him*

be seasoned with salt. | Salt is good, but if the salt has lost its saltiness, with what will you season it? Have salt in yourselves, and be at peace with one another." (Mr 9:49,50)

We must not underestimate salt's importance. Of vital essence to the meal offering, it was called 'the salt of the covenant':

Le 2:13 – *"Every offering of your meal offering you shall season with salt. You shall not allow the salt of the covenant of your God to be lacking from your meal offering. With all your offerings you shall offer salt."*

Since the Gospels place us in the context of scripture, we do well to look for a scriptural meaning behind Jesus' words. If salt is the salt of the covenant, as we might reasonably suppose, then it seems striking that Jesus should speak of 'salt that has lost its flavor'.

4:41,42 – **"Therefore, salt is good. But if the salt becomes tasteless, with what will you season it? It is fit for nothing, except, having been cast out, to be trampled underfoot by men. Have salt in yourselves, and be at peace with one another."**

Job 6:6,7 – *"Can that which has no flavor be eaten without salt? Or is there any taste in the white of an egg? | My soul refuses to touch them. They are as loathsome food to me."*

The reader is free to disagree with me, but I draw a link here to Job's remark about flavourless things being loathsome food – *"My soul refuses to touch them."* If things that have no flavour cannot be eaten without salt, then we may infer that the covenant itself is unpalatable, since it needs to be salted, as per Leviticus 2:13. Indeed, going a step further, we might argue that since the covenant was a covenant of salt, the salt of the covenant itself has become unpalatable – but salt that has lost its flavour *"is then good for nothing, but to be cast out and trodden under the feet of men."*

Jesus says *"Salt is good"* and *"Have salt in yourselves."* Salt is good; have salt, have goodness, in yourselves, and be at peace with one another.

4:43,44 THEY WERE NOT ABLE TO EVEN EAT BREAD

Mark twice reports that Jesus and his disciples didn't even have time to eat, because there were so many people coming and going – see Mark 3:20, 6:31. One imagines the hungry disciples wishing they could take some time off for a few *'Follow me!'* parties.

4:45-52 "BEHOLD, MY MOTHER AND MY BROTHERS"

By this time, word had gotten back to Nazareth that Jesus was drawing crowds in Capernaum. Mark tells us that *'When his friends* [lit., 'those belonging to him'] *heard it, they went out to seize him: for they said, "He is insane."'* (Mr 3:21) The Greek is very plain on this point: they thought Jesus was out of his mind. We are left to wonder. Did they consider him out of his mind simply because he was preaching to crowds? Or was it the message he was preaching that alarmed them? In view of the strong wording that is used – that his people came to seize him (*krateó* –'to lay hold of') and were saying that he was mad (*existémi* – 'to be insane') – I think it reasonable to infer that Jesus' teachings, though perhaps not phrased in such a way as to directly and openly challenge the Torah, were nevertheless perceived as being errant and tacitly opposed to it.

Joseph is notably absent from the posse, but Jesus' mother and brothers arrive in Capernaum intent on seizing him. One supposes they had a plan: haul him back to Nazareth, bring him to his senses and nip all of this nonsense in the bud. Standing outside the door, they call for him and send in word that they are there. Those present in the crowd say to Jesus, *"Behold, your mother and your brothers are outside looking for you."* (Mr 3:32) And what does he reply?

He answered them, "Who are my mother and my brothers?" | *Looking around at those who sat around him, he said, "Behold, my mother and my brothers!"* (Mr 3:33,34)

his mind,^{v} because he has an unclean spirit."^{w}

46 And his mother and his brothers arrived, and they were standing outside;^{x} and they sent *word* to him, calling him.^{y}

47 And a crowd was sitting around him, and they said to him, "Behold, your mother and your brothers^z are outside, and are asking for you."^{a}

48 And answering them, he said, "Who is my mother, and *who are* my brothers?"^{b}

49 And having looked about on those who were sitting around him in a circle, he said, "Behold, my mother^c and my brothers."^{d}

50 But answering, he said to them, "My mother and my brothers are those who are hearing and doing the word of God."^{e}

51 And a certain woman from the crowd, having raised *her* voice, said to him, "Blessed *is* the womb that bore you, and *the* breasts at which you nursed!"^{f}

52 But he said, "On the contrary, blessed are they who hear the word,^{g} and keep watch *over it*."^{h}

v Ho 9:7
  Na 1:11
w Ps 69:9
  Mr 3:21,30
x Mt 12:46
  Lu 8:19
  Jn 7:5
y Mr 3:31
z Ps 69:8
  Mt 13:55
a Mt 12:47
  Mr 3:32
  Lu 8:20
b Ps 69:8
  Mt 12:48
  Mr 3:33
c Jn 19:25
d Ps 113:9
  Mt 12:49
  Mr 3:34
e Mt 12:50
  Mr 3:35
  Lu 8:21
f Lu 11:27
g Mr 4:14
h Lu 11:28

This answer is striking for two reasons. In the first place, it seems that Jesus blatantly refused to speak with or even see his own mother. He stays in the house while his mother and brothers cool their heels outside; he can't be bothered. We could see this as speaking volumes about the relationship he had with his family, echoed by Psalms 69:8 – *I have become a stranger to my brothers, an alien to my mother's children.* As John 7:5 informs us, *'even his brothers didn't believe in him.'*

Further, we should note that in looking around the room, Jesus declares, *"Behold, my mother and my brothers!"* This may have been more than just rhetorical flourish. Rejecting his own family, Jesus says for all to hear, 'This is my mother, and these are my brothers.' We may guess that he considered a few of his closest disciples to be his 'brothers' and was looking at them as he said this. But more importantly, it would appear that there was a woman present in the room whom Jesus looked upon as being his mother: *"Behold, my mother!"*

Who was she? Based on an incongruity that is found in John 19:25 – where it is said that *'there were standing by the cross of Jesus his mother, and his mother's sister, Mary the wife of Clopas, and Mary Magdalene'* – it is my conjecture that this unnamed woman may have been the Salome mentioned in Mark 15:40 and 16:1. See my commentary below, THE WOMEN BESIDE THE CROSS, page 332.

4:51 – And a certain woman from the crowd, having raised *her* voice, said to him, "Blessed *is* the womb that bore you, and *the* breasts at which you nursed!"

This verse is taken from a passage in Luke where Jesus is preaching to the crowd about demons and signs. Out of the blue, a 'certain woman' pipes up and says, *"Blessed is the womb that bore you, and the breasts which nursed you!"* (Lu 11:27)

In Luke, this odd remark, which has nothing to do with either signs or demons, seems wholly out of context; it rather feels as if has been lifted from somewhere else and inserted therein to create a short break in the narrative. In using it here, I am inviting the reader to imagine that Mary herself – distraught that her firstborn son should look upon another woman as more deserving than she of being called his mother – may have shouted this in a desperate bid to remind Jesus that it was she who bore and suckled him. His reply was a firm rebuff: *"On the contrary, blessed are they who hear the word, and keep watch over it."*

5   The women who were serving them

CHAPTER 5

a *Lu 8:1*
b *Lu 8:2*
c *Lu 8:3*
d *Mt 13:1,2*
   Mr 4:1
e *Mt 13:3*
   Mr 4:2
f *Mt 13:3*
   Mr 4:3
   Lu 8:5

AND it came about, soon afterwards, that he journeyed through city and village, proclaiming and announcing the good news of the kingdom of God; and the twelve *were* with him,[a]

2   and certain women *as well*, who had been healed from evil spirits and weaknesses — Mary who is called Magdalene, from whom seven demons had gone out,[b]

3   and Joanna, *the* wife of Chuza, Herod's steward, and Susanna, and many others — who were serving them out of their own means.[c]

4   And again, he began to teach by the sea. And the crowd that was gathered together became so great, that he got into a boat on the sea and sat down; and all the crowd was on the shore, close to the sea.[d]

5   And he was teaching them many things in parables, and saying to them in his teaching,[e]

6   "Listen! Behold, the sower went out to sow.[f]

5

The kingdom of God

5:1-3 THE WOMEN WHO WERE SERVING THEM

Jesus was clearly popular with the women: there were many who were following him, and what's more, some were giving financial support to the group out of their own means. Then as now, spiritual mentors are often attended to by groupies and wealthy benefactresses. As the Bible says, *'there is nothing new under the sun.'* (Ec 1:9)

5:4-12 THE PARABLE OF THE SOWER

5:12 – And he was saying, "He who has ears to hear [...] "

De 29:4 – *But Yahweh has not given you a heart to know, eyes to see, and ears to hear, to this day.*

Isa 6:9,10 – *He said, "Go, and tell this people, 'You hear indeed, but don't understand; and you see indeed, but don't perceive.' | Make the heart of this people fat. Make their ears heavy, and shut their eyes; lest they see with their eyes, and hear with their ears, and understand with their heart, and turn again, and be healed."*

Is it YHWH who prevents his people from hearing, who does not give them ears? Nevertheless, while Jesus knows his words may in most cases be devoured by birds or scorched by the sun or choked by thorns, he can hope that at least in some instances his teachings will take root in fertile soil and yield a bountiful crop of wisdom and understanding.

5:12 – " […] let him hear."

Pr 2:2,10 – *So as to turn your ear to wisdom, and apply your heart to understanding | For wisdom will enter into your heart. Knowledge will be pleasant to your soul.*

5:13-21 JESUS EXPLAINS THE PARABLE OF THE SOWER

5:15 – "The sower sows the word."

Jesus is sowing new teachings with new words. However:

De 4:2 – *You shall not add to the word which I command you […]*

What's more, his teachings and actions appear to have the deliberate aim of bringing about the abrogation of Israel's covenant with YHWH.

De 13:1-5 – *If a prophet or a dreamer of dreams arises among you, and he gives you a sign or a wonder, | […] you shall not listen to the words of that prophet, or to that dreamer of dreams. […] |*

5:16 – "And these are the ones who are beside the road […] "

Isa 35:8 – *A highway will be there, a road, […] called The Holy Way. […]*

Those who are diligently following 'The Holy Way', YHWH's well-worn path of obedience, aren't likely to hear the word. But those who are beside the road – those who have wandered off track, as it were, and become like 'lost sheep' – might be more receptive. Certainly, they're in a better position to heed the word and set off in a new direction.

5:16 – " […] and when they hear *it*, immediately Satan comes and takes away the word that has been sown in them."

Job 9:12 – *"Behold, he snatches away. Who can hinder him? Who will ask him, 'What are you doing?'"*

Ah, but it won't be that easy! YHWH will swoop down like a crow and snatch away the word that has been sown in them.

7   "And it came to pass, as he sowed, that some *seed* fell beside the road, and the birds came and devoured it.[g]

8   "And other *seed* fell on the rocky *ground*, and where it had not much soil; and immediately it sprang up, because it had no depth of soil.[h]

9   "And after the sun rose, it was scorched; and because it had no root, it withered.[i]

10   "And other *seed* fell among the thorns, and the thorns grew up, and choked it, and it gave no fruit.[j]

11   "And other *seed* fell into the good soil, and gave fruit, growing up and increasing, and bore in one thirty, and in one sixty, and in one a hundred."[k]

12   And he was saying, "He who has ears to hear,[l] let him hear."[m]

13   And when he was alone, those about him, with the twelve, asked him *about* the parable.[n]

14   And he said to them, "You do not understand this parable? And how will you understand all the parables?[o]

15   "The sower sows the word.[p]

16   "And these are the ones who are beside the road[q] where the word is sown: and when they hear *it*,

g   Mt 13:4
    Mr 4:4
    Lu 8:5
h   Mt 13:5
    Mr 4:5
    Lu 8:6
i   Mt 13:6
    Mr 4:6
    Lu 8:6
j   Mt 13:7
    Mr 4:7
    Lu 8:7
k   Mt 13:8
    Mr 4:8
    Lu 8:8
l   De 29:4
    Isa 6:9,10
m   Pr 2:2,10
    Mt 13:9
    Mr 4:9
    Lu 8:8
n   Mt 13:10
    Mr 4:10
    Lu 8:9
o   Mr 4:13
p   De 4:2
    De 13:1-5
    Mr 4:14
q   Isa 35:8
    Jer 6:16
    Jer 18:15

r De 12:32
  Job 9:12
s Mt 13:19
  Mr 4:15
  Lu 8:12
t Mt 13:20
  Mr 4:16
  Lu 8:13
u Ex 32:33
  Le 26:14-33
  De 28:15-68
  De 29:18,20
  Jer 11:3,4
v Job 9:3,14
  Job 9:32-35
  Mt 13:21
  Mr 4:17
  Lu 8:13
w Mt 13:22
  Mr 4:18
  Lu 8:14
x Ge 17:8
  Nu 14:8
  De 7:12-14
  De 11:13-15
  De 28:1-14
  De 30:9,10
y Mt 13:22
  Mr 4:19
  Lu 8:14
z Isa 53:10
  Mt 13:23
  Mr 4:20
  Lu 8:15
a Mt 5:15
  Mr 4:21
  Lu 8:16
  Lu 11:33
b De 4:11,12
  Ps 18:11
c Job 12:22
  Ec 12:14
d De 29:29

immediately Satan comes and takes away the word[r] that has been sown in them.[s]

17 "And likewise, these are the ones who upon the rocky *ground* are sown: who, when they hear the word, immediately receive it with joy;[t]

18 and they have no root in themselves, but are temporary — then affliction or persecution having arisen[u] on account of the word immediately causes them to stumble.[v]

19 "And these are the ones who among the thorns are sown: these are the *ones*, having heard the word;[w]

20 and the worries of the age, and the illusion of riches, and desires for the rest enter in,[x] choking the word, and it becomes unfruitful.[y]

21 "And these are the ones who upon the good ground have been sown: those who hear the word and receive it, and bring forth fruit, in one thirty, and in one sixty, and in one a hundred."[z]

22 And he was saying to them, "Is a lamp brought to be put under the basket, or under the bed? *Is it* not *brought* that it might be put upon the lampstand?[a]

23 "For nothing is hidden,[b] except that it should be brought to light;[c] nor has *anything* secret[d] come into

5:18 – " [...] then affliction or persecution having arisen [...] "

Ex 32:33 – *Yahweh said to Moses, "Whoever has sinned against me, him will I blot out of my book."*

De 29:18,20 – *Lest there should be among you man, woman, family, or tribe whose heart turns away today from Yahweh our God | Yahweh will not pardon him, but then Yahweh's anger and his jealousy will smoke against that man, and all the curse that is written in this book will fall on him, and Yahweh will blot out his name from under the sky.*

Talk about a threat of persecution…

5:18 – " [...] immediately causes them to stumble."

Job 9:3,14 – *"If he is pleased to contend with him, he can't answer him one time in a thousand. | How much less shall I answer him, and choose my words to argue with him?"*

Job 9:32-35 – *"For he is not a man, as I am, that I should answer him, that we should come together in judgment. | There is no umpire between us, that might lay his hand on us both. | Let him take his rod away from me. Let his terror not make me afraid; | then I would speak, and not fear him, for I am not so in myself."*

Faced with YHWH's rod and terror, even the righteous and blameless Job – who had every reason to balk at YHWH's ill-treatment – stumbled and caved in. Affliction and persecution are powerful deterrents to being independent in thought and deed.

5:20 – "and the worries of the age, and the illusion of riches, and desires for the rest enter in [...] "

Nu 14:8 – *If Yahweh delights in us, then he will bring us into this land, and give it to us; a land which flows with milk and honey.*

De 28:1-14 – *[...] | All these blessings will come upon you, and overtake you, if you listen to Yahweh your God's voice. | You shall be blessed in the city, and you shall be blessed in the field. | You shall be blessed in the fruit of your body, the fruit of your ground, the fruit of your animals, the increase of your livestock, and the young of your flock. | [...] | Yahweh will cause your enemies who rise up against you to be struck before you. [...] | Yahweh will command the blessing on you in your barns, and in all that you put your hand to. He will bless you in the land which Yahweh your God gives you. | [...] | Yahweh will grant you abundant prosperity [...] | Yahweh will make you the head, and not the tail. You will be above only, and you will not be beneath [...]*

Seriously, who wouldn't be waylaid by promises such as these?

5:21 – "And these are the ones who upon the good ground have been sown: those who hear the word and receive it, and bring forth fruit, in one thirty, and in one sixty, and in one a hundred."

Isa 53:10 – *Yet it pleased Yahweh to bruise him. He has caused him to suffer. When you make his soul an offering for sin, will see his seed. [...]*

Even so, the sower sows the word, with a mission to bring his fellow Jews to an awareness of the truth. As Isaiah's 'Suffering Servant', Jesus will see his own seed bring forth fruit when his followers in turn begin to spread his teachings, some bringing freedom to thirty, others to sixty, and still others to a hundred.

5:22,23 WHAT IS HIDDEN WILL BE BROUGHT TO LIGHT

5:23 – "For nothing is hidden [...]"

De 4:11,12 – *[...] The mountain burned with fire to the heart of the sky, with darkness, cloud, and thick darkness. | Yahweh spoke to you out of the middle of the fire: you heard the voice of words, but you saw no form; you only heard a voice.*

Ps 18:11 – *[...] He made darkness his hiding place, his pavilion around him, darkness of waters, thick clouds of the skies.*

The kingdom of God   5

being, but that it should come to light.[e]

24 "Therefore, look at how you hear. For whoever might have, *more* will be given to him, and whoever might not have, even what he seems to have will be taken *away* from him."[f]

25 And he was saying, "The kingdom of God is in this way like a man who should cast the seed upon the earth,[g]

26 and should sleep and rise night and day; and the seed should sprout and grow — he knows not how.[h]

27 "The earth itself brings forth fruit — first a blade, then a head of grain, then full grain in the head.[i]

28 "But when the fruit should be handed over, immediately he sends the sickle, for the harvest stands ready.[j]

29 "Therefore, to what shall we liken the kingdom of God, or with what parable shall we describe it?[k]

30 "It is like a mustard seed, which is the smallest of all the seeds upon the earth,[l]

31 yet when it is full grown, it is larger than all the garden plants, and forms large branches, and the birds of the sky find shelter in its shade."[m]

32 And again he was saying, "To what will I liken

e Mt 10:26
  Mr 4:22
  Lu 12:2
  Jn 3:20
  Jn 8:32
f Mr 4:25
  Lu 8:18
g Mr 4:26
h Ec 7:24
  Ec 8:17
  Ec 11:5
  Mr 4:27
i Mr 4:28
j Mr 4:29
k Isa 40:18
  Mr 4:30
  Lu 13:18
l Mt 13:31
  Mr 4:31
  Lu 13:19
m Mt 13:32
  Mr 4:32
  Lu 13:19

5:23 – " […] except that it should be brought to light; […] "

Job 12:22 – *He uncovers deep things out of darkness, and brings out to light the shadow of death.*

5:23 – " […] nor has *anything* secret come into being […] "

De 29:29 – *The secret things belong to Yahweh our God […]*

5:23 – " […] but that it should come to light."

Jn 3:20 – *For everyone who does evil hates the light, and doesn't come to the light, lest his works would be exposed.*

To expose what is evil is to bring the truth to light. Knowing the truth, one may free oneself of evil.

Jn 8:32 – *"You will know the truth, and the truth will make you free."*

5:25-33 THE KINGDOM OF GOD

What is the kingdom of God? Jesus does not speak of an earthly kingdom to come. He does not preach that there will be an anointed king sitting on the throne of David in Jerusalem, nor that YHWH himself will reside in Zion and rule over the nations, as anticipated by his co-religionists and promised by the prophets – *"So you will know that I am Yahweh, your God, dwelling in Zion, my holy mountain. Then Jerusalem will be holy, and no strangers will pass through her any more."* (Joe 3:17)

Rather, Jesus says that the kingdom of God may be likened to a man who casts seed on the earth. The earth itself brings forth fruit, and all he has to do is reap the harvest. It's as simple as that. Jesus does not teach his followers that they must observe the Law or undertake a *'baptism of repentance for forgiveness of sins'* to receive God's blessings.

Further, Jesus says that the kingdom of God may be likened to a mustard seed – though it is the smallest of all the seeds upon the earth, yet it grows to be larger than all of the other garden plants. Or again, to leaven – one hides but a small quantity in three large measures of flour, and yet it all becomes leavened. Hence, the kingdom of God, like the mustard seed, though small at first, will grow and surpass everything else; like the leaven, it will come to permeate our whole being.

5:34,35 JESUS TEACHES IN PARABLES

It is not true that Jesus was only speaking in parables when teaching in public – see chapter 4, where Jesus imparts many of his teachings quite openly, without recourse to allegory.

But Jesus did convey certain teachings exclusively via parables, and it is notable that he was apparently unwilling to elucidate their meaning in public – only his disciples were privy to an explanation, in private. In *The Gospel of Jesus of Nazareth*, it is shown that many of Jesus' parables may be seen as calling into question YHWH's reign over Israel. If this reading is correct, then it would be no wonder that Jesus would seek to cloak his dangerously subversive message in parables that would be hard for his listeners to grasp, lest traditionalists seize upon his words and find cause to challenge or detain him.

Nevertheless, the word he sowed in parables would be received and understood by those who were upon the good ground, who were ready to hear and understand and see things differently. The others, who were beside the road or on rocky soil or caught in the thorns, would remain subjugated to YHWH's commands – *Make the heart of this people fat. Make their ears heavy, and shut their eyes; lest they see with their eyes, and hear with their ears, and understand with their heart.* (Isa 9:10)

5:36-40 JESUS GIVES ORDERS TO DEPART

Considering that Mark's account jumps from my verse 36 directly to verse 41, a footnote tells us that *Verses 37-40 are not found in the best*

5   Jesus gives orders to depart

n *Mt 13:33*
    Lu 13:20
o *Mt 13:33*
    Lu 13:21
p *Mr 4:33*
q *Mt 13:34*
r *Mr 4:34*
s *Mt 8:18*
    Mr 4:35
    Lu 8:22
t *Mt 8:19*
    Lu 9:57
u *Mt 8:20*
    Lu 9:58
v *Mt 8:21*
    Lu 9:59
w *Mt 8:22*
    Lu 9:60

the kingdom of God?[n]

33 "It is like leaven, which a woman took and hid in three [1]measures of flour, until it was all leavened."[o]

34 And with many such parables was he speaking the word to them, as they were able to hear *it*;[p]

35 nor was he speaking to them without parables;[q] *yet* he was explaining everything in private to his own disciples.[r]

36 And on that day, when evening had come, he said to them, "Let us go over to the other side."[s]

37 [2][And having come up to him, one scribe said to him, "Teacher, I will follow you wherever you might go."[t]

38 And Jesus said to him, "Foxes have holes, and the birds of the air have nests, but the son of man has not where he might rest *his* head."[u]

39 But another of his disciples said to him, "Master, allow me to first go and bury my father."[v]

40 But Jesus said to him, "Follow me, and leave the dead to bury the dead themselves."[w]]

41 And sending away the crowd, they took him

---

1 Gr., *sata*; a measure for dry goods, a *sáton* amounted to roughly twelve litres
2 Verses 37-40 are not found in the best ancient mss.

THE KINGDOM OF GOD

ancient mss. If only for stylistic reasons, the two brief exchanges related by Matthew and Luke – with Jesus replying to the scribe, *"The foxes have holes, and the birds of the sky have nests, but the Son of Man has nowhere to lay his head"*, and to the disciple, *"Follow me, and leave the dead to bury their own dead"* – would seem to have been inserted at a later date.

These sayings are melodramatically hyperbolic. Jesus certainly found a place to lay his head every night – he seems to have been given lodging wherever he went, and we never hear about him sleeping *à la belle étoile.* And what's with this callous attitude towards a disciple who wants to first go and bury his dead father?[23] It boggles the mind. Jesus can't have been that hard-hearted; after all, we read in John 11:35 that *'Jesus wept'* when faced with Mary's grief over her dead brother Lazarus.

No, this is just overblown holiness, unfortunately of a stripe that sets the stage for spiritual fanaticism. Amounting to a sensational invitation to imitate Jesus through self-denial and the renunciation of all family ties, these sayings make one's decision to *'Follow Jesus'* a full bore, all-or-nothing commitment tinged with personal drama. What better way for a growing movement to inculcate self-importance among its converts? Many cults are known to do the same.

5:41-46 A STORM ARISES

This tale likely reflects a genuine experience that the boys had out there on the lake. Unpredictable and sometimes violent squalls are known to occasionally stir up waves on the Sea of Galilee, and since Andrew and Simon and James and John were fishermen, the group had easy access to boats. It should come as no surprise that their teacher would content himself with sleeping in the stern: coming from Nazareth, Jesus was no sailor. He was just along for the ride.

Readers will be well acquainted with the parallels that may be drawn between this sailing adventure and Psalm 107:23-30 – *Those who go down to the sea in ships, who do business in great waters; | These see Yahweh's deeds, and his wonders in the deep. | For he commands, and raises the stormy wind which lifts up its waves. | They mount up to the sky; they go down again to the depths. Their soul melts away because of trouble. | They reel back and forth, and stagger like a drunken man, and are at their wits' end. | Then they cry to Yahweh in their trouble, and he brings them out of their distress. | He makes the storm a calm, so that its waves are still. | Then they are glad because it is calm, so he brings them to their desired haven.*

In the text, however, a footnote informs us that *Verses 44 and 46 are not found in the best ancient mss.* If we compare what Jesus says to the sea in Mark 4:39 – *"Peace! Be still!" The wind ceased, and there was a great calm* – with Psalm 107:29 – *He makes the storm a calm, so that its waves are still* – we might rightly conclude that the evangelists retail this stormy incident with the not-so-subtle intention of portraying Jesus as being on a par with the YHWH of Psalm 107.

That said, we could also draw a parallel for this story with the mishap that befell the sailors with whom Jonah was sailing, when YHWH was after him: *But Yahweh sent out a great wind on the sea, and there was a mighty storm on the sea, so that the ship was likely to break up. | Then the mariners were afraid, and every man cried to his god. They threw the cargo that was in the ship into the sea to lighten the ship. But Jonah had gone down into the innermost parts of the ship, and he was laying down, and was fast asleep. | So the ship master came to him, and said to him, "What do you mean, sleeper? Arise, call on your God! Maybe your God will notice us, so that we won't perish." | Nevertheless the men rowed hard to get them back to the land; but they could not, for the sea grew more and more stormy against them.* (Jon 1:4,5,6,13) Who's to say this stormy bout of weather on the Sea of Galilee wasn't one of those 'opportune' times that Satan – read YHWH – had been looking for since Luke 4:13? Maybe it was YHWH who whipped up the winds, hoping that Jesus would cave in and call out to his tribal god in fear, lest he and his disciples perish.

along, as he was in the boat, and other boats were also with him.[x]

42   And there arose a great squall;[y] and the waves were breaking over the boat, so that it was filling with water.[z]

43   And he was in the stern, sleeping on the cushion; and they woke him, saying, "Teacher, does it not concern you, that we perish?"[a]

44   [3][And having been woken, he rebuked the wind, and said to the sea, "Hush, be quiet!" And the wind abated, and there was a great calm.[b]]

45   And he said to them, "Why are you timid? Have you still no faith?"[c]

46   [3][But having been afraid, they wondered, saying to one another, "Who is this, then, that he gives orders even to the winds and the water, and they obey him?"[d]]

47   And they came to the other side of the sea, into the land of the Gerasenes.[e]

48   And having come out of the boat, immediately *there* came out of the tombs to meet him a man with an unclean spirit.[f]

x Ps 107:23,24
   Mr 4:36
y Ps 107:25,26
z Jon 1:4
   Mt 8:24
   Mr 4:37
   Lu 8:23
a Ps 107:27,28
   Jon 1:5,6,13
   Mt 8:25
   Mr 4:38
   Lu 8:24
b Ps 107:29
   Mt 8:26
   Mr 4:39
   Lu 8:24
c Ec 3:1,2
   Ec 8:8
   Mr 4:40
d Mt 8:27
   Mr 4:41
   Lu 8:25
e Ps 107:30
   Mt 8:28
   Mr 5:1
   Lu 8:26
f Mt 8:28
   Mr 5:2
   Lu 8:27

---

3 Verses 44 and 46 are not found in the best ancient mss.

5 The herd of swine

g *Mt 8:29*
   Mr 5:7
   Lu 8:28
h *Mr 5:8*
   Lu 8:29
i *Mt 8:30*
   Mr 5:11
   Lu 8:32
j *Mt 8:32*
   Mr 5:13
   Lu 8:33
k *Mt 8:33*
   Mr 5:14
   Lu 8:34,35
l *Mt 8:34*
   Mr 5:15
m *Mr 5:16*
   Lu 8:36
n *Mt 8:34*
   Mr 5:17
   Lu 8:37
o *Mr 5:18*
   Lu 8:38
p *Mr 5:19*
   Lu 8:38

49 And having seen Jesus from a distance, he was crying out with a loud voice, saying, "What have I to do with you? Go away!"[g]

50 For he was saying to him, "Come forth, *you* unclean spirit!"[h]

51 Now near the mountain, there was a large herd of swine grazing;[i] and immediately the herd rushed down the steep bank into the sea.[4][j]

52 And those who fed them fled, and reported it to the city; and they went out to see what it was that had happened.[k]

53 And they came to Jesus,[l] and those who had seen it related to them how it happened to the one possessed by demons, and about the swine.[m]

54 And they began to implore him to go away from their region.[n]

55 And having gotten into the boat, the man with the unclean spirit was admonishing him, that he might be with him.[o]

56 And he did not let him, but sent him away.[p]

---

4 Certain later mss. add, *about two hundred, and they were drowned in the sea*

No such luck for YHWH, though. Jesus is unfazed by the storm. He even chides his disciples for their timidity – *"Have you still no faith?"* His casual, easygoing acceptance of what is and what will be is remarkable.

Ec 3:1,2 – *For everything there is a season, and a time for every purpose under heaven: | a time to be born, and a time to die* [...].

Ec 8:8 – *There is no man who has power over the spirit to contain the spirit; neither does he have power over the day of death.* [...]

5:47-56 THE HERD OF SWINE

Anyone who has been to the eastern shores of the Sea of Galilee knows that there are no steep banks leading down to the lake, so I don't think those crazed swine rushed in and drowned – they would have run out of steam before they'd reached the water's edge. But maybe they stampeded a bit, spooked by all that yelling over near the tombs. Jesus raised a ruckus and the pigs ran off. Who needs that kind of trouble? The fellows who were tending and feeding the pigs went to get help, and *'the people came to see what it was that had happened.'* (Mr 5:14)

I don't quite buy the Gospels' version of events. If their local demon-possessed loony had indeed been miraculously dispossessed of his unclean spirits and rendered sane by Jesus, then surely the people would have been suitably awed, and even eager to bring him their other hard-luck cases for on-the-spot healing. Nothing doing: *'they began to beg him to depart from their region.'* (Mr 5:14)

No, I think the whole thing boils down to this: furious about the pigs, the locals concluded that Jesus and his friends were an unwelcome band of errant troublemakers. As for the loony, he was probably still just as obnoxious as before – which explains why Jesus kicked him off the boat when he tried to board, emphatically refusing to let the crazy man accompany them. One must needs deal firmly with would-be tag-alongs.

6

The things that defile a man

6:1-6 A KINGDOM DIVIDED AGAINST ITSELF CANNOT STAND

YHWH was at daggers with his holy nation and kingdom of priests for their rebellious ways – this was clearly a house and a kingdom divided against itself. Here again, I feel that Jesus is speaking in parables so as to hide his deeper, subversive meaning.

6:4 – "And if a kingdom [...] "
Ex 19:5,6 – "[...] *you shall be my own possession from among all peoples* [...] | *and you shall be to me a kingdom of priests, and a holy nation.* [...]"

6:4 – " [...] is divided against itself [...] "
De 32:20 – *He said, "I will hide my face from them. I will see what their end will be; for they are a very perverse generation, children in whom is no faithfulness."*
Isa 1:2 – *Hear, heavens, and listen, earth; for Yahweh has spoken: "I have nourished and brought up children, and they have rebelled against me."*
Isa 30:9 – *For it is a rebellious people, lying children, children who will not hear Yahweh's law.*

6:5 – "And if a house is divided against itself [...] "
Jer 11:10,11 – " [...] *the house of Israel and the house of Judah have broken my covenant which I made with their fathers.* | *Therefore Yahweh says,*

CHAPTER 6

AND when Jesus had again crossed over to the other side,[a] a great crowd gathered around him, and he was by the sea.[b]

2   But some of them were saying, "By Beelzebul, the ruler of the demons, he casts out the demons."[c]

3   And having called them to himself, he was saying to them in parables,[d] "How can Satan cast out Satan?[e]

4   "And if a kingdom[f] is divided against itself,[g] that kingdom is not able to stand.[h]

5   "And if a house is divided against itself,[i] that house is not able to stand.[j]

6   "And if Satan[k] has risen up against himself, and has been divided,[l] he is not able to stand, but has *come to* an end."[m]

7   And behold, while he was saying these things to them, there came one of the rulers of the synagogue, named Jarius; and having seen him, he fell at his feet,[n]

a   Mt 9:1
b   Mr 5:21
    Lu 8:40
c   Mt 12:24
    Mr 3:22
    Lu 11:15
d   Mt 13:34
e   Mr 3:23
f   Ex 19:5,6
g   De 32:20
    Isa 1:2
    Isa 30:9
h   Mt 12:25
    Mr 3:24
    Lu 11:17
i   Isa 5:1-7
    Jer 11:10,11
    Eze 8:6
    Eze 18:25,29
    Eze 33:20
j   Mt 12:25
    Mr 3:25
    Lu 11:17
k   2Sa 24:1
    1Ch 21:1
l   Eze 28:2,16
m   Eze 28:18,19
    Mt 12:26
    Mr 3:26
    Lu 11:18
n   Mt 9:18
    Mr 5:22
    Lu 8:41

6   Jarius' daughter   The ailing woman in the crowd

o Mt 9:18
   Mr 5:23
   Lu 8:41
p Mt 9:19
   Mr 5:24
   Lu 8:42
q Mt 9:20
   Mr 5:25,27
   Lu 8:43,44
r Mt 9:21
   Mr 5:28
s Lu 8:46
t Mr 5:30
u Mr 5:31
   Lu 8:45
v Mr 5:32
w Mr 5:33
   Lu 8:47

8   and he exhorted him much, saying, "My little daughter is extremely *ill*; come and lay the hands on her, that she might be healed and live."^o

9   And he departed with him, and a great crowd followed him, and was pressing on him *from all sides.*^p

10   And a woman, being with a flow of blood *for* ¹many years, having heard about Jesus, came in the crowd behind him and touched his cloak.^q

11   For she was saying, "If I shall but touch his outer garments, I will be healed."^r

12   And immediately Jesus, knowing in himself that power had gone out of him,^s *and* having turned around in the crowd, said, "Who touched my outer garments?"^t

13   And his disciples said to him, "You see the crowd pressing on you *from all sides*, and you say, 'Who touched me?'"^u

14   And he looked around to see who had done this.^v

15   And the woman, having been frightened and trembling, came and fell down before him, and told him all the truth.^w

16   And he said to her, "Daughter, your faith has

---

1 According to the best ancient mss.; most later mss. read, *twelve*

'Behold, I will bring evil on them, which they shall not be able to escape; and they shall cry to me, but I will not listen to them.'"

Eze 18:25,29 – *"Yet you say, 'The way of the Lord is not equal.' Hear now, house of Israel: Is my way not equal? Aren't your ways unequal? | Yet the house of Israel says, 'The way of the Lord is not fair.' House of Israel, aren't my ways fair? Aren't your ways unfair?"*

6:6 – "And if Satan [...] "

The comparison of these two verses neatly suggests that YHWH and Satan are one and the same:

2Sa 24:1 – *Again Yahweh's anger burned against Israel, and he moved David against them, saying, "Go, count Israel and Judah."*

1Ch 21:1 – *Satan stood up against Israel, and moved David to take a census of Israel.*

6:6 – " [...] has risen up against himself, and has been divided [...] "

The margin notes link this to the passage from Ezekiel that appears in the prologue.

Eze 28:2,16 – *"Son of man, tell the prince of Tyre, 'Thus says the Lord Yahweh: "Because your heart is lifted up, and you have said, 'I am a god, I sit in the seat of God, in the middle of the seas;' yet you are a man, and not God, though you set your heart as the heart of God. | [...] Therefore I have cast you as profane out of God's mountain; and I have destroyed you, covering cherub, from the middle of the stones of fire."'"*

It is not my contention that Jesus' true God – the God of the kingdom of God or heaven of which he speaks – would be concerned with bringing about the fall of YHWH-Satan. Rather, it would be YHWH himself rising up against his own dark side that would bring this about.[24]

6:6 – " […] he is not able to stand, but has *come to* an end."

Eze 28:18,19 – " […] *Therefore I have brought out a fire from the middle of you. It has devoured you. I have turned you to ashes on the earth in the sight of all those who see you. | All those who know you among the peoples will be astonished at you; […] and you shall exist no more."*

6:10-16 THE AILING WOMAN IN THE CROWD

6:16 – And he said to her, "Daughter, your faith has healed you. Go your way."

Nowhere do we read that Jesus prayed in conjunction with a healing. This may be contrasted with the *modus operandi* of other holy men of his time, whose prayers to YHWH on behalf of suppliants were in many instances the key element that brought results.[25]

In the Gospels, Jesus only engages in prayer when he is alone, or in the presence of his disciples.[26] While there are people who bring him their children *'that he should lay his hands on them and pray'*, it is only said that *'He laid his hands on them, and departed from there'* – not that he prayed for them. (Mr 19:13,15) There is no recorded instance of Jesus addressing himself to YHWH in prayer for a healing to occur, be it for sickness or for those with unclean spirits. Indeed, it may have been his omission to invoke YHWH that struck the people of Capernaum so forcefully, causing them to exclaim, *"What is this? A new teaching? For with authority he commands even the unclean spirits, and they obey him!"* (Mr 1:27)

In other words, Jesus dispenses with YHWH altogether. If the healing occurs, it is not because YHWH has been invoked; nor because the woman has declared *mea culpa* and repented of sin; nor because she has surreptitiously touched Jesus' cloak; nor because there has been a transfer of power; but simply because the woman has faith:

Mt 9:22 – *But Jesus, turning around and seeing her, said, "Daughter, cheer up! Your faith has made you well."* […]

healed you. Go your way."[x]

17 And while he was still speaking, they came from the ruler of the synagogue's *house*, saying, "Your daughter has died. Why do you still trouble the teacher?"[y]

18 But Jesus, disregarding what was spoken, said to the ruler of the synagogue, "Fear not, only have faith."[z]

19 And he allowed no one to follow him; and he came to the ruler of the synagogue's house, and he beheld a commotion, and much weeping and wailing.[a]

20 And entering in, he said to them, "Why do you make a commotion and weep? The child is not dead, but is asleep."[b]

21 And they scorned him. But having put them all out, he took the child's father and mother with him and entered in where the child was.[c]

22 And having taken the child by the hand, he said to her, "Talitha koum."[2][d]

23 And at that moment, the girl got up and walked; and immediately they were greatly bewildered.[e]

24 And he admonished them many *times*, that no one should know *of* it; and he said *something* should be

x Mt 9:22
   Mr 5:34
   Lu 8:48
y Mr 5:35
   Lu 8:49
z Mr 5:36
   Lu 8:50
a Mt 9:23
   Mr 5:37,38
   Lu 8:52
b Mt 9:24
   Mr 5:39
   Lu 8:52
c Mr 5:40
   Lu 8:53
d Mt 9:25
   Mr 5:41
   Lu 8:54
e Mt 9:25
   Mr 5:42
   Lu 8:55,56

---

2 Certain later mss. add, *which is translated, "Little girl, I say to you, arise"*

f   *Mr 5:43*
    Lu 8:55,56
g   *Mt 11:2*
    Lu 7:18
h   *Isa 40:3*
    Mal 3:1
    Mal 4:5,6
i   *Lu 7:19*
j   *Mt 11:3*
    Lu 7:20
k   *Isa 32:3,4*
    Lu 7:21
l   *Mt 11:4*
    Lu 7:22
m   *Isa 42:18-20*
    Mt 11:6
    Lu 7:23
n   *1Ki 14:15*
    Mt 11:7
    Lu 7:24

given her to eat.[f]

25   And word was brought to John by his disciples, concerning all of these things.[g]

26   And having summoned a certain two of his disciples, John sent them to Jesus, saying "Are you the coming one?[h] Or should we wait for *someone who is* different?"[i]

27   And having come to him, the men said, "John the Baptist has sent us to you, saying 'Are you the coming one? Or should we expect someone else?'"[j]

28   At that hour, he was healing many of diseases and afflictions and evil spirits, and to many blind *people*, he showed favor to see.[k]

29   And answering, he said to them, "Go, report to John what you have seen and heard,[l] and *say*, he is blessed who shall not be offended by me."[m]

30   And when John's messengers had departed, he began to speak to the crowds about John. "What have you gone out into the wilderness to gaze at? A reed shaken by *the* wind?[n]

31   "But what have you gone out to see? A man dressed in soft clothes? Behold, those who *are dressed* in splendid clothes and *who* are living in luxury are in

Mr 5:34 – *He said to her, "Daughter, your faith has made you well. Go in peace, and be cured of your disease."*

Lu 8:48 – *He said to her, "Daughter, cheer up. Your faith has made you well. Go your way."*

YHWH has thus had no hand whatsoever in the outcome.

6:7-9, 17-24 Jairus' daughter

Jesus does not pray to YHWH to revive the girl. Instead, he tells her father to have faith, and when he comes to the little girl, he takes her by the hand and says to her, *"Talitha koum."* Here again, Jesus acts on his own authority.

6:25-37 John the Baptist's query

John the Baptist did not send two of his disciples to ask Jesus, 'Are you the Messiah?', but rather, 'Are you the coming one?', i.e., 'Elijah':

Isa 40:3 – *The voice of one who calls out, "Prepare the way of Yahweh in the wilderness! Make a level highway in the desert for our God."*

Mal 3:1 – *"Behold, I send my messenger, and he will prepare the way before me; and the Lord, whom you seek, will suddenly come to his temple; and the messenger of the covenant, whom you desire, behold, he comes!" says Yahweh of Armies.*

Mal 4:5,6 – *"Behold, I will send you Elijah the prophet before the great and terrible day of Yahweh comes. | He will turn the hearts of the fathers to the children, and the hearts of the children to their fathers, lest I come and strike the earth with a curse."*

This suggests that John did not consider himself to be the 'messenger' promised by the prophets. Given the reports of healings that were reaching him, the Baptist perhaps wondered if the man he had baptised in the Jordan River were someone to reckon with after all.

Yet as Jesus explains to his followers, *"This is the one of whom it has been written, 'Behold, I send my messenger before Me, and he will prepare the way before Me.'"* (Mt 11:10, Lu 7:27)

My reference to Isaiah suggests why he would tell the two disciples to report to John what they have seen and heard, and to say, *"he is blessed who shall not be offended by me"*:

Isa 42:18-20 – *"Hear, you deaf, and look, you blind, that you may see. | Who is blind, but my servant? Or who is as deaf as my messenger whom I send? Who is as blind as he who is at peace, and as blind as Yahweh's servant? | You see many things, but don't observe. His ears are open, but he doesn't listen."*

Hopefully, John – who according to Jesus was the messenger – would not be offended to discover that he is deaf and blind, that he sees many things but does not observe; that his ears are open, but that he does not listen.

6:34 – "I say to you, among those born of women, no one is greater than John; but *one who is* least in the kingdom of God is greater than he."

Now, isn't that a remarkable statement? Jesus tells his listeners that John is not only a prophet, but *"much more than a prophet"* – yet *"one who is least in the kingdom of God is greater than he."* (Mt 11:9,11) To my ear, it sounds as if Jesus is saying that while John may be looked upon as the apotheosis of the prophets, he and his ilk are wholly unversed in the kingdom of God.

6:35 – "The Law and the prophets *were preached* until John. Since then, the good news of the kingdom of God is proclaimed, and everyone is ardently jostling to get into it."

In Luke 16:16, Jesus seems to be contrasting the way people are eagerly responding to the good news of the kingdom of God – they

One who is least in the kingdom of God is greater than John 6

palaces.[o]
32 "But what have you gone out to see? A prophet? Yes, I say to you, and *one* considerably more than a prophet.[p]
33 "This is the one of whom it has been written, 'BEHOLD, I SEND MY MESSENGER BEFORE ME, AND HE WILL PREPARE THE WAY BEFORE ME.'[q]
34 "I say to you, among those born of women, no one is greater than John; but *one who is* least in the kingdom of God is greater than he.[r]
35 "The Law and the prophets *were preached* until John.[s] Since then, the good news of the kingdom of God is proclaimed, and everyone is ardently jostling to get into it.[t]
36 "And if you are willing to accept it, he is Elijah, the one who is to come.[u]
37 "He who has ears,[v] let him hear.[w]
38 "But to what will I liken this generation? It is like little children sitting in the markets and calling out to others who are different,[x]
39 saying, 'We played the flute for you, and you did not dance. We lamented for you, and you did not mourn.'[y]

o 1Ki 7:1-8 2Ch 9:3,4 *Mt 11:8* *Lu 7:25*
p *Mt 11:9* *Lu 7:26*
q Mal 3:1 *Mt 11:10* *Lu 7:27*
r *Mt 11:11* *Lu 7:28*
s De 31:24-29 Isa 30:9 Jer 5:23 Jer 13:8-11 Eze 2:4,5,7 Eze 3:7 Mal 3:1
t *Mt 11:12* *Lu 16:16*
u Mal 4:5 *Mt 11:14*
v Ex 21:5,6 De 15:16,17
w *Mt 11:15*
x *Mt 11:16* *Lu 7:31,32*
y *Mt 11:17* *Lu 7:32*

are trying to force their way into it – with the evident reluctance with which they have received the Law and the prophets, as suggested by the margin notes:

Isa 30:9 – *"For this is a rebellious people, lying children, children who will not hear Yahweh's law."*

Jer 5:23 – *"But this people has a revolting and a rebellious heart; they have revolted and departed."*

Eze 3:7 – *"But the house of Israel will not listen to you, for they will not listen to me; for all the house of Israel are obstinate and hard-hearted."*

Clearly, Jesus' kingdom of God trumps the Law and the prophets.

6:37 – "He who has ears, let him hear."

De 15:16,17 – *It shall be, if he tells you, "I will not go out from you," because he loves you and your house, because he is well with you; | then you shall take an awl, and thrust it through his ear to the door, and he shall be your slave forever. Also to your female slave you shall do likewise.*

If you still have your ears – intact, that is, unlike those slaves who have had their ears pierced with an awl – it could signify that you have not yet committed yourself to being enslaved by YHWH forever.

6:38-42 TO WHAT SHALL I LIKEN THIS GENERATION?

One gathers that orthodox Jews wished John the Baptist would lighten up a bit – *'We played the flute for you, and you did not dance.'* The ascetic hard-liner's approach was hardly any fun; the loon was probably possessed by a demon!

But Jesus was no better. With his carousing and feasting and *'Follow me!'* parties, he went too far in the other direction for their tastes. *'We lamented for you, and you did not mourn'* – surely, they must have reasoned, a good, conscientious Jew should wear sackcloth and ashes now and then.

6:42 – "And the wisdom was justified by her children."

Mt 15:1,2 – *Then Pharisees and scribes came to Jesus from Jerusalem, saying,* | *"Why do your disciples disobey the tradition of the elders? For they don't wash their hands when they eat bread."*

Mr 2:16,18,24 – *The scribes and the Pharisees, when they saw that he was eating with the sinners and tax collectors, said to his disciples, "Why is it that he eats and drinks with tax collectors and sinners?"* | *John's disciples and the Pharisees were fasting, and they came and asked him, "Why do John's disciples and the disciples of the Pharisees fast, but your disciples don't fast?"* | *The Pharisees said to him, "Behold, why do they do that which is not lawful on the Sabbath day?"*

Lu 16:14,15 – *The Pharisees, who were lovers of money, also heard all these things, and they scoffed at him.* | *He said to them, "You are those who justify yourselves in the sight of men, but God knows your hearts. For that which is exalted among men is an abomination in the sight of God."*

The wisdom of criticising Jesus is justified by the children of that wisdom, the Pharisees.

6:43-56 THE THINGS THAT DEFILE A MAN

6:53 – "Do you not yet understand that everything which enters into the mouth goes into the belly, and is made to go out in the privy, making all foods clean?"

Is Jesus making a claim that all foods are clean? Is pork on the menu? Or is Jesus just saying that whatever goes into the mouth is purged by the digestive tract and then pooped out into the latrine, thus 'purifying' the body of all foods that are eaten?

The debate has simmered for two millennia, for good cause. To begin with, the original Greek wording apparently confused the copyists. From the grammar, they couldn't make heads or tails of who or what was doing the purifying. Was the latrine doing it? Yuck! To clean things

6   A Pharisee invites Jesus to dine with him

z *Mt 11:18*
Lu 7:33
a *De 21:20*
Pr 21:17
Pr 23:20
Mt 11:19
Lu 7:34
b *Mt 9:34*
Mt 11:19
Mt 12:2,24
Mt 15:1,2
Mr 2:16,18,24
Mr 7:1-5
Lu 5:21,30
Lu 6:2
Lu 7:35
Lu 15:1,2
Lu 16:14,15
c *Lu 11:37*
d *Mt 15:2*
Mr 7:3
Lu 11:38
e *Mt 23:25*
Lu 11:39
f *Mt 23:26*
g *Mt 15:10*
Mr 7:14
h *Mt 15:11*
Mr 7:15

40 "Indeed, John came, neither eating nor drinking, and they say, 'He has a demon!'[z]

41 "The son of man came, eating and drinking, and they say, 'Behold, a man, a glutton and a drinker of wine, a friend of tax collectors and of sinners!'[a]

42 "And the wisdom was justified by her children."[b]

43 Now as he was speaking, a Pharisee asked him to dine with him, and having entered, he reclined.[c]

44 But the Pharisee wondered, having seen that he had not first washed before the meal.[d]

45 But the master said to him, "Now you Pharisees, you cleanse the outside of the cup and the plate, but inside they are full of pillaging and self-indulgence.[e]

46 "Blind Pharisee, first make the inside of the cup clean, that the outside of it might also become clean."[f]

47 And having summoned the crowd, he said to them, "Hear and understand —[g]

48 not that which enters into the mouth defiles the man, but that which comes forth from the mouth, this *is what* defiles the man."[h]

49 Then, having come near, the disciples said to him, "Do you know that the Pharisees, having heard

up, it seems some scribe somewhere took it upon himself to modify the verb *katharizó* (to purify, to make clean) so that it could imply it was the body (unmentioned, but a neuter noun) and its digestive processes that were purging the foods. This was good news for those who didn't like the idea of Jesus messing around with Judaism's kosher food industry. (To bolster this view, they like to cite Matthew 5:17,18.)

But in the older manuscripts, *katharizó*'s conjugation points to a masculine noun as its referent. The trouble is, apart from 'latrine', the only other masculine noun in the neighborhood is 'Jesus'. Does Jesus purify the foods? Can't be – the guy doesn't even wash his hands. So the translators decided that Mark, in an aside, must be telling us that Jesus had 'declared' all foods to be clean. Pork lovers cheered.

So, pork? or no pork? Along with a host of other forbidden foods, that is the question. And here, my friends, is my answer:

Mr 7:15 – *"There is nothing from outside of the man, that going into him can defile him […]."*

The operative word here is 'nothing'. Be it kosher or not kosher, it's not what goes *into* your mouth that can defile you; it's what comes forth *out* of your mouth.[27]

6:54 – "But the things which go forth out of the mouth come forth out of the heart, and those defile the man."

Pr 27:19 – *Like water reflects a face, so a man's heart reflects the man.*

Eze 28:2 – *"Son of man, tell the prince of Tyre, 'Thus says the Lord Yahweh: "Because your heart is lifted up, and you have said, 'I am a god, I sit in the seat of God, in the middle of the seas;' yet you are a man, and not God, though you set your heart as the heart of God.""*

6:55,56 – "For out the heart come forth evil thoughts, slaughters, malice, deceit, *the* evil eye, slander, pride, recklessness. All these evils come forth from within, and defile the man."

So what words come out of YHWH's mouth? Let's listen in…

Le 26:16-39 – *"I will appoint terror over you. […] | I will set my face against you, and you will be struck before your enemies. […] | You will eat the flesh of your sons, and you will eat the flesh of your daughters. […] | I will scatter you among the nations, and I will draw out the sword after you. Your land will be a desolation, and your cities shall be a waste. | […]"*

Ps 55:20,21 – *He raises his hands against his friends. He has violated his covenant. | His mouth was smooth as butter, but his heart was war. His words were softer than oil, yet they were drawn swords.*

Pr 21:23,24 – *Whoever guards his mouth and his tongue keeps his soul from troubles. | "Proud", "Haughty", "Scorner" is his name, who works in the arrogance of pride.*

Isa 45:23 – *"I have sworn by Myself. The word has gone out of My mouth in righteousness, and will not be revoked, that to Me every knee shall bow, every tongue shall take an oath."*

Jer 23:19,20 – *"Behold, Yahweh's storm, his wrath, has gone out. Yes, a whirling storm. It shall burst on the head of the wicked. | Yahweh's anger shall not turn back, until he has executed, and until he has performed the intents of his heart. In the latter days, you will understand it perfectly."*

6:57-64 THE CANAANITE WOMAN

6:57 – But having risen up from that place, he went away into the region of Tyre.

Eze 28:2,9 – *"Son of man, tell the prince of Tyre, 'Thus says the Lord Yahweh: "Because your heart is lifted up, and you have said, 'I am a god.' […] | Will you yet say before him who kills you, 'I am God'? but you are man, and not God, in the hand of him who wounds you."""*

If Jesus hiked all the way down to Tyre, I think it was to ensure that his disciples would not overlook Ezekiel's prophesy. Of course, getting in a bit of Mediterranean seaside R & R wouldn't have hurt, either.

this speech, were offended?"[i]

50 But he answered, saying, "Leave them alone; they are blind guides who strain out the gnat, but swallow *the* camel.[j] But if a blind guide guides a blind man, both will fall into a pit."[k]

51 But having answered, Simon said to him, "Explain this parable to us."[l]

52 And he said, "Are you also still without understanding?[m]

53 "Do you not yet understand that everything which enters into the mouth goes into the belly, and is made to go out in the privy, making all foods clean?[n]

54 "But the things which go forth out of the mouth come forth out of the heart, and those defile the man.[o]

55 "For out the heart come forth evil thoughts,[3] slaughters, malice, deceit, *the* evil eye, slander, pride, recklessness.[p]

56 "All these evils come forth from within, and defile the man."[q]

57 But having risen up from that place, he went away into the region of Tyre.[r]

---

3 Certain later mss. add, *adulteries, fornications, thefts*

i   Mt 15:12
j   Mt 23:24
k   Mt 15:14
    Lu 6:39
l   Mt 15:15
m Mt 15:16
n   Mt 15:11
    Mt 15:17
    Mr 7:15
    Mr 7:19
o   Pr 27:19
    Eze 28:2
    Mt 15:18
    Mr 7:20
p   Ex 32:9
    Le 26:14-39
    De 6:15
    Jg 11:29-40
    Job 1:12-19
    Job 2:3
    Ps 55:20,21
    Pr 21:23,24
    Isa 45:23
    Jer 23:19,20
    Eze 23:3
    La 2:20-22
    Mt 15:19
    Mr 7:21,22
q   Mt 15:20
    Mr 7:23
r   Ps 45:2,7,17
    Eze 28:2,9
    Eze 28:11-19
    Mt 15:21
    Mr 7:24

6 The Canaanite woman

s *Mt 15:22*
   Mr 7:25,26
t *Mt 15:23*
u *Ps 74:1*
   Jer 12:7
   Eze 34:5,6
   Mt 9:36
   Mt 15:24
   Mt 18:11
v *Mt 15:25*
w *Mt 15:26*
   Mr 7:27
x *Ps 45:10-12*
   Mt 15:27
   Mr 7:28
y *Mt 9:22*
   Mr 5:34
   Mr 10:52
   Lu 8:48
   Lu 18:42
z *Mt 15:28*
   Mr 7:29,30

58 And behold, a Canaanite woman, having come out from that region, cried out, saying, "Have mercy on me, Master [4] – my daughter is grievously demon-possessed!" [s]

59 But he answered her not a word. And having come near, his disciples solicited him, saying, "Send her away, for she is shouting behind us." [t]

60 But answering, he said, "I was not sent, except to the lost sheep of the house of Israel." [u]

61 But the *woman*, having come, knelt down and kissed *his hand*, saying, "Master, help me!" [v]

62 But answering, he said, "It is not good to take the children's bread and throw it to puppies." [w]

63 But she said, "Master, even puppies eat from the crumbs which fall under their master's table." [x]

64 Then, answering, he said to her, "O woman, great *is* your faith. [y] Be it to you as you wish." And her daughter was healed from that hour. [z]

---

4 Certain later mss. add, *son of David*

6:60 – But answering, he said, "I was not sent, except to the lost sheep of the house of Israel."

Ps 74:1 – *God, why have you rejected us forever? Why does your anger smolder against the sheep of your pasture?*

We could read 'lost sheep' as meaning the sheep of the house of Israel who have been 'cut off', rejected by Yʜwʜ.

Jer 12:7 – *"I have forsaken my house. I have cast off my heritage. I have given the dearly beloved of my soul into the hand of her enemies."*

Eze 34:5,6 – *"They were scattered, because there was no shepherd; and they became food to all the animals of the field, and were scattered. | My sheep wandered through all the mountains, and on every high hill. Yes, my sheep were scattered on all the surface of the earth; and there was no one who searched or sought."*

Mt 9:36 – *But when he saw the multitudes, he was moved with compassion for them, because they were harassed and scattered, like sheep without a shepherd.*

His message of liberation, though, was only intended for the Jews. Gentiles were of no concern to him, so it's no wonder that Jesus ignores the Canaanite woman at first. Besides, he's on vacation at the seashore; who wants to be pestered by hawkers and hard-luck cases? Yet she persists. Implored by his exasperated disciples to send her away, Jesus rebuffs the woman with a decidedly disparaging remark.

6:63 – But she said, "Master, even puppies eat from the crumbs which fall under their master's table."

Ps 45:10-12 – *Listen, daughter, consider, and turn your ear. Forget your own people, and also your father's house. | So the king will desire your beauty, honor him, for he is your lord. | The daughter of Tyre comes with a gift. [...]*

Nevertheless, 'the daughter of Tyre comes with a gift' – her self-abasing rejoinder softens Jesus' uncharacteristically hard heart.

7

Prayer and good gifts

7:1-14 PRAYER, AND GOOD GIFTS GIVEN TO THOSE WHO ASK

7:1 – And having departed from there, Jesus went along the sea of Galilee; and having gone up the mountain, he was sitting there.

Time and again, it is said that Jesus has gone up 'the mountain'; I've wondered if that mountain might have been Mount Arbel, on the western shores of the Sea of Galilee. It commands a beautiful view of the lake, it's just a few hours' walk south of Capernaum, and along the way Jesus would have conveniently passed right by Magdala – where some people think his sweetheart Mary Magdalene lived.

7:2 – [...] "Master, teach us to pray, just as John taught his disciples."
Lu 5:33 – *"Why do John's disciples often fast and pray, likewise also the disciples of the Pharisees, but yours eat and drink?"*
Jesus' disciples must have felt like spiritual black sheep. Their teacher was always going off by himself to pray, but he'd never told them how they should pray. Figure it out for themselves? Not these sheep...

We may note, though, that these *'Follow me!'* party animals never once ask their teacher for instructions about fasting.

7:4 – "give us this day our daily bread."
If I reduce the so-called Lord's Prayer to one simple demand – 'give us this day our daily bread' – it is because Jesus' elucidation deals only

CHAPTER 7

A ND having departed from there, Jesus went along the sea of Galilee; and having gone up on the mountain, he was sitting there.[a]

2   And it came about, as he was praying in a certain place, that when he ceased, one of his disciples said to him, "Master, teach us to pray, just as John taught his disciples."[b]

3   But he said to them, "When you pray, say, 'Our Father, who *is* in heaven,[1][c]

4   give us today our daily bread.'"[d]

5   And he said to them, "Who among you will have a friend, and will go to him at midnight, and say to him, 'Friend, lend me three loaves of bread,[e]

6   for a friend of mine has come to me on a journey, and I have nothing to set before him.'[f]

7   "And he, answering from within, will say, 'Do

a Mt 15:29
b Lu 5:33
   Lu 11:1
c Mt 6:9
   Lu 11:2
d Pr 30:8
   Mt 6:11
   Lu 11:3
e Lu 11:5
f Lu 11:6

1 Certain later mss. add, *hallowed be your name*

with getting what you want by pounding on doors and being persistent. Besides, the rest of the Lord's Prayer – *'May your name be kept holy. May your Kingdom come. May your will be done on earth, as it is in heaven';* *'Forgive us our sins, as we ourselves also forgive everyone who is indebted to us. Bring us not into temptation, but deliver us from the evil one'* – does not find its place in the passage's chiastic structure.[28] In my view, it was dreamed up by someone else and inserted at a later date.

7:5 – " […] 'Friend, lend me three loaves of bread.'"

In the chiastic structure, the three loaves pair with the bread, fish and egg in verses 11-13.

7:7 – " […] 'I cannot get up to give you *anything*.'"

Pr 3:27,28 – *Do not withhold good from those to whom it is due, when it is in the power of your hand to do it. | Do not say to your neighbor, "Go, and come again; tomorrow I will give it to you," when you have it by you.*

7:8 – "I say to you, […] having *been* woken, he will give him as much as he needs."

Ps 78:18,21 – *They tempted God in their heart by asking food according to their desire. | Therefore Yahweh heard, and was angry […] against Israel.*

Ps 78:23-25,29 – *Yet he commanded the skies above, and opened the doors of heaven. | He rained down manna on them to eat, and gave them food from the sky. | Man ate the bread of angels. He sent them food to the full. | So they ate, and were well filled. He gave them their own desire.*

Ps 105:40 – *They asked, and he brought quails, and satisfied them with the bread of the sky.*

The squeaky Hebrew gets the feast…

7:9,10 – "And I say to you, ask, and it will be given to you; seek, and you will find; knock, and it will be opened to you. For everyone who

asks, receives; and everyone who seeks, finds; and to everyone who knocks, it will be opened."

If we consider passages such as Leviticus 26:3-33 and Deuteronomy 28:1-68, we may gauge the degree to which obedience to the Law was the *sine qua non* for receiving Yhwh's blessings. The Jewish god's gifts were straightforwardly contingent on a *quid pro quo*. Markedly different, therefore, is Jesus' approach to getting good gifts from God in heaven, the indefinable 'God' of all who *"makes his sun to rise on the evil and the good, and sends rain on the just and the unjust."* (Mt 5:45) Ask. You will receive. Seek. You will find. Knock. It will be opened to you. This is a singular teaching; so far as I know, it has no parallel in Jesus' time.

In the verses that follow, Jesus seems to be making oblique ironic reference to Israel's father Yhwh, when he speaks of stones, serpents and scorpions:

7:11 – "But which of you who is a father, to a son who will ask for a loaf of bread, will give him a stone?"

De 9:9-11 – *When I had gone up onto the mountain to receive the stone tablets, even the tablets of the covenant which Yahweh made with you, then I stayed on the mountain forty days and forty nights. I neither ate bread nor drank water. | Yahweh delivered to me the two stone tablets written with God's finger. […]*

Mt 4:3 – *The tempter came and said to him, "If you are the Son of God, command that these stones become bread."*

7:12 – "Or *who will ask for* a fish, and instead of a fish, will give him a serpent?"

Nu 21:6 – *Yahweh sent venomous snakes among the people, and they bit the people. Many people of Israel died.*

7

Good gifts given to those who ask

g Pr 3:27,28
   Lu 11:7
h Ps 78:18,21
   Ps 78:23-25,29
   Ps 105:40
   Lu 11:8
i Mt 7:7
   Lu 11:9
j Mt 7:8
   Lu 11:10
k Ex 4:22
l De 9:9-11
   Mt 4:3
   Mt 7:9
m Nu 21:6
   Mt 7:10
   Lu 11:11
n 2Ch 10:11,15
   Lu 11:12
o Ge 6:5
   Ps 53:2,3
   Ec 9:3
   Jer 16:12
p Ps 16:10
   Mt 7:7
   Mt 7:11
   Mt 26:39
   Mt 27:46
   Mr 14:36
   Mr 15:34
   Lu 11:10
   Lu 11:13
   Lu 22:42

not cause me trouble! The door has already been shut, and my children are in bed with me. I cannot get up to give you *anything*.'[g]

8 "I say to you, even if he will not get up and give him *anything* on account of being his friend, yet because of his shameless importunity, having *been* woken, he will give him as much as he needs.[h]

9 "And I say to you, ask, and it will be given to you; seek, and you will find; knock, and it will be opened to you.[i]

10 "For everyone who asks, receives; and everyone who seeks, finds; and to everyone who knocks, it will be opened.[j]

11 "But which of you who is a father,[k] to a son who will ask for a loaf of bread, will give him a stone?[l]

12 "Or *who will ask for* a fish, and instead of a fish, will give him a serpent?[m]

13 "Or if he should ask for an egg, will give him a scorpion?[n]

14 "Therefore, if you, being evil,[o] know *how* to give good gifts to your children, how much more will your Father, who *is* in the heavens, give good *gifts* to those who ask Him?"[p]

7:13 – "Or if he should ask for an egg, will give him a scorpion?"

2Ch 10:11,15 – *"Now whereas my father burdened you with a heavy yoke, I will add to your yoke. My father chastised you with whips, but I will chastise you with scorpions." | So the king didn't listen to the people; for it was brought about by God, that Yahweh might establish his word […].*

7:14 – "Therefore, if you, being evil […]"

Ge 6:5 – *Yahweh saw that the wickedness of man was great in the earth, and that every imagination of the thoughts of man's heart was continually only evil.*

Ps 53:2,3 – *God looks down from heaven on the children of men […] | […] There is no one who does good, no, not one.*

Ec 9:3 – *[…] the heart of the sons of men is full of evil, and madness is in their heart while they live […]*

Jer 16:12 – *"You have done evil more than your fathers; for, behold, you walk every one after the stubbornness of his evil heart, so that you don't listen to me."*

7:14 – " […] know *how* to give good gifts to your children, how much more will your Father, who *is* in the heavens, give good *gifts* to those who ask Him?"

Mr 14:36 – *"Abba, Father, all things are possible to you. Please remove this cup from me. However, not what I desire, but what you desire."*

Mr 15:34 – *At the ninth hour Jesus cried with a loud voice, saying, "Eloi, Eloi, lama sabachthani?" which is, being interpreted, "My God, my God, why have you forsaken me?"*

While he might have wryly anticipated that YHWH's answer to his Garden of Gethsemane prayer would hardly amount to a 'good gift' for himself, Jesus would no doubt have confidence that the true God gives good gifts to those who ask.

7:15-24 Jesus teaches in Nazareth

7:17 – "The spirit of the lord God is upon me, because God has anointed me to bring good news to the meek; to bind up the crushed, to proclaim release to the captives and freedom to the bound."

Who are the crushed? Any Jew who does not keep YHWH's commandments will be crushed:

De 7:9,10 – *Know therefore that Yahweh your God himself is God, the faithful God, who keeps covenant and loving kindness with them who love him and keep his commandments to a thousand generations, | and repays those who hate him to their face, to destroy them. He will not be slack to him who hates him. He will repay him to his face.*

Jer 19:1-11 – *Thus said Yahweh, "Go, and buy a potter's earthen bottle, and take some of the elders of the people, and of the elders of the priests [...]. | Then you shall break the bottle in the sight of the men who go with you, | and shall tell them, 'Yahweh of Armies says: "Even so will I break this people and this city, as one breaks a potter's vessel [...]."'"*

Who are the captives in need of release? Who are the bound, the bondservants in need of freedom?

Le 25:55 – *"For to me the sons of Israel are slaves; they are my slaves whom I brought out of the land of Egypt. I am Yahweh your God."*

7:19 – And he began to say to them, "Today this Scripture is fulfilled in your ears."

Isa 42:1,5-7 – *"Behold, my servant, whom I uphold; my chosen, in whom my soul delights – I have put my Spirit on him. [...] | Thus says God Yahweh, he who created the heavens and stretched them out, he who spread out the earth and that which comes out of it, he who gives breath to its people and spirit to those who walk in it. | I, Yahweh, have called you in righteousness, and will hold your hand, and will keep you, and make you a covenant for the*

15 And he went out from there and came into his own country, where he was brought up. And according to his custom, on the day of the Sabbath, he entered into the synagogue and stood up to read.[q]

16 And the scroll of the prophet Isaiah was handed to him, and having unrolled the scroll, he found the place where it was written,[r]

17   "THE SPIRIT OF THE LORD GOD IS UPON ME,
      BECAUSE GOD HAS ANOINTED ME
      TO BRING GOOD NEWS TO THE MEEK;
      TO BIND UP THE CRUSHED,[s]
      TO PROCLAIM RELEASE TO THE CAPTIVES
      AND FREEDOM TO THE BOUND."[t]

18 And having rolled up the scroll and given it back to the attendant, he sat down, and all eyes in the synagogue were staring at him.[u]

19 And he began to say to them, "Today this Scripture is fulfilled in your ears."[v]

20 And many *of those* listening were astounded, saying, "From where *do* these things *come* to him, and what *is* the wisdom that has been given to him, and do such works of power come about by his hands?[w]

21 "Is this not the carpenter, the son of Mary, and *the* brother of James, and Joses, and Judas, and

q Mt 13:54
  Mr 6:1,2
  Lu 4:16
r Lu 4:17
s Le 26:14-19
  De 7:9,10
  Jer 19:1-11
  La 3:1-16
t Le 25:55
  Isa 44:21
  Isa 61:1
  Ho 10:10
  Lu 4:18
u Lu 4:20
v Isa 42:1,5-7
  Lu 4:21
w Isa 40:14
  Mt 13:54
  Mr 6:2

7   Jesus sends out the disciples in pairs

x *Mt 13:55,56*
   Mr 6:3
y *De 13:1,3,5*
   Jer 23:16
   Mr 6:3
z *Mt 13:57*
   Mr 6:4
   Lu 4:24
   Jn 4:44
a *Mt 13:58*
   Mr 6:5
b *Mt 9:22*
   Mr 5:34
   Mr 5:36
   Mr 10:52
   Lu 8:48
   Lu 8:50
   Lu 17:19
   Lu 18:42
c *Mr 6:6*
d *Mt 10:5*
   Mr 6:7
   Lu 9:1
e *Mt 10:7*
   Lu 9:2
f *Mt 10:9*
   Mr 6:8
   Lu 9:3
   Lu 22:35
g *Mt 10:10*
   Mr 6:9
   Lu 9:3
h *Mt 10:11*
   Mr 6:10
   Lu 9:4

Simon? And are not his sisters here with us?"[x]

22   And they took offense at him.[y] But he said to them, "A prophet is not without honor, except in his own country, among his own relatives and in his own house."[z]

23   And he was not able to do there any work of power, except for a few sick people he healed, having laid the hands on *them*.[a]

24   And he wondered at their lack of faith.[b] And he went about the surrounding villages, teaching.[c]

25   And summoning the twelve, he began to send them out two *by* two, and he gave them authority *over* the unclean spirits,[d]

26   and he sent them to proclaim the kingdom of God, and to heal the sick.[e]

27   And he said to them, "Take nothing for the journey, except a staff only — neither bread nor bag nor money in the belt —[f]

28   but *go* wearing sandals, and do not put on two tunics."[g]

29   And he said to them, "Wherever you enter into a house, stay there until you go out from there.[h]

30   "And any place that will not receive you, not even

people, as a light for the nations; | to open the blind eyes, to bring the prisoners
out of the dungeon, and those who sit in darkness out of the prison."

My own view is that Jesus felt he was called by the true God – as he
might have seen him, the one who truly did create the heavens and the
earth, who gave breath to its peoples – to free the people of Israel from
their tribal god, from their bondage to YHWH; to open their blind eyes;
to bring them out of religious darkness, out of their spiritual prison.

7:20 – And many *of those* **listening were astounded, saying, "From**
where *do* **these things** *come* **to him, and what** *is* **the wisdom that has**
been given to him, and do such works of power come about by his
hands?"

Isa 40:14 – *Who did he take counsel with, and who instructed him, and*
taught him in the path of justice, and taught him knowledge, and showed him
the way of understanding?

Jesus seems to have acted with an assurance that confounded his listeners. As for the 'works of power', the locals were probably reacting
to reports or rumors they had heard, not actual healings that Jesus had
done in their midst: both Mark and Matthew relate that Jesus could do
no miracles while in Nazareth.

7:21 – "Is this not the carpenter, the son of Mary, and *the* **brother of**
James, and Joses, and Judas, and Simon? And are not his sisters here
with us?"

To keep Mary a perpetual virgin, great efforts have been made over
the centuries to explain why these four brothers and two or more sisters cited by Matthew and Mark are not Jesus' direct relations. My own
view is that Mary and Joseph enjoyed a normal, healthy union that produced a fine family, as would befit any orthodox Jewish couple.

With regard to why Jesus may have been known as 'the son of Mary',
see above, THE ANGEL OF THE LORD COMES TO MARY, page 12.

7:22 – And they took offense at him. [...] [29]

Luke alone recounts that the congregation in the synagogue was *'filled with wrath'* and *'rose up, threw him out of the city, and led him to the brow of the hill that their city was built on, that they might throw him off the cliff.'* (Lu 4:28,29)

This is highly unlikely, given the lay of the land around Nazareth. The crowd would have been all tuckered out by the time they got to the top of Mount Kedumim, traditionally identified as the hill in question and more than a kilometer to the south. What's more, there's no cliff off of which they could have thrown Jesus; there's just a steep bank, down which he wouldn't have rolled very far. One pictures the crowd, winded and dismayed – 'Confound it! There's no cliff up here...' – and Jesus, quite unperturbed, passing through their midst and going his way.

7:23,24 – And he was not able to do there any work of power, except for a few sick people he healed, having laid the hands on *them*. And he wondered at their lack of faith. [...]

Since the people lacked faith, it is no wonder that Jesus could perform no works of power. For healings to occur, people needed to have faith – cf. the reference verses for note *b* in the margin.

7:25-31 JESUS SENDS OUT THE DISCIPLES IN PAIRS

7:26 – and he sent them to proclaim the kingdom of God, and to heal the sick.

In Matthew 10:7, the disciples are told to go and proclaim, *'The kingdom of the heavens has drawn near.'* In contrast, Luke 9:2 simply states that they are sent *to proclaim the kingdom of God* – a rendering that to my ear more closely concurs with Jesus' teaching that the kingdom of God is not a kingdom to come, but one that is already present.

hear you, going out from there, shake off the dust which *is* under your feet, as a testimony for them."[i]

31 And going out, they passed through the villages, announcing *the* good news and healing everywhere.[j]

32 Now [2]Herod the tetrarch heard of all the things being done, and was perplexed, because it was said by some that John had been raised from among *the* dead;[k]

33 but by some, that Elijah had appeared; but by others that a prophet, one of the ancients, had arisen.[l]

34 But Herod said, "John, I beheaded. But who is this, about whom I hear such *things*?"[m]

35 [3][For Herod himself, having sent *soldiers*, seized John and bound him in prison on account of Herodias, the wife of his brother Philip, because he had married her.[n]

36 Yet John was saying to Herod, "It is not lawful for you to have your brother's wife."[o]

37 And Herodias held it against him and wanted to kill him, and *yet* was not able *to*;[p] for Herod feared the multitude, because they held John to be a prophet.[q]

38 And an opportune day came, when Herod on

i Isa 52:2
   Mt 10:14
   Mr 6:11
   Lu 9:5
j Lu 9:6
k Mt 14:1
   Mr 6:14
   Lu 9:7
l Mt 16:14
   Mr 6:15
   Lu 9:8
m Lu 9:9
n Mt 14:3
   Mr 6:17
   Lu 3:20
o Le 18:16
   Le 20:21
   Mt 14:4
   Mr 6:18
   Lu 3:19
p Mr 6:19
q De 18:15,18
   Mt 14:5
   Mt 21:26
   Mr 11:32
   Lu 20:6

---

2 Herod Antipas, tetrarch of Galilee and Perea from 4 BCE – 39 CE, and son of Herod the Great
3 Verses 35-46 are not found in the best ancient mss.

7   John the Baptist is beheaded

r Mr 6:21
s Mt 14:6,7
   Mr 6:22
t Mr 6:23
u Mt 14:8
   Mr 6:24
v Mt 14:8
   Mr 6:25
w Mt 14:9
   Mr 6:26
x Mt 14:10
   Mr 6:27
y Mt 14:11
   Mr 6:28

his birthday gave a banquet for lords, and his military commanders, and the notables of Galilee;[r]

39 and the daughter of he *and* Herodias having come in, and having danced, she pleased Herod and his guests, and the king said to the girl, "Ask *of* me whatever you want, and I will give *it* to you."[s]

40 And he swore to her, "Whatever you might ask of me, I will give to you, up to half of my kingdom."[t]

41 And having gone out, she said to her mother, "What shall I ask *for*?" And she said, "The head of John the Baptist."[u]

42 And having entered in immediately with haste before the king, she asked, saying, "I want that you at once give to me the head of John the Baptist on a platter."[v]

43 And although the king was greatly grieved, on account of the oaths *he had made* and his guests, he would not annul it.[w]

44 And immediately the king sent an executioner, and commanded that his head be brought; and he went and beheaded him in the prison,[x]

45 and brought the head upon a platter, and gave it to the girl, and the girl gave it to her mother.[y]

7:27,28 – And he said to them, "Take nothing for the journey, except a staff only – neither bread nor bag nor money in the belt – but go wearing sandals, and do not put on two tunics."

There's nothing like hands-on experience for learning how God's providence works. Jesus sends out his disciples without provisions, without money, and with only one tunic.

Lu 22:35 – *He said to them, "When I sent you out without purse, and wallet, and sandals, did you lack anything?" They said, "Nothing."*

7:30 – "And any place that will not receive you, not even hear you, going out from there, shake off the dust which *is* under your feet, as a testimony for them."

Isa 52:2 – *Shake yourself from the dust! Arise, sit up, Jerusalem! Release yourself from the bonds of your neck, captive daughter of Zion!*

7:32-46 HEROD AND JOHN THE BAPTIST

The detailed account of Herod's birthday party and Herodias' daughter asking for the head of John the Baptist on a platter as a gift is here said to be absent from the best ancient manuscripts. It makes for great reading, but it strikes me as being quite off-topic insofar as Jesus goes. I prefer Luke's three verse digression; it supplies the needed break in the narrative, but then lets us get back to the story without further delay.

Matthew and Mark relate that Herodias wanted to kill John because he had told Herod that it was not lawful for him to have taken her as a wife (cf. Le 20:21). For his part, Josephus puts it down to prevention: *'Herod, who feared lest the great influence John had over the people might put it into his power and inclination to raise a rebellion, (for they seemed ready to do any thing he should advise,) thought it best, by putting him to death, to prevent any mischief he might cause.'* [30]

7:47-50 JESUS AND THE DISCIPLES WITHDRAW TO A SOLITARY PLACE

At this stage, Jesus' preaching about the kingdom of God seems to have attracted so many people in search of healing and spiritual insight that he and his disciples couldn't find the time to sit down together for their traditional *'Follow me!'* feasts. Giving the crowds the slip, Jesus and the disciples sail off in 'the boat'. But they don't go far – the crowds are able to follow them on foot. Since it is said later on that Jesus goes up on 'the mountain' to pray (Mt 14:23, Mr 6:46), we could guess that they put ashore not far from Mount Arbel (see above, page 120).

7:51-60 THE CROWD COMES TO JESUS AND IS FED

7:51 – And having gone out *of the boat,* **he saw** *a* **great crowd, and he was moved with compassion for them, for they were like sheep without a shepherd [...]**

Ps 23:1 – *Yahweh is my shepherd: I shall lack nothing.*

Really? Wanna bet?

Ps 44:9-22 – *But now you rejected us, and brought us to dishonor, [...] | You have made us like sheep for food [...]. | Yes, for your sake we are killed all day long. We are regarded as sheep for the slaughter.*

Eze 34:4-6 – *"You haven't strengthened the diseased, neither have you healed that which was sick, neither have you bound up that which was broken, neither have you brought back that which was driven away, neither have you sought that which was lost; but with force and with rigor you have ruled over them. | They were scattered, because there was no shepherd; and they became food to all the animals of the field, and were scattered. | My sheep wandered through all the mountains, and on every high hill. Yes, my sheep were scattered on all the surface of the earth; and there was no one who searched or sought."*

46 And having heard *of it*, his disciples came and took away the corpse and laid it in a tomb.[z]]

47 And having returned, the disciples related to him how much they had done.[a]

48 And he said to them, "Come away by yourselves to a solitary place, and rest a little while." For there were many who were coming and who were going, and they did not even have time to eat.[b]

49 So they went away in the boat to a solitary place by themselves.[c]

50 And *many* saw them going, and recognized *them*, and *they* ran there together on foot from all the towns and went before them.[d]

51 And having gone out *of the boat*, he saw *a* great crowd, and he was moved with compassion for them, for they were like sheep without a shepherd;[e] and he began to teach them many things.[f]

52 And already the hour having become much, the disciples, having come to him, said, "The place is desolate, and the hour *is* already much;[g]

53 send them away, that having gone to the surrounding farms and villages, they might buy for themselves something to eat."[h]

z Mt 14:12
   Mr 6:29
a Mr 6:30
   Lu 9:10
b Mr 6:31
c Mt 14:13
   Mr 6:32
   Jn 6:1
d Mt 14:13
   Mr 6:33
   Lu 9:11
   Jn 6:2
e Ps 23:1
   Ps 44:9-22
   Ps 74:1
   Ps 78:52
   Ps 80:1
   Jer 12:7
   Eze 34:4-6
   Mt 9:36
   Jn 10:11
f Mr 6:34
   Lu 9:11
g Mt 14:15
   Mr 6:35
   Lu 9:12
h Mt 14:15
   Mr 6:36
   Lu 9:12

7   The crowd comes to Jesus and is fed

i *Mt 14:16*
  Mr 6:37
  Lu 9:13
j *Mt 14:17*
  Mr 6:38
  Lu 9:13
k *Mt 14:18*
  Lu 11:5,6
l *Mt 6:9,11*
  Mt 7:11
m *Mt 14:19*
  Mr 6:41
  Lu 9:16
  Jn 6:11
n *Mt 14:20*
  Mr 6:42
  Lu 9:17
o *Mt 14:20*
  Mr 6:43
  Lu 9:17
  Jn 6:13
p *Mt 14:21*
  Mr 6:44
  Lu 9:14
  Jn 6:10
q *Mt 14:22*
  Mr 6:45
r *Mt 14:23*
  Mr 6:46

54 But Jesus said to them, "They have no need to go away — you give them *something* to eat!"[i]

55 But they said to him, "We have nothing here, except [4]three loaves and a few small fish."[j]

56 But he said, "Bring them to me here."[k]

57 And having ordered the crowds to sit down on the grass, having taken the [4]loaves, having looked up to heaven,[l] he blessed *the loaves*; and having broken *them*, he gave the loaves to the disciples, and the disciples *gave them* to the crowds.[m]

58 And all ate and were satisfied.[n]

59 [5][And they picked up the broken pieces that were left over, twelve baskets full.[o]

60 But those who were eating were about five thousand men, besides women and children.[p]]

61 And immediately, he compelled his disciples to enter into the boat, and to go ahead to the other side, until he should dismiss the crowds.[q]

62 And having dismissed the crowds, he went up by himself on the mountain to pray.[r]

63 And evening having come, the boat was in the

---

4 According to the best ancient mss.; later mss. read, *five loaves and two fish*
5 Verses 59 and 60 are not found in the best ancient mss.

7:55 – But they said to him, "We have nothing here, except three loaves and a few small fish."

On this point, a footnote informs us that later manuscripts read *'five loaves and two fish'*. One would guess that esoteric Gnostics had been fiddling with the text.[31]

With only a few loaves of bread and a couple of fish on hand, though, the disciples have been caught short – clearly, no one had planned to be out on the hills for a sunset picnic. Quite a pickle they find themselves in, all because Jesus has been talking to the crowds interminably, paying no attention whatsoever to the time going by while he's been *'teaching them many things'*.

7:56 – But he said, "Bring them to me here."

Lu 11:5,6 – *He said to them, "Which of you, if you go to a friend at midnight, and tell him, 'Friend, lend me three loaves of bread, | for a friend of mine has come to me from a journey, and I have nothing to set before him.'"*

7:57 – And [...] having taken the loaves, having looked up to heaven, he blessed *the loaves*; and having broken *them*, he gave the loaves to the disciples, and the disciples *gave them* to the crowds.

Jesus looks up to heaven when he blesses the loaves, a gesture that calls to mind his teaching about prayer:

Mt 6:9,11 – *"Pray like this: 'Our Father in heaven, may your name be kept holy. | Give us today our daily bread."*

Mt 7:11 – *"If you then, being evil, know how to give good gifts to your children, how much more will your Father who is in heaven give good things to those who ask him."*

Despite the meager offerings, we're told that everyone ate and was satisfied. We only hear about the fish and the loaves, but who's to say? – maybe the other people in the crowd shared what they had brought along, too.

7:61-69 FROM THEIR BOAT, THE DISCIPLES SEE JESUS

It seems that Jesus is trying to give the crowds the slip once more. First he sends the disciples off in the boat; then he dismisses the crowds and goes up the mountain to pray, alone. Some while later, the evening having come and the crowds having no doubt departed, Jesus comes down from the mountain and reaches the shore, where the disciples see him walking near the sea and cry out, thinking he is a ghost. Calming their fears with a few words of reassurance,[33] Jesus boards the boat. They immediately sail from there to Gennesaret (itself but a short distance from Magdala) and moor at the shore.

7:70-74 MARTHA AND MARY

Bread and fish alone wouldn't have made a proper feast anyway, so the troup heads off to where there's some good food to be had. With no doubt twelve very happy disciples in tow, Jesus enters a 'certain village' (Magdala?) and shows up at the house of a 'certain woman' for an impromptu meal.

Now, it so happens that this woman named Martha has a sister named Mary (Magdalene? that would neatly explain how Jesus knows Martha) who spends her time sitting *at the master's feet* and listening to him talk, leaving her sister to do all the work. One can easily imagine Jesus and the disciples lounging about, quite content to be waited on hand and foot. Greatly troubled by so much serving, Martha complains.

Downplaying her concerns, Jesus tells her with irrefutable wisdom that only one thing is necessary, which her sister Mary has chosen – *"indeed, the good part"* – and which won't be taken away from her.

What part is that?

Being with Jesus, of course, and listening to his word.

(Cool, huh?)

midst of the sea, and he was alone upon the land.[s]

64 And having seen them, he came towards them, walking near the sea.[t]

65 And having seen him walking near the sea, they thought that he was a ghost, and they cried out.[u]

66 For *the disciples* all saw him, and were troubled. But immediately he spoke with them, and he said to them, "Be of good cheer, fear not!"[v]

67 And having come out of their boat, and having immediately recognized him,[w]

68 then they were willing to receive him into the boat. And immediately the boat was at the land to which they were going.[x]

69 And having crossed over to the land, they came to Gennesaret, and moored *at the shore*.[y]

70 Now as they went *along*, he entered into a certain village, and a certain woman named Martha received him.[z]

71 And she had a sister called Mary, and *who*, having sat down at the master's feet, was listening to his word.[a]

72 But Martha was greatly troubled about *so* much serving; and confronting him, she said, "Master, is it

s Mt 14:24
  Mr 6:47
  Jn 6:17
t Mt 14:25
  Mr 6:48
u Mt 14:26
  Mr 6:49
  Jn 6:19
v La 3:57
  Mt 14:27
  Mr 6:50
  Jn 6:20
w Mt 14:34
  Mr 6:54
x Mr 8:10
  Jn 6:21
y Mt 14:34
  Mr 6:53
  Mr 8:10
z Lu 10:38
a Lu 10:39

7, 8   Martha and Mary   The Pharisees ask Jesus for a sign

z *Lu 10:40*
a *Lu 10:41*
b *Lu 10:42*

of no concern to you, that my sister has left me to serve *all* alone? Speak to her, therefore, that she might help me!"ᶻ

73 But answering, he said to her, "Martha, Martha, you are anxious and greatly disturbed about *so* much.ᵃ

74 "But one is necessary, or one Mary – indeed, the good part – chose, which will not be taken from her."ᵇ

CHAPTER 8

a *De 18:20-22*
   Mt 16:1
b *Mt 16:2*
c *Isa 53:1-12*
   Mt 16:3
   Lu 12:56

AND the Pharisees, having come to him, testing *him*, asked him to show them a sign from heaven.ᵃ

2 But answering, he said to them, "When evening has come, you say, 'Fair weather, for the sky is red.'ᵇ

3 "And at dawn, 'A storm today, for the sky is red.' Truly, you have learned how to distinguish the face of the sky, but the signs of the appointed times, you are not able."ᶜ

4 But having been questioned by the Pharisees *as to* when the kingdom of God would come, he

8

Who do the people say that I am?

8:1-5 THE PHARISEES ASK JESUS FOR A SIGN

8:1 – And the Pharisees, having come to him, testing *him*, asked him to show them a sign from heaven.

The Jews must have wondered – what was this kingdom of God that Jesus kept talking about? Yʜwʜ's kingdom was nowhere to be seen. Israel had no anointed king, and the country was everywhere occupied by the Romans. To the Pharisees, it might well have seemed that Jesus was leading the people astray; certainly his teachings were at variance with the Law. Perhaps he was trying to seduce people with a kingdom ruled by another god. Hence this test, to see if he will show them a sign. For if it comes true, then perhaps this Jesus fellow has a mandate from Yʜwʜ after all:

De 18:20-22 – [...] | *When a prophet speaks in Yahweh's name, if the thing doesn't follow, nor happen, that is the thing which Yahweh has not spoken. The prophet has spoken it presumptuously. You shall not be afraid of him.*

In typical fashion, though, our wily Galilean shifts things to a different level altogether. He chides the Pharisees for being able to read the sky,[34] but not the signs of the appointed times. Those may perhaps be found in a passage that I imagine Jesus knew by heart; indeed, I suspect that he saw his own life presaged in Isaiah 53, and that he orchestrated his fate to coincide with the prophesy.

Isa 53:1,2 – *Who has believed our message? To whom has the arm of Yahweh been revealed? | For he grew up before him as a tender plant, and as a root out of dry ground. He has no good looks or majesty. When we see him, there is no beauty that we should desire him.*

Nowadays, our collective imagination sees Jesus as having been a drop-dead gorgeous, long-haired hippie. But who's to say? What if he wasn't such a hottie after all?

Isa 53:3 – *He was despised, and rejected by men; a man of suffering, and acquainted with disease. He was despised as one from whom men hide their face; and we didn't respect him.*

Maybe that 'son of Mary' epithet meant that Jesus grew up as a bit of a social outcast – not unlike David, who, lamenting, *'Behold, I was born in iniquity; in sin my mother conceived me'* (Ps 51:5), may have been born of an adulterous union, too. Or maybe Jesus was a sickly child. At any rate, in his public life he was well acquainted with disease through his healing activities.

Isa 53:4 – *Surely he has borne our sickness, and carried our suffering; yet we considered him plagued, struck by God, and afflicted.*

The public who watched him die on the cross would have surely felt that Jesus was plagued and afflicted, stricken by God.

Isa 53:5 – *But he was pierced for our transgressions. He was crushed for our iniquities. The punishment that brought our peace was on him; and by his wounds we are healed.*

In my view, Jesus believed that his death on the cross would lead to the abrogation of the Mosaic covenant, which would free the Jews from their bondage to YHWH. This would bring peace at last to the people of Israel. No longer would they suffer YHWH's vengeance for all their transgressions of the Law.

Isa 53:6 – *All we like sheep have gone astray. Everyone has turned to his own way; and Yahweh has laid on him the iniquity of us all.*

As Jesus says in Matthew 15:24, "I was sent only to the lost sheep of the house of Israel." (Mt 15:24) These are the ones he seeks to redeem.

Isa 53:7 – *He was oppressed, yet when he was afflicted he didn't open his mouth. As a lamb that is led to the slaughter, and as a sheep that before its shearers is silent, so he didn't open his mouth.*

Jesus was silent before the Sanhedrin (Mark 14:61), Pilate (Matthew 15:4,5), and Herod (Luke 23:9).

Isa 53:8,9 – *He was taken away by oppression and judgment; and as for his generation, who considered that he was cut off out of the land of the living and stricken for the disobedience of my people? | They made his grave with the wicked, and with a rich man in his death; although he had done no violence, nor was any deceit in his mouth.*

Jesus was crucified along with two robbers – wicked men indeed. He was taken down from the cross and placed in a tomb cut out of stone – such tombs were costly and in general belonged to wealthy families. Aside from knocking over a few moneychangers' tables, there is no record of Jesus ever being violent, and so far as we know, he was a scrupulously honest man. (cf. Mark 12:14)

Isa 53:10 – *Yet it pleased Yahweh to bruise him. He has caused him to suffer. When you make his soul an offering for sin, [...]*

When Jesus prayed in the garden of Gethsemane – *"Abba, Father, all things are possible to you. Please remove this cup from me. However, not what I will, but what you will."* (Mr 14:36) – he was making it abundantly clear that whatever followed would be Yhwh's will. Likewise, as evidenced by Yhwh's silence in the face of Jesus' crucifixion – *"My God, my God, why have you forsaken me?"* – the God of Israel tacitly accepted Jesus' life, and thus made his soul 'an offering for sin.'

Isa 53:10-12 – *When you make his soul an offering for sin, he will see his seed. He will prolong his days, and Yahweh's pleasure will prosper in his hand. | After the suffering of his soul, he will see the light and be satisfied. My righteous servant will justify many by his knowledge; and he will bear their iniquities. |Therefore will I give him a portion with the great, and he will divide the plunder with the strong; because he poured out his soul to death, and was counted with the transgressors; yet he bore the sin of many, and made intercession for the transgressors.*

Jesus no doubt believed his sacrifice would prove worthwhile. When YHWH had made his soul an offering for sin by silently accepting his death on the cross, then Jesus would see his seed – his word, his teachings – spread far and wide. Israel, heretofore YHWH's pleasure, would come to prosper in his – Jesus' – hand. Following his sacrificial death, he would see the light of truth prevail and be satisfied. He would have justified many by his knowledge of both the truth and of himself, as being the one destined to overthrow YHWH. He would pour out his soul to death and be counted with the lost sheep, the sinners, the ones whom YHWH judged and rejected; yet he would bear their sins and redeem them all, by laying down his life for his friends.

8:4 – But having been questioned by the Pharisees *as to* when the kingdom of God would come, he answered them and said, "The kingdom of God does not come with observation."

The Pharisees would have had every reason to categorically disagree with Jesus on this score, for the Scriptures taught that observable signs would precede YHWH's coming:

Joe 2:30,31 – *I will show wonders in the heavens and in the earth: blood, fire, and pillars of smoke. | The sun will be turned into darkness, and the moon into blood, before the great and terrible day of Yahweh comes.*

Mic 7:15 – *"As in the days of your coming out of the land of Egypt, I will show them marvelous things."*

answered them and said, "The kingdom of God does not come with observation.^d

5 "Nor will they say, 'Behold, *it is* here, or there.' For behold, the kingdom of God is within you."^e

6 And having left them, *and* having embarked again, he went away to the other side.^f

7 And they forgot to take bread, and except for one loaf, they had none with them in the boat.^g

8 And he enjoined them, saying, "Behold! Take heed of the leaven of the Pharisees, and the leaven of Herod."^h

9 And they debated with one another, because they did not have bread.ⁱ

10 And realizing this, he said to them, "Why do you debate because you have no bread?^j

11 "How *is it that* you do not understand that I was speaking to you not about bread, but to beware of the leaven of the Pharisees?"^k

12 Then they understood that he had not said to beware of the leaven of bread, but of the teaching of the Pharisees.^l

13 And they came to Bethsaida. And they brought him a blind man, and exhorted him, so that he might

d Joe 2:30,31
  Mic 7:15
e Ps 82:6
  Lu 17:20
  Lu 17:21
  Jn 10:33,34
f Mr 8:13
g Mt 16:5
  Mr 8:14
h Jer 32:21
  Da 4:3
  Da 6:27
  Mt 16:1
  Mt 16:6
  Mr 8:15
  Lu 23:8
i Mt 16:7
  Mr 8:16
j Mt 16:8
  Mr 8:17
k Mt 16:11
l Mt 16:12

8

m *Mr 8:22*
n *Mr 8:23*
o *Mr 8:24*
p *Mr 8:25*
q *Mr 8:26*
r *Mt 16:13*
  Mr 8:27
  Lu 9:18
s *Mal 4:5*
t *Mt 16:14*
  Mr 8:28
  Lu 9:19
u *Mt 16:15*
  Mr 8:29
  Lu 9:20
v *De 17:15*
  1Sa 10:24
  Ps 2:6,7
  Ps 89:20,27
  Ec 10:12,13
  Mt 16:16
  Mt 24:11
  Mr 8:29
  Lu 9:20
  Lu 24:12

touch him.[m]

14   And having taken hold of the blind man's hand, he led him forth out of the village; and having spat upon his eyes, *and* having laid the hands upon him, he asked him, "Do you see anything?"[n]

15   And having looked up, he said, "I see the men, because as trees I see *them*, walking."[o]

16   Then he again laid the hands upon his eyes; and he opened his eyes and was restored, and saw all clearly.[p]

17   And he sent him to his home, saying, "Do not enter the village, nor tell *it* to anyone in the village."[q]

18   And Jesus and his disciples went forth into the villages of Caesarea Philippi; and on the way, he was questioning his disciples, saying to them, "Who do men say me to be?"[r]

19   But they spoke to him, saying, "John the Baptist; and others, Elijah;[s] but others, one of the prophets."[t]

20   And he questioned them, "But you, who do you say me to be?"[u]

21   But Simon answered, saying, "You are the [1]messiah."[v]

22   And he sternly told them that they should tell

8:5 – "Nor will they say, 'Behold *it is* here, or there.' For behold, the kingdom of God is within you."

Ps 82:6 – *I said, "You are gods, all of you are sons of the Most High."*

Jn 10:33,34 – *The Jews answered him, "We don't stone you for a good work, but for blasphemy: because you, being a man, make yourself God." | Jesus answered them, "Isn't it written in your law, 'I said, you are gods?' [...]"*

This is one of Jesus' singular teachings. In stark contrast to those who view the kingdom of God as an external, earthly paradise that will come with observable signs, Jesus states that kingdom of God is within us. It is not a kingdom of this world, but a kingdom of the soul. And if the kingdom of God is within us, then God, too, is within us. In short, that we are, each of us, God.

8:6-12 BEWARE OF THE LEAVEN OF THE PHARISEES

8:8 – And he enjoined them, saying, "Behold! Take heed of the leaven of the Pharisees, and the leaven of Herod."

Mt 16:1 – *The Pharisees and Sadducees came, and testing him, asked him to show them a sign from heaven.*

Lu 23:8 – *Now when Herod saw Jesus, he was exceedingly glad, for he [...] hoped to see some miracle done by him.*

As this exchange between Jesus and his disciples follows on the heels of the Pharisees' expressed interest in signs and a coming kingdom of God, I interpret Jesus as warning his disciples against being focused on such things. As for Herod, his interest was in miracles.

8:13-17 JESUS HEALS A BLIND MAN

8:14,15 – And [...] he asked him, "Do you see anything?" And having looked up, he said, "I see the men, because as trees I see *them*, walking."

This episode, which is only to be found in Mark's gospel, the earliest written, is unique in the canon of miracles: Jesus' intervention is not wholly successful the first time round. Isn't that odd? I guess the blind guy saw no reason to have faith at first sight...

8:18-22 "WHO DO MEN SAY ME TO BE?"

8:21 – But Simon answered, saying, "You are the messiah." [35]
Ec 10:12,13 – *The words of a wise man's mouth are gracious; but a fool is swallowed by his own lips. | The beginning of the words of his mouth is foolishness; and the end of his talk is mischievous madness.*
Mt 24:11 – *"Many false prophets will arise, and will lead many astray."*
Lu 24:12 – *But Peter [...] saw the strips of linen lying by themselves, and he departed to his home, wondering what had happened.*

8:22 – And he sternly told them that they should tell no one this, that he was the messiah.
In my view, simply because he knew it was not true. He was not the anointed messiah. Nor did he want to be. Rather, Jesus saw himself as being the son of man, and he intended to offer himself up, like Isaac, as a sacrifice. If YHWH *accepted* this sacrifice, then the God of Israel would be seen to transgress his own law.

8:23-26 JESUS REBUKES SIMON

8:23 – And he began to teach them that it was necessary for him to go away to Jerusalem, and to suffer many things from the elders and the chief priests and the scribes, and to be put to death and to be raised up.
Ge 22:2-4 – *He said, "Now take your son, your only son, whom you love, even Isaac, and go into the land of Moriah. Offer him there as a burnt offering*

no one this, that he was the [1]messiah.[w]

23 And he began to teach them that it was necessary for him to go away to Jerusalem, and to suffer many things from the elders and the chief priests and the scribes, and to be put to death and [2]to be raised up.[x]

24 And he spoke the word forthrightly. And Simon, having taken him aside, began to rebuke him,[y] saying, "*God be* merciful to you, Master![z] This will never happen to you!"[a]

25 But having turned around, and having seen his disciples, he rebuked Simon, and said, "Get behind me, [3]Cephas![b] You are a stumbling block to me! For you are not thinking *about* the things of God, but the things of men."[c]

26 But he said to his disciples, "It is impossible that stumbling blocks should not come, but woe *to him* by whom they come."[d]

27 And having summoned the crowd with his disciples, he said to them, "Truly I say to you, unless you eat the flesh of the son of man, and drink his

w Ps 146:3,4
   Mt 16:20
   Mr 8:30
   Lu 9:21
x Ge 22:2-4
   De 21:22,23
   Ps 25:1
   Mt 16:21
   Mr 8:31
   Lu 9:22
   Jn 8:36
   Jn 12:32
y Mr 8:32
z Ge 22:8,13,14
a De 12:31
   Mt 16:22
b De 32:4
   Jos 24:27
   Ps 18:31
   Jn 1:42
c Mt 16:23
   Mr 8:33
d Mt 18:7
   Lu 17:1

---

1 Gr., *messias*, for the Hebrew *mashiach*; certain later mss. read, *christos*
2 Certain later mss. add, *after three days*
3 Gr., *Képhas*; lit., *stone*; certain mss. read, *Satana*, or Satan

on one of the mountains which I will tell you of." | Abraham rose early in the morning, and saddled his donkey, and took two of his young men with him, and Isaac his son. He split the wood for the burnt offering, and rose up, and went to the place of which God had told him. | On the third day Abraham lifted up his eyes, and saw the place far off. [36]

Whether Jesus went so far as to spell out to his disciples that all this was to be a reprise of the sacrifice of Isaac is anybody's guess.

De 21:22,23 – *If a man has committed a sin worthy of death, and he is put to death, and you hang him on a tree; | [...] ; for he who is hanged is accursed of God [...].*

What is clear, though, is that Jesus was apparently explicit about how things were going to be played out in Jerusalem, and what the denouement would be. Knowing that he would be put to death because of the deliberate blasphemy of the Name that he intended to commit before the Sanhedrin, Jesus could foresee that he would be 'raised up', that is, either hung on a 'tree' as per Deuternomy 21:22, or, even worse (but definitely in the spirit of the times[37]), crucified alive – for being hanged is the ignominy that the Scriptures spell out for all those who, according to the Mishnah,* are accursed of, or who have cursed the name of, God:[38]

'ALL WHO ARE STONED ARE [AFTERWARDS] HANGED: THIS IS R. ELIEZER'S VIEW, THE SAGES SAY: ONLY THE BLASPHEMER AND THE IDOLATER ARE HANGED.' The Gemara adds, 'Our Rabbis taught: [Scripture states,] And if he be put to death, then thou shalt hang him on a tree (Deut. XXI, 22): [...] For he is hanged [because of] a curse against God. (E.V. *"For he that is hanged is a reproach unto God,"* is so interpreted by the Mishnah, i.e., he was a blasphemer.) Just as the blas-

---

* While I cite the Talmud in several places throughout this work, it must be emphasized that the Mishnah postdates Jesus' period by nearly 200 years; as such, it – and the Gemara, written even later – cannot be used as firm support for arguments made about Jewish affairs in the first century CE. We may use it as a springboard for conjectures, but not as evidence for drawing conclusions.

phemer in question is executed by stoning, so all who are stoned [must be subsequently hanged]: this is R. Eliezer's view.'[39]

'How is he hanged (*after being stoned*)? The post is sunk into the ground with a [cross-] piece branching off [at the top].' '[...] his body shall not remain all night upon the tree, but thou shalt surely bury him the same day for he is hanged [because of] a curse against God, (*Deut. XXI, 23. is interpreted by the Mishnah as an objective genitive – 'a curse against God*') – as if to say why was he hanged? – because he cursed the name [of God]; and so, (*if his body be left hanging a considerable time, thus reminding men of his blasphemy*) the name of heaven [God] is profaned.'[40]

In my view, then, when Jesus spoke of his being 'raised up', he was '*signifying by what kind of death he should die*' (Jn 12:33) – that is, that his death would be the death of one who was accursed of God.

In the Gospels, though, Jesus is always speaking of being 'raised up' "after three days". This notion clearly derives from the words of the prophet Hosea:

Ho 6:2 – *After two days he will revive us. On the third day he will raise us up, and we will live before him.*

In my opinion, duly inspired by Hosea, the Jesus-movement wrote its unswerving conviction that Jesus had been 'raised up' and resurrected from death 'on the third day' into the story – hence, a footnote here suggests that '*after three days*' was inserted by copyists at a later date.

8:24 – And he spoke the word forthrightly. And Simon, having taken him aside, began to rebuke him, saying, "God be merciful to you, Master! This will never happen to you!"

It's no wonder Simon Peter balked. His good teacher, put to death and 'raised up' like one who is accursed of God? This could never be!

Besides, if Jesus had been telling them that he would be going up to Jerusalem – that is, Mount Moriah – in the same spririt as Isaac, then that too would never happen: the God of Israel utterly abhors human sacrifice; he would never consent to it. Indeed, YHWH would forcefully step in to preclude such an outcome, just as he stayed Abraham's hand and provided a ram for the offering:

Ge 22:8,13,14 – *Abraham said, "God will provide himself the lamb for a burnt offering, my son." […] | Abraham lifted up his eyes, and looked, and saw that behind him was a ram caught in the thicket by his horns. Abraham went and took the ram, and offered him up for a burnt offering instead of his son. | Abraham called the name of that place Yahweh Will Provide. As it is said to this day, "On Yahweh's mountain, it will be provided."*

8:25 – **But having turned around, and having seen his disciples, he rebuked Simon, and said, "Get behind me, Cephas! You are a stumbling block to me! For you are not thinking about the things of God, but the things of men."**

In the Gospels, Simon's sobriquet 'Cephas' – properly *stone* – appears only once, in John 1:42. The evangelist gives no explanation. However, I have found it of note in Matthew 16:23 that Jesus says to Simon, *"You are a stumbling block to me."* From this, I imagine that Jesus may have called Simon a 'stone' in conjunction with his being a 'stumbling block'. What would this stumbling block be?

De 12:31 – *The Rock, his work is perfect, for all his ways are just. A God of faithfulness who does no wrong, just and right is he.*

Jos 24:27 – *Joshua said to all the people, "Behold, this stone shall be a witness against us, for it has heard all Yahweh's words which he spoke to us. It shall be therefore a witness against you, lest you deny your God."*

Ps 24:27 – *For who is God, except Yahweh? Who is a rock, besides our God?*

We may equate stone and rock with both the God of Israel and his covenant. In calling Simon a 'cephas', a stone, Jesus may have been thinking of the stone that Joshua set up to remind Israel of its covenant with YHWH. If Jesus is hoping through his death to liberate Israel from that covenant, then Simon – with his *'Far be it from you, Lord! This will never be done to you'* objections and his misguided view that Jesus is the messiah – would indeed be a stumbling block. Hence the sharpness of Jesus' reproach, which is conveyed equally well by the epithet 'Satan'… with whom I equate YHWH anyway, so it amounts to the same thing.

8:27-34 MANY OF JESUS' DISCIPLES WITHDRAW

8:27,28 – And having summoned the crowd with his disciples, he said to them, "Truly I say to you, unless you eat the flesh of the son of man, and drink his blood, you have no life in yourselves. For whoever might wish to save his soul shall lose it, but whoever will lose his soul on account of me shall save it."

Le 3:17 – *"It shall be a perpetual statute throughout your generations in all your dwellings, that you shall eat neither fat nor blood."*

Le 17:10,14 – *"Any man of the house of Israel [...] who eats any kind of blood, I will set my face against that soul [...] and will cut him off from among his people. | For as to the life of all flesh, its blood is with its life: therefore I said to the children of Israel, 'You shall not eat the blood of any kind of flesh; for the life of all flesh is its blood. Whoever eats it shall be cut off.'"*

Le 18:5 – *"You shall therefore keep my statutes and my ordinances; which if a man does, he shall live in them. I am Yahweh."*

De 30:19,20 – *[...] I have set before you life and death [...]. Therefore choose life, that you may live, you and your descendants; | to love Yahweh your God, to obey his voice, and to cling to him; for he is your life. [...]*

Eze 18:4 – *"Behold, all souls are mine; as the soul of the father, so also the soul of the son is mine: the soul who sins, he shall die."*

For a Jew, to keep YHWH's covenant is to chose life; and to be cut off from that covenant is to lose one's life, one's soul – *'the soul who sins, he shall die.'* Hence, any Jew who sins by deliberately drinking blood

8   Many of Jesus' disciples withdraw

e Le 3:17
   Le 17:10
f Mr 9:50
   Lu 12:57
   Jn 6:53
g Le 18:5
   De 30:19,20
   De 32:46,47
h Le 7:25,27
   Le 17:10,14
   Eze 18:4
i Mt 16:25
   Mr 8:35
   Lu 9:24
   Jn 12:47
j Ge 13:14,15
   Ge 17:6-8
   De 11:22-24
   Jos 1:3
k De 6:5
   De 10:12
   De 26:16
   De 30:6
   Mt 16:26
   Mr 8:36
   Lu 9:25
l Le 17:11
   Ps 49:8
   Mt 16:26
   Mr 8:37
   Mr 10:45
   Jn 15:13
m De 13:3,4
   Jn 6:60
n Nu 15:30,31
   Jn 6:61
o Jn 6:66
p Jn 8:31
q Isa 14:12-17
   Eze 28:18,19
   Jn 8:32

blood,[e] you have no life in yourselves.[f]

28 "For whoever might wish to save his soul[g] shall lose it, but whoever will lose his soul[h] on account of me shall save it.[i]

29 "For what shall it profit a man if he should gain the whole world,[j] and *yet* forfeit his soul?[k]

30 "For what shall a man give in exchange for his soul?"[l]

31 Then many of his disciples, having heard, were saying, "This is a hard word. Who can listen to it?"[m]

32 But Jesus, knowing in himself that his disciples were grumbling about this, said to them, "Does this cause you to stumble?"[n]

33 And because of this, many of his disciples withdrew and were no longer walking with him.[o]

34 Jesus was therefore saying to those *who were* Jewish *who had* believed him, "If you abide in my word, *then* you are truly my disciples,[p]

35 and you will know the truth, and the truth will [4]set you free."[q]

36 But it came to pass, about eight days after *saying* these words, *that* Jesus, having taken *with him* Simon

---

4 Or, *liberate you*

– which is precisely what Jesus proposes – knows in advance that he will be cut off from the covenant and the Chosen People and will die. Yet Jesus teaches his followers that they must eat the flesh of the son of man and drink his blood to have *life in themselves*. That, indeed, by doing so – which can only result in their being cut off from the Chosen People forever – they will save their souls. Clearly, Jesus does not hold with the idea that keeping YHWH's covenant is the way to life.

Mr 9:50 – "*[…] Have salt in yourselves […]."*

Lu 12:57 – *"Why don't you judge for yourselves what is right?"*

I read Jesus as saying, Do not look to the covenant and obedience to YHWH's commandments for your life; rather, have life in yourselves, have salt in yourselves, and judge for yourselves what is right.

8:29 – "For what shall it profit a man if he should gain the whole world […] "

Ge 13:14,15 – *Yahweh said to Abram, after Lot was separated from him, "Now, lift up your eyes, and look from the place where you are, northward and southward and eastward and westward, | for all the land which you see, I will give to you, and to your offspring forever."*

Ge 17:6-8 – *"I will make you exceedingly fruitful, and I will make nations of you. Kings will come out of you. | I will establish my covenant between me and you and your offspring after you throughout their generations for an everlasting covenant, to be a God to you and to your offspring after you. | I will give to you, and to your offspring after you, the land where you are traveling, all the land of Canaan, for an everlasting possession. I will be their God."*

De 11:22-24 – *For if you shall diligently keep all these commandments which I command you, to do them, to love Yahweh your God, to walk in all his ways, and to cling to him; | then will Yahweh drive out all these nations from before you, and you shall dispossess nations greater and mightier than yourselves. | Every place whereon the sole of your foot treads shall be yours:*

from the wilderness, and Lebanon, from the river, the river Euphrates, even to the western sea shall be your border.

8:29 – " […] and yet forfeit his soul?"

De 6:5 – *You shall love Yahweh your God with all your heart, with all your soul, and with all your might.*

De 10:12 – *Now, Israel, what does Yahweh your God require of you, but to fear Yahweh your God, to walk in all his ways, and to love him, and to serve Yahweh your God with all your heart and with all your soul?*

8:30 – "For what shall a man give in exchange for his soul?"

YHWH's everlasting covenant with Israel contained no provisions by which a Jew might obtain his emancipation. Indeed, there was only one way to get out of the covenant: to be cut off. But the soul who is cut off, says YHWH, will die. With what could a Jew redeem his life?

Le 17:11 – *"For the life of the flesh is in the blood; and I have given it to you on the altar to make atonement for your souls: for it is the blood that makes atonement by reason of the life."*

Ps 49:8 – *For the redemption of their life is costly, no payment is ever enough.*

Mr 10:45 – *"For the Son of Man also came not to be served, but to serve, and to give his life as a ransom for many."*

Jn 15:13 – *"Greater love has no one than this, that someone lay down his life for his friends."*

8:31 – Then many of his disciples, having heard, were saying, "This is a hard word. Who can listen to it?"

De 13:3,4 – *You shall not listen to the words of that prophet, or to that dreamer of dreams; for Yahweh your God is testing you, to know whether you love Yahweh your God with all your heart and with all your soul. | You*

*shall walk after Yahweh your God, fear him, keep his commandments, and
obey his voice, and you shall serve him, and cling to him.*

It is likely that Jesus' teaching about eating flesh and drinking blood
was more than many of his disciples could bear.

**8:32 – But Jesus, knowing in himself that his disciples were grum-
bling about this, said to them, "Does this cause you to stumble?"**

'Crimony, Jesus, you bet! You're going to get us all axed!'

Nu 15:30,31 – *"But the soul who does anything with a high hand* [i.e.
intentionally, deliberately], *whether he is native-born or a foreigner, the
same blasphemes Yahweh. That soul shall be cut off from among his people.
| Because he has despised Yahweh's word, and has broken his commandment,
that soul shall utterly be cut off. His iniquity shall be on him."*

No wonder many of his disciples withdrew and were no longer walking with him.

**8:34,35 – Jesus was therefore saying to those *who were* Jewish *who
had* believed him, "If you abide in my word, *then* you are truly my
disciples, and you will know the truth, and the truth will set you
free."**

It is of note that Jesus singles out his Jewish followers in John 8:31,
and there seems to be a good reason for this – after all, to abide in Jesus'
word, a Jew would have to overcome his innate revulsion towards the
idea of eating human flesh and drinking blood.

Jesus promises that *"you will know the truth, and the truth will set you
free."* The Greek word here is *eleutheroó*, which specifically means to
release from bondage – and indeed, this is the precise meaning that
Jesus' interlocutors understood when they objected, *"We are Abraham's
offspring, and have never been in bondage to anyone. How do you say, 'You
will be made free'?"*

8:36-48 Jesus brings Simon, John and James to a high mountain

8:36 – But it came to pass, about eight days after *saying* these words, *that* Jesus, having taken *with him* Simon and John and James, brought them up to a high mountain by themselves.

Why did Jesus choose these three particular disciples to accompany him on this outing? I think it was to impress upon his arguably most reactionary Jewish disciples[41] that he was truly Yhwh's son, an understanding essential for grasping the full implications of his death.

Ps 89:12 – *The north and the south, you have created them. Tabor and Hermon rejoice in your name.*

Christian tradition holds that the Transfiguration occurred on Mount Tabor. The pairing of Tabor with Hermon in the psalm offers us a link to the latter, which will figure in chapter 18 as the mountain to which I believe Jesus instructed his disciples to go following his death.

Why choose a 'high mountain'?[42] Just for the view? Or did Jesus, as a proclaimer of good news about the kingdom of God, take his cue from Isaiah's injunction:

Isa 40:9 – *You who tell good news to Zion, go up on a high mountain. You who tell good news to Jerusalem, lift up your voice with strength. Lift it up. Don't be afraid. Say to the cities of Judah, "Behold, your God!"*

By making evident the truth about Yhwh – "Behold, your God!" – Jesus is bringing Zion the good news of her liberation from bondage.

Na 1:15 – *Look, on the mountains the feet of him who brings good news, who publishes peace! […] For the wicked one will no more pass through you. He is utterly cut off.*

In my reading, of course, Jesus would have envisaged the 'wicked one' to be Yhwh himself.

and John and James, brought them up to a high mountain by themselves.[r]

37　And it came to pass, that the appearance of his face was different,[s] and his clothing gleamed white.[t]

38　And behold, two men were talking with him, who were Moses and Elijah,[u]

39　who, having appeared in glory, were speaking of his exodus, which he was about to fulfill in Jerusalem.[v]

40　Now Simon and those who were with him were heavy with sleep;[w] and he came and found them sleeping, and he said, "Simon, are you asleep?"[x]

41　And answering, Simon said to Jesus, "Rabbi, it is good for us to be here; and let us make three tabernacles, one for you, and one for Moses, and one for Elijah."[y]

42　For he knew not what he should answer.[z]

43　But as he was saying these things, a cloud came, overshadowing them;[a] but they were terrified as they entered into the cloud.[b]

44　And a voice came out of the cloud,[c] "This is my beloved son.[d] Listen to him!"[e]

45　And having heard, the disciples fell upon their faces, and were frightened out of their wits.[f]

r　Ps 89:12
　　Isa 40:9
　　Na 1:15
　　Mt 17:1
　　Mr 9:2
　　Lu 9:28
s　Ex 34:29,35
t　Mt 17:2
　　Mr 9:3
　　Lu 9:29
u　Am 3:3
　　Mt 17:3
　　Mr 9:4
　　Lu 9:30
v　Mr 9:31
　　Mr 10:33,34
　　Lu 9:31
　　Lu 9:44
w　Lu 9:32
x　Mr 14:37,40
y　Mt 17:4
　　Mr 9:5
　　Lu 9:33
z　Mr 9:6
a　Ex 24:15,16
　　Mt 17:5
　　Mr 9:7
b　Lu 9:34
c　Ex 19:9
d　Ge 22:2
　　Ps 2:7
e　Mt 17:5
　　Mr 9:7
　　Lu 9:34,35
f　Ge 17:3
　　Nu 20:6
　　1Ki 18:39
　　Mt 17:6

8:37 – And it came to pass, that the appearance of his face was different, and his clothing gleamed white.

Three elements of the Transfiguration – here, the change observed in the appearance of Jesus' face; later, the cloud, and the voice that comes out of the cloud – form a direct scriptural link to Moses speaking with YHWH on Mount Sinai (note *a* in verse 43; note *c* in verse 44):

Ex 24:15,16 – *Moses went up on the mountain, and the cloud covered the mountain. | Yahweh's glory settled on Mount Sinai, and the cloud covered it six days. The seventh day he called to Moses out of the middle of the cloud.*

Ex 19:9 – *Yahweh said to Moses, "Behold, I come to you in a thick cloud, that the people may hear when I speak with you [...]."*

It is notable, however, that the gleaming white appearance of Jesus' clothing finds no parallel in Exodus. For his part, Luke says that Jesus' clothing *'became white and dazzling'*; Mark reports that it *'became glistening, exceedingly white, like snow, such as no launderer on earth can whiten them'* (the lucky devil...he must have had a divinely appointed launderer); and Matthew seems to top them both by saying that *'His face shone like the sun, and his garments became as white as the light.'*

8:38,39 – And behold, two men were talking with him, who were Moses and Elijah, who [...] were speaking of his exodus, which he was about to fulfill in Jerusalem.

If we follow Luke, then it appears that Jesus attended a prearranged meeting with two men to discuss his 'exodus', which is how I translate the Greek *exodos* found in Luke 9:31 (a word choice that is not without significance, given that Jesus' death is to coincide with the Passover).

This is fascinating. If this meeting truly took place, then it is the only hint we have in the Gospels to suggest that Jesus may have been influenced in his thinking – possibly even abetted in his design? – by like-minded compadres. Who were these two men? Apparitions of the prophets?[43] Terrestrial friends? Had Jesus perhaps met them for the first time when he was out in the wilderness?[44] If so, over the course of forty meditative days, the three of them would have had time to hatch a plan for abrogating the covenant. In my freewheeling imagination, 'Moses' and 'Elijah' (cool *noms de guerre*? a facetious inside joke?) were behind-the-scenes allies who shared in Jesus' quest to liberate Israel once and for all from her bondage to YHWH.

The discussion they have together of the exodus he is about to fulfill in Jerusalem would have likely covered in depth points that Jesus would later relate to his disciples:

Mr 9:31 – *For he was teaching his disciples, and said to them, "The Son of Man is being handed over to the hands of men, and they will kill him; and when he is killed, on the third day he will rise again."*

Mr 10:33,34 – *"Behold, we are going up to Jerusalem. The Son of Man will be delivered to the chief priests and the scribes. They will condemn him to death, and will deliver him to the Gentiles. | They will mock him, spit on him, scourge him, and kill him. On the third day he will rise again."*

They could have also discussed donkeys and upper rooms and post-crucifixion transport to Galilee (more about those later on).

8:39 – [...] who, having appeared in glory [...]

It is notable that Mark and Matthew do not echo Luke's report that the two men *'appeared in glory'*. Did Luke make this up on his own, or was it a detail that came to him from the oral tradition?

Some might imagine that the two men appeared with a sort of incandescent glow about them. However, in the Scriptures, only YHWH appears in fiery glory – cf. Exodus 24:17, Leviticus 9:23,24, Numbers 16:19-21,35, and 2 Chronicles 7:1-3.[45]

Moreover, on the one occasion when a deceased prophet does return to speak with the living, it is not said that he appears in glory, but rather in a robe – *He said to her, "What does he look like?" She said, "An old man comes up. He is covered with a robe."* [...] (1Sa 28:14)

It therefore seems reasonable to conclude that the 'appeared in glory' formulation does not refer to some ethereal aura these two men were emanating, but simply to the rich appearance of their robes. In support of this, we may note that Jesus uses the word 'glory' in that very sense – *"even Solomon in all his glory"* (Luke 12:27, and retained by Matthew, 6:29) – when he compares king Solomon's glorious attire to that of the lilies (who, though they neither toil nor spin, still trump the Davidic king hands down in the fashion stakes).

It would appear, then, that 'Moses' and 'Elijah' were dressed to the nines. To any casual observer, this little meeting would have surely looked incongruous up there on the mountain. Jesus the itinerant preacher trading his trail-dusty mantle for dazzling white attire? Two unusually monikered men, gloriously garbed? It begs the question: were these two guys head honchos connected to one of the secretive mystery religions that were widespread throughout the Mediterranean in those days?[46] Was Jesus engaged in some sort of high summit conference with two sumptuously attired hierophants?[47] If they read that the two men *'appeared in glory'*, those familiar with the mystery religions might deduce that Jesus' contacts were pagans. For this reason, when it came to writing their own accounts, Mark and Matthew may have preferred to keep mum about the two men's appearance.

8:40 – Now Simon and those who were with him were heavy with sleep [...]

They were probably tuckered out from the strenuous hike up the high mountain. Besides, if things were dragging on interminably, as tends to happen in the Middle East (think of all those endless prayers in the Garden of Gethsemane), the tired disciples' attention couldn't help but flag. Is it any wonder they dozed off?

8:40 – [...] and he came and found them sleeping, and he said, "Simon, are you asleep?"

In the original Greek of Matthew 17:4 and Mark 9:5, Simon is said to 'answer', yet in the texts Jesus has asked him no question. For this reason, borrowing from Mark 14:37, I have here taken the liberty of creating a question for Simon to answer.

8:41,42 – And answering, Simon said to Jesus, "Master, it is good for us to be here; and let us make three tabernacles, one for you, and one for Moses, and one for Elijah." For he knew not what he should answer.

Isn't this cute? Like a sleepy-eyed kid who's been caught napping, Simon blurts out the first inanity that pops into his head.

8:43,44 – But as he was saying these things, a cloud came, overshadowing them; but they were terrified as they entered into the cloud. And a voice came out of the cloud, "This is my beloved son. Listen to him!"

Ge 22:2 – *He said, "Now take your son, your only son, whom you love, even Isaac, and go into the land of Moriah. Offer him there as a burnt offering on one of the mountains which I will tell you of."*

Ps 2:7 – *I will tell of the decree. Yahweh said to me, "You are my son. Today I have become your father."*

If Jesus is YHWH's son, then his being sacrificed in Jerusalem – where Solomon built the temple on Mount Moriah[48] – likens him to Isaac. This plainly puts the million shekel question on the altar: as he did once before, when Isaac was about to die in sacrifice at the hand of his father, will YHWH intervene at the last moment to spare his own son?

Now, did YHWH himself say these words, booming out *'This is my beloved son. Listen to him!'* in a celestially thundering baritone? Or again, when the cloud descended upon the party, was it maybe 'Moses' or 'Elijah', hidden from view by the swirling mists, who piped up with the pronouncement for the disciples' benefit? Regardless, Jesus was a Jew, and the Jews were the sons of their tribal god, so the assertion *'This is my beloved son'* holds whether YHWH on high said it himself or not.

It is interesting to consider the injunction, 'Listen to him!' To begin with, the Chosen People were honor bound to listen to YHWH:

De 13:4 – *You shall walk after Yahweh your God, fear him, keep his commandments, and obey his voice, and you shall serve him, and cling to him.*

De 26:17 – *You have declared today that Yahweh is your God, and that you would walk in his ways, and keep his statutes, and his commandments, and his ordinances, and listen to his voice.*

That said, the Jews were terrified of their tribal god's voice; hearing it, they feared they would die. So they asked Moses to be a middleman:

Ex 20:18,19 – *All the people perceived the thunderings, the lightnings, the sound of the trumpet, and the mountain smoking. When the people saw it, they trembled, and stayed at a distance. | They said to Moses, "Speak with us yourself, and we will listen; but don't let God speak with us, lest we die."*

For this reason, YHWH promised Moses that he would raise up a prophet, one who would be his personal spokesman:

De 18:18 – *"I will raise them up a prophet from among their brothers, like you. I will put my words in his mouth, and he shall speak to them all that I shall command him."*

All well and good. But what about prophets who don't speak YHWH's word, but their own?

De 18:20-22 – *"But the prophet who speaks a word presumptuously in my name, which I have not commanded him to speak, or who speaks in the name of other gods, that same prophet shall die." | You may say in your heart, "How shall we know the word which Yahweh has not spoken?" | When a prophet speaks in Yahweh's name, if the thing doesn't follow, nor happen,* *that is the thing which Yahweh has not spoken. The prophet has spoken it presumptuously. You shall not be afraid of him.*

Let's fast-forward to Jesus' discourse concerning the end times:

Mr 13:30 – *"Most certainly I say to you, this generation will not pass away until all these things happen."*

Since the apocalyptic end did not happen as billed, we might hazard to draw two conclusions: one, that Jesus did not have a mandate from YHWH; and two, by extension, that it was not YHWH who said *'Listen to him!'* up there on the high mountain, but rather one of those two men who were present.

8:45 – And having heard, the disciples fell upon their faces, and were frightened out of their wits.

Folks were always falling on their faces whenever YHWH appeared on the scene.

Ge 17:3 – *Abram fell on his face, and God spoke with him [...]*

Nu 20:6 – *Moses and Aaron went from the presence of the assembly to the door of the Tent of Meeting, and fell on their faces. Yahweh's glory appeared to them.*

1Ki 18:39 – *When all the people saw it, they fell on their faces. They said, "Yahweh, he is God! Yahweh, he is God!"*

Of course, the disciples did not see YHWH, nor his glory; they just heard a voice. But that was enough to scare the bejesus out of them.

8:46,47 – And Jesus, having come near, and having touched them, said, "Rise up, and do not be afraid." And suddenly, having looked around, they no longer saw anyone with themselves, except Jesus.

With the cloud to cover their departure, 'Moses' and 'Elijah' have apparently skedaddled unseen.

8:48 – And as they were coming down the mountain, he ordered them that they should tell no one what they had seen.

Jesus perhaps felt that he'd already had enough trouble with Simon Peter thinking he was the messiah. If his three disciples started telling people that he'd met with a couple of guys named Moses and Elijah up there on the high mountain, who knew how much further such nonsense might go. Better to nip such indiscretions in the bud.

But we could also explain Jesus' injunction in another way. Hearing that he had met with two strikingly attired men on a high mountain, certain skeptical listeners might infer that Jesus had been rubbing elbows with one of the mystery religions or idolatrous cults. After all, high places were where forbidden practices were found:

2Ch 28:3,4 – *Moreover he burned incense in the valley of the son of Hinnom, and burned his children in the fire, according to the abominations of the nations whom Yahweh cast out before the children of Israel. | He sacrificed and burned incense in the high places, and on the hills, and under every green tree.*

Isa 57:7 – *On a high and lofty mountain you have set your bed. You also went up there to offer sacrifice.*

For the Jews, such practices contravened the first and second commandments. If word of this meeting spread, Jesus might find himself accused of being in league with idolaters. He sure didn't want to be crowned as the messiah, but he didn't want to be suspected of being a pagan, either – with murderous mobs easily mustered, you could find yourself getting stoned for that:

De 17:2-6 – *If there is found among you, within any of your gates which Yahweh your God gives you, a man or woman who does that which is evil in Yahweh your God's sight, in transgressing his covenant, | and has gone and served other gods, and worshiped them, or the sun, or the moon, or any of the stars of the sky, which I have not commanded; | and you are told, and you have heard of it, then you shall inquire diligently. Behold, if it is true, and the* *thing certain, that such abomination is done in Israel, | then you shall bring out that man or that woman, who has done this evil thing, to your gates, even that same man or woman; and you shall stone them to death with stones. | At the mouth of two witnesses, or three witnesses, he who is to die shall be put to death. At the mouth of one witness he shall not be put to death.*

I think it unlikely that Jesus had surreptitious dealings with paganism to hide, but with three eye-witnesses – enough to convict, if suspicions were aroused – Jesus probably felt it more prudent to tell Simon Peter, John and James to keep quiet about what they had seen.

While Christianity, in both its rites and beliefs, seems to have drawn considerable inspiration from the era's mystery religions, notably the cult of Dionysus, I do not see Jesus as having intended to launch such a cult for the Jews with his teachings and death. The fact that he was contemporaneous with such cults might prompt us to wonder whether he were conversant with those mysteries, or even perhaps an initiate himself at one point; nevertheless, in my view, Jesus' own teachings are distinct from those of the pagan religions, as well as from the Gnosticism that was attributed to him in John's gospel and which informs the basis of Paul's spirituality. Hence, I do not hold that Jesus was an adept of either Gnosticism, paganism, or any other mystery religion.

g Mt 17:7
h Mt 17:8
   Mr 9:8
   Lu 9:36
i Mr 9:9

46   And Jesus, having come near, and having touched them, said, "Rise up, and do not be afraid." [g]

47   And suddenly, having looked around, they no longer saw anyone with themselves, except Jesus.[h]

48   And as they were coming down the mountain, he ordered them that they should tell no one what they had seen.[i]

CHAPTER 9

a Mr 9:14
   Lu 9:37
b Mr 9:15,16
c Jn 8:3
d Jer 3:6
   Eze 16:2,7,8
   Eze 16:15-17
   Eze 23:1-21
   Lu 1:38
   Jn 8:4

AND it came to pass the next day, when they had come down from the mountain, that he saw a great crowd, and *some* scribes disputing with them.[a]

2   And immediately, having seen him, they were astounded, and running to him, they greeted him. And he asked them, "What are you disputing with them?" [b]

3   And they brought a woman who had been caught in adultery, and having stood her in the midst,[c]

4   they said to him, "Teacher, this woman was caught in the very act of committing adultery.[d]

9

Neither do I condemn you

9:1-11 The woman caught in adultery

The story of Jesus dealing kindly with an adulteress has troubled more than one. Though it was likely circulating in one form or another in the early oral tradition, it seems the *pericope adulterae* itself had a hard time gaining scriptural admission to John's gospel.

John situates this episode in Jerusalem, but I have here transposed it to Galilee. Having come down from the high mountain, on the next day Jesus finds a crowd arguing with some scribes or his disciples.

9:3,4 – And they brought a woman who had been caught in adultery, and having stood her in the midst, they said to him, "Teacher, this woman was caught in the very act of committing adultery."

Jer 3:6 – Moreover, Yahweh said to me in the days of Josiah the king, "Have you seen that which backsliding Israel has done? She has gone up on every high mountain and under every green tree, and has played the prostitute there."

Eze 16:15-17 – "But you trusted in your beauty, and played the prostitute because of your renown, and poured out your prostitution on everyone who passed by. It was his. | You […] made for yourself images of men, and played the prostitute with them."

Eze 23:1-21 – " […] Yet she multiplied her prostitution, remembering the days of her youth, in which she had played the prostitute in the land of

169

Egypt. | *She lusted after their paramours, whose flesh is as the flesh of donkeys, and whose issue is like the issue of horses.* [...]"

Let us not forget that YHWH accused Jerusalem and Israel of playing the harlot and committing adulteries.

9:5 – "Now in the Law, Moses commanded *that* **such** *a woman* **be stoned; what say you, therefore?"**

De 22:23,24 – *If there is a young lady who is a virgin pledged to be married to a husband, and a man finds her in the city, and lies with her;* | *then you shall bring them both out to the gate of that city, and you shall stone them to death with stones; the lady, because she didn't cry, being in the city; and the man, because he has humbled his neighbor's wife. So you shall remove the evil from among you.*

According to the Mishnah, 'the Divine Law ordained stoning for an *arusah*,'[50] a woman who is betrothed to be married. In contrast, a *nesu'ah* – that is, a woman who is married and is now living in her husband's house – was to be strangled.[51] Hence, if the scribes were calling for the woman to be stoned as opposed to strangled, it implies that she was an *arusah* (as was Mary, by the way).

Now, where is the man with whom they caught her 'in the very act'? They're supposed to stone him as well. Why haven't they brought him along, too? Well, the guilty 'man' may have turned out to be a mere boy – the Gemara tells us that minors are excluded from punishment (in the scale of judgment, youthful age apparently outweighs randy precociousness). Or again, perhaps the man was a Gentile – in that same exclusionary passage, the Talmud stipulates that *"'he that committeth adultery with his neighbor's wife" excludes the wife of a heathen.'*[52] That in itself does not say whether a Jewish woman's pagan paramour is excluded as well, but if they've caught the *arusah* in bed with a heathen, then they may have let the ne'er-do-well goy get away scot-free, with no questions asked.

5   "Now in the Law, Moses commanded *that* such *a woman* be stoned;[e] what say you, therefore?"[f]

6   But Jesus, having stooped down, with *his* finger wrote on the ground.[g]

7   Yet as they continued to ask him, having straightened himself up, he said to them, "The one among you who is without sin,[h] let him cast the first stone at her."[i]

8   And again, having stooped down, he wrote on the ground.[j]

9   But having heard *this*, they went out, one by one, beginning with the older men, and he was left alone, and the woman was in the midst.[k]

10   And having straightened up, Jesus said to her, "Woman, where are they? Has no one condemned you?"[l]

11   And she said, "No one, sir." And Jesus said to her, "Neither do I condemn you. Go in peace."[m]

12   And behold, a man from the crowd cried out, saying, "Master, I implore you, look upon my son, for he is [1]epileptic.[n]

13   "And behold, a spirit takes him, and suddenly

---

1 Lit., *moonstruck*

e De 22:23,24
f Jn 8:5
g Ex 24:12
   Ex 31:18
   Jn 8:6
h Ex 20:14
   Lu 1:28-31
   Lu 1:34,35,38
   Lu 6:41
i De 17:7
   Jn 8:7
j Mt 7:1
   Jn 8:8
k Jn 8:9
l Pr 20:9
   Ec 7:20
   Jn 8:10
m Jn 8:11
   Jn 8:15
n Mt 17:14,15
   Mr 9:17
   Lu 9:38

9:7 – Yet as they continued to ask him, having straightened himself up, he said to them, "The one among you who is without sin, let him cast the first stone at her."

Ex 20:14 – *"You shall not commit adultery."*

Lu 1:28-31,34,35,38 – *Having come in, the angel said to her, "Rejoice, you highly favored one! The Lord is with you. Blessed are you among women!" | But when she saw him, she was greatly troubled at the saying, and considered what kind of salutation this might be. | The angel said to her, "Don't be afraid, Mary, for you have found favor with God. | Behold, you will conceive in your womb, and give birth to a son, and will call his name 'Jesus.'" | Mary said to the angel, "How can this be, seeing I am a virgin?" | The angel answered her, "The Holy Spirit will come on you, and the power of the Most High will overshadow you. Therefore also the holy one who is born from you will be called the Son of God." | Mary said, "Behold, the slave of the Lord; let it be done to me according to your word." [...]*

Lu 6:41 – *"Why do you see the speck of chaff that is in your brother's eye, but do not consider the beam that is in your own eye?"*

9:8 – And again, having stooped down, he wrote on the ground.

Jesus writing with his finger recalls YHWH having done the same when he codified the Law (Exodus 24:12, 31:18); so, to pique his listeners' consciences, perhaps Jesus was spelling out one of the precepts from the Torah that they themselves may have already transgressed – something like *"You shall not covet your neighbor's house; you shall not covet your neighbor's wife, nor his male slave, nor his female slave, nor his ox, nor his donkey, nor anything that is your neighbor's"* (Ex 20:17), or *"You shall not take vengeance, nor bear any grudge against the children of your people; but you shall love your neighbor as yourself. [...]"* (Le 19:18)

We have no idea what he wrote, of course, so it's anybody's guess. This is mine:

Mt 7:1 – *"Don't judge, so that you won't be judged."*

9:10 – And having straightened up, Jesus said to her, "Woman, where are they? Has no one condemned you?"

Pr 20:9 – *Who can say, "I have made my heart pure. I am clean and without sin?"*

Ec 7:20 – *Surely there is not a righteous man on earth, who does good and doesn't sin.*

9:11 – And she said, "No one, sir." And Jesus said to her, "Neither do I condemn you. Go in peace."

Jn 8:15 – *"You judge according to the flesh. I judge no one."*

On a temporal level, for those who judge 'according to the flesh', the pericope is about a betrothed woman who has unfortunately been surprised in bed and caught in *flagrante delicto* with (one supposes) a man who is not her husband. Jesus does not condemn her. Indeed, two verses later he says he judges no one. Curious, no? Does he consider YHWH's Law to be irrelevant?

But as is often the case, we can read the pericope on a different level altogether if we look at it once again in light of the Scriptures. YHWH has accused Israel and Judah of infidelity. Yet in the Gospels, by coming upon Mary in Most High fashion with his Holy Spirit, it is he himself who commits adultery with a betrothed woman (see above, THE ANGEL OF THE LORD COMES TO MARY, page 12). Not that you can lay hands on a fly-by-night guy like that…which may explain why, although they supposedly caught the woman *'in the very act'*, they were apparently unable to apprehend her lover and bring him along for the stoning party.

We might like to consider, incidentally, that Jesus has first said to those gathered, *"He who is without sin among you, let him throw the first stone."* No one has stayed to cast a stone. Jesus now says to the woman, *"Neither do I condemn you."* Should we infer from this that Jesus, too, was not without sin? [53]

9   The epileptic boy

o *Mr 9:18*
   Lu 9:39
p *Mt 17:16*
   Mr 9:18
   Lu 9:40
q *Mt 17:17*
   Mr 9:19
   Lu 9:41
r *Mr 9:20*
   Lu 9:42
s *Mr 9:21*
t *Mr 9:22*
u *Mt 17:18*
   Mr 9:25
   Lu 9:42
v *Mr 9:26*
w *Mr 9:27*

he cries out, and it throws him into convulsions, with foaming *at the mouth*; and *it* departs from him with difficulty, and *it* batters him.°

14 "And I brought him to your disciples, and they were not able to heal him."ᵖ

15 And answering, he said, "Bring me to him."�q

16 And they brought him to him. And immediately, the spirit threw him into convulsions, and having fallen upon the ground, he rolled *about* and foamed *at the mouth*.ʳ

17 And he asked his father, "How long has it been this way with him?" And he said, "Since childhood,ˢ

18 and *it happens* often, and it casts him into the fire, and into the waters, that it might destroy him. But if you are able to do anything, help us, have pity on us!"ᵗ

19 But Jesus, having seen that a crowd was rapidly gathering, rebuked the unclean spirit.ᵘ

20 And having cried out and thrown him into many convulsions, it came out; and he became as if dead, so that many said that he was dying.ᵛ

21 But Jesus, having taken him by the hand, raised him up, and he arose.ʷ

22 And having entered into a house, his disciples

9:12-23 THE EPILEPTIC BOY

The boy had epilepsy. Despite Hippocrates' rejection of the idea that the affliction was the result of spiritual causes,[54] it was still widely held that such attacks were brought on by demons, or by goddesses associated with the moon (hence Matthew's term 'moonstruck').

Since an epileptic seizure generally lasts at most not more than a few minutes, it is curious to note what Mark relates:

Mr 9:25 – When Jesus saw that a multitude came running together, he rebuked the unclean spirit, saying to him, "You mute and deaf spirit, I command you, come out of him, and never enter him again!"

Was this a deliberate bid to turn the circumstances to his advantage? Playing to the gallery, Jesus dishes out a dramatic rebuke and so makes himself look like a whiz-bang healer. Of course, the seizure would have ended in a few minutes anyway. This is no miracle.

9:22,23 – And having entered into a house, his disciples asked him in private, "Why were we not able to cast it out?" And he said to them, "This kind can be made to come out by nothing, except by prayer."

I would argue that Jesus understood that even faith was powerless to cure this sort of affliction – so far as he knew, all one could do was pray and hope for the best. Interestingly, though, he is not said to have offered a prayer to YHWH on the boy's behalf.

9:24-26 THE SON OF MAN IS TO BE HANDED OVER

The Transfiguration episode has marked a turning point. Jesus' exodus is now in the works. From here on, he will speak again and again with his inner circle about what is to come. But unlike the first time he spoke about it, when Simon Peter upbraided him for saying such things (see above, page 151), the disciples are now too afraid to question him.

Once again, when it comes to Jesus saying that he would be 'raised up', it is my view that the subsequent Jesus-movements misunderstood him to mean that he would be resurrected; rather, I read him as having told his disciples that he would be *raised up* – i.e., lifted up, hung up – on a tree or cross, per Deuteronomy 21:22. On this score, we should keep in mind that our Galilean likely spoke with his disciples in Aramaic; so if Jesus said he was going to be 'raised up', how would a translator put that into Greek? Not with *kremannumi* (cf. Act 5:30, 10:39; Gal 3:13), but with a word that would convey instead, as befits Christian belief, that Jesus had arisen or awoken from death: either *anistémi* (Mark's choice in 9:31) or *egeiró* (Matthew's in 17:23).

9:27-30 THE TEMPLE TAX

The half-shekel tribute was paid by every Jewish male, twenty or older, to ransom his soul:

Ex 30:12-16 – *"When you take a census of the sons of Israel, according to those who are counted among them, then each man shall give a ransom for his soul to Yahweh [...] | They shall give this, everyone who passes over to those who are counted, half a shekel after the shekel of the sanctuary [...] half a shekel for an offering to Yahweh. | [...] | You shall take the atonement money from the sons of Israel, and shall appoint it for the service of the Tent of Meeting; that it may be a memorial for the sons of Israel before Yahweh, to make atonement for your souls."*

This tribute money was then earmarked for the upkeep of the temple. Simon Peter blithely assumes that his teacher is happy to pay up, but when he comes into the house, Jesus seems to raise an objection:

Mt 17:25 – *" [...] What do you think, Simon? From whom do the kings of the earth receive toll or tribute? From their sons, or from strangers?"*

asked him in private, "Why were we not able to cast it out?"[x]

23 And he said to them, "This kind can *be made to* come out by nothing, except by prayer."[y]

24 And from there, having gone forth, they passed through Galilee, and he did not want that anyone should know,[z]

25 for he was teaching his disciples, and was saying to them, "The son of man is to be delivered into *the* hands of men; and they will kill him and [2]he will be raised up."[a]

26 But they did not understand the statement, and they were afraid to ask him.[b]

27 Now when they had come to Capernaum, those who receive the [3]didrachma approached Simon and said, "Does your teacher not pay the didrachma?"[c]

28 He said, "Yes." And when he had come into the house, Jesus anticipated him, saying, "What do you think, Simon? The kings of the earth,[d] from whom do they receive customs or poll-tax? From their sons,[e] or from strangers?"[f]

x *Mt 17:19*
   Mr 9:28
y *Mt 17:21*
   Mr 9:29
z *Mr 9:30*
a *Mt 17:22,23*
   Mt 26:45-47
   Mt 27:22,26,31
   Mr 9:31
   Mr 14:41-43
   Mr 15:10,13,15
   Lu 9:44
b *Mr 9:32*
   Lu 9:45
c *Ex 30:12-16*
   Mt 17:24
d *Ps 24:1,10*
   Ps 47:2
   Ps 103:19
e *Ex 4:22*
   Ex 6:5-7
   De 14:1,2
   Ps 82:6
   Jer 3:19
   Ho 11:1
f *Le 25:23*
   Le 25:39,40,42
   Le 25:55
   1Ch 29:15
   Job 41:4
   Ps 39:12
   Isa 44:21
   Mt 17:25

---

2 Certain later mss. add, *on the third day*
3 A Greek coin, the didrachm was equivalent to half a Tyrian shekel, and paid
  as a temple tax

9   "The one who wishes to become great will be your servant"

g Mt 17:26
h Mt 17:27
i Mr 9:33
j Mt 18:1
   Mr 9:34
   Lu 9:46
   Lu 22:24
k Mt 19:30
   Mr 3:19
   Mr 9:35
   Jn 13:26-30
l 1Ch 29:11
   2Ch 20:6
   Ps 22:28
   Ps 47:8
m Le 25:55
   De 28:48
   Jer 27:8
n Ge 45:8
   De 5:1
   Jos 1:16-18
   2Sa 22:44,45
   Ps 2:8,9
   Ps 18:43,44
   Mt 20:25
   Mr 10:42
o Mt 20:26
   Mt 23:11
   Mr 10:43

29 But he having said, "From strangers", Jesus said to him, "Therefore, the sons are [4]free.[g]

30 "But so that we might not offend them, having gone to the sea, cast *in* a hook, and take the first fish having come up; and having opened its mouth, you will find a [5]stater. Having taken that, give *that* to them for me and you."[h]

31 And in the house, it happened *that* he asked them, "What were you debating on the way?"[i]

32 But they kept silent, for on the way, they had been debating with one another who *was* greatest.[j]

33 And having sat down, he called the twelve and said to them, "If anyone wishes to be first, he will be last of all, and servant of all.[k]

34 "You know that those who suppose they rule over the nations[l] subjugate them,[m] and those *who are* their great ones have power over them.[n]

35 "But it shall not be so among you; however, the one who wishes to become great among you will be your servant.[o]

36 "For who is greater — the *one* that reclines at

---

4 Or, *unbound*; i.e., not a slave
5 A Greek coin, the stater was equivalent to a Tyrian shekel, itself equivalent to a tetradrachm and used for the payment of the temple tax

YHWH is a king of the earth:

Ps 47:2 – *For Yahweh Most High is awesome. He is a great King over all the earth.*

So, are the Jews the sons of YHWH…

Ex 4:22 – *"Israel is my son, my firstborn."*

De 14:1 – *You are the sons of Yahweh your God. […]*

…or strangers?

Le 25:23 – *"The land shall not be sold in perpetuity, for the land is mine; for you are strangers and live as foreigners with me."*

Le 25:55 – *"For to me the sons of Israel are slaves; they are my slaves whom I brought out of the land of Egypt. I am Yahweh your God."*

1Ch 29:15 – *"For we are strangers before you, and foreigners, as all our fathers were. […]"*

Simon Peter answers that the kings of the earth receive tribute from strangers. *"Therefore the sons are free,"* rejoins Jesus. The Hebrew *ebed* used in Leviticus 25:55 means slave, or bond-servant, while the Greek *eleutheros* used in Matthew 17:26 primarily means free or freeborn, or released from slavery. This neatly raises the point that if the Jews are indeed the sons of YHWH, then they must be exempt, or free, from paying the tax.

That, of course, is hardly the case: YHWH imposes the tax, and – as the God of Israel plainly states in Leviticus – the sons of Israel are his slaves.

9:30 – "But so that we might not offend them, having gone to the sea, cast *in* a hook, and take the first fish having come up; and having opened its mouth, you will find a stater. Having taken that, give *that* to them for me and you."

Jesus may consider himself absolved from paying the tax since, as a Jew, he can claim to be a son of YHWH; but to supposedly avoid offending 'them' (one supposes the tax-collectors), he sends Simon Peter off to the sea to throw in a hook, pull out a fish, open its mouth and find a stater with which to pay the tax.[55]

While this story is traditionally read as a miracle, we should note that in marked contrast to every other miracle story concerning Jesus, its fulfillment is neither related nor even implied. Given that Simon Peter seems to have been the most dull-witted disciple of the bunch, I wonder if Jesus wasn't just having a bit of a lark here, sending his all too gullible follower off on a wild fish chase. Much to the amusement of his fellow disciples, the hapless fellow – thinking he was on an errand to find a free coin – would have pulled up a fish and found nothing more in its mouth than the hook by which he had landed it.[56]

In like manner, this is the only story in which Jesus is uncharacteristically portrayed as being concerned about 'offending' others, to the point of even making a concession so as to not ruffle their sensibilities.[57] This too leads me to think that the fish bit was said tongue-in-cheek.

If we conclude that Jesus sent Simon Peter on a fool's errand and had no intention of paying the tax, then he was once again flouting the Law. If we instead conclude that Jesus *did* pay the tax with a fishy stater – or even with the fish itself, or a few coins prosaically fished from the group's money bag – then we must allow that his doing so refers us to the point he has just made: whereas sons are exempt, strangers pay. In other words, the Jews are indeed strangers and slaves under YHWH.

9:31-37 HE WHO WISHES TO BECOME GREAT AMONG YOU WILL BE YOUR SERVANT

9:33 – And having sat down, he called the twelve and said to them, "If anyone wishes to be first, he will be last of all, and servant of all."

Mr 3:19 – *And Judas Iscariot, who also betrayed him.*

Jn 13:26-30 – *Jesus therefore answered, "It is he to whom I will give this piece of bread when I have dipped it." So when he had dipped the piece of bread, he gave it to Judas, the son of Simon Iscariot. | [...] Then Jesus said to him, "What you do, do quickly." | [...]*

As presented here, Jesus' response may be read as first addressing the question of who among the disciples is the greatest – the greatest, says Jesus, is he who will be last of all, and the servant of all. In the Gospels that were written later, Judas' name was always the last to appear in the lists of disciples. Likewise, it is Judas who served Jesus, and by extension everyone in the group, by being the one to arrange for his arrest.

9:34 – "You know that those who suppose they rule over the nations subjugate them, and those *who are* their great ones have power over them."

Who rules over the nations?

1Ch 29:11 – *"Yours, Yahweh, is the greatness, the power, the glory, the victory, and the majesty! For all that is in the heavens and in the earth is yours. Yours is the kingdom, Yahweh, and you are exalted as head above all."*

2Ch 20:6 – *And he said, "Yahweh, the God of our fathers, aren't you God in heaven? Aren't you ruler over all the kingdoms of the nations? Power and might are in your hand, so that no one is able to withstand you."*

Ps 22:28 – *For the kingdom is Yahweh's. He is the ruler over the nations.*

Whom does he subjugate?

Le 25:55 – *"For to me the sons of Israel are slaves; they are my slaves whom I brought out of the land of Egypt. I am Yahweh your God."*

Likewise, his great ones have power over them:

De 5:1 – *Moses called to all Israel, and said to them, "Hear, Israel, the statutes and the ordinances which I speak in your ears today, that you may learn them, and observe to do them."*

Jos 1:16-18 – *They answered Joshua, saying, "All that you have commanded us we will do, and wherever you send us we will go. | Just as we* listened to Moses in all things, so will we listen to you. Only may Yahweh your God be with you, as he was with Moses. | Whoever rebels against your commandment, and doesn't listen to your words in all that you command him shall himself be put to death. Only be strong and courageous."

9:35 – "But it shall not be so among you; […]"[58]

In other words, among the disciples, it will not be this way, for they will be freed from the covenant – they will no longer be ruled over by YHWH, nor by his great ones like Moses or Joshua.

9:35,36 – " […] however, the one who wishes to become great among you will be your servant. For who is greater – the *one* that reclines at table, or the *one* that serves? Is *it* not he that reclines at table? But I am in your midst, as the *one* that serves."

However, says Jesus, there is one exception: me. I am among you, but wishing to become great, I will be your servant.

9:37 – "For the son of man did not come to be served, but to serve, and to give his life as a ransom for many."

Ex 4:22 – *"Israel is my son, my firstborn."*

Le 25:55 – *"For to me the sons of Israel are slaves; they are my slaves whom I brought out of the land of Egypt. I am Yahweh your God."*

Ps 25:1 – *To you, Yahweh, do I lift up my soul.*

Ps 49:6-8 – *Those who trust in their wealth, and boast in the multitude of their riches – | none of them can by any means redeem his brother, nor give God a ransom for him. | For the redemption of their life is costly, no payment is ever enough.*

Ps 106:10 – *He saved them from the hand of him who hated them, and redeemed them from the hand of the enemy.*

Jn 8:36 – *"If therefore the Son makes you free, you will be free indeed."*

table, or the *one* that serves? *Is it* not he that reclines at table? But I am in your midst, as the *one* that serves.[p]

37 "For the son of man did not come to be served, but to serve, and to give his [6]life as a ransom for many."[q]

38 Now one of the [7]Pharisees asked him, so that he should eat with him, and having entered into the [8]Pharisee's house, he reclined *at table.*[r]

39 And behold, *there was* a woman, who was *such a one as* in the city, a sinner; and having learned that he had reclined *at table*, and having brought an alabaster phial of ointment — [s]

40 and having stood behind him, at his feet, weeping — *with* tears began to wet his feet, and with the hair of her head was wiping *them*; and *she* was kissing his feet, and was anointing *them* with the ointment.[t]

41 But having seen this, the *one* having invited him spoke within himself, saying, "If this were a prophet, he would have known who and what kind of woman touches him, for she is a sinner."[u]

42 And answering, Jesus said to him, "Simon, I

p *Lu 22:27*
q Ex 4:22
   Le 25:55
   Ps 25:1
   Ps 49:6-8
   Ps 106:10
   Mt 20:28
   Mr 10:45
   Jn 8:36
   Jn 15:13
r *Lu 7:36*
s *Lu 7:37*
t *Lu 7:38*
u Eze 16:25,32-34
   Eze 23:45
   Lu 7:39

---

6 Or, *soul*
7 Certain early mss. read, *disciples*
8 Certain early mss. read, *disciple's*

9   "He to whom little is forgiven, loves little"

v *Lu 7:40*
w *Lu 7:41*
x *Lu 7:42*
y *Lu 7:43*
z *Lu 7:44*
a Isa 26:5,6
   Lu 7:45
b Ec 9:8
c *Lu 7:46*
d De 5:9
   De 29:14-21
   Jos 24:19
   Job 7:21
   Job 10:14
   La 3:42,43
   Ho 1:6
e 1Sa 8:7
   Ps 78:40
   Isa 9:13
   Jer 5:3,7,9,23
   Am 4:6-11
   Hag 2:17
   Lu 7:47

have something to say to you." And he said, "Say it, Teacher."[v]

43 "A certain moneylender had two debtors: one owed *him* five hundred [9]denarii, and *the* other, fifty."[w]

44 "They not having the means to repay *their debt*, he forgave them both. Which of them therefore will love him most?"[x]

45 Answering, Simon said, "I suppose the one to whom he forgave the most." And he said to him, "Rightly have you judged."[y]

46 And having turned to the woman, he said to Simon, "Do you see this woman? I came into your house. You gave me no water for my feet, but she has wet my feet with her tears, and wiped *them* with her hair."[z]

47 "You did not give me a kiss, but she, from *the time* that I came in, has not ceased kissing my feet."[a]

48 "You did not anoint my head with olive oil,[b] but she anointed my feet with ointment."[c]

49 "On account of this I say to you, her many sins have been forgiven, for she loved much. On the other hand, *he* to whom little is forgiven,[d] loves little."[e]

---

9 A Roman coin, the denarius was equivalent to the wages for a day's work

Jn 15:13 – *"Greater love has no one than this, that someone lay down his life for his friends."*

Jesus offers himself as the first Son, the firstborn to be sanctified and sacrificed to YHWH on behalf of the Jews, all of whom are his slaves, that they might go free. The redemption of their lives is costly – wealth alone could never buy their freedom – but if the Son himself is sacrificed, then they will be free. His soul will serve as a ransom for many.

9:38-49 A SINFUL WOMAN ANOINTS JESUS' FEET

Personally, I suspect that the 'Simon' here named was in fact Jesus' disciple Simon Peter – not a card-carrying Pharisee, but, as I see him, the most conservatively Jewish member of the apostolic inner circle.[59]

9:46-48 – " [...] she has wet my feet with her tears, and wiped them with her hair. You did not give me a kiss, but she, from *the time* that I came in, has not ceased kissing my feet. You did not anoint my head with olive oil, but she anointed my feet with ointment."

It is highly significant that the woman does not anoint Jesus' *head* – as one would expect, and which would have been the first place to start (see below, THE COSTLY SPIKENARD, page 259) – but rather is portrayed as bestowing her every attention on his *feet*, washing and kissing and anointing them with a perfumed oil or ointment. Jesus' feet are thus deliberately glorified. These are the feet, suggests the margin note, that will bring low YHWH, who dwells in the lofty city of Jerusalem:

Isa 26:5,6 – *"For he has brought down those who dwell on high, the lofty city. He lays it low [...] even to the ground. He brings it even to the dust. | The foot shall tread it down; even the feet of the poor, and the steps of the needy."*

9:49 – "On account of this I say to you, her many sins have been forgiven, for she loved much. On the other hand, *he* to whom little is forgiven, loves little."

The Jews were forgiven little by Yʜᴡʜ:

De 5:9 – "[…] *I, Yahweh, your God, am a jealous God, visiting the iniquity of the fathers on the children, and on the third and on the fourth generation of those who hate me.*"

De 29:14-21 – […] *Yahweh will not pardon him* […] | *Yahweh will set him apart for evil out of all the tribes of Israel, according to all the curses of the covenant that is written in this book of the law.*

Jos 24:19 – *Joshua said to the people, "*[…] *Yahweh* […] *is a holy God. He is a jealous God. He will not forgive your disobedience nor your sins."*

Job 10:14 – *If I sin, then you mark me. You will not acquit me from my iniquity.*

Ho 1:6 – *She conceived again, and bore a daughter. Then he said to him, "Call her name Lo-Ruhamah ['not loved'] ; for I will no longer have mercy on the house of Israel, that I should in any way pardon them."*

Not pardoned, not forgiven, not loved… "*He to whom little is forgiven, the same loves little.*" Is it any wonder, then, if the Jews rebelled and rejected their god?

1Sa 8:7 – *Yahweh said to Samuel, "Listen to the voice of the people in all that they tell you; for they have not rejected you, but they have rejected me as the king over them."*

Ps 78:40 – *How often they rebelled against him in the wilderness, and grieved him in the desert!*

Isa 9:13 – *Yet the people have not turned to him who struck them, neither have they sought Yahweh of Armies.*

Jer 5:3,7,9,23 – *O Yahweh, don't your eyes look on truth? You have stricken them, but they were not grieved. You have consumed them, but they have refused to receive correction. They have made their faces harder than a rock. They have refused to return.* | "*How can I pardon you? Your children have forsaken me, and sworn by what are no gods. When I had fed them to the full, they committed adultery, and assembled themselves in troops at the prostitutes' houses. | Shouldn't I punish them for these things?" says Yahweh; "and shouldn't my soul be avenged on such a nation as this? | But this people has a revolting and a rebellious heart; they have revolted and gone."*

Am 4:6-11 – [...] | *"I sent plagues among you like I did Egypt. I have slain your young men with the sword, and have carried away your horses; and I filled your nostrils with the stench of your camp, yet you haven't returned to me," says Yahweh.*

Hag 2:17 – *"I struck you with blight, mildew, and hail in all the work of your hands; yet you didn't turn to me," says Yahweh.*

Morally supercilious, Simon has opined to himself that if Jesus were a prophet, he would never consent to being touched by a woman such as this – a sinner![60] Yet in marked contrast to Simon, this unnamed woman has come into the house and showered Jesus' feet with loving attention, wetting them with her tears, drying them with her hair and anointing them with ointment. Jesus turns the tables on his host by observing that if the woman is able to love much, it is because "her many sins have been forgiven" – thus neatly implying that Simon, who has shown him so little consideration since he arrived, no doubt loves little because his many sins have *not* been forgiven.

Since the woman came expressly to the house to see Jesus when she learned that he was there, we might suppose that it was he who had told her one day that her sins were forgiven. He freed her, as it were, from the Law...and she loves him for it. Whereas the Pharisaic Simon, still very much under the Law, remains subject to YHWH and his unforgiving wrath.

10

Search first for the kingdom of God

10:1-13 DIVORCE

"Is it lawful for a man to divorce his wife?" They're at it again, those Pharisees, testing Jesus. But why ask? What's the test? What's at stake?

En route for Jerusalem, Jesus has left Galilee. To say that he is in 'the region of Judea, and beyond the Jordan' suggests that he will soon enter – or indeed, has perhaps already entered – Perea, which was under Herod Antipas' jurisdiction. This also brings to mind John the Baptist, whom Herodias, say the Gospels, had maneuvered to have executed on account of the prophet's open contestation of her marriage to Herod Antipas – marriage for which she had divorced her first husband, Herod II.[61]

It would seem, then, that the test goes like this: 'Is divorce lawful? If you say yes, then you dishonor the teachings and memory of the prophet John, who was killed for his beliefs – and the people will have reason to reject you. If you say no, then Herodias will learn of it and will seek to silence you as she did John.'[62]

As he will do later when asked whether or not the Jews should pay tax to Caesar, Jesus here places the argument on a hallowed footing: *"From the beginning of the creation, God made them male and female. For this cause a man will leave his father and mother, and will join to his wife, | and the two will become one flesh, so that they are no longer two, but one flesh. | What therefore God has joined together, let no man separate."* (Mr 10:6-8)

Divorce **10**

CHAPTER 10

AND having risen up from there, he came into the region of Judea, and beyond the Jordan. And crowds were again journeying together with him, and again, as he had been accustomed, he was teaching them.[a]

2   And having come to him, *some* Pharisees questioned him, whether it is lawful for a husband [1]to divorce a wife, testing him.[b]

3   But he answering, said to them, "What did Moses command you?"[c]

4   But they said, "Moses allowed a certificate of divorce to be written, and [1]to divorce *her*."[d]

5   But Jesus said to them, "For your hardness of heart, he wrote this commandment for you.[e]

6   "But since *the* beginning of creation, he made them MALE AND FEMALE.[f]

7   "'FOR THIS A MAN WILL LEAVE HIS FATHER

a Mt 19:1
   Mr 10:1
b Mt 19:3
   Mr 10:2
c Mr 10:3
d De 24:1
   Mt 1:19
   Mt 5:31
   Mt 19:7
   Mr 10:4
e Mal 2:14-16
   Mt 19:8
   Mr 10:5
f Ge 1:27
   Mt 19:4,8
   Mr 10:6

---

1 Or, *to send away*

10   Divorce

g   Ge 2:24
    Mt 19:5
    Mr 10:7
h   Ge 2:24
    Mt 19:5,6
    Mr 10:8
i   Mal 2:14-16
    Mt 19:6
    Mr 10:9
j   Mr 10:10
k   Isa 50:1
    Jer 12:7,8
l   Ezr 1:1,2
    Isa 44:28
    Isa 45:1-3
m   Jer 31:31,32
    Ho 2:16,19,20
n   Jer 3:8
o   De 24:1,2,4
    Mt 5:32
    Mt 19:9
p   Mt 19:10
q   Pr 19:8
    Mt 19:11
r   Mt 19:13
    Mr 10:13
    Lu 18:15
s   Mt 19:14
    Mr 10:14
    Lu 18:16

AND MOTHER, AND SHALL CLEAVE TO HIS WIFE;[g]

8   AND THE TWO WILL BECOME ONE FLESH' — so that they are no longer two, but one flesh.[h]

9   "What God has therefore yoked together, *let* man not separate."[i]

10   And in the house, the disciples again asked him about this.[j]

11   And he said to them, "Whoever [2]divorces his wife[k] and should marry another,[l] commits adultery against her; and whoever might marry[m] *a woman* who is divorced[n] commits adultery."[o]

12   His disciples said to him, "If this is the case of the man with the woman, it is better not to marry!"[p]

13   But he said to them, "Not all *men* make room for this statement, but those to whom it has been given."[q]

14   And they were bringing little children to him, that he might touch them. But *the* disciples rebuked them.[r]

15   But having seen *this*, Jesus was indignant, and said to them, "Permit the little children to come to me. Do not hinder them, for the kingdom of God is such *as they*.[s]

2 Or, *sends away*

The disciples were apparently surprised by their teacher's strict reading of the Scriptures. Wasn't Jesus the guy who preached 'Judge not', and who'd let an adulteress off the hook? So they ask for clarification.

10:11 – And he said to them, "Whoever divorces his wife and should marry another, commits adultery against her; and whoever might marry *a woman* who is divorced commits adultery."

YHWH, of course, had already divorced Israel:

Isa 50:1 – *Yahweh says, "Where is the bill of your mother's divorce, with which I have put her away? Or to which of my creditors have I sold you? Behold, you were sold for your iniquities, and your mother was put away for your transgressions."*

Israel's god had also cast his favour on another, whom he had anointed and called his shepherd – Cyrus (who was not even a Jew):

Isa 45:1-3 – *Yahweh says to his anointed, to Cyrus, whose right hand I have held, to subdue nations before him, and strip kings of their armor; to open the doors before him, and the gates shall not be shut: | "I will go before you, and make the rough places smooth. […] | I will give you the treasures of darkness, and hidden riches of secret places, that you may know that it is I, Yahweh, who call you by your name, even the God of Israel."*

Nonetheless, YHWH declares that he will marry Israel once again:

Jer 31:31,32 – *"Behold, the days come," says Yahweh, "that I will make a new covenant with the house of Israel, and with the house of Judah: | not according to the covenant that I made with their fathers in the day that I took them by the hand to bring them out of the land of Egypt; which my covenant they broke, although I was a husband to them," says Yahweh.*

Ho 2:16,19,20 – *"It will be in that day," says Yahweh, "that you will call me 'my husband,' and no longer call me 'my master.' | I will betroth you to me forever. Yes, I will betroth you to me in righteousness, in justice, in loving kindness, and in compassion. | I will even betroth you to me in faithfulness; and you shall know Yahweh."*

Yet Israel is a divorced woman, one whom Yhwh has repudiated:

Jer 3:8 – *"I saw when, for this very cause, that backsliding Israel had committed adultery, I had put her away and given her a bill of divorce, yet treacherous Judah, her sister, had no fear; but she also went and played the prostitute."*

Hence, under the law, to take her back would be to commit adultery:

De 24:1,2,4 – *When a man takes a wife and marries her, then it shall be, if she finds no favor in his eyes, because he has found some unseemly thing in her, that he shall write her a bill of divorce, and put it in her hand, and send her out of his house. | When she has departed out of his house, she may go and be another man's wife. | Her former husband, who sent her away, may not take her again to be his wife, after that she is defiled; for that is abomination before Yahweh. […]*

10:12 – His disciples said to him, "If this is the case of the man with the woman, it is better not to marry!"

The apostles were evidently nonplussed by their teacher's unyielding stance. Each disciple may have been an aspirant saint-in-the-making, but the thought of finding oneself in an unhappy union and barred from divorce to rectify one's plight must have seemed utterly beyond the pale to these all-too-human mortals. (At least one, Simon Peter, was married. Odd that we never hear about his poor wife, left at home…)

10:13 – But he said to them, "Not all *men* make room for this statement, but those to whom it has been given."

Pr 19:8 – *He who gets wisdom loves his own soul. He who keeps understanding shall find good.*

On one level, we may interpret Jesus here as saying that it would be better if Israel were neither married nor betrothed to Yhwh, no less than to any other god. Not all men can make room for such a statement; only those to whom such a capacity (for unfettered spiritual freedom) has been given.

In like manner, on a more temporal level, we may interpret Jesus as saying it would be better if couples did not marry at all. His view may have been due to the disgrace his mother incurred when she was pregnant with him,[63] or to his Jewish society's unforgiving stance towards adulterers, as evidenced by John 8:1-11. It may even have been due to a romantic relationship that he may have had with one of his followers, if their love were constrained by one or both of them being married.[64] For any of these reasons, Jesus could have come to the conclusion that men and women would be better off without marriage altogether, be it the spiritual union of a people with its tribal god, or the sanctified union of two consenting adults. After all, things change, sooner or later.

10:14-17 RECEIVE THE KINGDOM OF GOD LIKE A CHILD

10:14 – And they were bringing little children to him, that he might touch them. But *the* disciples rebuked them.

I should think it common in that day and age for parents to ask men of spiritual stature to touch their children and bestow a blessing – the practice, after all, has roots in the Hebrew Scriptures (cf. Ge 48:14-16, Le 9:22, De 34:9) – so I wonder why the disciples rebuked them. It may be they felt children were of no importance, as is often supposed; yet to me that seems dubious: Jesus had clearly shown through his healing activities – per Mark 2:5, 5:41, 7:30 – that he was concerned with the welfare of children. One supposes that the disciples therefore had some other unspoken reason for shooing away the parents with their kids.

10:15 – But having seen *this*, Jesus was indignant, and said to them, "Permit the little children to come to me. Do not hinder them, for the kingdom of God is such *as they*."

Earlier (see above, THE KINGDOM OF GOD, page 94), Jesus has taught that the kingdom of God is like a man who has only to cast seed on the ground in order to reap a plentiful harvest; or like a mustard seed which grows to be larger than all the other garden plants; or like a small quantity of leaven that leavens three large measures of flour. Here, Jesus states that the kingdom of God is 'such as' children.

Many commentators feel that children here exemplify the supposed virtues of humility, docility and obedience, and conclude that Jesus was commending such traits. I can only disagree. In my view, it is the fact that children have not yet attained the age of 'religious maturity' – the point at which a child becomes a son or daughter 'of the commandment' (*bar* or *bat mitzvah*) and must assume the full panoply of religious and legal obligations that are incumbent upon adults – that sets them apart. Prior to this, children are not beholden to the Law. They have not yet been roped into religious duty, with tefillin strapped onto their heads and arms; their perceptive spirits have not yet been dulled by dogma, hampered by traditions and laws. They are not yet Jews in the fullest sense of being 'subject to the Law'.[65] Their vows are not binding, and they are not held to account for their sins[66] (though they can certainly be scapegoated for their fathers' sins – cf. Numbers 14:18). If Jesus equates the kingdom of God with children, then it suggests that the kingdom of God is beyond the reach of the Law.

10:16,17 – "Truly I say to you, whoever shall not receive the kingdom of God as *he receives* a child, shall never enter into it." And having taken them in his arms, he blessed them, having laid the hands on them.

By welcoming the children with open arms, Jesus shows his disciples how they should welcome the kingdom of God.

Receive the kingdom of God like a child   **10**

16   "Truly I say to you, whoever shall not [3]receive the kingdom of God as *he receives* a child, shall never enter into it."[t]

17   And having taken them in his arms, he blessed them, having laid the hands on them.[u]

18   And *he* going forth on his way, one having run up and having fallen on his knees before him asked him, "Good Teacher, what shall I do, so that I might inherit eternal life?"[v]

19   But Jesus said to him, "Why do you call me good?[w] No one *is* good, except one – God.[x]

20   "You know the commandments: YOU SHOULD NOT MURDER. YOU SHOULD NOT COMMIT ADULTERY. YOU SHOULD NOT STEAL. YOU SHOULD NOT BEAR FALSE WITNESS. HONOR YOUR FATHER AND YOUR MOTHER."[y]

21   But he said, "Teacher, all these I have kept from *my* youth."[z]

22   But Jesus, having looked upon him, loved him, and said to him, "One thing to you is lacking. Go, sell whatever you have, and give to the poor, and you will have treasure in heaven. And come, follow me!"[a]

---

3 Or, *welcome*

t   Mr 10:15
    Lu 18:17
u   Mr 10:16
v   Job 33:28
    Ps 16:10,11
    Ps 21:2,4
    Isa 25:7-9
    Mt 19:16
    Mr 10:17
    Lu 10:25
    Lu 18:18
w   Ge 1:4
    Ec 11:7
    Jn 1:4
    Jn 9:5
x   Am 5:18,20
    Mt 19:17
    Mr 10:18
    Lu 18:19
y   De 4:40
    De 30:15-20
    De 32:47
    Eze 18:9
    Mt 19:17-19
    Mr 10:19
    Lu 18:20
z   Mt 19:20
    Mr 10:20
    Lu 18:21
a   Pr 23:4,5
    Ec 7:11
    Jn 8:12
    Mt 19:21
    Mr 10:21
    Lu 18:22

10   Parable of the rich man

b Pr 18:11
Mt 19:22
Mr 10:22
Lu 18:23
c Mt 19:23
Mr 10:23
Lu 18:24
d Mt 10:9
Mt 19:23
Mr 10:24
Lu 6:20
Lu 22:35
e Mt 19:24
Mr 10:25
Lu 18:25
f Mt 19:25
Mr 10:26
Lu 18:26
g Pr 3:10
Lu 12:16
h Lu 12:17
i Lu 12:18

23 But the *man*, having been saddened by the word, went away vexed, for he had many possessions.[b]

24 But Jesus, having seen him, said, "How hard shall *it be for* those having riches to enter into the kingdom of God."[c]

25 Now the disciples were astonished by his words. But Jesus, having answered again, said to them, "Children, how difficult it is, to enter into the kingdom of God.[d]

26 "It is easier *for* a camel to pass through the eye of a needle, than *for* a rich man to enter into the kingdom of God."[e]

27 But they were exceedingly thunderstruck, saying among themselves, "And who is able to be saved?"[f]

28 But he told them a parable, saying, "The field of a certain rich man brought *forth* a good harvest.[g]

29 "And he was reasoning within himself, saying, 'What shall I do? For I have no place where I may gather together *all of* my fruits.'[h]

30 "And he said, 'I will do this: I will pull down my granaries and I will build larger ones, and there I will gather together all of my grain and my goods.[i]

31 "'And I will say to my soul, "Soul, you have

10:18-27 "IT IS EASIER FOR A CAMEL…"

10:18 – And *he* going forth on his way, one having run up and having fallen on his knees before him asked him, "Good Teacher, what shall I do, so that I might inherit eternal life?"

Job 33:28 – *"He has redeemed my soul from going into the pit. My life shall see the light."*

Ps 16:10,11 – *For you will not leave my soul in Sheol, neither will you allow your holy one to see corruption. | You will show me the path of life. In your presence is fullness of joy. In your right hand there are pleasures forever.*

Ps 21:2,4 – *You have given him his heart's desire, and have not withheld the request of his lips. | He asked life of you, you gave it to him, even length of days forever and ever.*

Isa 25:7-9 – *He will destroy in this mountain the surface of the covering that covers all peoples, and the veil that is spread over all nations. | He has swallowed up death forever! […] | It shall be said in that day, "Behold, this is our God! We have waited for him, and he will save us! This is Yahweh! We have waited for him. We will be glad and rejoice in his salvation!"*

The Jewish belief in a resurrection of the dead and an eternal life to come had underpinnings in scripture. See below, THE RESURRECTION OF THE DEAD, page 232.

10:19 – But Jesus said to him, "Why do you call me good? […] "

Ge 1:4 – *God saw the light, and saw that it was good. […]*

Ec 11:7 – *Truly the light is sweet, and a pleasant thing it is for the eyes to see the sun.*

Jn 1:4 – *In him was life, and the life was the light of men.*

Jn 9:5 – *"While I am in the world, I am the light of the world."*

10:19 – " […] No one *is* good, except one – God."

Am 5:18,20 – *"Woe to you who desire the day of Yahweh! Why do you long for the day of Yahweh? It is darkness, and not light. | Won't the day of Yahweh be darkness, and not light? Even very dark, and no brightness in it?"*

We may give this an ironic turn. Seen in this light, is YHWH good? Maybe it is Jesus who is good, and not the God of Israel.

At any rate, the standard reply to the question – certainly the one that John the Baptist would have given – is that to inherit life, a Jew need only observe the commandments.

De 30:15-20 – *Behold, I have set before you today life and prosperity, and death and evil. | For I command you today to love Yahweh your God, to walk in his ways, and to keep his commandments, his statutes, and his ordi-nances, that you may live […] | But if your heart turns away, […] you will surely perish. […] Therefore choose life, that you may live […].*

In answer, the fellow tells Jesus that he has kept all of the command-ments since his youth. One wonders, therefore, whether the man had come to feel that the Law was not enough. Did he have a sense that something was lacking? That somehow, the Law was not the answer to his question and that he needed to do something else to obtain life?

10:22 – But Jesus, having looked upon him, loved him, and said to him, "One thing to you is lacking. Go, sell whatever you have, and give to the poor, and you will have treasure in heaven. And come, follow me!"

Pr 23:4,5 – *Don't weary yourself to be rich. In your wisdom, show restraint. | Why do you set your eyes on that which is not? For it certainly sprouts wings like an eagle and flies away to heaven.*

Ec 7:11 – *Wisdom is as good as an inheritance. Yes, it is more excellent for those who see the sun.*

Jn 8:12 – *Again, therefore, Jesus spoke to them, saying, "I am the light of the world. He who follows me will not walk in the darkness, but will have the light of life."*

It seems Jesus rather liked this fellow. In the wording of the Gospels, 'Follow me!' amounts to an invitation to join up as a disciple.

10:23 – But the *man*, having been saddened by the word, went away vexed, for he had many possessions.

Pr 18:11 – *The rich man's wealth is his strong city, like an unscalable wall in his own imagination.*

Can you beat that? The guy turned down a personal invitation to join the exclusive Jesus Fun Club.

10:24,25 – But Jesus, having seen him, said, "How hard shall *it be for* those having riches to enter into the kingdom of God." Now the disciples were astonished by his words. But Jesus, having answered again, said to them, "Children, how difficult it is, to enter into the kingdom of God."

Mt 10:9 – *"Don't take any gold, silver, or brass in your money belts."*

Lu 6:20 – *He lifted up his eyes to his disciples, and said, "Blessed are you who are poor, God's Kingdom is yours."*

Lu 22:35 – *He said to them, "When I sent you out without purse, and wallet, and shoes, did you lack anything?" They said, "Nothing."*

When he sent them out without purse or wallet, Jesus had ensured his disciples would experience the kingdom of God firsthand, and so learn for themselves that they need not worry about wealth.

In the Gospels, only Mark relates that Jesus addressed his disciples as *"Children"*. Coming from Jesus, and given the context, this is surely a mark of esteem. Yet it has been neatly excised in Matthew and Luke. Perhaps they felt calling the disciples 'children' was unbecoming.

10:28-32   THE PARABLE OF THE RICH MAN

10:32 – "But God said to him, 'Fool! This night, they demand back your soul. But what you prepared, to whom will *it* be?'"

Ps 39:5,6 – *"Behold, you have made my days hand widths. My lifetime is as nothing before you. Surely every man stands as a breath. | Surely every man walks like a shadow. Surely they busy themselves in vain. He heaps up, and doesn't know who shall gather."*

Ec 2:21 – *For there is a man whose labor is with wisdom, with knowledge, and with skillfulness; yet he shall leave it for his portion to a man who has not labored for it. This also is vanity and a great evil.*

10:33-44   DO NOT BE ANXIOUS FOR YOUR LIFE

Jesus' teaching resonates with truth, yet it is still a challenge to heed. Then as now, the prevailing view was that man must toil, and that God rewards man according to his deeds. Yet Jesus asserts that if we but seek the kingdom of God, *"all these things will be added to you."* His followers must have thought him mad.

10:35 – "Consider the ravens, since they neither sow nor reap, for whom there is no granary nor storeroom; and God feeds them. How much more different are you than the birds!"

Ps 147:9 – *He provides food […] for the young ravens when they call.*

10:36 – "But which of you, being anxious, is able to add a cubit to his lifespan?"

Ec 3:1,2 – *For everything there is a season, and a time for every purpose under heaven: | a time to be born, and a time to die; a time to plant, and a time to pluck up that which is planted.*

many good *things* laid up for years — take your ease, eat, drink, *and* be of good cheer!"[j]

32 "But God said to him, 'Fool! This night, they demand back your soul.[k] But what you prepared, to whom will *it* be?'"[l]

33 And he said to his disciples, "Through this, I say to you, do not be anxious for *your* life, what you should eat, nor for your body, what you should put on.[m]

34 "For life is more than food, and the body *more than* clothing.[n]

35 "Consider the ravens, since they neither sow nor reap, for whom there is no granary nor storeroom; and God feeds them.[o] How much more different are you than the birds![p]

36 "But which of you, being anxious, is able to add a cubit to his [4]lifespan?[q]

37 "Therefore, if you are not able *to do* even a very little thing, why are you anxious about the rest?[r]

38 "Consider the lilies, how they grow: they neither toil nor spin — but I say to you, not even Solomon in all his glory was clothed as one of these.[s]

39 "But if God so clothes the grass — which is in

---

4 Or, *stature*

j Lu 12:19
k Ps 90:3
   Ps 104:29
   Ec 12:7
l Ps 39:5,6
   Ec 2:21
   Lu 12:20
m Mt 6:25
   Lu 12:22
n Mt 6:25
   Lu 12:23
o Ps 104:27,28
   Ps 136:25
   Ps 147:9
p Mt 6:26
   Lu 12:24
q Job 14:5
   Ps 139:16
   Ec 3:1,2
   Ec 8:7,8
   Mt 6:27
   Lu 12:25
r Lu 12:26
s 1Ch 29:25
   Mt 6:28,29
   Lu 12:27

10 Search first for the kingdom of God

t *Mt 6:30*
   Lu 12:28
u *Mt 6:19*
v *Mt 6:21*
   Lu 12:34
w *Mt 6:31*
   Lu 12:29
x *Mt 6:32*
   Lu 12:30
y *Ps 37:4*
   Ps 127:2
   Ps 145:15,16
   Mt 6:33
   Lu 12:31
y *Pr 27:1*
z *Mt 6:34*
a *Mt 20:1*
b *Mt 20:2*

the field today, and tomorrow is cast into a furnace —
how much more *so* you, of little faith?[t]

40 "Do not store up for yourselves treasures on
earth, where moth and rust destroy, and where thieves
break in and steal —[u]

41 for where your treasure is, there your heart will
be, too.[v]

42 "Therefore, do not be anxious, saying 'What
might we eat?' or 'What might we drink?' or 'With
what might we clothe ourselves?'[w]

43 "But search first for the kingdom of God, and
all these things will be added to you.[y]

44 "Therefore, do not be anxious about tomorrow,
for tomorrow will be anxious about itself.[y] Each day
has enough trouble of its own.[z]

45 "For the kingdom of God is like a man, the
master of a house, who went out early in the morning
to hire workers for his vineyard.[a]

46 "And having agreed with the workmen on a
denarius for the day, he sent them forth into his
vineyard.[b]

47 "And having gone out about the [5]third hour, he

---

5 I.e., 9 a.m.

Ec 8:7,8 – For he doesn't know that which will be; for who can tell him how it will be? | There is no man who has power over the spirit to contain the spirit; neither does he have power over the day of death. [...]

10:38 – "Consider the lilies, how they grow: they neither toil nor spin – but I say to you, not even Solomon in all his glory was clothed as one of these."

1 Ch 29:25 – Yahweh magnified Solomon exceedingly in the sight of all Israel, and gave to him such royal majesty as had not been on any king before him in Israel.

10:43 – "But search first for the kingdom of God, and all these things will be added to you."

Ps 37:4 – Also delight yourself in God, and he will give you the desires of your heart.

Ps 127:2 – It is vain for you to rise up early, to stay up late, eating the bread of toil; for he gives sleep to his loved ones.

Ps 145:15,16 – The eyes of all wait for you. You give them their food in due season. | You open your hand, and satisfy the desire of every living thing.

Again, it is my view that Jesus understood God as being distinct from Israel's tribal god. The principle here conveyed by Jesus is universal and wholly independent of YHWH; it may be experienced by any person who follows Jesus' recommendations. To drive the point home, Jesus now delivers a remarkable parable.

10:45-59 THE PARABLE OF THE VINEYARD WORKERS

10:54-56 – "And when those *hired* first came, they were thinking that they would receive more; yet they *too* each received a denarius. And having received *it*, they complained against the master of the house, saying, 'These *who came* last have worked one hour, and *yet* you have made them equal to us, the *ones* who have borne the burden of the day and the heat.'"

Job 34:11 – *"For the work of a man he will render to him, and cause every man to find according to his ways."*

Ps 62:12 – *Also to you, Lord, belongs loving kindness, for you reward every man according to his work.*

Jer 32:18,19 – *[...] The great, the mighty God, Yahweh [...]] ; whose eyes are open to all the ways of the sons of men, to give everyone according to his ways, and according to the fruit of his doings.*

Of course they expected that they would receive more...and why shouldn't they? Isn't it written that YHWH rewards a man according to his work? If the slackers who only toiled an hour get a denarius for their trouble, then the men who slaved away all day under the hot burning sun should by all rights get paid a great deal more.

10:57,58 – "But he answered to one of them, saying, 'Companion, I do not wrong you. Did you not agree with me *for* a denarius? Take what *is* yours and go. Yet I wish to give to this last *man*, even as *I have given* to you.'"

Mt 5:45 – *"[...] For he makes his sun to rise on the evil and the good, and sends rain on the just and the unjust."*

10:59 – "'Or is it not permitted for me to do as I wish with that which is mine? Or is your eye evil, because I am good?'"

Mr 10:18 – *Jesus said to him, "Why do you call me good? No one is good except one – God."*

Here we come full circle. The kingdom of God, says Jesus, is like the master of a house who is good – the master of the house is God, who is good. Not YHWH, but the God who bestows sunshine and rain on the evil and the good, on the just and the unjust. He gives, not according to a man's work, but freely. Simply because he is good.

saw others standing idle in the marketplace;[c]

48 and he said to them, 'Go also into the vineyard *to work*, and you will be paid whatever is just.'[d]

49 "And so they went. But again, having gone out about the [6]sixth and ninth hour, he did likewise.[e]

50 "But about the [7]eleventh *hour*, having gone out, he found others standing *there*, and said to them, 'Why are you standing here idle all day?'[f]

51 "They said to him, 'Because no one has hired us.' He said to them, 'You also, go into the vineyard, and whatever is right, you shall receive.'[g]

52 "But when the evening arrived, the master of the vineyard said to his foreman, 'Call the workmen and pay them their wages, beginning with the last until the first.'[h]

53 "And when those *hired* about the eleventh hour came, they each received a denarius.[i]

54 "And when those *hired* first came, they were thinking that they would receive more;[j] yet they *too* each received a denarius.[k]

55 "And having received *it*, they complained against

c Mt 20:3
d Mt 20:4
e Mt 20:5
f Mt 20:6
g Mt 20:7
h Mt 20:8
   Mt 20:16
i Mt 20:9
j Job 34:11
   Ps 62:12
   Jer 32:18,19
k Mt 20:10

---

6 I.e., noon and 3 p.m.
7 I.e., 5 p.m.

10

l   *Mt 20:11*
m *Ec 1:3*
    Ec 2:22
    Mt 20:12
n *Mt 20:13*
o *Mt 5:45*
    Mt 20:14
p *Mt 20:15*
    Mr 10:18
q *Ps 78:52-54*
    Ps 107:10,14
r *Mt 20:17*
    Mr 10:32
    Lu 18:31
s *Mic 6:7*
t *Mt 20:18,19*
    Mr 10:33
    Lu 18:32

the master of the house,[l]

56   saying, 'These *who came* last have worked one hour, and *yet* you have made them equal to us, the *ones* who have borne the burden of the day and the heat.'[m]

57   "But he answered to one of them, saying, 'Companion, I do not wrong you. Did you not agree with me *for* a denarius?[n]

58   "'Take what *is* yours and go. Yet I wish to give to this last *man*, even as *I have given* to you.[o]

59   "'Or is it not permitted for me to do as I wish with that which is mine? Or is your eye evil, because I am good?'"[p]

60 Now they were on the way, going up to Jerusalem, and Jesus was leading them forth,[q] and they were astonished; but those following were terrified. And once again, having taken the twelve, he began to tell them the things that were about to happen to him,[r]

61   because *he was saying*, "Behold, we are going up to Jerusalem, and the son of man will be handed over to the chief priests and to the scribes,[s] and they will condemn him to death.[t]

62   "And *they* will mock him and will spit upon him

10:60-62 JESUS LEADS HIS FOLLOWERS TO JERUSALEM

10:60 – Now they were on the way, going up to Jerusalem, and Jesus was leading them forth […]

Ps 78:52-54 – *But he led out his own people like sheep, and guided them in the wilderness like a flock. | He led them safely, so that they weren't afraid […]. | He brought them to the border of his sanctuary, to this mountain, which his right hand had taken.*

Ps 107:10,14 – *Some sat in darkness and in the shadow of death, being bound in affliction and iron. | He brought them out of darkness and the shadow of death, and broke away their chains.*

10:60-62 – […] and they were astonished; but those following were terrified. And once again, having taken the twelve, he began to tell them the things that were about to happen to him, because *he was saying,* "Behold, we are going up to Jerusalem, and the son of man will be handed over to the chief priests and to the scribes, and they will condemn him to death, and they will hand him over to the nations. And *they* will mock him and will spit upon him and will flog him, and *they* will kill *him* and he will be raised up."

Mic 6:7 – *Will Yahweh be pleased with thousands of rams? With tens of thousands of rivers of oil? Shall I give my firstborn for my disobedience? The fruit of my body for the sin of my soul?*

Speaking only to his closest disciples, Jesus spells out the program for the days to come. That those accompanying him to Jerusalem were scared out of their wits suggests they were overhearing at least some of these details. But which of his followers (including his disciples) could have made sense of such things at the time – that the priests would condemn him to death; that they would hand him over to the Gentiles; that Jesus would be mocked and mistreated, killed and 'raised up'? Such statements could only have boggled their minds.

11

Jesus comes to Jerusalem

11:1-7 ENTERING JERICHO, JESUS IS RECEIVED BY ZACCHAEUS

Ah, Jesus – always on the lookout, it seems, for a good table at which to eat. Zacchaeus was rich and received his guest with joy.

My guess is that Levi and Matthew knew their confrère and spoke to Jesus about him as they walked into Jericho.

'Master, we have a friend who lives in this town, a certain Zacchaeus. He's a tax collector, like us. We're sure he'd like to meet you, and we could all stay with him – he's rich, and he loves to eat and drink. Look, there he is! That's him, up in the tree.'

No surprise, then, that Jesus knows his name. *"Zacchaeus, hurry, come down! For today it behooves me to stay in your house."*

11:7 – And having seen *it*, they all grumbled, saying, "He has gone in to find lodging with a sinful man."

Jer 16:8 – *"You shall not go into the house of feasting to sit with them, to eat and to drink."*

Given what he's been saying about not being anxious for the morrow and life being more than food and drink, maybe they thought that Jesus should be showing himself indifferent to room and board, and all that.

and will flog him, and *they* will kill *him* and [8]he will be raised up."[u]

    u *Mt 20:19*
     Mr 10:34
     Lu 18:32,33

CHAPTER 11

AND having entered, he passed through Jericho.[a]

    2   And behold, there was a man named Zacchaeus, and he was a chief tax collector, and he was rich.[b]

    3   And he was seeking to see who Jesus was, and he was not able to from the crowd, because he was small in stature.[c]

    4   And having run to the front, he climbed up onto a sycamore fig tree, that he might see him, for he was about to pass that *way*.[d]

    5   And as he came to the place, having looked up, Jesus said to him, "Zacchaeus, hurry, come down! For today it behooves me to stay in your house."[e]

    6   And having hurried, he came down and received him as a guest, rejoicing.[f]

    a *Mr 10:46*
     Lu 19:1
    b *Lu 19:2*
    c *Lu 19:3*
    d *Lu 19:4*
    e *Lu 19:5*
    f *Lu 19:6*

---

8 Certain later mss. add, *on the third day*

11   The parable of the lost sheep

g Jer 16:8
    Lu 19:7
h Lu 15:3
i Mt 18:12
    Lu 15:4
j Mt 18:13
    Lu 15:5
k Lu 15:6
l Jer 12:7
    Mt 9:36
    Mt 15:24
    Mt 18:11
    Lu 19:10
m Mt 20:29
n Mr 10:46
o Mt 20:30
    Mr 10:47
    Lu 18:37,38

7   And having seen *it*, they all grumbled, saying, "He has gone in to find lodging with a sinful man."[g]

8   But he told them this parable, saying,[h]

9   "What man of you, having a hundred sheep, and having lost one of them, leaves not the ninety-nine in the wilderness, and goes after that *one* which has been lost, until he finds it?[i]

10   "And having found it, he lays it on his shoulders, rejoicing.[j]

11   "And having come to the house, he calls together *his* friends and neighbors, saying to them, 'Rejoice with me, for I have found my sheep, the *one that* was lost!'[k]

12   "For the son of man has come to search for and save that which has been lost."[l]

13   And as he was going out from Jericho, and his disciples and a large crowd,[m] *the* son of Timaeus, Bartimaeus, a blind beggar, was seated beside the road.[n]

14   And having heard that it was Jesus of Nazareth, he began to cry out and to say, "Jesus, son of David, have mercy on me!"[o]

15   And many rebuked him, that he should keep

11:8-12 THE PARABLE OF THE LOST SHEEP

11:9,12 – "What man of you, having a hundred sheep, and having lost one of them, leaves not the ninety-nine in the wilderness, and goes after that *one* which has been lost, until he finds it? For the son of man has come to search for and save that which has been lost."

Jer 12:7 – *"I have forsaken my house. I have cast off my heritage. I have given the dearly beloved of my soul into the hand of her enemies."*

Mt 9:36 – *But when he saw the multitudes, he was moved with compassion for them, because they were harassed and scattered, like sheep without a shepherd.*

Mt 15:24 – *But he answered, "I wasn't sent to anyone but the lost sheep of the house of Israel."*

YHWH may have been Israel's 'shepherd' in earlier times, but the God of Israel had since forsaken his people. Jesus felt compassion for all the sheep that were lost, all those who had been cut off. It was they whom he sought to redeem, to free, that they might have life. They need only turn away from their enslavement to YHWH and welcome the kingdom of God that is ever within them.

11:13-19 THE BLIND BEGGAR RECOVERS HIS SIGHT

11:14 – And having heard that it was Jesus of Nazareth, he began to cry out and to say, "Jesus, son of David, have mercy on me!"

Since Joseph was of the house of David, as Matthew (1:1-16) and Luke (1:27, 2:4, 3:23-31) both relate, it would have been natural for a Jew to address Jesus as the 'son of David'. Nevertheless, although he was entitled to Joseph's name, Jesus was not of Joseph's seed, and was thus not a true scion of the house of David. Jesus obviously knew this – see below, IS THE MESSIAH DAVID'S SON?, page 241.

11:19 – And Jesus said to him, "Go your way, your faith has healed you." And immediately, he recovered sight, and he followed him on the way.

The wording is from Mark 10:52. In contrast, Matthew 23:34 reads, *'Jesus, being moved with compassion, touched their eyes; and immediately their eyes received their sight, and they followed him'*; while Luke 18:42,43 reads, *'Jesus said to him, "Receive your sight. Your faith has healed you." | Immediately he received his sight, and followed him, glorifying God. […]'*

In Mark's account there is absolutely no physical contact nor verbal command to account for the miracle taking place. According to Jesus, it is the beggar's faith that has brought about the healing. In like manner, YHWH is not to be credited, either – see above, THE AILING WOMAN IN THE CROWD, page 106.

11:20-25 JESUS ENTERS JERUSALEM ON A DONKEY

Jesus sent two disciples to fetch – let's see, a donkey? A colt? The colt of a donkey? I favour a donkey.

Ge 22:2,3 – *Yahwah said, "Now take your son, your only son, whom you love, even Isaac, and go into the land of Moriah. Offer him there as a burnt offering on one of the mountains which I will tell you of." | Abraham rose early in the morning, and saddled his donkey, and took two of his young men with him, and Isaac his son. He split the wood for the burnt offering, and rose up, and went to the place of which God had told him.*

Zec 9:9 – *Rejoice greatly, daughter of Zion! Shout, daughter of Jerusalem! Behold, your King comes to you! He is righteous, and having salvation; lowly, and riding on a donkey, even on a colt, the foal of a donkey.*

Again, with the donkey it seems that Jesus was making an allusion, first and foremost, to his being Isaac – the firstborn son who is brought to Mount Moriah to be sacrificed by his Father. Thanks to Zechariah's prophesy, the same symbolism also identifies him as being YHWH's

silent; but he cried out much more, *saying,* "Son of David, have mercy on me!"[p]

16   And having stopped, Jesus said, "Summon him." And they called the blind *man,* saying to him, "Take heart, rise up – he calls you!"[q]

17   And having thrown aside his cloak, *and* having risen up, he came to Jesus.[r]

18   And answering him, Jesus said, "What do you wish, that I should do to you?" But the blind man said to him, "Rabboni, that I might recover *my* sight."[s]

19   And Jesus said to him, "Go your way, your faith has healed you." And immediately, he recovered sight, and he followed him on the way.[t]

20   And when they approached Jerusalem and came to Bethphage, on the mount of Olives, then Jesus sent two disciples,[u]

21   saying to them, "Go into the village that is opposite you, and immediately, entering into it, you will find [1]a donkey tied *there*; and having untied *it,* bring it.[v]

22   "And if anyone says anything to you, you will

p Mt 20:31
   Mr 10:48
   Lu 18:39
q Mr 10:49
   Lu 18:40
r Mr 10:50
s Mt 20:32,33
   Mr 10:51
   Lu 18:41
t Mt 20:34
   Mr 10:52
   Lu 18:42,43
u Mt 21:1
   Mr 11:1
   Lu 19:29
v Mt 21:2
   Mr 11:2
   Lu 19:30

---

1 According to the best ancient mss.; certain later mss. read, *a young ass*; one late ms. reads, *a colt*

11 Jesus enters Jerusalem on a donkey   The fig tree

w Mt 21:3
   Mr 11:3
   Lu 19:31
x Mt 21:6
   Mr 11:4-6
   Lu 19:32-34
y Ge 22:2,3
   Zec 9:9
   Mt 21:7
   Mr 11:7
   Lu 19:35
   Jn 12:14
z Mt 21:17
   Mr 11:11
a Mt 21:18
   Mr 11:12
b Mt 21:19
   Mr 11:13
c Jer 8:13
d Mt 21:19
   Mr 11:14

say, 'The teacher has need of it', and immediately he will send it back here.'"[w]

23 And the disciples, having gone, and having done as Jesus had arranged with them,[x]

24 brought the donkey, and they placed their cloaks upon *its back*, and he sat on them.[y]

25 And he entered into Jerusalem, into the temple. And having looked all around on all things *there*, the hour being now late, he went out to Bethany, with the twelve.[z]

26 And the following day, when they had gone out from Bethany, he was hungry.[a]

27 And having seen from a distance a fig tree having leaves, he went *to see* therefore if he will find any *fruit* on it; and having come to it, he found nothing except leaves, for it was not the season for figs.[b]

28 And he answered, saying to it, "No longer in this age, may *there be* from you *even* one fruit to eat."[c] And his disciples heard *this*.[d]

29 And they came to Jerusalem, and having entered into the temple, he began to drive out those selling and those buying in the temple, and he overturned the tables of the moneychangers and the seats of those

Chosen One, his anointed Son and King – and therefore all the more precious and worthy of his Father's consideration.

Interestingly, Jesus' need for a donkey was anticipated – perhaps his hierophant friends from the high mountain had made arrangements in advance – and the two disciples (why are they not named? was Judas one of the two?) have no trouble collecting the ass.[67]

11:25 – And he entered into Jerusalem, into the temple. And having looked all around on all things *there*, the hour being now late, he went out to Bethany, with the twelve.

Whoops! I seem to have skipped over Jesus' triumphal entry, with the joyful throngs shouting *"Hosanna in the highest!"* and cutting branches off trees and spreading them on the road along with their cloaks.[68] Well, to be honest, I read all that as being a Christian addition…

11:26-28 THE FIG TREE

11:28 – And he answered, saying to it, "No longer in this age, may *there be* from you *even* one fruit to eat." […]

Jer 8:13 – *"I will utterly consume them, says Yahweh: no grapes shall be on the vine, nor figs on the fig tree, and the leaf shall fade; and the things that I have given them shall pass away from them."*

Remembering what the prophets had said with regard to fig trees in the time of YHWH's wrath, Jesus here expresses his wish for these very events to come about.

11:29-31 THE CLEANSING OF THE TEMPLE

11:29 – And they came to Jerusalem, and having entered into the temple, he began to drive out those selling and those buying in the

temple, and he overturned the tables of the moneychangers and the seats of those selling the doves.

Quite a ruckus. Its purpose? To attract attention. Jesus is unknown in Jerusalem, and if he's going to merit scrutiny by the temple authorities, he needs to draw attention to himself as a troublemaker.

The trick here, though, is to not go too far. Jesus picks an easy target – my guess is that no one was particularly fond of the animal merchants and the moneychangers, who may have profited handsomely from the annual pilgrimage festivals. Moreover, he justifies his disturbance of the peace by citing the Scriptures, which gives him an air of authority and duly impresses the crowds. No one arrests him for vandalism – neither there and then nor in the days that followed, when he returned to the temple to teach in public – so it must have been a very minor altercation indeed. This is likewise supported by the fact that the incident was not given as evidence in his trial before the Sanhedrin.

11:31 – And the chief priests and scribes heard of it, for all the crowd was thunderstruck by his teaching.

Jesus undoubtedly came to the attention of the temple authorities early on, for his teachings, we're told, were making quite an impression on the crowds. Understandably unsettled by the reports that were reaching their ears, the temple authorities took the precaution of sending observers to find out what the Galilean upstart was up to.

11:33-37 THE WITHERED FIG TREE

11:33,34 – And passing by early in the morning, they saw the fig tree. And having remembered, Simon said to him, "Rabbi, look, the fig tree which you cursed is withered."

Joe 1:12,15,19 – *The vine has dried up, and the fig tree withered [...]. | Alas for the day! For the day of Yahweh is at hand, and it will come as destruc-*

selling the doves.[e]

30 And he was teaching and was saying to them, "Has it not been written, MY HOUSE WILL BE CALLED A HOUSE OF PRAYER FOR ALL THE NATIONS.[f] But you have made it A DEN OF ROBBERS."[g]

31 And the chief priests and scribes heard of *it*, for all the crowd was thunderstruck by his teaching.[h]

32 And whenever evening came, he went forth out of the city.[i]

33 And passing by early in the morning, they saw the fig tree, withered from the roots *up*.[j]

34 And having remembered, Simon said to him, "Rabbi, look, the fig tree which you cursed is withered!"[k]

35 And answering, Jesus said to them, "Have *the* faith of God.[l]

36 "Truly I say to you, whoever might say to this mountain,[m] 'Be you raised up and be cast into the sea',[n] and might not waver in his heart, but might believe that what he says takes place, it will be *thus* for him.[o]

37 "On account of this, I say to you, all *things* whatsoever – and praying[p] – *for which* you ask, keep believing that you have received *them*, and it will be

e Mt 21:12
   Mr 11:15
f Isa 56:7
g Jer 7:11
   Mt 21:13
   Mr 11:17
   Lu 19:46
h Mr 11:18
i Mr 11:19
   Lu 21:37
j Mr 11:20
k Joe 1:12,15,19
   Mr 11:21
l Eze 28:16
   Mr 11:22
m Ps 48:1
   Ps 125:1
   Isa 56:7
   Eze 20:40
   Joe 3:17
   Zec 8:3
n Re 8:8
o Jer 51:25,26
   Mt 21:21
   Mr 11:23
p Mt 26:39
   Mr 14:35,36
   Lu 22:41,42

q *Mt 21:22*
   Mr 11:24
r *Lu 21:38*
s *Mt 21:23*
   Mr 11:27
   Lu 20:1
t *Isa 40:14*
   Mt 21:23
   Mr 11:28
   Lu 20:2
u *Mt 21:24*
   Mr 11:29
   Lu 20:3
v *Mt 21:25*
   Mr 11:30
   Lu 20:4
w *Mt 21:25*
   Mr 11:31
   Lu 20:5
x *De 18:15,18*
   Mt 21:26
   Mr 11:32
   Lu 20:6
y *Mt 21:27*
   Mr 11:33
   Lu 20:7,8
z *Lu 20:9*
a *Isa 45:23*
   Lu 19:12

so for you." q

38 And it came to pass on one of the days, as he was teaching the people in the temple, r that the chief priests were present, and the scribes with the elders. s

39 And they spoke, saying to him, "Tell us by what authority you are doing these things, or who is the *one* who gave this authority to you?" t

40 But answering, he said to them, "I also will request *of* you a statement, and you tell me — u

41 the baptism of John, was it from heaven or from men?" v

42 And they reasoned among themselves, saying, "If we say, 'From heaven', he will say, 'So then, why did you not believe him?' w

43 "But if we say, 'From men', all the people will stone us, for they are persuaded *that* John was a prophet." x

44 And having answered Jesus, they said, "We do not know." And Jesus said to them, "Neither *then will* I tell you by what authority I do these things." y

45 But he began to say this parable to the people: z "A certain well-born man went to a distant region to take a kingdom for himself and to return." a

tion from the Almighty. | Yahweh, I cry to you, for the fire has devoured the pastures of the wilderness, and the flame has burned all the trees of the field.

Has the tree withered overnight? Or was the impressionable Simon reading more into a few dry leaves than was really there? In the end, since we're echoing Scripture here, it makes no difference – the unlucky fig tree's fate is signed, sealed, delivered: no figs!

11:36 – "Truly I say to you, whoever might say to this mountain [...]"

Ps 48:1 – *Great is Yahweh, and greatly to be praised, in the city of our God, in his holy mountain.*

Ps 125:1 – *Those who trust in Yahweh are as Mount Zion, which can't be moved, but remains forever.*

Eze 20:40 – *"For in my holy mountain, in the mountain of the height of Israel," says the Lord Yahweh, "there shall all the house of Israel, all of them, serve me in the land. There I will accept them, and there I will require your offerings and the first fruits of your offerings, with all your holy things."*

Joe 3:17 – *"So you will know that I am Yahweh, your God, dwelling in Zion, my holy mountain. [...]"*

11:36 – " [...] 'Be you raised up and be cast into the sea', and might not waver in his heart, but might believe that what he says takes place, it will be *thus* for him."

Jer 51:25,26 – *"Behold, I am against you, destroying mountain," says Yahweh, "which destroys all the earth. I will stretch out my hand on you, roll you down from the rocks, and will make you a burned mountain. | They shall not take cornerstone from you, nor a stone for foundations; but you will be desolate for ever," says Yahweh.* [69]

Re 8:8 – *The second angel sounded, and something like a great burning mountain was thrown into the sea. [...]*

If you decide to overthrow YHWH, your tribal god, you will surely succeed. Just have faith, the faith of God:

Eze 28:16 – "[…] *Therefore I have cast you as profane out of God's mountain; and I have destroyed you, covering cherub, from the middle of the stones of fire.*"

11:38-44 THE CHIEF PRIESTS QUESTION JESUS

11:39 – And they spoke, saying to him, "Tell us by what authority you are doing these things, or who is the *one* who gave this authority to you?"

Isa 40:7 – *Who did he take counsel with, and who instructed him, and taught him in the path of justice, and taught him knowledge, and showed him the way of understanding?*

It was a reasonable question. With whom had Jesus studied? Whose teaching was he propounding? Was he speaking presumptuously?

Ever so clever, Jesus turns the tables and puts the chief priests a question, but they dare not answer. To which he replies, "Neither *then will* I tell you by what authority I do these things."

Ballsy guy, this Jesus fellow, standing up to the chief priests like that.

11:45-59 THE PARABLE OF THE MINAS

11:45,46 – But he began to say this parable to the people: "A certain well-born man went to a distant region to take a kingdom for himself and to return. Now having summoned ten of his slaves […] "

Le 25:55 – *"For to me the sons of Israel are slaves; they are my slaves whom I brought out of the land of Egypt. I am Yahweh your God."*

Nu 18:21 – *"To the children of Levi, behold, I have given all the tithe in Israel for an inheritance, in return for their service which they serve […]."*

In this parable, the 'well-born man' would be the God of Israel himself, and the slaves would be the priests, the 'children of Levi', who were named to serve him.

46 "Now having summoned ten of his slaves,[b] he gave to them ten [2]minas,[c] and said to them, 'Do business *with this* until I return.'[d]

47 "But his citizens hated him,[e] and they sent an emissary[f] after him, saying, 'We do not wish this *man* to reign over us.'[g]

48 "And it came to pass upon his return *from* having taken the kingdom, that he called the slaves to whom he gave the money to be summoned, so that he might know what each had gained by trading.[h]

49 "Now the first *one* came, saying, 'Master, your mina has gained ten minas *more*.'[i]

50 "And he said to him, 'Well done, good slave. Since you were faithful with very little, be you having authority over ten cities.'[j]

51 "And the second *one* came, saying, 'Your mina, Master, has made five minas *more*.'[k]

52 "And he said to this *one* also, 'And you, be over five cities.'[l]

53 "And another *one* came, saying, 'Master, I knew that you are a harsh man,[m] reaping where you did not

b Le 25:55
   Nu 18:21
   Isa 44:21
c Eze 45:12
d Mt 21:45
   Mt 25:14
   Lu 19:13
e De 9:24
   Ne 9:26
   Ps 50:17
   Isa 1:2
   Isa 30:9
f Mt 20:28
   Mr 10:45
g 1Sa 8:7
   Ps 78:56
   Pr 29:2
   Jer 2:29-31
   Jer 5:3-5,23
   Lu 19:14
h Mt 25:19
   Lu 19:15
i Mt 25:20
   Lu 19:16
j Nu 35:2-7
   Jos 21:1-42
   Mt 25:21
   Lu 19:17
k Mt 25:22
   Lu 19:18
l Mt 25:23
   Lu 19:19
m De 29:20
   Jos 24:19,20
   Isa 27:11
   Jer 13:14
   Jer 16:3,4
   Eze 7:9
   Eze 8:18

---

2 An ancient Near Eastern measure of weight, one mina was equivalent to 100 drachmæ, or about 88 denarii

11:47 – "But his citizens hated him […] "

De 9:24 – *You have been rebellious against Yahweh from the day that I knew you.*

Ne 9:26 – *"Nevertheless they were disobedient, and rebelled against you, cast your law behind their back, killed your prophets […]."*

Isa 1:2 – *Hear, heavens, and listen, earth; for Yahweh has spoken: "I have nourished and brought up children, and they have rebelled against me."*

It sure doesn't sound as if the Chosen People were so very happy.

11:47 – " […] and they sent an emissary after him, saying, 'We do not wish this *man* to reign over us.'"

1 Sa 8:7 – *Yahweh said to Samuel, "Listen to the voice of the people in all that they tell you; for they have not rejected you, but they have rejected me as the king over them."*

Pr 29:2 – *When the righteous thrive, the people rejoice; but when the wicked rule, the people groan.*

Jer 2:29-31 – *"Why will you contend with me? You all have transgressed against me," says Yahweh. | "I have struck your children in vain. They received no correction. […] | […] Why do my people say, 'We have broken loose. We will come to you no more?'"*

The Jews had tried to break loose from their bondage to Y HWH more than once before, but without success – for under the everlasting covenant, there was no provision for a Jew to go free. They could rebel, but Y HWH would not let them go.

11:53 – "And another *one* came, saying, 'Master, I knew that you are a harsh man […] "

This is Y HWH to a T:

De 29:20 – *Yahweh will not pardon him, but then Yahweh's anger and his jealousy will smoke against that man, and all the curse that is written in this book will fall on him, and Yahweh will blot out his name from under the sky.*

Jer 13:14 – *"I will dash them one against another, even the fathers and the sons together," says Yahweh: "I will not pity, nor spare, nor have compassion, that I should not destroy them."*

Jer 16:3,4 – *For Yahweh says [...] : | "They shall die grievous deaths: they shall not be lamented, neither shall they be buried; they shall be as dung on the surface of the ground; and they shall be consumed by the sword, and by famine; and their dead bodies shall be food for the birds of the sky, and for the animals of the earth."*

11:53 – "' [...] reaping where you did not sow [...] '"

Le 27:30 – *"All the tithe of the land, whether of the seed of the land or of the fruit of the trees, is Yahweh's. It is holy to Yahweh."*

Jn 4:37 – *"For in this the saying is true, 'One sows, and another reaps.'"*

11:54 – "'And having been terrified, *you* having gone away [...] '"

Ps 115:2 – *Why should the nations say, "Where is their God, now?"*

Jer 12:7 – *"I have forsaken my house. I have cast off my heritage. I have given the dearly beloved of my soul into the hand of her enemies."*

11:54-56 – "' [...] I hid your mina in the ground; see then, *you* have what is yours.' | He said to him, 'Out of your own mouth will I judge you, wicked slave! [...] why did you not give my money to the bank; and having come, I might have collected it with interest?'"

The certain 'well-born man' complains, but his position is hardly defendable, in view of what is dictated to the Jews under the Law:

De 23:19 – *You shall not lend on interest to your brother; interest of money, interest of food, interest of anything that is lent on interest.*

Ps 15:2,5 – *He who walks blamelessly [...] doesn't lend out his money for usury, nor take a bribe against the innocent. [...]*

Jer 22:17 – *"But your eyes and your heart are only for your covetousness, and for shedding innocent blood, for oppression, and for doing violence."*

11 The parable of the minas

n Ex 23:16,19
Le 27:30
De 26:10
Jn 4:37
o Ex 13:2,12
Ex 22:29,30
Mt 25:24
Lu 19:21
p Ps 42:3,9,10
Ps 71:10,11
Ps 115:2
Isa 49:14
Jer 12:7
La 5:20
q Mt 25:25
Lu 19:20
r Pr 28:15
Ho 13:7,8
s Mal 3:8
Mt 25:26
Lu 19:22
t Ex 22:25
De 23:19
Ps 15:2,5
Pr 28:16
Jer 17:11
Jer 22:17
Mt 25:27
Lu 19:23
u Mt 25:28
Lu 19:24
v Ps 74:23
w De 7:10
De 32:41
Ps 21:8
Isa 59:18
Isa 65:2,12,15
Isa 66:6
Jer 11:3,4,8,11
La 3:42,43
Lu 19:27
x Mt 21:45

sow,[n] and gathering together from where you did not scatter.[o]

54 "'And having been terrified, *you* having gone away,[p] I hid your mina in the ground; see then, *you* have what *is* yours.'[q]

55 "He said to him, 'Out of your own mouth will I judge you, wicked slave! You knew that I am a harsh man,[r] reaping where I have not sowed, and gathering together from where I have not scattered.[s]

56 "'And on account of this, why did you not give my money to the [3]bank; and having come, I might have collected it with interest?'[t]

57 "And to those standing there, he said, 'Take the mina away from him, and give *it to* the *one who* has the ten minas.[u]

58 "'Moreover, these enemies of mine[v] — the *ones who* have not been willing for me to reign over them — bring them here and slay them before me.'[w]

59 And having heard his parables, the chief priests realized that he was speaking about them.[x]

---

3 Lit., *table*; i.e., a money-changer's stall

11:57,58 – "And to those standing there, he said, 'Take the mina away from him, and give *it to* the *one who* has the ten minas. Moreover, these enemies of mine [...] '"

Ps 78:23 – *Don't forget the voice of your adversaries. The tumult of those who rise up against you ascends continually.*

11:58 – "' [...] the *ones who* have not been willing for me to reign over them – bring them here and slay them before me.'"

De 32:41 – "*[...] I will take vengeance on my adversaries, and will repay those who hate me.*"

Isa 65:2,12,15 – *"I have spread out my hands all day to a rebellious people, who walk in a way that is not good, after their own thoughts; | I will destine you to the sword, and you will all bow down to the slaughter [...] | [...] and the Lord Yahweh will kill you. [...]"*

Jer 11:3,4,8,11 – *"Say to them, Yahweh, the God of Israel says: 'Cursed is the man who doesn't hear the words of this covenant, | which I commanded your fathers [...],' saying, 'Obey my voice, and do them, according to all which I command you: so you shall be my people, and I will be your God.' | Yet they did not obey, nor turn their ear, but walked everyone in the stubbornness of their evil heart: therefore I brought on them all the words of this covenant, which I commanded them to do, but they didn't do them. | Therefore Yahweh says, 'Behold, I will bring evil on them, which they shall not be able to escape; and they shall cry to me, but I will not listen to them.'"*

11:59 – And having heard his parables, the chief priests realized that he was speaking about them.

As presented here, the parable of the minas may be read as a striking condemnation of the God of Israel. Likewise, the reference to giving cities to the good, faithful slaves clearly points to Aaron and the Levites, who were Yhwh's designated servants – cf. Exodus 28:1, Numbers 3:5-8 and Deuteronomy 10:8.

12

The foremost commandment

12:1-7 Is it lawful to pay tribute to Caesar?

12:1 – And having watched him closely, they sent spies, feigning themselves to be righteous, that they might take hold of him for *some* statement, so as to hand him over to the governor's rule and authority.

If Jesus had ruffled priestly feathers with his bold impertinence and his parable, then they may have rightly supposed that this maverick from Galilee would be stirring up trouble in the days to come. But the temple authorities had a Passover to put on: there were large crowds to cope with and logistics to oversee. Better to nip subversion in the bud. Trying to trap Jesus in a statement makes sense, since it would give the temple authorities a pretext to contain him before he got out of hand.

I question whether the Jews would have been under any specific obligation to involve the Romans, since it seems they enjoyed rather free rein in their religious affairs.[70] The idea of handing Jesus over to Pilate's authority may have only been for the priests' own convenience, so that they wouldn't have to deal with him during the Passover festivities.

12:3 – "Is it lawful for us to give tribute [...] "

Ezr 7:24 – *Also we inform you that it shall not be lawful to impose tribute, custom, or toll, on any of the priests, Levites, singers, gatekeepers, temple servants, or laborers of this house of God.*

CHAPTER 12

AND having watched him closely, they sent spies, feigning themselves to be righteous, that they might take hold of him *for some* statement, so as to hand him over to the governor's rule and authority.[a]

2   And they questioned him, saying, "Teacher, we know that you speak and teach rightly, and do not take sides, but teach the way of God on the basis of truth.[b]

3   "Is it lawful for us to give tribute[c] to Caesar, or not? Should we give, or not give?"[d]

4   But having perceived their craftiness,[e] he said to them,[f]

5   "Show me a [1]denarius. Whose likeness and inscription does it have?" And they said, "Caesar's."[g]

6   But he said to them, "Well then, give back the

a Mt 22:15,16
   Mr 12:13
   Lu 20:20
b Mt 22:16
   Mr 12:14
   Lu 20:21
c Ezr 7:24
   Ps 89:22
d Jer 27:1-8
   Jer 27:11-15
   Mt 22:17
   Mr 12:14
   Lu 20:22
e Mt 22:18
   Mr 12:15
f Lu 20:23
g Mt 22:19-21
   Mr 12:16
   Lu 20:24

---

1 A Roman coin, originally of silver; at that time, the denarius bore the portrait of Tiberius Caesar, whose reign lasted from 14 – 37 CE

h Ex 30:13
  Mt 17:24,25
  Mt 22:21
  Mr 12:17
  Lu 20:25
i Mt 22:22
  Mr 12:17
  Lu 20:26
j Mt 22:23
  Mr 12:18
  Lu 20:27
k De 25:5,6
  Mt 22:24
  Mr 12:19
  Lu 20:28
l Mt 22:25
  Mr 12:20
  Lu 20:29
m Mt 22:26
  Mr 12:21
  Lu 20:30
n Mt 22:26
  Mr 12:21,22
  Lu 20:31
o Mt 22:27
  Mr 12:22
  Lu 20:32

things of Caesar to Caesar, and the *things* of God to God."[h]

7   And they were not able to take hold of him in his discourse in the presence of the people; and having marveled at his answer, they were silent.[i]

8   But having come near, some of the Sadducees, who contend that there is no resurrection, questioned him,[j]

9   saying, "Teacher, Moses wrote to us, IF ANYONE'S BROTHER SHOULD DIE, having a wife, AND HE IS CHILDLESS, THAT HIS BROTHER SHOULD TAKE THE WIFE, AND SHOULD RAISE UP OFFSPRING TO HIS BROTHER.[k]

10   "Now then, there were seven brothers, and the first, having taken a wife, died childless.[l]

11   "And the second *took her as* wife, and he died childless.[m]

12   "And the third took her, and also in like manner the seven, *and they* did not leave behind children, and died.[n]

13   "And afterwards, the woman died.[o]

14   "Therefore, the wife, in the resurrection, whenever they rise up, *the* wife of which of them does

Although this decree was made by King Artaxerxes I some 500 years earlier, the Levite priests may have felt that it was good jurisprudence.

Ps 89:22 – *No enemy will tax him. No wicked man will oppress him.*

12:3 – " [...] to Caesar, or not? Should we give, or not give?"

It was a clever trap. His interlocutors must have felt sure that one way or another, Jesus couldn't help but compromise himself. If he publicly denounced the payment of tribute to Caesar, they'd be able to hand him over to the Romans and claim that he was being seditious. If however Jesus acquiesced to the practice,[71] he would alienate the crowds who were *'hanging on his words'* (Luke 19:48) – they resented being under Roman rule and they were longing for a messiah, not a quisling.

12:6 – But he said to them, "Well then, give back the *things* of Caesar to Caesar, and the *things* of God to God."

Ex 30:13 – *"They shall give this, everyone who passes over to those who are counted, half a shekel after the shekel of the sanctuary (the shekel is twenty gerahs); half a shekel for an offering to Yahweh."*

Mt 17:24,25 – *When they had come to Capernaum, those who collected the didrachma coins came to Peter, and said, "Doesn't your teacher pay the didrachma?" | He said, "Yes." When he came into the house, Jesus anticipated him, saying, "What do you think, Simon? From whom do the kings of the earth receive toll or tribute? From their children, or from strangers?"*

Jesus' answer is a gem...and we do well to note the parallel that it intimates: be it to Caesar or to YHWH, subjugated peoples pay tribute to their tyrant. YHWH, of course, wanted his half-shekel tribute in the coin of his realm, the shekel of the sanctuary[73] – that's what the money-changers were for.

12:8-21 THE SADDUCEES QUESTION JESUS

Ah, those mocking Sadducees, so sure of themselves! With its undertones of ribaldry, one fancies this question gave them a vicarious thrill.

Happily, and with remarkable assurance, Jesus cleverly counters the Sadducees' position with a scripturally-ironclad argument.

12:17 – "For neither are they still able to die, for they are equal to angels, and are sons of God, being sons of the resurrection."

Ge 28:12,13 – *He dreamed. Behold, a stairway set upon the earth, and its top reached to heaven. Behold, the angels of God ascending and descending on it. | Behold, Yahweh stood above it, and said, "I am Yahweh, the God of Abraham your father, and the God of Isaac. […]"*

Job 1:6 – *Now on the day when God's sons came to present themselves before Yahweh […].*

Using Jacob's ladder, the angels ascend from earth to heaven, where they are sons of YHWH.

12:18 – "But that the dead are raised up, Moses also showed at the bush, when the Lord called *Himself* THE GOD OF ABRAHAM, AND GOD OF ISAAC, AND GOD OF JACOB."

As is his wont, Jesus quotes directly from the Scriptures.

12:19 – "Now He is not the God of the dead, but of the living, for *they* all live *with* Him."

Ps 78:23-25 – *Yet he commanded the skies above, and opened the doors of heaven. | He rained down manna on them to eat, and gave them food from the sky. | Man ate the bread of angels. He sent them food to the full.*

That they're alive up there is shown by the bread, which is surely the bread of the living, not the dead.

she become? For the seven had her as wife."[p]

15 And Jesus said to them, "The sons of this age marry and are given in marriage.[q]

16 "But those having been deemed worthy to hit upon that age and the resurrection – the *resurrection* out from among the dead – neither marry nor are given in marriage.[r]

17 "For neither are they still able to die, for they are equal to angels, and are sons of God,[s] being sons of the resurrection.[t]

18 "But that the dead are raised up, Moses also showed at the bush, when the Lord called *Himself* THE GOD OF ABRAHAM, AND GOD OF ISAAC, AND GOD OF JACOB.[u]

19 "Now He is not the God of the dead, but of the living, for *they* all live *with* Him."[v]

20 But having answered, some of the scribes said *to him*, "Teacher, you have spoken well."[w]

21 Therefore the Jews were marveling, saying, "How does this man know written works, not having studied?"[x]

22 [2]But having drawn him aside privately, away

---

2 Most later mss. omit verses 22-26

p Mt 22:28
   Mr 12:23
   Lu 20:33
q Lu 20:34
r Mt 22:30
   Mr 12:25
   Lu 20:35
s Ge 28:12,13
   Gob 1:6
t Mt 22:30
   Mr 12:25
   Lu 20:36
u Ex 3:6,15
   Mt 22:31,32
   Mr 12:26
   Lu 20:37
v Ps 78:23-25
   Ps 148:2
   Mt 22:32
   Mr 12:27
   Lu 20:38
w Lu 20:39
x Jn 7:15

12:21 – Therefore the Jews were marveling, saying, "How does this man know written works, not having studied?"

Luke 20:39 takes us back to the question put to Jesus earlier by the chief priests: *"Tell us: by what authority do you do these things? Or who is giving you this authority?"* Everyone seems to have known that Jesus did not study the Scriptures under the authoritative guidance of a rabbi.

12:22-26 THE RESURRECTION OF THE DEAD

Oh, all right…I'm being naughty, here. These verses aren't from the Gospels. In the freewheeling spirit of *The Gospel of Jesus of Nazareth*, they were expunged when the need among Christians for Jesus to be resurrected gained the upper hand. Note, though, that it's only 'some of his disciples' who question him about this…Simon Peter and a few key others have perhaps wandered off to admire the temple.

12:22 – […] some of his disciples questioned him about this, saying, "When will this be, that the dead are raised up?"

The idea of bodily resurrection derives from the Scriptures, so it's no wonder that some of the disciples bought into it.

Ps 30:3 – *Yahweh, you have brought up my soul from Sheol. You have kept me alive, that I should not go down to the pit.*

Isa 26:19 – *Your dead shall live. My dead bodies shall arise. Awake and sing, you who dwell in the dust; for your dew is like the dew of herbs, and the earth will cast out the departed spirits.*

Eze 37:4-6 – *Again he said to me, "Prophesy over these bones, and tell them, 'You dry bones, hear Yahweh's word. | Thus says the Lord Yahweh to these bones: "Behold, I will cause breath to enter into you, and you shall live. | I will lay sinews on you, and will bring up flesh on you, and cover you with skin, and put breath in you, and you shall live; and you shall know that I am Yahweh."'"*

232

Eze 37:12-14 – *"Therefore prophesy, and tell them, 'Thus says the Lord Yahweh: "Behold, I will open your graves, and cause you to come up out of your graves, my people; and I will bring you into the land of Israel. | You shall know that I am Yahweh, when I have opened your graves, and caused you to come up out of your graves, my people. | I will put my Spirit in you, and you shall live, and I will place you in your own land: and you shall know that I, Yahweh, have spoken it and performed it," says Yahweh.'"*

Da 12:2 – *Many of those who sleep in the dust of the earth shall awake, some to everlasting life, and some to shame and everlasting contempt.*

12:23 – But having answered, he said *to them,* **"Do not be misled, for** HE WHO GOES DOWN TO SHEOL SHALL NOT COME UP,"

But the Scriptures are just as explicit about death being a one-way ticket to Sheol.

Job 7:9 – *"As the cloud is consumed and vanishes away, so he who goes down to Sheol shall come up no more."*

Ps 89:48 – *What man is he who shall live and not see death, who shall deliver his soul from the power of Sheol?*

12:24 – "NOR SHALL HE RETURN FROM THE LAND OF DARKNESS AND DEEP SHADOW."

2Sa 12:23 – *"But now he is dead, why should I fast? Can I bring him back again? I will go to him, but he will not return to me."*

Job 10:21,22 – *" […] I go where I shall not return from, to the land of darkness and of the shadow of death; | […]."*

Job 16:22 – *" […] I shall go the way of no return."*

Ps 78:39 – *He remembered that they were but flesh, a wind that passes away, and doesn't come again.*

Ps 103:15,16 – *As for man, his days are like grass. As a flower of the field, so he flourishes. | For the wind passes over it, and it is gone. Its place remembers it no more.*

12 The foremost commandment

y Ps 30:3
  Ps 44:25,26
  Isa 26:19
  Eze 37:4-6
  Eze 37:12-14
  Da 12:2
z Job 7:9
  Ps 89:48
a 2Sa 12:23
  Job 16:22
  Ps 78:39
  Ps 103:15,16
b Job 10:21,22
c Job 14:10-12
  Ps 89:48
  Isa 26:14
d Ge 3:19
  Ps 104:29
  Ec 3:19,20
  Ec 9:2-10
e Ge 1:2
  Ge 2:7
  Ps 104:30
  Ec 12:7
  Isa 42:5
f Mt 22:35,36
  Mr 12:28
g De 6:4
  Mr 12:29

from the crowd, some of his disciples questioned him about this, saying, "When will this be, *that* the dead are raised up?"[y]

23 But having answered, he said *to them*, "Do not be misled, for HE WHO GOES DOWN TO SHEOL SHALL NOT COME UP,[z]

24 NOR SHALL HE RETURN[a] FROM THE LAND OF DARKNESS AND DEEP SHADOW.[b]

25 "For the man who dies is not wakened from sleep, nor *is he* raised up;[c]

26 but all go to the same place,[d] and the spirit will return to God who gave *it*."[e]

27 And having come near, one of the [3]councilors — having heard them discussing *the matter* together *and* having seen that he answered them well — questioned him, "Which is the foremost commandment?"[f]

28 Jesus answered, "The foremost is, HEAR, O ISRAEL! THE LORD OUR GOD IS ONE;[g]

29 AND YOU WILL LOVE THE LORD YOUR GOD WITH ALL YOUR HEART, AND WITH ALL YOUR SOUL, AND WITH ALL YOUR MIND, AND WITH ALL YOUR

---

3 According to the best ancient mss.; subsequent mss. read, *scribes*; certain late mss. read, *lawyers*

12:25 – "For the man who dies is not wakened from sleep, nor *is he raised up;*"

Job 14:10-12 – *"But man dies, and is laid low. Yes, man gives up the spirit, and where is he? | As the waters fail from the sea, and the river wastes and dries up, | so man lies down and doesn't rise. Until the heavens are no more, they shall not awake, nor be roused out of their sleep."*

Ps 89:48 – *What man is he who shall live and not see death, who shall deliver his soul from the power of Sheol?*

Isa 26:14 – *The dead shall not live. The departed spirits shall not rise.* [...]

12:26 – "but all go to the same place, [...] "

Ge 3:19 – *"By the sweat of your face will you eat bread until you return to the ground, for out of it you were taken. For you are dust, and to dust you shall return."*

Ps 104:29 – *You hide your face: they are troubled; you take away their breath: they die, and return to the dust.*

Ec 3:19,20 – *For that which happens to the sons of men happens to animals. Even one thing happens to them. As the one dies, so the other dies. Yes, they have all one breath; and man has no advantage over the animals: for all is vanity. | All go to one place. All are from the dust, and all turn to dust again.*

Ec 9:2-10 – *All things come alike to all. There is one event to the righteous and to the wicked; to the good, to the clean, to the unclean, to him who sacrifices, and to him who doesn't sacrifice. As is the good, so is the sinner.* [...] *| For the living know that they will die, but the dead don't know anything,* [...] *| neither have they any more a portion forever in anything that is done under the sun. | Go your way – eat your bread with joy, and drink your wine with a merry heart;* [...] *| for there is no work, nor device, nor knowledge, nor wisdom, in Sheol, where you are going.*

12:26 – " […] **and the spirit will return to God who gave it."**

Ge 1:2 – *The earth was formless and empty. Darkness was on the surface of the deep and God's Spirit was hovering over the surface of the waters.*

Ge 2:7 – *God formed man from the dust of the ground, and breathed into his nostrils the breath of life; and man became a living soul.*

Ps 104:30 – *You send out your Spirit and they are created.* […]

Ec 12:7 – *And the dust returns to the earth as it was, and the spirit returns to God who gave it.*

Isa 42:5 – *Thus says God, he who created the heavens and stretched them out, he who spread out the earth and that which comes out of it, he who gives breath to its people and spirit to those who walk in it.*

12:27-34 THE FOREMOST COMMANDMENT

12:27 – And having come near, one of the councilors – having heard them discussing *the matter* **together** *and* **having seen that he answered them well – questioned him, "Which is the foremost commandment?"**

Mark says the man was one of the scribes; in Matthew, the term used is lawyer. Here, it is said that, in the best ancient manuscripts, he was one of the 'councilors'. Since Joseph of Arimathea was a councilor, my use of the term would suggest that it was perhaps Joseph who questioned Jesus on this occasion. Certainly, this is the sort of curiosity that a lawyer or councilor might show.

12:28,29 – Jesus answered, "The foremost is, HEAR, O ISRAEL! THE LORD OUR GOD IS ONE; AND YOU WILL LOVE THE LORD YOUR GOD WITH ALL YOUR HEART, AND WITH ALL YOUR SOUL, AND WITH ALL YOUR MIND, AND WITH ALL YOUR STRENGTH."

In Mark 12:30, 'mind' has been added to the commandment from Deuteronomy 6:4,5. Matthew 22:37 omits 'strength'. While the fault may lie with Jesus, we won't give the evangelists high marks for knowing their Torah – back to the yeshiva, you two!

The commandment to love YHWH with all one's heart and soul and strength is repeated time and again throughout the Torah; in stark contrast, the commandment to love one's neighbor appears but once.

12:30,31 – "This is the great and first commandment. But a second is like it: YOU WILL LOVE YOUR NEIGHBOR AS YOURSELF. There is not another commandment greater than these."

Le 19:18,33,34 – *"You shall not take vengeance, nor bear any grudge against the children of your people; but you shall love your neighbor as yourself. […] | If a stranger lives as a foreigner with you in your land, you shall not do him wrong. | The stranger who lives as a foreigner with you shall be to you as the native-born among you, and you shall love him as yourself; for you lived as foreigners in the land of Egypt. I am Yahweh your God."*

Le 25:23,55 – *"[…] For you are strangers and live as foreigners with me. | For to me the sons of Israel are slaves; they are my slaves whom I brought out of the land of Egypt. I am Yahweh your God."*

De 14:1 – *You are the sons of Yahweh your God. […]*

In other words, be it the children of your people or the foreigner – your sons or your slaves – you shall love them as you love yourself.

How does YHWH want to be loved? *You shall love Yahweh your God with all your heart, with all your soul, and with all your might.* (De 6:5)

It is interesting that YHWH should stipulate, *'You shall not take vengeance, nor bear any grudge against the children of your people…',* for on that score, Israel's god sure marches to a different drummer. But it doesn't matter. Jesus is here simply reducing the 613 commandments of the Law to one commandment, which he assimilates to a second. It is a compelling juxtaposition and, if rightly considered, tantamount to a challenge, for it effectively overthrows nearly the entire Law.

Agreeing with Jesus' view, the councilor opines that loving God and loving one's neighbor is *"greater than all the burnt offerings and sacrifices."* We must not underestimate the radicalism of such a statement. A perusal of the scriptural verses listed in margin note 'p' for verse 33 will serve to delineate the pervasive scope of sacrifice in the worship of YHWH.

12:34 – And Jesus, having seen that he answered wisely, said to him, "You are not far from the kingdom of God." […]

Ge 1:2 – *The earth was formless and empty. Darkness was on the surface of the deep and God's Spirit was hovering over the surface of the waters.*

Jn 3:5 – *Jesus answered, "Most certainly I tell you, unless one is born of water and spirit, he can't enter into God's Kingdom."*

Jn 4:24 – *"God is spirit, and those who worship him must worship in spirit and truth."*

In other words, Jesus perceives that his interlocutor is on the verge of grasping that all of the sacrifices dictated by YHWH are…irrelevant, and have nothing whatsoever to do with the spirit of God or his kingdom.[74]

It is from that point of awakening that it becomes possible for a man to step back, to free himself from the tenets of Judaism and to 'turn' – or 'turn around' – and enter into the kingdom of God, as in Matthew 18:3. This is why Jesus says to him, *"You are not far from the kingdom of God."*

12:34 – […] And none dared to question him any longer.

Is it any wonder? The legitimacy of sacrifice – inherent to Judaism, intrinsic to the worship of YHWH, indeed the temple's *raison d'être* – had just been called into question. The danger of apostasy was palpable.

STRENGTH.[h]

30 "This is the great and first commandment.[i]

31 "But a second is like it: YOU WILL LOVE YOUR NEIGHBOR AS YOURSELF.[j] There is not another commandment greater than these."[k]

32 And the [4]councilor said to him, "Right, Teacher, in accordance with truth have you said that HE IS ONE,[l] and THERE IS NO OTHER BESIDES HIM;[m]

33 and to LOVE HIM WITH ALL THE HEART, AND WITH ALL THE UNDERSTANDING, AND WITH ALL THE SOUL, AND WITH ALL THE STRENGTH,[n] and to LOVE ONE'S NEIGHBOR AS ONESELF,[o] is greater than all the burnt offerings and sacrifices."[p]

34 And Jesus, having seen that he answered wisely, said to him, "You are not far from the kingdom of God."[q] And none dared to question him any longer.[r]

35 Then *some* from the crowd, having heard these words, said, "This is truly the prophet."[s]

36 Others said, "This is the [5]messiah."[t] But the *others* said, "*Surely* not — for does the [5]messiah come out of Galilee?[u]

---

4 According to the best ancient mss.; subsequent mss. read, *scribe*; certain late
mss. read, *lawyer*
5 Gr., *messias*, for the Hebrew *mashiach*; certain later mss. read, *christos*

h De 6:5
   Mt 22:37
   Mr 12:30
i   Mt 22:38
j   Le 19:18,33,34
   Le 25:23,55
   De 14:1
   1Ch 29:15
k Mt 22:39,40
   Mr 12:31
l   De 6:4
m De 4:39
   Mr 12:32
n De 6:5
o Le 19:18
p Ex 13:2,12-15
   Ex 29:36-42
   Le 1:1-17
   Le 2:1-16
   Le 3:1-17
   Le 4:1-35
   Le 5:1-19
   Le 6:1-23
   Le 7:1-5
   Le 14:1-32
   Le 16:3-34
   Le 17:1-6
   Le 23:1-38
   Le 24:5-8
   Nu 28:1-31
   Nu 29:1-40
   2Ch 8:12,13
   Ezr 3:1-5
   Jer 33:18
   Eze 43:18-27
   Eze 45:13-25
   Eze 46:1-15
   Mal 1:11
   Mr 12:33
q Ge 1:2
   Mr 15:43
   Jn 3:5
   Jn 4:24
r   Mt 22:46
   Mr 12:34
   Lu 20:40
s Mt 21:11
   Jn 7:40
t   Jn 7:31
u   Jn 7:41

v 2Sa 7:5-16
   Ps 89:3,4
   Ps 89:20,26-29
   Ps 89:35,36
   Eze 34:23,24
   Eze 37:24,25
w 1Sa 17:12,15,58
   Mic 5:2
   Jn 7:42
x Jn 7:43
y Mt 22:42
   Mr 12:35
   Lu 20:41
   Lu 23:2
z Ps 110:1
   Mt 22:44
   Mr 12:36
   Lu 20:42,43
a Mt 22:45
   Mr 12:37
   Lu 20:44
b Mt 23:1
   Lu 20:45
c Mt 23:6,7
   Mr 12:38,39
   Lu 20:46
d Isa 3:14,15
   Isa 10:1,2

37 "Has not the Scripture said that the [6]messiah comes out from the offspring of David,[v] and from Bethlehem, the village where David was?"[w]

38 Then a dissension came about in the crowd on account of him.[x]

39 But he said to them, "Wherefore do they say *that* the [6]messiah is the son of David?[y]

40 "For David himself says in the book of Psalms,

'THE LORD SAID TO MY LORD,
"SIT AT MY RIGHT HAND,
UNTIL I MIGHT MAKE OF YOUR ENEMIES
A FOOTSTOOL FOR YOUR FEET.'"[z]

41 "So *if* David calls him LORD, then wherefore is he his son?" And the great crowd enjoyed listening to him.[a]

42 But *as* all the people were listening *to him*, he said to his disciples,[b]

43 "Beware of the scribes, who like to walk in long robes, and are fond of greetings in the marketplaces, and chief seats in the synagogues, and places of honor at the banquets;[c]

44 who wolf down the households of widows,[d] and

6 Gr., *messias*, for the Hebrew *mashiach*; certain later mss. read, *christos*

12:35-41 IS THE MESSIAH DAVID'S SON?

It is my opinion that Jesus had no genuine chromosomal connection to the House of David. The fact that people sometimes addressed him as the 'son of David' is immaterial – the epithet fits because Joseph was of the house of David (Lu 1:27, 2:4) and people viewed Jesus as his step-father's son…but that doesn't make him a *bona fide* descendant of the royal blood line. Besides, it wouldn't have taken long for the priests to learn that Jesus was 'the son of Mary'…which may be what prompted them to sneer, *"We were not born of sexual immorality."* (Jn 8:41)

Jesus knows that he lacks the proper pedigree for being a messiah – and it's not his aim anyway – but it serves his purpose to give the chief priests reason to *suspect* him of nonetheless claiming, if only indirectly, that he's the anointed king: it's a compelling charge that the priests will be able to use against him later, with the Romans.

Lu 23:2 – *They began to accuse him, saying, "We found this man perverting the nation, […] and saying that he himself is Christ, a king."*

Hence, Jesus skillfully wields the Scriptures to undercut the popular notion that the messiah must necessarily hail from David's line. Since Jesus is not by birth from the house of David, the chief priests understandably conclude from this discourse that he want the crowds to see him as having messianic sect-appeal.

12:42-45 JESUS LAMBASTES THE SCRIBES

12:43,44 – "Beware of the scribes […] who wolf down the households of widows […]."

Isa 3:14,15 – *Yahweh will enter into judgment with the elders of his people, and their leaders: "It is you who have eaten up the vineyard. The plunder of the poor is in your houses. | What do you mean that you crush my people, and grind the face of the poor?" says the Lord, Yahweh of Armies.*

Isa 10:1,2 – *Woe to those who decree unrighteous decrees, and to the writers who write oppressive decrees; | to deprive the needy from justice, and to rob the poor among my people of their rights, that widows may be their plunder, and that they may make the fatherless their prey!*

By aspersing the scribes' integrity, Jesus not only evokes a prophesy in passing, but he gets their goats as well. Wounded in their pride, these specialists of the law will now hardly be inclined to lift a finger in Jesus' defense when he appears before the Sanhedrin.

12:46-54 THE CHIEF PRIESTS AND THE PHARISEES SEEK TO ARREST JESUS

Enough was enough. This Jesus fellow was clearly seducing the crowds and leading them astray with his unorthodox public discourse. He was a menace to order and needed to be checked. Yet the attendants sent to lay hold of him come back empty-handed. Their excuse? *"No man ever spoke like this."*

Nicodemus' remark shows that at least one member of the Sanhedrin was phlegmatically evenhanded in his approach to dealing with the situation – *"Our Law does not judge the man, before it might hear from him first, and might know what he does."*

His peers remind him that the Scriptures make no mention of any prophet arising out of Galilee. We do well to note that if the priests only address the question of his being a prophet and not the messiah, it is for good reason: in those times, every Jew worth his scriptural salt knew that the messiah wouldn't be some yokel from the Galilean hinterlands, but a descendant of the House of David, born in Bethlehem.

pray at length to shine before *others*. These will receive judgment exceedingly."[e]

45 And there was much muttering about him among the crowds, for some said, "He is good"; but others said, "But no – he leads the people astray!"[f]

46 The Pharisees heard the crowd murmuring these things about him, and the chief priests and the Pharisees sent attendants, that they might lay hold of him.[g]

47 Now some of them were willing to lay hold of him, but no one laid hands on him.[h]

48 The attendants therefore came to the chief priests and the Pharisees, and they said to them, "Why did you not bring him?"[i]

49 The attendants answered, "No man ever spoke like this."[j]

50 Then the Pharisees answered, "Have you not also been led astray?[k]

51 "No one of the rulers has believed in him, nor of the Pharisees.[l]

52 "But this crowd, which does not know the Law, is accursed."[m]

53 Nicodemus said to them, "Our Law does not

e Mr 12:40
   Lu 20:47
f Jn 7:12
   Jn 10:20
g Jn 7:32
h Jn 7:44
i Jn 7:45
j Jn 7:46
k Jn 7:47
l Jn 7:48
m Jn 7:49

12, 13   The poor widow's gift to the treasury

n *Jn 7:50,51*
o *Jn 7:52*

judge the man, before it might hear from him first, and might know what he does."[n]

54 And they answered, saying to him, "Are you not also from Galilee? Search and see, because a prophet out of Galilee does not arise."[o]

CHAPTER 13

a *Mr 12:41*
   Lu 21:1
b *De 15:4*
   Mr 12:42
   Lu 21:2
c *Mr 12:43*
   Lu 21:3
d *Job 30:25*
   Mr 12:44
   Lu 21:4

AND having sat down opposite the treasury, he contemplated how the crowd cast money into the treasury; and many rich people were casting *in* much.[a]

2   And he saw a certain poor widow casting *in* two [1]small coins;[b]

3   and he said, "Truly I say to you, that this poor widow has cast *in* more than all.[c]

4   "For these all cast *in* gifts from out of their abundance – but she, from out of her penury, did cast *in* all *that* she had to live on."[d]

5   And as he was going forth out from the temple,

---

1 Gr., *lepta*; the *leptos* was a small copper or bronze coin

13

The tribulations to come

13:1-4 THE POOR WIDOW'S GIFT TO THE TREASURY

13:2 – And he saw a certain poor widow [...]

De 15:4 – *However there shall be no poor with you, for Yahweh will surely bless you* [...].

13:4 – " [...] she, from out of her penury, did cast *in* all *that* she had to live on."

Job 30:25 – *Didn't I weep for him who was in trouble? Wasn't my soul grieved for the needy?*

13:5,6 NOT A STONE UPON STONE SHALL BE LEFT

13:6 – And Jesus said to him, "Do you see these great buildings? Not a stone upon stone shall be left here, which shall not be thrown down."

Jer 51:25,26 – *"Behold, I am against you, destroying mountain," says Yahweh, "which destroys all the earth. I will stretch out my hand on you, roll you down from the rocks, and will make you a burned mountain.* | [...]"

The disciple admires the temple's splendor, but Jesus foresees a time when all the stones will be thrown down. In what follows, we do well to give full weight to the many ramifications that Jesus seems to have anticipated.

13:7-18 THE TRIBULATIONS TO COME

13:7 – And they questioned him, saying, "Teacher, how long therefore *until* these things, and what will be the sign when these things are about to happen?"

As we will see in just a moment, Jesus had every reason to expect the worst. Given the words of the prophets and all that had happened time and again in Israel's past, YHWH wasn't the sort of god who was going to let apostasy – much less open rebellion – go unpunished.

13:8 – But he said, "Take heed, lest you be led astray. For many will come in my name, saying 'I AM', and they will lead many astray."

Ex 3:14 – *God said to Moses, "I AM WHO I AM," and he said, "You shall tell the children of Israel this: 'I AM has sent me to you.'"*

Ex 20:7 – *"You shall not take the name of Yahweh your God in vain, for Yahweh will not hold him guiltless who takes his name in vain."*

Well intentioned but inaccurate translations of Mark and Luke aside, Jesus isn't foreseeing false Christs here, but rather copycat blasphemers. Claiming affiliation (they come in his name), these misguided glory seekers will be going wildly about saying 'I AM! I AM!', as if the mere act of blaspheming the Sacred Name – as they will have heard Jesus did before the Sanhedrin – were the key to triggering Armageddon.

But those who clamour 'I AM! I AM!' will have misunderstood. The blasphemy itself is of no consequence; rather, as we will see, it is by his sacrificial death on the cross and the rite of symbolically eating his flesh and blood that Jesus thinks to provoke YHWH's cataclysmic return.

Matthew 24:5, of course, reads very differently: *"For many will come in my name, saying, 'I am the Christ,' and will lead many astray."*

This is patently illogical. If Jesus says, *"many will come in my name"*,[75] then surely those many are not coming in his name to claim that they are the Christ: for that sort of endorsement, they would announce that

one of his disciples said to him, "Teacher, behold — such stones, and such buildings!"[e]

6   And Jesus said to him, "Do you see these great buildings? Not a stone upon stone shall be left here, which shall not be thrown down."[f]

7   And they questioned him, saying, "Teacher, how long therefore *until* these things, and what will be the sign when these things are about to happen?"[g]

8   But he said, "Take heed, lest you be led astray. For many will come in my name, saying 'I AM',[2][h] and they will lead many astray.[i]

9   "But when you might hear *of* battles and rumors of battles, do not be unsettled, for this must come to pass. However, it is not yet the end.[j]

10   "For nation will rise up against nation, and kingdom against kingdom;[k] there will be earthquakes in places *everywhere*;[l] there will be famines.[m]

11   "And a brother will hand over a brother to death, and a father *his* child, and children will rise up against parents, and will put them to death.[n]

12   "And you will be hated by all on account of my name, but the *one* having remained behind to the end,

---

2 Certain later mss. add, *the Christ*

e   Ezr 1:2-4
    Ezr 6:3-16
    Mt 24:1
    Mr 13:1
    Lu 21:5
f   1Ki 9:6-9
    Jer 51:25,26
    Mt 24:2
    Mr 13:2
    Lu 21:6
g   Isa 26:21
    Mt 24:3
    Mr 13:4
    Lu 21:7
h   Ex 3:14
    Ex 6:2,3
    Ex 20:7
i   Mt 24:4,5
    Mr 13:5,6
    Lu 21:8
j   Eze 7:2-4
    Mt 24:6
    Mr 13:7
    Lu 21:9
k   De 28:48,49
    2Ch 15:6
    Jer 5:15
    Joe 3:9,11,12
    Am 6:14
l   Jer 49:21
    Joe 2:1,10
    Am 8:8
k   De 28:53
    Eze 5:16,17
    Eze 7:15
m   Mt 24:7
    Mr 13:8
    Lu 21:10,11
n   Ex 32:25-29
    De 28:54,56
    Isa 9:19
    Mic 7:2,6
    Mr 13:12

they come in the name of someone who was known for heralding the coming of the messiah – John the Baptist, for example.[76] Or they would bypass credentials altogether, and simply declare themselves 'Christ' on their own authority.

It seems, therefore, that Matthew has added 'the Christ' to his source material, or that his source was corrupted before it reached him.

13:11 – "And a brother will hand over a brother to death, and a father _his_ child, and children will rise up against parents, and will put them to death."

This sort of internecine massacre had already happened before, at YHWH's behest:

Ex 32:25-29 – [...] | _He said to them, "Yahweh says, the God of Israel, 'Every man [...] kill his brother [...].'" | The sons of Levi did according to the word of Moses: and there fell of the people that day about three thousand men. | Moses said, "Consecrate yourselves today to Yahweh, yes, every man against his son, and against his brother [...]."_

13:13 – "But when you might see Jerusalem being encircled by armies, then know that her desolation has drawn near."

Jer 9:11 – _"I will make Jerusalem heaps, a dwelling place of jackals. I will make the cities of Judah a desolation, without inhabitant."_

Joe 2:1-11 – _Blow the trumpet in Zion, and sound an alarm in my holy mountain! [...] | Yahweh thunders his voice before his army; for his forces are very great [...]._

Some years later, when Titus and his Roman legions sacked Jerusalem in 70 CE, it looked as if the foretold destruction had indeed come true.

13:14,15 – "Then let those in Judea flee to the mountains, and let those in the midst of her depart, and do not let those in the country-side enter into her; because these are days of vengeance, [...]"

THE TRIBULATIONS TO COME

De 32:35,41 – *"Vengeance is mine, and recompense, at the time when their foot slides; for the day of their calamity is at hand. Their doom rushes at them. | If I sharpen my glittering sword, my hand grasps it in judgment; I will take vengeance on my adversaries, and will repay those who hate me."*

Pr 6:34 – *For jealousy arouses the fury of the husband. He won't spare in the day of vengeance.*

Hell hath no fury like a YHWH scorned.

13:15 – " […] and judgment […] "

Eze 5:8,15 – *"Therefore thus says the Lord Yahweh: 'Behold, I, even I, am against you; and I will execute judgments among you in the sight of the nations. | […] I shall execute judgments on you in anger and in wrath, and in wrathful rebukes – I, Yahweh, have spoken it.'"*

Eze 16:38 – *"I will judge you, as women who break wedlock and shed blood are judged; and I will bring on you the blood of wrath and jealousy."*

In both word and deed, Jesus teaches his followers to *'Judge not.'*

YHWH, in contrast, ruthlessly judges *'in anger and wrath'*.

13:19 – "for there will be great distress upon the land, and wrath upon this people."

Isa 10:23 – *For the Lord, Yahweh of Armies, will make a full end, and that determined, throughout all the earth.*

Isa 13:9,15,16 – *Behold, the day of Yahweh comes, cruel, with wrath and fierce anger; to make the land a desolation. […] | Everyone who is found will be thrust through. Everyone who is captured will fall by the sword. | Their infants also will be dashed in pieces before their eyes. Their houses will be ransacked, and their wives raped.*

Jer 11:11 – *"[…] and they shall cry to me, but I will not listen to them."*

As the Scriptures eloquently attest, there is no upper limit to YHWH's vengeance upon his people. But there is a hint here that those who are not found will escape. Hence Jesus' good advice to flee…

13   "If anyone says, 'Behold, the messiah!', do not believe it"

o *Mt 24:13*
   Mr 13:13
   Lu 17:23
   Lu 21:17,19
p *Jer 9:11*
   Jer 19:8
   Joe 1:15
   Joe 2:1-11
   Lu 21:20
q *Ge 19:17*
   Mt 24:16
   Mr 13:14
r *Lu 21:21*
s *De 32:35,41*
   Pr 6:34
   Na 1:2,6
t *Eze 5:8,15*
   Eze 11:10
   Eze 14:21
   Eze 16:38
u *Mt 5:17*
   Lu 18:31
   Lu 21:22
v *Mt 24:17*
   Mr 13:15
   Lu 17:31
w *Mt 24:18*
   Mr 13:16
   Lu 17:31
x *Mt 24:19*
   Mr 13:17
y *Isa 10:23*
   Isa 13:9,15,16
   Jer 11:11
   Eze 7:2-27
   Eze 21:31,32
   Eze 33:20,27-29
   Lu 21:23
z *Mr 13:21*
   Mr 16:9-13
   Mr 16:14
   Lu 24:32-35
   Jn 20:18,24,25
   Jn 20:30,31
   Jn 21:1,14
   Act 1:3
   Act 17:2,3
a *Mr 13:22*
   Act 2:38-43
   Act 5:12-16
   Act 6:7,8

he will be saved.[o]

13 "But when you might see Jerusalem being encircled by [3]armies, then know that her desolation has drawn near.[p]

14 "Then let those in Judea flee to the mountains,[q] and let those in the midst of her depart, and do not let those in the countryside enter into her;[r]

15 because these are days of vengeance,[s] and judgment,[t] that all things which have been written may be fulfilled.[u]

16 "But the *one* upon the housetop, let him not come down, nor go in to take anything out of his house;[v]

17 and the *one* in the field, let him not turn back to the things behind, to pick up his clothing.[w]

18 "But woe to those who are pregnant, and to those who are nursing in those days;[x]

19 for there will be great distress upon the land, and wrath *upon* this people.[y]

20 "And then, if anyone says to you, 'Behold, here is the [4]messiah! Behold, there!', do not believe it.[z]

---

3 Or, *hosts*; certain later mss. read, *encamped armies*
4 Gr., *messias*, for the Hebrew *mashiach*; certain later mss. read, *christos*

13:20-22 TAKE HEED OF FALSE PROPHETS

13:20 – "And then, if anyone says to you, 'Behold, here is the messiah! Behold, there!', do not believe it."

Well, we can give the disciples some credit – at the beginning, at least, they did heed Jesus' injunction:

Mr 16:9-13 – *Now when he had risen early on the first day of the week, he appeared first to Mary Magdalene […]. | She went and told those who had been with him […]. | When they heard that he was alive, and had been seen by her, they disbelieved. | After these things he was revealed in another form to two of them, as they walked, on their way into the country. | They went away and told it to the rest. They didn't believe them, either.*

But it wasn't long before a different tune was being sung…even by the resurrected Jesus himself.

Mr 16:14 – *Afterward he was revealed to the eleven themselves as they sat at the table, and he rebuked them for their unbelief and hardness of heart, because they didn't believe those who had seen him after he had risen.*

13:21 – "For false *messiahs* and false prophets will rise up, and will give signs and wonders, and lead many astray."

Not only the apostles generally (Acts 2:43, 5:12), but Peter, Stephen, Philip and Paul are all cited as performing attesting miracles. *The Gospel of Jesus of Nazareth* holds that these men, utterly misconstruing Jesus' intent, declared him to be the messiah and led many astray with their proselytising in favour of the newly emerging Jesus-movement.

13:22 – "But you, take heed, *for* I have told you all things in advance."

Mt 16:16,20 – *Simon Peter answered, "You are the Christ, the Son of the living God." | Then he commanded the disciples that they should tell no one that he was Jesus the Christ.*

Jesus' admonitions don't seem to have registered with Simon Peter, who went about performing attesting works of his own and proclaiming Jesus to be the messiah – see Acts 3:1-26 for one such episode.

1Jn 2:4 – *One who says, "I know him," and doesn't keep his commandments, is a liar, and the truth isn't in him.*

13:23-25 YOUR REDEMPTION DRAWS NEAR

13:25 – "But *when* these things are beginning to happen, then straighten yourselves and lift up your heads […] "

De 7:10 – *[Yahweh] repays those who hate him to their face. […]*

Ps 83:2 – *For, behold, […] those who hate you have lifted up their heads.*

Those who lift up their heads are those who hate Yhwh.

Isa 63:10 – *[…] Therefore he turned and became their enemy, and he himself fought against them.*

La 2:4,5 – *[…] He has bent his bow like an enemy, he has stood with his right hand as an adversary […] | The Lord has become as an enemy, he has swallowed up Israel […]*

13:25 – " […] because your redemption draws near."

Through his death, though, Jesus will redeem them from the hand of their enemy.

Ps 106:10 – *He saved them from the hand of him who hated them, and redeemed them from the hand of the enemy.*

Mr 10:45 – *"For the Son of Man also came not to be served, but to serve, and to give his life as a ransom for many."*

Jn 8:33 – *They answered him, "We are Abraham's offspring, and have never been in bondage to anyone. How do you say, 'You will be made free'?"*

Jn 8:35,36 – *"A slave does not live in the house forever. A son remains forever. If therefore the Son makes you free, you will be free indeed."*

21 "For false *messiahs* and false prophets will rise up, and will give signs and wonders, and lead many astray.[a]

22 "But you, take heed, *for* I have told you all things in advance.[b]

23 "But in those days, after that tribulation, THE SUN WILL BE DARKENED, AND THE MOON WILL NOT GIVE ITS LIGHT,[c]

24 AND THE STARS WILL FALL FROM HEAVEN, AND THE POWERS OF THE HEAVENS WILL BE SHAKEN.[d]

25 "But *when* these things are beginning to happen, then straighten yourselves and lift up your heads,[e] because your redemption draws near."[f]

26 And he told them a parable, *saying*, "Behold the fig tree, and all of the trees – already when they put forth buds, looking, you yourselves realize that the summer is already near.[g]

27 "And so, when you see these things coming to pass, realize that He[h] is near, at the doors.[i]

28 "Truly I say to you, that this generation shall not pass away, until all these things shall have happened.[j]

29 "Heaven and earth will pass away, but in no wise will my words pass away.[k]

a Act 8:6,7,13
Act 9:32-42
Act 14:1,3,8-10
Act 19:1-8,11,12
2Co 12:12
b Mt 16:16,20
Mr 13:23
1Jn 2:4
c Isa 13:10
Eze 32:7,8
Joe 2:10,30,31
Joe 3:14,15
Am 5:18,20
Mt 24:29
Mr 13:24
d Isa 13:13
Hag 2:6,21
Mt 24:29
Mr 13:25
Lu 21:25,26
e De 7:10
Ps 83:2
Isa 63:10
La 2:4,5
f Ps 106:10
Mt 20:28
Mr 10:45
Lu 21:28
Jn 8:33
Jn 8:35,36
g Mt 24:32
Mr 13:28
Lu 21:29,30
h Nu 16:20,21,33
Lu 12:5
Jn 14:30
i 1Ki 6:31,32
Eze 43:4-9
Mt 24:33
Mr 13:29
Lu 21:31
j Jer 16:9
Eze 12:25,28
Mt 24:34
Mr 13:30
Lu 21:32
k Mt 5:18
Mt 24:35
Mr 13:31
Lu 21:33

13:26,27   THE PARABLE OF THE FIG TREE

13:27 – "And so, when you see these things coming to pass, realize that He is near [...] "

Nu 16:20,21,33 – *Yahweh spoke to Moses and to Aaron, saying, |"Separate yourselves from among this congregation, that I may consume them in a moment!" | So they, and all that belonged to them went down alive into Sheol. The earth closed on them, and they perished from among the assembly.*

Lu 12:5 – *"But I will warn you whom you should fear. Fear him, who after he has killed, has power to cast into Gehenna. Yes, I tell you, fear him."*

Jn 14:30 – *"I will no more speak much with you, for the ruler of the world comes, and he has nothing in me."*

The one who is near, even at the doors, is the one whom the disciples should fear – the one who *"has power to cast into Gehenna."* That 'one' is none other than YHWH.

13:28-37   "BE VIGILANT!"

13:28 – "Truly I say to you, that this generation shall not pass away, until all these things shall have happened."

Jer 16:9 – *For Yahweh of Armies, the God of Israel says: "Behold, I will cause to cease out of this place, before your eyes and in your days, the voice of mirth and the voice of gladness, the voice of the bridegroom and the voice of the bride."*

Eze 12:25,28 – *"""For I am Yahweh. I will speak, and the word that I speak will be performed. It will be no more deferred; for in your days, rebellious house, I will speak the word, and will perform it," says the Lord Yahweh. | Therefore tell them, 'Thus says the Lord Yahweh: "None of my words shall be deferred any more, but the word which I speak will be performed," says the Lord Yahweh.'"*

13:31,32– "But attend to yourselves, lest when your hearts be burdened with hangover and drunkenness, that day should come upon you suddenly – for like a snare it will come upon all those sitting upon the face of the earth."

Isa 24:17 – *Fear, the pit, and the snare, are on you who inhabit the earth.*

Hangover and drunkenness? I've a notion that Jesus and his disciples drank a lot more wine than we give them credit for.

13:34 – "*It is* like a man who went away from his people [...] "

Isa 49:14 – *But Zion said, "Yahweh has forsaken me, and the Lord has forgotten me."*

13:34 – " [...] and leaving his house, he charged his slaves with authority, to each one his work [...] "

Le 25:55 – *"For to me the sons of Israel are slaves; they are my slaves whom I brought out of the land of Egypt. I am Yahweh your God."*

13:34 – " [...] and commanded his doorkeepers to be vigilant."

Eze 10:19 – *The cherubim [...] stood at the door of the east gate of Yahweh's house; and the glory of the God of Israel was over them above.*

13:35 – "Therefore, be vigilant! For you do not know when the master of the house is coming [...] "

Jn 14:30 – *"I will no more speak much with you, for the ruler of the world comes, and he has nothing in me."*

13:37 – "But what I say to you, I say to all: be vigilant!"

Jesus obviously expected the worst – the end was going to be a trial to beat all trials. But as the prophets had made clear, freedom from YHWH wasn't going to come without a showdown.

13   "Be vigilant!"

l *Mt 24:35*
   Mr 13:31
m *Lu 21:34*
n *Isa 24:17*
   Zep 1:2,3,18
   Lu 21:35
o *Mt 24:42*
   Mr 13:33
p *Ps 13:1*
   Ps 22:2
   Ps 42:3
   Ps 71:10,11
   Ps 115:2
   Isa 49:14
   Jer 12:7
q *Le 25:55*
   Isa 44:21
r *Ge 3:24*
   Ex 25:18-20
   Eze 10:19
s *Mr 13:34*
t *2Ch 2:4,5*
   2Ch 7:1,2
   Eze 43:4,5
u *Jn 14:30*
v *Mr 13:35*
w *Mr 13:36*
x *Mr 13:37*
y *Ex 12:1-20,24*
   Le 23:5-7
   Nu 9:2,3
   De 16:1,12
z *Lu 22:1*

30 "But with regard to that day and hour, no one knows.[l]

31 [5]["But attend to yourselves, lest when your hearts be burdened with hangover and drunkenness, that day should come upon you suddenly – [m]

32 for like a snare it will come upon all those sitting upon the face of the earth.[n]]

33 "Look! Be awake! For you do not know on what sort of day your master comes.[o]

34 "*It is* like a man who went away from his people,[p] and leaving his house, he charged his slaves[q] with authority, to each one his work, and commanded his doorkeepers[r] to be vigilant.[s]

35 "Therefore, be vigilant! For you do not know when the master of the house[t] is coming[u] – whether in the evening, or at midnight, or at cockcrow, or in the morning –[v]

36 lest, having come suddenly, he might find you sleeping.[w]

37 "But what I say to you, I say to all: be vigilant!"[x]

38 Now the feast of Unleavened *Bread*[y] was approaching.[z]

---

5 Verses 31 and 32 are not found in the best ancient mss.

13:38-41 CAIAPHAS

13:38 – Now the feast of Unleavened *Bread* was approaching.

De 16:1,12 – *Observe the month of Abib, and keep the Passover to Yahweh your God; for in the month of Abib, Yahweh your God brought you out of Egypt by night. | You shall remember that you were a slave in Egypt. [...]*

That year, as every year, the Feast of Unleavened Bread would have begun as the sun was setting on the 14th of Nisan:

Ex 12:18 – *In the first month, on the fourteenth day of the month at evening, you shall eat unleavened bread, until the twenty first day of the month at evening.*

The paschal lamb would have been sacrificed 'at evening' on that day:

Ex 12:3,6 – *"Speak to all the congregation of Israel, saying, 'On the tenth day of this month, they shall take to them every man a lamb, according to their fathers' houses, a lamb for a household; | and you shall keep it until the fourteenth day of the same month; and the whole assembly of the congregation of Israel shall kill it at evening.'"*

In practice, 'The animal was slain on the eve of the Passover, on the afternoon of the 14th of Nisan, after the Tamid sacrifice had been killed, i.e., at three o'clock, or, in case the eve of the Passover fell on Friday, at two.'[77]

A holy assembly was convoked on the 15th of Nisan, which, properly speaking, is the first day of the Passover:

Ex 12:16 – *"In the first day there shall be to you a holy convocation. [...]"*

This is explained again in Leviticus:

Le 23:5-7 – *"In the first month, on the fourteenth day of the month in the evening, is Yahweh's Passover. | On the fifteenth day of the same month is the feast of unleavened bread to Yahweh. Seven days you shall eat unleavened bread. | In the first day you shall have a holy convocation. You shall do no regular work."*

Ultimately, there is little point arguing about the date of that year's Passover, for the Gospels do not concur and so support contradictory conclusions. It is my view, though, that Jesus intended for his death to be intimately associated with the symbolic meaning of the Passover, and so would have wished for his crucifixion to coincide as closely as possible with the sacrificing of the paschal lambs. For this reason, I have chosen to follow John's account, which states that *'They led Jesus therefore from Caiaphas into the Praetorium. It was early, and they themselves didn't enter into the Praetorium, that they might not be defiled, but might eat the Passover'* (Jn 18:28); and likewise, *'Therefore the Jews, because it was the Preparation Day, so that the bodies wouldn't remain on the cross on the Sabbath – for that Sabbath was a special one'* [...]. (Jn 19:31)

In John, then, the day that Jesus was crucified was a Preparation Day – i.e., the day before the Sabbath. This means that the lambs would have been sacrificed on a Friday afternoon, and the first day of the Feast of Unleavened Bread, with its holy convocation, would have fallen that year on the Sabbath, making it a 'high' or great day.[78]

With his unorthodox teachings and calculated provocations, Jesus has given the priests more than enough cause for concern and certainly sufficient reason to seek to restrain him. It is time now to set in motion the events that will lead to his being crucified on the 14th of Nisan, that he might yield up his spirit at the precise moment in the afternoon when the paschal lambs were being sacrificed in the temple.

13:41 – but they were saying, "Not during the feast, so that there not be an uproar among the people."

With the Passover due to begin in four or five days time, the temple authorities would have understandably hoped to be able to detain him beforehand. It wouldn't have been to anyone's liking to have to deal with a miscreant once the festival got underway. Besides, it would have been bad form – who wants to go around airing dirty laundry like that in public during a major festival, when Jerusalem is playing host to hundreds of thousands of pilgrims?

13:42-47 THE COSTLY SPIKENARD

13:43,44 – But having seen this, the disciples became indignant, saying, "What is the point of this waste? For this could have been sold for much, and the proceeds given to the poor!" [...]

De 15:4-6,10 – *However there shall be no poor with you [...] | if only you diligently listen to Yahweh your God's voice, to observe to do all this commandment which I command you today. | [...]*

The disciples are just being mindful of Moses' injunctions. If there are still so many poor people in need of alms, it is perhaps because the Jews have not conscientiously observed all of the commandments.

13:45,46 – But Jesus, having realized this, said to them, "Leave her alone. Why do you give her trouble? For she did a good deed to me. For the poor you have with you always [...]."

De 15:11 – *For the poor will never cease out of the land. [...]*

Oddly enough, Moses says this just seven verses after saying that there will be no poor in the land...*if* the people observe Yʜwʜ's commandments. Maybe he had an inkling of how well they'd do.[79]

13:47 – "For this woman, having poured this ointment on my body, has anointed my body for burial."

More than once, Jesus has told his disciples that he will die; here he makes it explicit by saying that this woman *"has anointed my body for burial."*[80] Unless all of these statements are false, Jesus knew full well that he was going to his death; yet he has committed no crime to warrant capital punishment. It seems fair to conclude, therefore, that he had a surefire plan for getting himself condemned to death. Since the first step in that plan would be for him to be arrested and put on trial, it is my view that he deliberately charged Judas with the delicate mission of contacting the temple authorities.

We should not conclude too hastily that the woman's act of anointing Jesus' head with the costly spikenard was done to signify that he was the messiah, as the Jesus-movement was wont to believe. After all, to anoint someone's head with oil was a common gesture of welcome, as indicated by Luke 7:46.[81]

13:48-50 JUDAS MEETS WITH THE CHIEF PRIESTS

13:49 – [...] And they reckoned to him thirty silver coins.

Ex 12:3 – *"Speak to all the congregation of Israel, saying, 'On the tenth day of this month, they shall take to them every man a lamb, according to their fathers' houses, a lamb for a household.'"*

Zec 11:12 – *I said to them, "If you think it best, give me my wages; and if not, keep them." So they weighed for my wages thirty pieces of silver.*

It may or may not have been the 10th of Nisan, but the priests have in one sense unwittingly negotiated for a sacrificial paschal lamb on behalf of their father YHWH's house, the temple. This is paid in advance to Judas, who will bring them the lamb.

13:50 – And he agreed, and was seeking a fitting time to hand him over to them, apart from the crowd.

In my mind, it was both he *and* Jesus, in cahoots, who worked this out, with Jesus calling the shots and both knowing in advance where and at what time each would find the other in the Garden of Gethsemane. Judas takes the rap, but Jesus can't appear before the Sanhedrin without first being arrested. It's the kind of thankless mission you'd only ask your most trusted and closest friend to carry out – which perhaps speaks volumes about Jesus' rapport with Simon Peter.

39 Then the chief priests and the scribes and the elders of the people were gathered together in the court of the high priest, who was called [6]Caiaphas.[a]

40 And they were seeking how to lay hold of him;[b]

41 but they were saying, "Not during the feast, so that there not be an uproar among the people."[c]

42 And as he was in Bethany, in the house of Simon the leper, he reclined at his table, *and there* came a woman who had an alabaster *phial* of very costly pure spikenard ointment; and having broken the alabaster *phial's seal,* she poured *it* on his head.[d]

43 But having seen *this,* the disciples became indignant, saying, "What is the point of this waste?[e]

44 "For this could have been sold for much, and *the proceeds* given to the poor!"[f] And they admonished her sternly.[g]

45 But Jesus, having realized *this,* said to them, "Leave her alone. Why do you give her trouble? For she did a good deed to me.[h]

46 "For the poor you have with you always,[i] and whenever you wish, you are always able to do good

a Mt 26:3
b Mt 26:4
   Mr 14:1
c Mt 26:5
   Mr 14:2
d Ca 1:12,13
   Mt 26:6,7
   Mr 14:3
e Mt 26:8
   Mr 14:4
f De 15:4-6,10
   Pr 19:17
   Pr 28:27
   Mt 26:9
   Jn 12:5
g Mr 14:5
h Mt 26:10
   Mr 14:6
i De 15:11

---

6 Joseph Caiaphas, a high priest of the Jews from 18 – 36 CE and presumably presider, or *Nasi,* of the Great Sanhedrin at the trial of Jesus

j Mt 26:11
  Mr 14:7
  Jn 12:8
k Mt 26:12
  Mr 14:8
l Mt 26:14
  Mr 14:10
  Jn 18:15
m Ex 12:3
  Zec 11:12
  Mt 26:15
  Mr 14:11
  Lu 22:4,5
n Mt 26:16
  Mr 14:11
  Lu 22:6

to them; but you do not always have me.[j]

47 "For this woman, having poured this ointment on my body, has anointed my body for burial."[k]

48 Then one of the twelve,[7] having gone to the chief priests,[l]

49 was saying, "What are you willing to give me? And I will hand him over to you." And they reckoned to him thirty silver coins.[m]

50 And he agreed, and was seeking a fitting time to hand him over to them, apart from the crowd.[n]

CHAPTER 14

a De 16:3
b Ho 6:2,3
  Ho 6:6
  Mt 26:2
  Mr 14:1
c Mr 14:13
d Ex 12:19
  Ex 13:7
  Lu 22:8

Now it was to be the Passover and the unleavened *loaves*[a] after two days.[b]

2 And he sent two of his disciples,[c] having said *to them*, "Having gone, make ready the Passover for us, that we might eat *it*."[d]

3 But they said to him, "Where do you wish *that*

7 Certain later mss. add, *who is called Judas Iscariot*

14
This is my commandment

14:1-7 TWO DISCIPLES ARE SENT TO PREPARE FOR THE PASS-
OVER MEAL

14:1 – Now it was to be the Passover and the unleavened *loaves* after
two days.

Ho 6:2,3 – *"After two days he will revive us. On the third day he will raise
us up, and we will live before him. | Let us acknowledge Yahweh. Let us press
on to know Yahweh. As surely as the sun rises, Yahweh will appear. […]"*

We here draw attention to Hosea – '*After two days he will revive us. On
the third day he will raise us up, and we will live before him.*' The record is
iffy, but why complain – if the chronology of events were straightforward, we'd have fewer dissertations to read. Suffice it to say that in my
book, we're now the 11th of Nisan. After two days have passed, we will
be the 14th. On that day, the third day, Jesus will be raised up on the
cross in sacrifice. Whether he will live remains to be seen.

'*Let us press on to know Yahweh.*' Yes, let us press on to know YHWH,
for *"every good tree produces good fruit; but the corrupt tree produces evil
fruit. Therefore by their fruits you will know them."* (Mt 7:17,20) '*As surely
as the sun rises, Yahweh will appear.*' As we have seen above (THE TRIBU-
LATIONS TO COME, page 246), Jesus anticipates that YHWH will return,
without fail.

Ho 6:6 – *"For I desire mercy, and not sacrifice; and the knowledge of God
more than burnt offerings."*

So says, according to the prophet, the God of Israel. Really? Well then, if YHWH truly does prefer mercy to sacrifice, Jesus has nothing to worry about.

14:2 – And he sent two of his disciples, having said *to them,* **"Having gone, make ready the Passover for us, that we might eat** *it.*"

Ex 13:7 – "[…] *No yeast shall be seen with you, within all your borders.*"

Getting things ready for a Passover feast is not something one leaves to the last minute. There's food and wine to obtain, and it takes time to ensure that a house is effectively devoid of leaven. If we follow Luke, then it was Simon and John who were sent to do this – it's nice to think of these two on their hands and knees, scrubbing the cupboards and the corners clean, no? At least, we can hope they did it themselves…I'd feel badly for Martha if those two scalawags roped her into doing this job.

14:3 – But they said to him, "Where do you wish *that* **we should prepare** *for it?*"

The two disciples are sent into the city on a mission to meet with the mysterious contact whom they would identify by the pitcher of water he carried. No less than the donkey that was tethered and waiting for Jesus in Bethphage, the furnished upper room for 'the teacher' and his disciples is a prearranged affair. Clearly, Jesus had contacts outside his circle of followers and behind the scenes, who were making arrangements on his behalf.

14:8-10 THE LAST SUPPER

14:8 – But evening having come, he reclined *at table* **with the twelve disciples.**

A good many people read this as a straightforward statement that Jesus had come into the city and was eating the Passover meal with his

The Last Supper

we should prepare *for it*?"[e]

4   And he said to them, "Behold, *upon* you having gone into the city, a man carrying a pitcher of water will meet you. Follow him into the house that he enters.[f]

5   "And you will say to the master of the house, 'The teacher says to you, "Where is the lodge, where I might eat the Passover with my disciples?"'[g]

6   "And he will show you a large upper room *that is* furnished. Prepare *for it* there."[h]

7   And having gone away from *there*, they found *it* just as he had said it to them, and they prepared *for* the Passover.[i]

8   But evening having come, he reclined *at table* with the twelve.[j]

9   And he said to them, "With passionate yearning, I longed to eat this Passover with you, before I suffer.[k]

10   "For I say to you, that I will never eat it, until it be fulfilled[l] in the kingdom of God."[m]

11   And he rose from the supper, and laying aside the outer garments, and having taken a towel, he girded himself.[n]

12   Then he poured water into the basin, and he

e Mt 26:17
    Mr 14:12
    Lu 22:9
f Mr 14:13
    Lu 22:10
g Mt 26:18
    Mr 14:14
    Lu 22:11
h Mr 14:15
i Mt 26:19
    Mr 14:16
    Lu 22:13
j Mt 26:20
    Mr 14:17
    Lu 22:14
k Ps 22:14-18
    Isa 53:4-6,10
    Lu 22:15
    Heb 10:30,31
l Ex 6:6
    Ex 12:26,27,42
    Ex 13:3
m Lu 22:16
n Jn 13:4

twelve disciples in the furnished upper room. Such a view overlooks an oft repeated motif, namely that mention is made of it when Jesus changes locale;[82] given the importance of the Last Supper, it therefore seems incongruous not to mention that Jesus has gone into Jerusalem for dinner that evening. Thus, in my view, Jesus is still in Bethany, at the house of Simon the leper, and this is not the Passover meal.

14:9 – And he said to them, "With passionate yearning, I longed to eat this Passover with you, before I suffer."

I think Jesus had a very good idea of the suffering that he was about to undergo, and which he trusted would fulfill the Scriptures.

Isa 53:4-6,10 – [...] *Yahweh has laid on him the iniquity of us all. | Yet it pleased Yahweh to bruise him. He has caused him to suffer.* [...]

14:10 – "For I say to you, that I will never eat it, until it be fulfilled in the kingdom of God."

"Until it be fulfilled" – what does the Passover represent?

Ex 6:6 – *"Therefore tell the children of Israel, 'I am Yahweh, and I will bring you out from under the burdens of the Egyptians, and I will rid you out of their bondage, and I will redeem you with an outstretched arm [...].'"*

Ex 12:26,27,42 – *"[...] | It is a night to be much observed to Yahweh for bringing them out from the land of Egypt. [...]"*

Ex 13:3 – *Moses said to the people, "Remember this day, in which you came out of Egypt, out of the house of bondage. [...]"*

In other words, the Passover stands for a liberation from bondage – and in the view of *The Gospel of Jesus of Nazareth*, the Jews are the slaves of YHWH. Jesus says that although he has longed to eat this Passover with his disciples (one understands before his death), *"I will never eat it, until it be fulfilled [...]"* It is by his sacrificial death, timed to coincide with the Passover, that he hopes to free his coreligionists from their bondage under the covenant and so fulfill the Passover's promise of freedom.

14:11-23 JESUS WASHES HIS DISCIPLES' FEET

Providing a guest with water with which to wash his feet was a mark of hospitality,[83] but the washing of feet was done when one entered a house, and certainly before sitting down to a meal. Hence, Jesus' pedal ministrations are singular indeed, for dinner has already been served; yet it is precisely at this point that Jesus 'rises from the supper' to strip off his clothes, gird himself with a towel, and fill the footwashing basin with water.

We need to see this in context. As related in the Gosepls, the disciples were known to flout convention when it came to washing their hands before meals (Mt 15:2, Mr 7:5); my guess is that they weren't too fastidious about washing their feet when they came into a house, either. Jesus himself dispensed with washing, too – *He went in, and sat at the table. When the Pharisee saw it, he marveled that he had not first washed himself before dinner.* (Lu 11:37,38)[84] So Jesus' remark that *"someone who has bathed only needs to have his feet washed, but is completely clean"* suggests that on this occasion – one could almost say exceptionally – the disciples have all bathed. This, it seems reasonable to suppose, would have been the traditional immersion in a mikveh to achieve ritual purity prior to a festival.[85] Thus, for the approaching Passover, everyone is ritually clean …with the exception of their feet, which they would wash when they sat down for the traditional Seder in a few days' time.

While we know from the Gospels that the disciples did not normally wash their hands before a meal, on this particular evening their hands are clean. Indeed, they are all clean, save for their feet. But now that they're seated for dinner, Jesus gets up to wash his disciples' feet, an act that recalls the way a wife was to look after her husband. His deed serves two purposes. The foremost is to set an example – *"For I have given you an example, that you also should do as I have done to you."* (Jn 13:15) He will shortly follow this with a 'fresh' commandment, *"that you love*

14   Jesus washes his disciples' feet

o Jn 13:5
p Jn 13:6
q Lu 7:38,44-46
   Jn 13:7
r Isa 52:2
   Jn 13:8
s Jn 13:9
t Jn 13:10
u Jn 13:12
v Jn 13:13

began to wash the disciples' feet, and to wipe *them* with the towel with which he was girded.°

13 Then he came to Simon, who said to him, "Master, do you wash my feet?"ᵖ

14 And Jesus answered him, saying, "What I do, you do not see just now, but you will come to know after these *examples*."�q

15 And Simon said to him, "Never should you wash my feet, ¹*not* ever!" Jesus answered him, "If I do not wash you, you have no part with me."ʳ

16 Simon said to him, "Master, not only my feet, but also *my* hands and *my* head!"ˢ

17 Jesus said to him, "The one who has bathed has no *other* need except to wash the feet; otherwise, he is completely clean. And you are clean, but not all *of you*."ᵗ

18 Therefore, when he had washed their feet, and taken his outer garments, and having reclined again at table, he said to them, "Do you realize what I have done to you?ᵘ

19 "You call me 'the teacher' and 'the master', and you say *so* correctly, for *I* am.ᵛ

---

1 Lit., *to the age*

one another. Just as I have loved you, you also love one another." Jesus shows his disciples that their love must be based on a sense of active caring and genuinely expressed equality. No one is 'above' another, and we should look after each other and serve each other's needs.

The second purpose is to render his disciples ritually pure, from head to toe. For at this point, the meal they are enjoying is about to become more than just the last supper they will share before his arrest – it is going to become The Last Supper. Not only is Jesus going to impart his Last Teachings and his One and Only Commandment, he is going to formally free his disciples from the bonds of the Mosaic covenant, via a ritual that is still celebrated to this day.

14:16 – Simon said to him, "Master, not only my feet, but also my hands and my head!"

It may have been too much for Simon Peter, to see his teacher acting like a woman: '[The washing of feet] was a service which the wife was expected to render her husband (Yer. Ket. v. 30a); according to Rab Huna, it was one of the personal attentions to which her husband was entitled, no matter how many maids she may have had; likewise, according to the Babylonian Talmud (Ket. 61a), besides preparing his drink and bed, the wife had to wash her husband's face and feet.'[86] Or again, to see him behaving not at as master should, tended to by others for his needs (cf. Lu 7:38, 10:40), but conducting himself like a slave.[87]

At any rate, the brash Simon once again distinguishes himself as being the only disciple to challenge his teacher.

14:20 – "Therefore, if I, the 'master' and the 'teacher', have washed your feet, *then* you also ought to wash one another's feet."

The ancient world was rife with pecking orders of every stripe that set one man over another, and especially masters (or gods) over slaves. With his foot-washing ritual, it seems that Jesus is seeking to upend the usual distinction between teacher and disciple, master and slave…one supposes with the hope of dealing a blow to such hierarchies.

While Jesus' example necessarily recalls that of the 'sinful' woman in Luke 7:36-47 who washed his feet with her tears, it is not clear whether he felt such favors should be extended to women. Sadly, we have no reports of Jesus ever kneeling before a woman to wash her feet.

14:22 – "Truly, truly, I say to you, a teacher is not above the disciple, nor a master above his slave."

Confound it, there I go again, messing with the Scriptures. Matthew 10:24 doesn't say that at all; echoing Malachi 1:6, it reads, *"A disciple is not above the teacher, nor a slave above his lord."* Matthew's formulation does not say that the disciple and teacher are equal; rather, it stresses that the disciple is not *above* his teacher, and that a slave is not *above* his master – which is the normal state of affairs (cf. Eph 6:5). But does that sound like Jesus? Surely not. With his footwashing example, it seems he wants to stress that he is equal to his disciples, not above them.

For my part, I think Jesus might well have said, *'a teacher is not above the disciple'*. But if he had added the logical second part – *'nor a master above his slave'* – the statement would have been untenably revolutionary in the Roman and Greek world. The Jesus-movement was already fending off fierce oppression; they did not need to appear as challenging the *status quo* any more than necessary. Hence, in the context of *The Gospel of Jesus of Nazareth*, Jesus' original wording would have been altered in 'subsequent mss.', and the verse eventually omitted altogether.

14:24-27 The bread and wine

14:24 – And as they were eating of them, having taken bread, and having blessed *it*, he broke *it*, and gave *it* to them, and said, "Take, eat – this is my body."

20 "Therefore, if I, the 'master' and the 'teacher', have washed your feet, *then* you also ought to wash one another's feet."[w]

21 "For I have given you an example, so that just as I have done to you, you also should do."[x]

22 "Truly, truly, I say to you, [2]a teacher is not above the disciple, nor *is* a master above his slave."[y]

23 "If you know these things, you are blessed if you do them."[z]

24 And *as* they were eating of them, having taken bread, and having blessed *it*, he broke *it*, and gave *it* to them, and said, "Take, eat – this is my body."[a]

25 And having taken a cup, *and* having given thanks, he gave *it* to them, and they all drank of it.[b]

26 And he said to them, "This is my blood[c] of the covenant, which is being poured out for many.[d]

27 "Truly I say to you, that I will never again drink of the fruit of the vine, until that day when I might drink it fresh in the kingdom of God.[e]

28 "I give to you a fresh commandment,[f] that *you* love one another – just as I have loved you, so that you

w Jn 13:14
x Jn 13:15
   Jn 13:16
y Mt 10:24
   Jn 13:16
z Jn 13:17
a Le 3:17
   Le 7:25
   Mt 26:26
   Mr 14:22
   Lu 22:19
   Jn 6:55,56
b Le 3:17
   Le 7:27
   Mt 26:27
   Mr 14:23
   Lu 22:17
   Jn 6:55,56
c Le 17:10,11,14
d Ex 24:4-8
   De 12:16
   Ps 49:7,8
   Isa 53:10,11
   Zec 9:11
   Mt 20:28
   Mt 26:28
   Mr 10:45
   Mr 14:24
   Lu 22:20
   Jn 19:34
e Job 3:19
   Mt 26:29
   Mr 14:25
   Lu 22:18
f De 4:2

---

2 According the best ancient mss.; subsequent mss. read, *a disciple is not above the teacher, nor a slave above his master*; certain late mss. omit verse 22

Le 3:17 – *"It shall be a perpetual statute throughout your generations in all your dwellings, that you shall eat neither fat nor blood."*

Le 7:25 – *"For whoever eats the fat of the animal, of […] an offering made by fire to Yahweh, even the soul who eats it shall be cut off from his people."*

Jesus here initiates his disciples into a symbolic transgression of the prohibition against eating fat and blood.

To understand why bread might be equivalent to fat, consider Psalm 147:14 – *He fills you with the finest of the wheat.* The Hebrew word for 'finest', *cheleb*, means 'fat', and is so translated regarding the myriad sacrifices offered to YHWH.

Incidentally, the bread that Jesus breaks here is *artos* – not *azumos*, or unleavened bread. If this were a Seder meal, it seems an odd oversight to speak of ordinary bread.

14:25 – And having taken a cup, *and* having given thanks, he gave *it* to them, and they all drank of it.

Le 7:27 – *"Whoever it is who eats any blood, that soul shall be cut off from his people."*

By daring to eat flesh and drink blood, the disciples are at this point effectively and irrevocably severing themselves from the covenant with YHWH. We must not underestimate the significance of this symbolism. For a Jew, there could be no greater apostasy than the anthropophagy[88] which Jesus proposed, and it was undoubtedly for this reason that *'many of his disciples went back, and walked no more with him'* when he expressed the idea for the first time – cf. John 6:53,60,66.

14:26 – And he said to them, "This is my blood of the covenant, which is being poured out for many."

Ex 24:4-8 – […] | *Moses took the blood, and sprinkled it on the people, and said, "Look, this is the blood of the covenant, which Yahweh has made with you concerning all these words."*

De 12:16 – *Only you shall not eat the blood. You shall pour it out on the earth like water.*

Ps 49:7,8 – *None of them can by any means redeem his brother, nor give God a ransom for him. | For the redemption of their life is costly, no payment is ever enough.*

Isa 53:10,11 – *Yet it pleased Yahweh to bruise him. He has caused him to suffer. When you make his soul an offering for sin, he will see his seed. […] | After the suffering of his soul, he will see the light and be satisfied. My righteous servant will justify many by the knowledge of himself; and he will bear their iniquities.*

Zec 9:11 – *As for you also, because of the blood of your covenant, I have set free your prisoners from the pit in which is no water.*

Mr 10:45 – *"For the Son of Man also came not to be served, but to serve, and to give his life as a ransom for many."*

Jn 19:34 – *However one of the soldiers pierced his side with a spear, and immediately blood and water came out.*

It is by giving his life unto death and pouring out his blood that Jesus will ransom his fellows. If the redemption of their lives is costly, it is because their lives can only be redeemed with life itself. No payment that amounted to less than life itself could ever be enough. The life is in the blood, and *'it is the blood that makes atonement by reason of the life.'*

14:27 – "Truly I say to you, that I will never again drink of the fruit of the vine, until that day when I might drink it fresh in the kingdom of God."

The Greek word here used is *kainos* – if ever Jesus were to drink wine again, it would not be just a 'new' wine, but a 'fresh' wine, different in nature. (See below, page 274)

However, I think we too easily overlook the first part of this verse, in which Jesus clearly states that he will *"never again drink of the fruit of the vine"*. That is quite a declaration from a man who *"came eating and* drinking", who was judged '*a gluttonous man and a drunkard.*' (Mt 11:19) From this point on, Jesus is to be the sacrificial offering before YHWH. On the one hand, his abstinence ensures that he cannot be accused of defiling himself with wine that is not kosher. More pragmatically, he will need to keep his head in the days to come. Not only is Jesus going to his death, but he is to endure one of the most torturous methods ever devised for execution. So much hinges on his being clearheaded and in command of his senses; if he forgets himself, he could fail in his quest to secure freedom for his friends.

14:28-35 A FRESH COMMANDMENT

14:28 – "I give to you a fresh commandment [...] "

Here again, the Greek is *kainos*. Vine says that '*kainos* denotes "new," of that which is unaccustomed or unused, not "new" in time, recent, but "new" as to form or quality, of different nature from what is contrasted as old.' Thus *kainos* has to do with being new in **quality**, whereas '*neos* signifies "new" in respect of time, that which is recent; [...] accordingly what is *neos* may be a reproduction of the old in quality or character.'[89] Jesus is therefore giving his disciples a commandment that is wholly new in form and quality – it is original, unprecedented. It does not derive from what has come before. It is not a 'new' commandment to be added to the 613 commandments found in the Torah, but rather a 'fresh' commandment – one with which his disciples can start afresh.

14:28 – "I give to you a fresh commandment, that *you* love one another – just as I have loved you, so that you also love one another."

Jesus enjoins his disciples to love one another, not '*as you love yourselves*' – a yardstick that would concur with the Torah (Leviticus 19:18) – but rather, "*as I have loved you.*" It is by his own example, distinct from the Law, that Jesus sets the measure for their conduct.

In what way did Jesus love his disciples during the time they were together? It's anybody's guess; his conduct as reported in the Gospels has
mostly to do with other people, so we have little to go on. We could say
that one hallmark of his love is the way he seems to have eschewed all
judgment; taking people as they are, he condemned no one. Likewise,
in almost all instances, he responded to those who entreated him. He
did not set himself above others; he might argue with the scribes and
Pharisees, but he did not disdain them and would eat at their table. And
of course, he welcomed children with open arms. But this is how Jesus
was with others. How he actually loved his disciples is a mystery.

The only thing we can say for sure is that the washing of each other's
feet, at least among men, counted for something. Kitchen duties, on the
other hand, were not part of his program – as we've noted, Jesus himself
was indifferent to household chores (see above, JESUS HEALS SIMON'S
MOTHER-IN-LAW, page 48, and MARTHA AND MARY, page 138).

14:31 – "Greater love than this no one has, that one might lay down his life for his friends."

Ge 22:2,8 – [...] | *Abraham said, "God will provide himself the lamb for
a burnt offering, my son." [...]*

Zep 1:7 – [...] *The day of Yahweh is at hand. For Yahweh has prepared
a sacrifice. He has consecrated his guests.*

Zec 12:10 – [...] *They will look to me whom they have pierced; and they
shall mourn for him, as one mourns for his only son, [...] his firstborn.*

Mr 10:45 – *"For the Son of Man also came not to be served, but to serve,
and to give his life as a ransom for many."*

Jn 1:36 – *And he looked at Jesus [...] and said, "Behold, the Lamb of God!"*

Jn 8:35,36 – *"A slave does not live in the house forever. A son remains
forever. If therefore the Son makes you free, you will be free indeed."*

Jn 10:11 – *"I am the good shepherd. The good shepherd lays down his life
for the sheep."*

14 — A fresh commandment

g Jn 13:34
h Jn 13:35
i Jn 15:12
j Ge 22:2,8
   Job 29:13
   Mic 6:6,7
   Zep 1:7
   Zec 12:10
   Mt 20:28
   Mr 10:45
   Jn 1:36
   Jn 8:35,36
   Jn 10:11
   Jn 15:13
k Jn 15:14
l Le 25:55
   Isa 44:21
   Jn 8:33
m Eze 12:28
   Am 3:2
n Jn 8:32
   Jn 15:15
o Mr 3:14
   Lu 6:13
p Jn 15:16
q De 12:32
   Jn 15:17
r Jn 13:21

also love one another.[g]

29 "By this, all will know that you are my disciples, if you might have love among yourselves.[h]

30 [3]["This is my commandment – that you love one another, just as I have loved you.[i]

31 "Greater love than this no one has, that one might lay down his life for his friends.[j]

32 "You are my friends, if you do what I command you.[k]

33 "No longer do I call you slaves,[l] for the slave does not know what his master is doing. But I have called you friends, for all things which I heard from my Father,[m] I have made known to you.[n]

34 "You did not choose me, but I chose you, and appointed you,[o] that you might [4]go away, and *that* you might bear fruit, and *that* your fruit might endure.[p]

35 "This I command you, that you love one another."[q]]

36 And having said these things, Jesus was troubled in spirit.[r]

37 And as they were eating, he said to them, "Truly

---

3 Verses 30-35 are not found in the best ancient mss.
4 Or, *depart*

Truly, Jesus gave his life for his friends, to set them free. They were the slaves of YHWH, but they need not remain in the house of Israel forever. Whereas Jesus, fully assuming the yoke of being a son of YHWH – "*a son remains forever*" – laid down his life in sacrifice, "*for the sheep.*"

That said, while there is certainly no greater act of love than self-sacrifice in a situation where it is done to save a friend's life, I think it likely these words were put in Jesus' mouth by the early Jesus-movement in a bid to glorify its martyrs. After all, laying down one's life in martyrdom has nothing to do with saving other people's lives; rather, it serves to secure meaning for one's own life, within the context of a story one fervently believes to be true. Martyrs die out of love for their own beliefs.

14:32 – "You are my friends, if you do what I command you."

The Greek word *philos* connotes endearment…something that is noticeably absent from all the promises that YHWH makes for following his commandments.

14:33 – "No longer do I call you slaves […] "

Le 25:55 – "*For to me the sons of Israel are slaves; they are my slaves whom I brought out of the land of Egypt. I am Yahweh your God.*"

Jn 8:33 – *They answered him, "We are Abraham's offspring, and have never been in bondage to anyone. How do you say, 'You will be made free'?"*

14:33 – " […] for the slave does not know what his master is doing. But I have called you friends, for all things which I heard from my Father, I have made known to you."

Eze 12:28 – "*Therefore tell them, 'Thus says the Lord Yahweh: "None of my words shall be deferred any more, but the word which I speak will be performed," says the Lord Yahweh.'*"

Am 3:2 – "*I have only chosen you of all the families of the earth. Therefore I will punish you for all of your sins.*"

Jn 8:32 – *"You will know the truth, and the truth will make you free."*

My point here is that Jesus has made known to his disciples all that YHWH is doing and will do to his slaves, his Chosen People. He has revealed to his disciples the truth about their tribal god, and in so doing, counted them as friends. Armed with that truth, they will be made free.

14:35 – "This I command you, that you love one another."

This is Jesus' one and only 'rule', and its threefold enunciation – in John 13:34, 15:12, and 15:17 – employs the ancient world's shorthand (see below, page 291) to underscore its overarching significance.

What should strike us above all is that in stark contrast to the Law, which stipulates *'You shall not wrong one another, but you shall fear your God'* (Le 25:17), neither here nor elsewhere does Jesus ever command his disciples to either love or to worship or to fear God. By comparison, in Judaism – and more broadly still, the religious traditions of the Mediterranean – the paramount rule was that men must love, worship, and, most especially, *fear* God. There was a compelling reason for this: the fear of God was seen as the only sure way to deter men from wrongful conduct. If they had no fear of divine retribution, chaos would ensue, for men would do as they pleased with no regard for others.[90] But with his 'fresh' commandment to love one another, Jesus renders this fear of God unnecessary – for if we love one another, we will treat each other well. Men will not need to coerce themselves into good behavior with a fear of otherworldly punishment for their misdeeds; rather, guided by love, they will naturally seek what is good for others and do no harm. Seen thus in the context of antiquity's prevalent fear of gods, and its rites of placatory worship, Jesus' commandment appears revolutionary in its approach to life and community. Since God *"makes his sun to rise on the evil and the good, and sends rain on the just and the unjust"* (Mt 5:45), it arguably makes no difference whether men love God or not – whereas if they love one another, it will truly make a world of difference.

14:36-46 JESUS HONORS JUDAS WITH THE MORSEL

14:36 – And having said these things, Jesus was troubled in spirit.

This is a man who is sealing his own fate. He is about to set in motion the final act of his life, and with the possible exception of Judas, his disciples are probably in the dark about his true intentions. They may well not realize that Jesus is about to be arrested, and that this is their very last meal together.

14:39 – Now there was one of his disciples reclining upon Jesus' bosom, whom Jesus loved.

Pr 18:24 – [...] *there is a friend who sticks closer than a brother.*

I believe that, among the disciples, Judas was Jesus' closest confident and friend. The strongest evidence for this is found in the very act for which he is condemned: his betrayal of Jesus.[91] Utterly failing to grasp the importance of Jesus being tried by the Sanhedrin, a disciple such as Simon Peter – fervidly objecting, *"Far be it from you, Lord! This will never be done to you!"* – might have refused, or deliberately botched the job.

Judas had arranged for Jesus to be handed over to the temple authorities. Jesus clearly had full knowledge of this – the rendezvous in the Garden of Gethsemane can only have been mutually agreed – and he had entrusted the mission to the one person in whom he must have had full confidence. Isn't the fact that Judas was responsible for the group's money bag (John 12:6) yet another modest sign of the trust that Jesus had already placed in him?

14:41 – And so, having leaned in this way upon Jesus' bosom, he said to him, "Rabbi, who is it?"

Ps 41:9 – *Yes, my own familiar friend, in whom I trusted, who ate bread with me, has lifted up his heel against me.*

Ps 55:13 – *But it was you, [...] my companion, and my familiar friend.*

Lu 18:31 – *He took the twelve aside, and said to them, "Behold, we are going up to Jerusalem, and all the things that are written through the prophets concerning the Son of Man will be completed."*

Jesus would have explained to Judas that the betrayal he was asking him to commit counted for one of the many Scriptures it was necessary to fulfill.

14:42 – Then Jesus answered him, saying, "It is he to whom I, having dipped the morsel, will also give it." Then he took the morsel, and – having dipped *it* himself – he gave it to him.

We understand this as being a mark of affection and honor. Sharing one's morsel is touchingly portrayed in 2 Samuel 12:3 – *The poor man had nothing, except one little ewe lamb, which he had bought and raised. It grew up together with him, and with his children. It ate of his own morsel, drank of his own cup, and lay in his bosom, and was like a daughter to him.*

14:43-45 – And then, after *giving him* the morsel, Jesus said to him, "What you do, do swiftly." But this, none of those reclining at table knew to what *end* he said *this* to him. For some thought, because he had the money bag, that Jesus was saying to him, "Buy what *things* we have need of for the feast" – or that he should give something to the poor.

Let us consider this passage carefully. Jesus says to Judas, *"What you do, do swiftly."* They both know he is sending Judas to bring the temple guards to the Garden of Gethsemane. This has been prearranged. But none of those reclining at the table know why he says this to Judas. This suggests that Jesus had not told the others what was going to happen that night. They were all in the dark. Even his statement, *"Most certainly I tell you that one of you will betray me"* – and his clear designation of Judas as being that very person – has failed to make an impression.

I say to you, that one of you will hand me over."[s]

38　The disciples were looking at one another, at a loss *to know* of whom he was speaking.[t]

39　Now there was one of his disciples reclining upon Jesus' bosom, whom Jesus loved.[u]

40　Therefore Simon nodded to him, to ask *him* whom it was he was speaking about.[v]

41　And so, having leaned in this way upon Jesus' bosom, he said to him, "Rabbi, who is it?"[w]

42　Then Jesus answered him, saying, "It is he to whom I, having dipped the morsel, will also give it." Then he took the morsel, and — having dipped *it* himself — he gave it to [5]him.[x]

43　And then, after *giving him* the morsel, Jesus said to him, "What you do, do swiftly."[y]

44　But this, none of those reclining at table knew to what *end* he said *this* to him.[z]

45　For some thought, because he had the money bag, that Jesus was saying to him, "Buy what *things* we have need of for the feast", or that he should give something to the poor.[a]

46　Then, having received the morsel, he went out

---

5 Certain later mss. read, *Judas*

s　Mt 26:21
　　Mr 14:18
　　Jn 13:21
t　Mt 26:22
　　Mr 14:19
　　Jn 13:22
u　Pr 18:24
　　Jn 13:23
v　Jn 13:24
w　Ps 41:9
　　Ps 55:13
　　Lu 18:31
　　Jn 13:25
x　Jn 13:26
y　Jn 13:27
z　Jn 13:28
a　De 15:11
　　Jn 13:29

14   "The word concerning me has an end"

b *Jn 13:30*
c *Lu 22:35*
d *Lu 22:36*
e *Isa 53:12*
f *Ps 40:7*
   Lu 22:37
g *Lu 22:38*

immediately, even though it was night.[b]

47 And he said to them, "When I sent you forth without purse and bag and sandals, did you lack anything?" And they said, "Nothing."[c]

48 And he said to them, "But now, let the *one* who has a purse pick it up, and likewise a bag. And the *one* who does not have, let him sell his cloak, and buy a dagger.[d]

49 "For I say to you, that this which has been written must be accomplished in me — AND WITH THE LAWLESS HE WAS RECKONED[e] — for the *word* concerning me has an [6]end."[f]

50 But they said, "Master, behold, here *are* two daggers." And he said to them, "It is enough."[g]

---

6 Or, *fulfillment; purpose*

No wonder, then, that Jesus was troubled in spirit. Here he is, going to his death, and his other disciples are all too busy eating and drinking and having a good time to realise what's really afoot. They even suppose he's just sending Judas out to buy provisions for the approaching Seder meal, or to give something to the poor (even though we never hear of Jesus telling his disciples to give alms to the poor). Well, it may be that the disciples were too tipsy that night to think this one through; or, more likely, that they were just glad to see Judas go. I've a notion the guy was the black sheep of the apostolic family.[92]

14:47-50 "THE WORD CONCERNING ME HAS AN END"

14:49 – "For I say to you, that this which has been written must be accomplished in me – AND WITH THE LAWLESS HE WAS RECKONED – for the *word* concerning me has an end."

Isa 53:12 – […] *because he poured out his soul to death, and was counted with the transgressors* […]

Ps 40:7 – *Then I said, "Behold, I have come. It is written about me in the book in the scroll."*

Jesus would have been scrupulously attentive to seeing that his sacrifice fulfilled as many prophesies as possible. His death could only have the meaning he intended within the context of the Scriptures.

14:48,50 – And he said to them, "But now, let the *one* […] who does not have, let him sell his cloak, and buy a dagger. But they said, "Master, behold, here are two daggers." And he said to them, "It is enough."

This is almost comical. Some outlaw bunch these guys make – two daggers!

The daggers are just for show, of course, so that the Scripture about Jesus being reckoned with the lawless may be symbolically fulfilled.

15

Jesus is handed over

15:1-9 JESUS FORESEES THAT SIMON WILL DENY HIM

15:3,4 – "Nevertheless, after being raised up, I will go before you into Galilee." And they answered, saying to him, "Where, Master?" And he said to them, "Where the corpse is, there the vultures will be gathered together."

De 28:26 – *Your dead body will be food to all birds of the sky, and to the animals of the earth […]* [93]

Jer 7:33 – *"The dead bodies of this people shall be food for the birds of the sky, and for the animals of the earth […]"*

Jer 19:7 – *"[…] I will cause them to fall by the sword before their enemies, and by the hand of those who seek their life: and their dead bodies will I give to be food for the birds of the sky, and for the animals of the earth."*

Eze 32:4-6 – *"I will leave you on the land, I will cast you out on the open field, and will cause all the birds of the sky to settle on you, and I will satisfy the animals of the whole earth with you. | I will lay your flesh on the mountains, and fill the valleys with your height. | […]"*

Eze 39:17,19 – *"You, son of man, thus says the Lord Yahweh: 'Speak to the birds of every sort, and to every animal of the field, "Assemble yourselves, and come; gather yourselves on every side to my sacrifice that I do sacrifice for you, even a great sacrifice on the mountains of Israel, that you may eat meat and drink blood. | You shall eat fat until you be full, and drink blood until you are drunk, of my sacrifice which I have sacrificed for you.""*

CHAPTER 15

AND having sung hymns, they went out to the Mount of Olives.[a]

2   And Jesus said to them, "All of you will be made to stumble, for it has been written, 'I WILL STRIKE THE SHEPHERD, AND THE SHEEP WILL BE THOROUGHLY SCATTERED.'[b]

3   "Nevertheless, after being raised up, I will go before you into Galilee."[c]

4   And they answered, saying to him, "Where, Master?" And he said to them, "Where the corpse is, there the vultures will be gathered together."[d]

5   But Simon said to him, "Even if they all will be made to stumble, nevertheless I *will* not."[e]

6   But Jesus answered, saying to him, "Where I go, you are not able to follow now;[f] but you will follow later."[g]

7   And he said to him, "Master, why am I not able to

a Mt 26:30
   Mr 14:26
   Lu 22:39
b Zec 13:7
   Mt 26:31
   Mr 14:27
c Mt 26:32
   Mr 14:28
   Mr 16:7
d De 28:26
   Job 39:26-30
   Isa 14:13
   Jer 7:33
   Jer 16:4
   Jer 19:7
   Eze 32:3-6
   Eze 39:17,19
   Mt 24:28
   Mt 28:16
   Lu 17:37
e Pr 27:1
   Mt 26:33
   Mr 14:29
f Mr 14:50
g Jer 34:18,20
   Mt 26:32
   Mt 28:16
   Lu 17:37
   Jn 13:36

Mt 26:32 – *"But after I am raised up, I will go before you into Galilee."*

Mt 28:16 – *But the eleven disciples went into Galilee, to the mountain where Jesus had sent them.*

Mr 16:7 – *"But go, tell his disciples and Peter, 'He goes before you into Galilee. There you will see him, as he said to you.'"*

Lu 17:37 – *They, answering, asked him, "Where, Lord?" He said to them, "Where the body is, there will the vultures also be gathered together."*

I am convinced that Jesus sought to fulfill the Scriptures by having his body left as food for the birds of the sky and the animals of the earth.

To achieve this end, he would have needed accomplices. The two men he met on the high mountain and with whom he discussed his coming exodus may have been the same men the women met when they came to the tomb early in the morning and found the stone rolled aside – cf. Luke 24:2-4. It may have been to these two men that Jesus entrusted the task of conveying his corpse to Galilee, where they had met before.

At any rate, he had told his disciples in advance on which mountain they would find him. And in the event, they did find him there…but not perhaps in a way that made sense to them – or so one infers – which left some with doubts. We will return to this in chapter 18.

15:5 – But Simon said to him, "Even if they all will be made to stumble, nevertheless I *will* not."

Pr 27:1 – *Don't boast about tomorrow; for you don't know what a day may bring.*

15:6 – But Jesus answered, saying to him, "Where I go, you are not able to follow now; but you will follow later."

Jer 34:18,20 – *"I will give the men who have transgressed my covenant, who have not performed the words of the covenant which they made before me […] | I will even give them into the hand of their enemies, and into the* hand of those who seek their life. Their dead bodies will be food for the birds of the sky, and for the animals of the earth."

We may read this on two levels. In saying that Simon will follow him later to where he goes, Jesus may be simply indicating that his disciple will come to the mountain which he has designated, as above. We may also read this, however, as a reference to the prophesy: having eaten blood and so transgressed YHWH's covenant, Simon may find himself, like Jesus, slain and exposed on a mountain to be 'food for the birds of the sky, and for the animals of the earth.'

15:7 – And he said to him, "Master, why am I not able to follow you just now? I will lay down my life for you!"

1Ki 20:11 – *The king of Israel answered, "Tell him, 'Don't let him who puts on his armor brag like he who takes it off.'"*

It seems that Simon, maybe a bit tipsy from all that wine, has been inspired to greatness by his teacher's stirring words: *"Greater love has no one than this, that someone lay down his life for his friends."*

15:8,9 – And Jesus said to him, "You will lay down your life for me? Truly I say to you, not a cock will crow, until you have utterly disowned me three times." But he said vehemently, *"Even* if it be necessary for me to die with you, I will never disown you!" And in like manner, they all spoke as well.

Pr 20:6 – *Many men claim to be men of unfailing love, but who can find a faithful man?*

Simon's bravado notwithstanding, Jesus seems to have had a pretty fair notion of his disciple's true mettle.

In addition to being a sorry commentary on his disciple's character, the prediction that Simon will deny him introduces the chiasmus that will now follow: Jesus' thrice repeated prayer to YHWH and Simon's thrice repeated denial.

15 Jesus prays in the garden of Gethsemane

h 1Ki 20:11
   Lu 22:33
   Jn 13:37
   Jn 15:13
i Mt 26:34
   Mr 14:30
   Lu 22:34
   Jn 13:38
j Pr 20:6
   Mt 26:35
   Mr 14:31
k Mt 26:36
   Mr 14:32
l Mt 26:37
   Mr 14:33
m Ps 31:9
   Jn 12:27
n Mt 26:38
   Mr 14:34
o Ps 54:2
   Ps 55:1,5,16
   Ps 84:12
   Mt 26:39
   Mr 14:35
   Lu 22:41
p Ge 22:7
   Ex 4:22
   Ps 89:26
q Ps 28:2,6,8
   Ps 34:4,6,19
   Ps 55:18,22
   Ps 86:1-7,16
   Mic 7:7
   Mt 7:9-11
   Mt 26:39
   Mr 14:36
   Lu 22:42
   Jn 14:30,31

follow you just now? I will lay down my life for you!"[h]

8 And Jesus said to him, "You will lay down your life for me? Truly I say to you, not a cock will crow, until you have utterly disowned me three times."[i]

9 But he said vehemently, *"Even if it be necessary for me to die with you, I will never disown you!"* And in like manner, they all spoke as well.[j]

10 And they came to a place by the name of Gethsemane, and he said to his disciples, "Sit down here, while I pray."[k]

11 And he took Simon and James and John with him, and he began to be deeply grieved and distressed.[l]

12 And he said to them, "My soul is overwhelmed with sorrow, to the point of death.[m] Wait here and stay awake with me."[n]

13 And having gone forward a little *ways*, he fell upon the earth and prayed that, if it were possible, the hour might pass by, away from him.[o]

14 And he said, "Abba! Father![p] All things are possible for You. Remove this cup from me. But not what I will, but what You *will*."[q]

15 And he came and found them sleeping. And he

15:10-21 JESUS PRAYS IN THE GARDEN OF GETHSEMANE

This is the first and only time that Jesus openly prays to YHWH within earshot of his disciples, ostensibly for the benefit of the same disciples who accompanied him up the high mountain. For these three – Simon, the slowest of the bunch to comprehend his meanings, and the thunderous James and John – Jesus may have wanted to take special care to point up that all that was to follow was indeed YHWH's will.

15:12 – And he said to them, "My soul is overwhelmed with sorrow, to the point of death. Wait here and stay awake with me."

Ps 31:9 – *Have mercy on me, Yahweh, for I am in distress. My eye, my soul, and my body waste away with grief.*

Jn 12:27 – *"Now my soul is troubled. What shall I say? 'Father, save me from this time?' But for this cause I came to this time."*

15:13 – And having gone forward a little *ways*, he fell upon the earth and prayed that, if it were possible, the hour might pass by, away from him.

Ps 54:2 – *Hear my prayer, God. Listen to the words of my mouth.*

Ps 55:1,5,16 – *Listen to my prayer, God. Don't hide yourself from my supplication. | Fearfulness and trembling have come on me. Horror has overwhelmed me. | As for me, I will call on God. Yahweh will save me.*

15:14 – And he said, "Abba! Father! [...] "

Ge 22:7 – *Isaac spoke to Abraham his father, and said, "My father?" He said, "Here I am, my son." He said, "Here is the fire and the wood, but where is the lamb for a burnt offering?"*

Ex 4:22 – *" [...] 'Yahweh says, Israel is my son, my firstborn.'"*

Ps 89:26 – *He will call to me, 'You are my Father, my God, and the rock of my salvation!'*

289

15:14 – " […] All things are possible for You. Remove this cup from me. But not what I will, but what You *will*."

Ps 86:1-7,16 – *Hear, Yahweh, and answer me, […] | […] save your servant who trusts in you. | Be merciful to me, Lord, for I call to you all day long, | […] to you, Lord, do I lift up my soul. | For you, Lord, are good […] to all those who call on you. | Hear, Yahweh, my prayer. Listen to the voice of my petitions. | In the day of my trouble I will call on you, for you will answer me. | Turn to me, and have mercy on me! […] Save the son of your servant.*

Mic 7:7 – *But as for me, I will look to Yahweh. I will wait for the God of my salvation. My God will hear me.*

Mt 7:9-11 – *"Or who is there among you, who, if his son asks him for bread, will give him a stone? | Or if he asks for a fish, who will give him a serpent? | If you then, being evil, know how to give good gifts to your children, how much more will your Father who is in heaven give good things to those who ask him!"*

Jesus clearly asks YHWH to remove this cup from him. *"However, not what I desire, but what you desire."* Thus, the stage is set: when the hour comes, if Jesus dies on the cross, then the blame lies with YHWH.

15:17 – And having gone away again for *a* second *time*, he prayed, saying, "My Father, if it not be possible for this *cup* to pass by, except I drink it, Your will be done."

Ps 17:6 – *I have called on you, for you will answer me, God. […]*

Ps 77:1,2 – *My cry goes to God! Indeed, I cry to God for help, and for him to listen to me. | In the day of my trouble I sought the Lord. My hand was stretched out in the night, and didn't get tired. My soul refused to be comforted.*

Ps 109:21,22 – *But deal with me, Yahweh the Lord, for your name's sake, because your loving kindness is good, deliver me. | […]*

Ps 145:18,19 – *Yahweh is near to all those who call on him, to all who call on him in truth. | He will fulfill the desire of those who fear him. He also will hear their cry, and will save them.*

15:19 – And having left them, having gone away again, for the third time he prayed […]

In the ancient world, an action performed only once or twice was not necessarily sufficient; performed three times, though, it was supposed to cinch the deal.[94]

For example, to fulfill their spiritual duty, the Jews were required to appear before YHWH three times each year:

Ex 23:14 – *"You shall observe a feast to me three times a year."*

Likewise, had the donkey only balked twice, YHWH's angel might have ended up slaying Balaam:

Nu 22:32,33 – *Yahweh's angel said to him, "Why have you struck your donkey these three times? Behold, I have come out as an adversary, because your way is perverse before me. | The donkey saw me, and turned aside before me these three times. Unless she had turned aside from me, surely now I would have killed you, and saved her alive."*

And if Elijah had only performed his prostration twice instead of thrice, who can say whether YHWH would have answered his prayer to revive the boy:

1Ki 17:21,22 – *He stretched himself on the child three times, and cried to Yahweh, and said, "Yahweh my God, please let this child's soul come into him again." | Yahweh listened to the voice of Elijah; and the soul of the child came into him again, and he revived.*

By repeating his prayer to YHWH three times, Jesus shows that he has been careful to fulfill all the prayerful obligations of a suppliant.[95] There can now be no reason on earth why the God of Israel should refuse to 'remove this cup' from him…unless it is indeed YHWH's desire that Jesus be offered up in sacrifice.

15:19 – […] having said the same utterance again.

Ps 9:10 – *Those who know your name will put their trust in you, for you, Yahweh, have not forsaken those who seek you.*

Ps 20:6,9 – […] | *Save, Yahweh! Let the King answer us when we call!*

Ps 31:2,4 – *Bow down your ear to me. Deliver me speedily. Be to me a strong rock, a house of defense to save me.* | *Pluck me out of the net that they have laid secretly for me, for you are my stronghold.*

Ps 37:5,7 – […] | *Rest in Yahweh, and wait patiently for him. Don't fret because of […] the man who makes wicked plots happen.*

Ps 141:1,8,9 – *Yahweh, I have called on you. Come to me quickly! […] Don't leave my soul destitute.* | *Keep me from the snare which they have laid for me, from the traps of the workers of iniquity.*

Ps 142:1-7 – […] *On the path in which I walk, they have hidden a snare for me.* | […] *Listen to my cry, for I am in desperate need.* […]

If Jesus is seeking to fulfill the Scriptures, as seems quite evident, then part of that picture would be to paint the impression that someone has laid a snare for him on the path that he walks, as per the last four Psalms quoted above. Hence, it may well have been part of Jesus' design that Judas' role and the actions of the chief priests at least be perceived as base and underhanded, with Jesus being snared by 'persecutors' and imprisoned.[96]

15:21 – "Wake up! Let us be led away. Behold, he who hands me over has come near."

Joe 1:5 – *Wake up, you drunkards, and weep! Wail, all you drinkers of wine, because of the sweet wine; for it is cut off from your mouth.*

Simon and the others were small comfort to Jesus in his hour of need. A bit too much wine with supper, boys?

15:22-39 JESUS IS SEIZED

15:24 – And immediately, having come up to Jesus, he said, "Rejoice, Rabbi!" – and he kissed him.

Pr 24:26 – *An honest answer is like a kiss on the lips.*

said to Simon, "Are you sleeping? Were you not able to stay awake one hour?"[r]

16   "Be vigilant, and pray that you might not come into temptation!"[1][s]

17   And having gone away again for *a* second *time,* he prayed, saying, "My Father, if it not be possible for this *cup* to pass by, except I drink it, Your will be done."[t]

18   And having come again, he found them sleeping, for their eyes were heavy.[u]

19   And having left them, having gone away again, for *the* third *time* he prayed, having said the same utterance again.[v]

20   Then he came to the disciples and said to them, "At least you are sleeping, and taking your rest.[2][w]

21   "Wake up! Let us be led away. Behold, he who hands me over has come near."[x]

22   And at that moment, even as he was speaking of him, behold,[3] one of the twelve approached; and with him a crowd with daggers and clubs, from the chief

r	Mt 26:40
	Mr 14:37
	Lu 22:45
s	Mt 26:41
	Mr 14:38
	Lu 22:46
t	Ps 5:1,4
	Ps 17:6
	Ps 77:1,2
	Ps 105:8,14,15
	Ps 106:44,45
	Ps 109:21,22
	Ps 145:18,19
	Isa 45:17,19,21
	Isa 51:21,22
	Jer 29:12,13
	Joe 2:32
	Mt 26:42
	Mr 14:39
u	Mt 26:43
	Mr 14:40
v	Ps 9:10
	Ps 20:6,9
	Ps 31:2,4
	Ps 37:5,7
	Ps 141:1,8,9
	Ps 142:1-7
	Mt 26:44
w	Mt 26:45
	Mr 14:41
x	Joe 1:5
	Mt 26:46
	Mr 14:42
	Jn 18:2

---

1 Certain later mss. add, *For the spirit is willing, but the flesh is weak*
2 Certain later mss. add, *The hour has come – behold, the son of man is handed over, into the hands of sinners*
3 Certain later mss. add, *Judas*

15

y Mt 26:47
Mr 14:43
Lu 22:47
Jn 18:3
z Mt 26:48
Mr 14:44
Lu 22:47
a Pr 24:26
Mt 26:49
Mr 14:45
b Mt 26:50
c Jn 18:4
d Ex 3:14
Jn 18:5
e Jn 18:6
f Jn 18:7
g Jn 18:8
h Mt 26:50
Mr 14:46

priests and the scribes and the elders.[y]

23   Now he who was handing him over had given an indication, saying to them, "Whomever I kiss, is he. Lay hold of him, and lead *him* away safely."[z]

24   And immediately, having come up to Jesus, he said, "Rejoice, Rabbi!" – and he kissed him.[a]

25   But Jesus said to him, "Friend, for whom have you come?"[b]

26   [4][Then Jesus, knowing all the things that were coming to him, came forth and said to them, "Whom do you seek?"[c]

27   They answered him, "Jesus of Nazareth." He said to them, "I AM."[d]

28   Therefore, as soon as he said to them, "I AM", they drew back among the *trees* and fell on the ground.[e]

29   Therefore he asked them again, "Whom do you seek?" And they said, "Jesus of Nazareth."[f]

30   Jesus answered, "I said to you, I AM. Therefore, if you seek me, permit these *others* to go away."[g]]

31   Then, having approached, they threw *their* hands upon Jesus and laid hold of him.[h]

32   But those around him, having seen what was

4 Verses 26-30 are not found in the best ancient mss.

I think that Judas dearly loved Jesus and knew what his teacher was trying to do. He would have held his friend in the highest esteem, and hoped with all his heart that Jesus' plan would bring about the abrogation of the covenant, and thus spiritual freedom for all Jews.

15:26-28 – Then Jesus, knowing all the things that were coming to him, came forth and said to them, "Whom do you seek?" They answered him, "Jesus of Nazareth." He said to them, "I AM." Therefore, as soon as he said to them, "I AM", they drew back among the *trees* and fell on the ground.

Ex 3:14 – *God said to Moses, "I AM WHO I AM," and he said, "You shall tell the children of Israel this: 'I AM has sent me to you.'"*

Here, verses 26-30 would have been added later for the sole purpose of elucidating the nature of Jesus' blasphemy before the Sanhedrin.[97]

We can be sure that Jesus never said 'I AM' to the men who came to arrest him, because not one of them gave evidence of such blasphemy before the Sanhedrin. Yet their reaction – *they drew back and fell on the ground* – clearly conveys that Jesus has pronounced the Sacred Name.[98]

15:32,33 – But those around him, having seen what was going to happen, said, "Master, if we will strike with the dagger?" Then Simon the Zealous drew *his* dagger and struck the high priest's slave, and cut off his ear; and the slave's name was Malchus.

De 15:17 – *It shall be, if he tells you, "I will not go out from you," because he loves you and your house, because he is well with you; | then you shall take an awl, and thrust it through his ear to the door, and he shall be your slave forever. Also to your female slave you shall do likewise.*

Malchus is a slave, perhaps one whose ear has been pierced to make him a permanent slave. Therefore, if someone (one could imagine Simon the Zealous…unless it were Judas himself?) cuts off Malchus' ear, it is coarse way of freeing Malchus from his slavery.

15:34 – Then Jesus said to him, "Put your dagger away in its place. The cup which my Father has given me, will I not drink it?"

Jer 25:28 – *It shall be, if they refuse to take the cup at your hand to drink, then you shall tell them, 'Yahweh of Armies says: "You shall surely drink."'*

15:35 – "How *else* then might the Scriptures be fulfilled, since it must come about in this way?"

Chopping off ears is certainly not what Jesus has in mind, in terms of freeing the Jews from their slavery to YHWH. The Scriptures have foretold the way things must come about for freedom to be achieved.

15:38 – And having left him *behind*, they all fled.

Pr 24:10,11 – *If you falter in the time of trouble, your strength is small. | Rescue those who are being led away to death! Indeed, hold back those who are staggering to the slaughter!*

Well, against a crowd wielding clubs and daggers, they did only have two knives of their own. It was time to skedaddle!

15:39,40 A CERTAIN YOUNG MAN FLEES NAKED

15:39,40 – And a certain young man was following along with him, having thrown a linen cloth about *his* naked *body*, and they laid hold of him. But the *young man*, having left the linen cloth behind, fled naked.

What? Who's this guy? Where does he come from? What's he doing there?

This little detail, only related by Mark, is a doozie. It's so incongruous that it smacks of real life. Absent from the other Synoptics and certainly from John, this little sideshow somehow kept its place in Mark's gospel, though it serves no narrative purpose. It just seems to

going to happen, said, "Master, if we will strike with the dagger?"[i]

33 Then [5]Simon the Zealous drew *his* dagger and struck the high priest's slave, and cut off his ear;[j] and the slave's name was Malchus.[k]

34 Then Jesus said to him, "Put your dagger away in its place.[l] The cup which my Father has given me, will I not drink it?[m]

35 "How *else* then might the Scriptures be fulfilled, since it must come about in this way?"[n]

36 And having answered, Jesus said to them, "As against a robber, have you come out with daggers and clubs to apprehend me?[o]

37 "Every day I was with you in the temple, teaching, and you did not lay hold of me, but that the Scriptures might be fulfilled."[p]

38 And having left him *behind*, they all fled.[q]

39 And a certain young man was following along with him, having thrown a linen cloth about *his* naked *body*, and they laid hold of him.[r]

40 But the *young man*, having left the linen cloth behind, fled naked.[s]

i Lu 22:49
j Ex 21:6
   De 15:17
   Mt 26:51
   Mr 14:47
   Lu 22:50
k Jn 18:10
l Mt 26:52
m Jer 25:28
   Jn 18:11
n Mt 26:54
o Mt 26:55
   Mr 14:48
   Lu 22:52
p Mt 26:55,56
   Mr 14:49
   Lu 22:53
q Pr 24:10,11
   Mt 26:56
   Mr 14:50
r Mr 14:51
s Mr 14:52

---

5 According to the best ancient mss.; most later mss. read, *a certain one of them*

15   Simon is questioned by those standing in the courtyard

t   *Lu 22:54*
u   *Mt 26:47*
    Mr 14:43
v   *Mt 26:14*
    Mr 14:10
    Lu 22:3,4
w   *Jn 18:15*
x   *Jn 18:16*
y   *Mr 14:54*
    Lu 22:55
    Jn 18:18
z   *Mr 14:66*
a   *Mt 26:69*
    Mr 14:67
    Lu 22:56
    Jn 18:17
b   *Mt 26:70*
    Lu 22:57
    Jn 18:17
c   *Mr 14:68*

41 And having apprehended him, they led him away and brought him into the high priest's house.[t]

42 And Simon and the other disciple[u] were following Jesus; but that disciple was known to the high priest,[v] and he entered with Jesus into the courtyard of the high priest.[w]

43 But Simon stood at the door outside. Therefore the other disciple, who was known to the high priest, went out and spoke to the doorkeeper, and brought Simon in.[x]

44 But the slaves and the attendants were standing there, having made a heap of burning coals, since it was cold, and they were warming themselves. And Simon was standing with them, and warming himself.[y]

45 And Simon was below, in the courtyard; and one the high priest's slave-girls came,[z]

46 and having seen Simon warming himself, and having peered at him, *she* said *to him*, "You also were with Jesus, the Galilean."[a]

47 But he denied *it* before *them* all, saying, "I do not know what you are saying."[b] And he went out to the porch.[c]

be a comical incident that happened to occur as Jesus was being hauled off to the high priest's house.

Without wanting to read too much into these two verses from Mark, let us nevertheless duly note the following:

1) The only disciples who will be in a position to recount this episode afterwards are Judas (if he accompanied the crowd that led Jesus away) and possibly Simon (if he were following closely enough to see) and the 'certain disciple' who was with Simon (more about him shortly).

2) This is a 'certain' young man. The wording implies that he was not just someone who happened to be there, but someone who was known to the group.

3) He was stark naked and had grabbed a linen cloth to cover himself as he ran after the crowd that had arrested Jesus.

Let's see...while Jesus was busy praying and while Simon and James and John were catching forty winks, what *were* the other disciples doing out there in the Garden of Gethsemane?

15:41-52 SIMON DENIES JESUS THREE TIMES

15:42 – And Simon and the other disciple [...].

I am here following the Stephanus Textus Receptus 1550, which reads 'the other disciple' (versus 'another disciple'). If we understand this as designating someone who has been recently mentioned in John's text, then there are only two contenders: the disciple who cut off Malchus' ear (who John says was Simon Peter, so it can't be him)...and Judas.

15:42 – [...] were following Jesus; but that disciple was know to the high priest, and he entered with Jesus into the courtyard of the high priest.

Mt 26:14 – Then one of the twelve, who was called Judas Iscariot, went to the chief priests.

Mr 14:10 – *Judas Iscariot, who was one of the twelve, went away to the chief priests, that he might deliver him to them.*

Lu 22:3,4 – *Satan entered into Judas, who was also called Iscariot, who was counted with the twelve. | He went away, and talked with the chief priests and captains about how he might deliver him to them.*

There is only one disciple who can be said to have known the high priest – Judas, who went to discuss with the chief priests the matter of how they might take Jesus into custody. That he 'entered with Jesus into the courtyard' suggests that he was accompanying Jesus; Judas would have been able to do just that. And unlike the others, Judas would have had no consequences to fear from being identified as one of Jesus' followers.

15:43 – But Simon stood at the door outside. Therefore the other disciple, who was known to the high priest, went out and spoke to the doorkeeper, and brought Simon in.

Having failed to live up to the brazen promises he'd made earlier in front of everyone else, Simon has mustered the courage to follow as Jesus has been led away. Maybe he calculated that the others would be less likely to razz him about his earlier overweening bravado, when they learned that he'd later gone to the high priest's house.

15:51 – But he began to curse, and to swear, "I do not know this man of whom you speak!" And immediately a cock crowed.

The fact that Simon denies Jesus three times in a row serves to underscore just how complete and utter his denial is.

We may wonder…did a cock really crow? Once? Twice? The historicity of the episode is not the point – the three denials form a chiastic match with Jesus' three prayers in the Garden of Gethsemane, around the centerpiece of Jesus' arrest.

48 And the slave-girl, having seen him, again began to say to those standing by, "This *fellow* is one of them."^d

49 And again he denied *it* with an oath – "Since I do not know the man!"^e

50 But after a little *while*, those who stood *there*, having come near, said to Simon, "Truly, you also are from them, for even your speech makes you plainly clear."^f

51 But he began to curse, and to swear, "I do not know this man of whom you speak!" And immediately a cock crowed.^g

52 And Simon remembered Jesus' statement, he having said to him, "Before a cock crows, you will deny me three times." And having gone out, he wept bitterly.^h

d Mt 26:71
   Mr 14:69
   Lu 22:58
   Jn 18:25
e Mt 26:72
   Mr 14:70
   Lu 22:58
   Jn 18:25
f Mt 26:73
   Mr 14:70
   Lu 22:59
   Jn 18:26
g Mt 26:74
   Mr 14:71
   Lu 22:60
   Jn 18:27
h Mt 26:75
   Mr 14:72
   Lu 22:61,62

16   Jesus is brought before the Sanhedrin

CHAPTER 16

a *Lu 22:66*
b *Ex 12:3*
   Le 22:20
   Job 31:6
   Mr 14:55
c *De 19:15*
   Mr 14:56
d *De 19:15*
e *Ps 27:12-14*
   Ps 35:11,12
   Mt 26:60
   Mr 14:57
f *Mt 24:2*
   Mr 13:2
   Lu 21:6
g *Ps 109:1-5*
   Pr 12:17
   Mt 26:61
   Mr 14:58
h *Ex 23:1*
   De 19:16-19
   Mr 14:59

AND when it became day, the council of the elders of the people, both the chief priests and the scribes, were gathered together, and they led him away into their [1]Sanhedrin.[a]

2   And the chief priests and all the [1]Sanhedrin sought evidence against Jesus, but did not find *any*.[b]

3   For many [2]were bearing witness against him, but the testimonies were not [3]equal.[c]

4   But some *other witnesses*,[d] having come forward, were bearing false witness against him, saying,[e]

5   "Since we heard him saying, 'I will overthrow this temple,[f] the *one* made with hands, and in three days I will build another, not made by hands.'"[g]

6   And not even in this manner was their evidence [3]equal.[h]

1 Gr. *synedrion*; lit., *a sitting together*
2 Certain later mss. read, *were bearing false witness*
3 Or, *consistent*

16

Jesus is condemned to death

16:1-6 JESUS IS BROUGHT BEFORE THE SANHEDRIN

16:1 – And when it became day, the council of the elders of the people, both the chief priests and the scribes, were gathered together, and they led him away into their Sanhedrin.

Nowhere do the Gospels explicitly say that the Sanhedrin convened in the middle of the night; indeed, Luke 22:66 states that it assembled *'when it became day'*. The reason for imagining the contrary is derived from the other three Gospels, which in typical chiastic fashion break the story of Simon Peter's denial into two parts and sandwich the interrogation of Jesus between them. Since the cock's crow after Peter's third denial implies that dawn is approaching, the trial, recounted before this, easily appears to have been conducted at night; and because such a notion dovetails so nicely with the popular Christian belief that the chief priests were deviously plotting to kill Jesus and cloaking their machinations with secrecy, Luke's plain as day statement that the Council convened *'when it became day'* goes by the wayside. The other three Evangelists add a further element by stating that Jesus was taken to Pilate in the morning; but again, it is an assumption to say that it was the morning following a nocturnal trial.

Since the early Jesus-movement never accused the Jews of having violated proper judicial procedure, we might deduce that the Sanhedrin's proceedings in the Jesus case complied with its judicial policies.

What would those policies have been? Would they have precluded a nocturnal trial? If we look to the oral traditions of the Mishnah compiled by Judah ha-Nasi ca. 200 CE, we learn that the process of a criminal could only be conducted in daytime and that a sentence of death could not be pronounced until the day after the trial. Trials were furthermore forbidden to take place on the Preparation Day for a Sabbath or festival (cf. *Tractate Sanhedrin*, chapter IV, folios 32a and 35a). Of course, we cannot affirm that these precepts were in force two centuries earlier, for the traditions that inform the Mishnah stem from the court of justice at Jamnia, which was dominated by the Pharisees and was the successor, after the destruction of the temple in 70 CE, to the Sanhedrin, which in Jesus' time was strongly influenced by the Sadducees.[99] While admitting that the procedural conduct of the two courts probably differed in certain respects, it nevertheless does seem reasonable to suppose that the traditions of the earlier Sanhedrin could have provided at least a framework for the later court at Jamnia, in which case certain elements of the aforementioned precepts may have existed as part of the Sanhedrin's rules – such as the requirement that trials be conducted during the day.[100]

We do not know which charges were brought against Jesus, so we cannot be sure whether the Sanhedrin that was convened was composed of 3, 23 or 71 members. The *Tractate Sanhedrin* states that 'CIVIL SUITS [ARE TRIED] BY THREE; CAPITAL CASES BY TWENTY-THREE' and that 'A TRIBE, FALSE PROPHET AND A HIGH PRIEST CAN ONLY BE TRIED BY A COURT OF SEVENTY-ONE. WAR OF FREE CHOICE CAN BE WAGED ONLY BY THE AUTHORITY OF A COURT OF SEVENTY-ONE.'[101]

Finally, what day are we? In my view, Jesus was handed over on the 11th or 12th of Nisan, and tried when day had come. The trial may of course have lasted only a few hours, but we might allow that the dearth of reliable witnesses required that more be sought for, and that Jesus' silence hindered judgment as well. The proceedings may have even dragged on for the better part of a day. At any rate, it is Jesus who sets the pace with his silence, and he can be sure the trial will end abruptly when he opens his mouth for the first time.

16:2 – And the chief priests and all the Sanhedrin sought evidence against Jesus, but did not find *any*.

Le 22:20 – *"But whatever has a defect, that you shall not offer; for it shall not be acceptable for you."*

Job 31:6 – *Let me be weighed in an even balance, that God may know my integrity.*

Jesus, as it were, is found to have no defect. This can only mean that he is ritually pure and suitable for sacrifice.

16:3 – For many were bearing witness against him, but the testimonies were not equal.

De 19:15 – *One witness shall not rise up against a man for any iniquity, or for any sin, in any sin that he sins. At the mouth of two witnesses, or at the mouth of three witnesses, shall a matter be established.*

If the chief priests were maliciously determined to put Jesus to death, as they have been accused of by Christians, then why did they not prepare a better sham trial? You'd think they'd have lined up suitable witnesses in advance, no? Yet the testimonies do not agree, and in the context of the trial this means that none of the evidence is so far admissible. In my view, this alone proves that the chief priests were not seeking to 'destroy' Jesus, as Matthew *et al.* assert.[102] Rather, the priests were acting with due authority in a case of public disturbance that called for clarification. And if Jesus were suspected of being a false prophet – a crime punishable by death (see Deuteronomy 13:5) – then their concerns were not only legitimate, but of urgent import.

16:4,5 – But some *other witnesses,* having come forward, were bearing false witness against him, saying, "Since we heard him saying, 'I will overthrow this temple, the *one* made with hands, and in three days I will build another, not made by hands.'"

Ps 27:12-14 – *Don't deliver me over to the desire of my adversaries, for false witnesses have risen up against me, such as breathe out cruelty. | [...]*

Ps 109:1-5 – *God of my praise, don't remain silent, for they have opened the mouth of the wicked and the mouth of deceit against me. They have spoken to me with a lying tongue. | [...]*

Matthew is surely inventing his facts here, for if there were two witnesses, as he says, and if their testimony were consistent – as one would expect – then the Sanhedrin would have had its evidence. Barring that, these are the worst false witnesses to ever stand trial. They can't even get their false testimony straight. Imposters!

16:6 – And not even in this manner was their evidence equal.

Ex 23:1 – *"You shall not spread a false report. Don't join your hand with the wicked to be a malicious witness."*

De 19:16-19 – *If an unrighteous witness rises up against any man to testify against him of wrongdoing, | [...] | [...] and, behold, if the witness is a false witness, and has testified falsely against his brother; | then you shall do to him as he had thought to do to his brother. So you shall remove the evil from among you.*

The presence of 'false' witnesses may be said to 'fulfill' the Scriptures (as noted above, Psalms 27:12-14, 35:11,12 and 109:1-5), but in view of the risk they ran, as noted here in the margins, I can only think it unlikely that anyone would dare to testify falsely.[103]

At any rate, no charge against Jesus is upheld. Therefore, he was not found guilty of being a false prophet, which is the only charge for which a 71 member Sanhedrin would have been convened on his behalf.[104]

16:7-12 JESUS BLASPHEMES BEFORE THE SANHEDRIN

16:7 – And the high priest, having stood up in the midst *of the proceedings,* **questioned Jesus, saying, "Do you not answer, not even one** *thing,* **to what these** *witnesses* **give** *as* **evidence against you?"**

Jn 7:51 – *"Does our law judge a man, unless it first hears from him personally and knows what he does?"*

16:8 – But he was silent, and did not answer, not one *thing.* **[...]**

Ps 17:3 – *You have proved my heart. [...] You have tried me, and found nothing. I have resolved that my mouth shall not disobey.*

Isa 53:6,7,10 – *[...] Yahweh has laid on him the iniquity of us all. | He was oppressed, yet when he was afflicted he didn't open his mouth. As a lamb that is led to the slaughter, and as a sheep that before its shearers is silent, so he didn't open his mouth. | Yet it pleased Yahweh to bruise him. He has caused him to suffer. When you make his soul an offering for sin [...]*

16:8 – [...] Again the high priest was questioning him, and said to him, "Are you the messiah, the son of the Blessed *One?"*

De 17:15 – *You shall surely set him king over yourselves, whom Yahweh your God chooses. You shall set as king over you one from among your brothers. You may not put a foreigner over you, who is not your brother.*

1Ch 17:11-14 – *"It will happen, when your days are fulfilled that you must go to be with your fathers, that I will set up your offspring after you, who will be of your sons; and I will establish his kingdom. | [...]"*

Ps 89:20,26,27 – *"I have found David, my servant. I have anointed him with my holy oil. | [...] | I will also appoint him my firstborn, the highest of the kings of the earth."*

No harm in asking, right? The high priest may have thought to himself, 'He's from Galilee, not Bethlehem, and I don't suppose he comes from the house of David either, but we may as well give him a chance and cover all the bases.'

Keep in mind that it would have been in no way blasphemous for Jesus to have answered him that yes, he was the Messiah, the anointed Son of YHWH. If he had, the high priest would have just wanted to know in that case who had anointed him and so given him that authority.

16:9 – And Jesus said, "I AM."

Ex 3:14 – *God said to Moses, "I AM WHO I AM," and he said, "You shall tell the children of Israel this: 'I AM has sent me to you.'"*

Ex 6:2,3 – *God spoke to Moses, and said to him, "I am Yahweh; | and I appeared to Abraham, to Isaac, and to Jacob, as God Almighty; but by my name Yahweh I was not known to them."*

To say you were the Son of God and his Messiah was no blasphemy …but to say the Sacred Name aloud was![105]

While the exact pronunciation of the Ineffable Name was supposedly only known to the high priest, we may infer from the Mishnah that it was more widely known than that.[106]

16:10,11 – But the high priest, having torn his robes, said, "What need have we any more of witnesses? You heard the blasphemy! [...] "

Ex 20:7 – *"You shall not take the name of Yahweh your God in vain, for Yahweh will not hold him guiltless who takes his name in vain."*

Upon hearing the Ineffable Name, the high priest immediately tears his robes. One imagines that the others all present did the same.[107] Had Jesus pronounced the Sacred Name in the Garden of Gethsemane, as John recounts, those who had heard it would have been called to give evidence;[108] but since Jesus blasphemes in front of the gathered priests, there is no need at all to hear testimony from witnesses.

7 And the high priest, having stood up in the midst *of the proceedings*, questioned Jesus, saying, "Do you not answer, not even one *thing*, *to* what these *witnesses* give *as* evidence against you?"[i]

8 But he was silent, and did not answer, not one *thing*.[j] Again the high priest was questioning him, and said to him, "Are you the [4]messiah, the son of the Blessed *One*?"[k]

9 And Jesus said, [5]"I AM."[l]

10 But the high priest, having torn his robes, said, "What need have we any more of witnesses?"[m]

11 "You heard the blasphemy![n] How does it seem to you?" And they all condemned him *as* liable, to be *put to* death.[o]

12 And some began to spit on him,[p] and to cover up his face and to strike him with their fists,[q] and to say to him, "Prophesy!"[r] And *with* blows the attendants took hold of him.[s]

i Mt 26:62
   Mr 14:60
   Jn 7:51
j Ps 17:3
   Ps 39:9
   Isa 53:6,7,10
k De 17:15
   2Sa 7:12-16
   1Ch 17:11-14
   1Ch 28:4-7
   Ps 2:7
   Ps 89:20,26,27
   Mt 26:63
   Mr 14:61
   Lu 22:70
l Ex 3:14
   Ex 6:2,3
   Mr 14:62
   Lu 22:70
m Mt 26:65
   Mr 14:63
   Lu 22:71
n Ex 20:7
o Le 24:16
   De 17:6
   Ps 109:7
   Mt 26:66
   Mr 14:64
p Job 30:10
q Isa 50:6
r De 18:22
s Eze 7:9
   Mt 26:67
   Mr 14:65

---

4 Gr., *messias*, for the Hebrew *mashiach*; certain later mss. read, *christos*

5 Lit., יהוה, or *YHWH*, and appearing thus in the best ancient mss.; the Hebrew Tetragrammaton signifies the Hebrew tribal name for God, which the Jews ceased to pronounce about 300 BCE, considering it too sacred and fearing desecration; when entering the Holy of Holies once each year on the Day of Atonement, the high priest was permitted to say aloud the sacred name, a privilege reserved to him alone; for all others, enunciation of the sacred name was judged blasphemous; certain mss. read, IAΩ ; certain mss. read, ΠΙΠΙ ; most later mss. read, Ἐγώ εἰμι, or, *I am*

16:11 – " [...] How does it seem to you?" And they all condemned him *as* liable, to be *put to* death.

Le 24:16 – *"He who blasphemes Yahweh's name, he shall surely be put to death. All the congregation shall certainly stone him. The foreigner as well as the native-born, when he blasphemes the Name, shall be put to death."*

Ps 109:7 – *When he is judged, let him come out guilty. Let his prayer be turned into sin.*

They all condemn him as being *liable* to be put to death, but they have not yet passed sentence. For that, they must wait one day.[109]

16:12 – And some began to spit on him, and to cover up his face and to strike him with their fists [...].

Job 30:10 – *They abhor me, they stand aloof from me, and don't hesitate to spit in my face.*

Isa 50:6 – *I gave my back to those who beat me, and my cheeks to those who plucked off the hair. I didn't hide my face from shame and spitting.*

No doubt about it: when it comes to blasphemy, people see red.

16:12 – [...] and to say to him, "Prophesy!" [...]

De 18:22 – *When a prophet speaks in Yahweh's name, if the thing doesn't follow, nor happen, that is the thing which Yahweh has not spoken. The prophet has spoken it presumptuously. You shall not be afraid of him.*

It's a mocking challenge, but one that makes sense: if Jesus were to prophesy something in YHWH's name and this thing were to come true, only then might they consider that he had YHWH's sanction to say aloud the Sacred Name.

16:12 – [...] And *with* blows the attendants took hold of him.

Eze 7:9 – *"My eye won't spare, neither will I have pity. [...] and you will know that I, Yahweh, strike."*

16:13,14 JESUS IS CONDEMNED TO DEATH

My view is that the Sanhedrin was reconvened the following day, to formally sentence Jesus to death for blasphemy.[110] This would concur with the Mishnah, which states that 'CAPITAL CHARGES MUST BE TRIED BY DAY AND CONCLUDED BY DAY. [...] CAPITAL CHARGES MAY BE CONCLUDED ON THE SAME DAY WITH A FAVOURABLE VERDICT, BUT ONLY ON THE MORROW WITH AN UNFAVOURABLE VERDICT (*in case points in the accused's favour are discovered during the night*).'[111]

Having been condemned to death, Jesus was led forth, likewise per the Mishnah: 'WHEN THE TRIAL IS ENDED (*and the accused is found guilty*), HE [THE CONDEMNED] IS LED FORTH TO BE STONED (*if he be so sentenced*).'[112] However, the priests take him, not outside of the city to be stoned, but to Pilate, for reasons that we will see shortly.

16:15-17 JUDAS RETURNS THE THIRTY SILVER COINS

16:16 – saying, "I am guiltless of this *man's* blood. You will see!" [...][113]

Mr 14:36 – *He said, "Abba, Father, all things are possible to you. Please remove this cup from me. However, not what I desire, but what you desire."*

Judas is indeed guiltless. YHWH alone bears the responsibility.

16:16 – [...] But they said, "What *is that* to us? You will see!"

Sad, but true. Judas' fate was to be reviled for his crucial role.

16:17 – And having thrown the silver coins into the temple, he withdrew.

Ge 2:6,7 – *But a mist went up from the earth, and watered the whole surface of the ground. | Yahweh God formed man from the dust of the ground, and breathed into his nostrils the breath of life; and man became a living soul.*

16   Jesus is handed over to Pilate

t *Mt 27:1*
   Mr 15:1
u *Mt 27:2*
   Mr 15:1
   Lu 23:1
v *Mt 27:3*
w *Mt 26:39*
   Mr 14:36
   Lu 22:42
x *Mt 27:4*
y *Ge 2:6,7*
   Isa 64:8
   Zec 11:13
z *Isa 29:16*
   Mt 27:5
a *Jn 18:28*
b *Jn 18:29*

13 Now, morning having come, the chief priests and the elders of the people all took counsel against Jesus, so that they might put him to death;[t]

14 and having bound him, they led *him* away and handed him over to [6]Pilate, the governor.[u]

15 Then [7]*the one* having handed him over, having seen that he was condemned, returned the thirty silver coins to the chief priests and elders,[v]

16 saying, "[8]I am guiltless of this *man's* blood.[w] You will see!" But they said, "What *is that* to us? You will see!"[x]

17 And having thrown the silver coins into the temple,[y] he withdrew.[z]

18 Then they led Jesus from Caiaphas into the [9]Praetorium. Now it was early, and they did not enter into the Praetorium, that they might not be defiled, but might eat the Passover.[a]

19 Therefore Pilate went out to them, and said, "What accusation do you bring against this man?"[b]

20 And they answered, saying to him, "If he were

---

6 The cognomen of Pontius Pilate, the Roman prefect of Judea from 26 – 36 CE
7 Certain later mss. add, *Judas*
8 According to the best ancient mss.; certain later mss. read, *I have sinned, having handed over innocent blood*
9 The official residence, or palace, of the governor

Like a potter, YHWH forms man out of misty water and dusty earth.

Isa 64:8 – *But now, Yahweh, you are our Father. We are the clay, and you our potter. We all are the work of your hand.*

Zec 11:13 – *Yahweh said to me, "Throw it to the potter, the handsome price that I was valued at by them!" I took the thirty pieces of silver, and threw them to the potter, in Yahweh's house.*

Jesus no doubt told Judas to do this, with an eye to fulfilling the Scriptures. YHWH sure won't like being framed like that, though.

Isa 29:16 – *"You turn things upside down! Should the potter be thought to be like clay; that the thing made should say about him who made it, 'He didn't make me'; or the thing formed say of him who formed it, 'He has no understanding?'"*

16:18-30 JESUS IS HANDED OVER TO PILATE

16:18 – **Then they led Jesus from Caiaphas into the Praetorium. Now it was early, and they did not enter into the Praetorium, that they might not be defiled, but might eat the Passover.**

Caiaphas and the priests have brought Jesus to the gates of the governor's palace. From there, the palace guards would have escorted him into the Praetorium. The priests did not enter in, so as not to defile themselves before the coming Passover. In Luke's account, Jesus will be later this day sent to Herod's palace, before being returned to Pilate, who will then interrogate him further.

16:19,20 – **Therefore Pilate went out to them, and said, "What accusation do you bring against this man?" And they answered, saying to him, "If he were not evil, we would not have handed him over to you."**

Le 24:16 – *"He who blasphemes Yahweh's name, he shall surely be put to death. [...]"*

De 13:1-5 – *If a prophet or a dreamer of dreams arises among you* […] | *you shall not listen to the words of that prophet, or to that dreamer of dreams;* […] | *That prophet, or that dreamer of dreams, shall be put to death, because he has spoken rebellion against Yahweh your God,* […] *to draw you aside out of the way which Yahweh your God commanded you to walk in. So you shall remove the evil from among you.*

Let us be very clear: Jesus' teachings and conduct have called into question orthodox Judaism; his intent does indeed seem to be to draw his fellow Jews *'aside out of the way'* which YHWH commands. But far more importantly, and to top things off, he has blasphemed the Sacred Name. There can be no other outcome here: Jesus must die.

16:21 – **But they began to accuse him, saying, "We found this *man* perverting our nation, and forbidding to give tribute to Caesar, and saying *he* himself is Christ, a king."**

The chief priests surely had every right and reason to resort to expediency, for it was YHWH's law that mattered to them above all else. Pilate, who was not a Jew, could never have comprehended the gravity of Jesus' actions in their eyes, nor why he must die. Since the chief priests' reasons were not reasons that a Gentile like Pilate could allow, they have little choice but to deliberately misrepresent Jesus' 'crimes' so as to render him crucifiable under Roman law.[114]

16:27 – **"I have been born into this […] "**

Nu 27:16,17 – *"Let Yahweh, the God of the spirits of all flesh, appoint a man over the congregation,* | […] *that the congregation of Yahweh not be as sheep which have no shepherd."*

Zec 13:7 – *"Awake, sword, against my shepherd, and against the man who is close to me," says Yahweh of Armies. "Strike the shepherd, and the sheep will be scattered; and I will turn my hand against the little ones."*

not evil, we would not have handed him over to you."^c

21 But they began to accuse him, saying, "We found this *man* perverting our nation, and forbidding to give tribute to Caesar, and saying *he* himself is [10]Christ, a king."^d

22 Therefore Pilate went again into the Praetorium and summoned Jesus, and said to him, "Are you the king of the Jews?"^e

23 And Jesus answered, "Do you say this from yourself, or did others say *it* to you about me?"^f

24 And Pilate answered, "I am not a Jew. Your nation, and the chief priests, handed you over to me. What did you do?"^g

25 And Jesus answered, "My kingdom is not of this world. If my kingdom were of this world, my attendants would be striving that I might not be handed over now *by* the Jews. But my kingdom is not from this source."^h

26 Therefore Pilate said to him, "So then, you are a king?" And Jesus answered, "You say that I am a king.ⁱ

27 "I have been born into this,^j and for this I have come into the world, that I might bear witness to the

c Le 24:16
De 13:1-5
Jn 18:30
d Ps 109:2-5
Lu 23:2
e Mt 27:11
Mr 15:2
Lu 23:3
Jn 18:33
f Jn 18:34
g Jn 18:35
h Jn 18:36
i Mt 27:11
Mr 15:2
Lu 23:3
Jn 18:37
j Nu 27:16,17
Zec 13:7
Mt 9:36
Jn 10:11

---

10 Gr. *christon*; lit., *the anointed one*

16   Pilate sends Jesus to be questioned by Herod

k De 29:4
    Jn 8:31,32
    Jn 8:43
    Jn 18:37
l Lu 23:4
    Jn 18:38
m Lu 23:5
n Lu 23:6
o Lu 23:7
p Lu 23:8
q Ps 39:9
    Lu 23:9
r Ps 38:19,20
    Lu 23:10
s Lu 23:11

truth. Everyone who is of the truth, hears my voice." [k]

28 And Pilate said to him, "What is truth?" And having said this, he went out again to the Jews and said to them, "I find not one fault in him." [l]

29 But they were insisting, saying, "He stirs up the people, teaching throughout all of Judea, and has started *in* Galilee *before coming* as far as here." [m]

30 But having heard *this*, Pilate asked if the man were a Galilean; [n] and having realized that he was from Herod's jurisdiction, he sent him up to Herod, who was himself also in Jerusalem in those days. [o]

31 And Herod, having seen Jesus, rejoiced greatly, for he had been wanting to see him for a long time, on account of what he was hearing about him; and he was hoping to see some sign done by him. [p]

32 And he questioned him with many words, but he answered him not one. [q]

33 And the chief priests and the scribes had stood by, accusing him vehemently. [r]

34 But having disdained him – and Herod together with his troops having mocked *him*, and having thrown a brilliant robe about *him* – he sent him *back* up to Pilate. [s]

Mt 9:36 – *But when he saw the multitudes, he was moved with compassion for them, because they were [...] like sheep without a shepherd.*

Jn 10:11 – *"I am the good shepherd. The good shepherd lays down his life for the sheep."*

I think Jesus felt a personal sense of mission. In his view of the Scriptures, he would have felt that it was his destiny to be the good shepherd that Y HWH would strike.

It is of note that Jesus does not remain wholly silent before Pilate. He may not say a single word in his own defense – for his plan to work, it is essential that he be crucified – but he doesn't mind answering a few questions. To fulfill Isaiah's prophesy – *As a lamb that is led to the slaughter, and as a sheep that before its shearers is silent, so he didn't open his mouth* – maybe Jesus only needed to be silent with Jews. As a Gentile, Pilate didn't count.

16:27 – " [...] and for this I have come into the world, that I might bear witness to the truth. Everyone who is of the truth, hears my voice."

De 29:4 – *But Yahweh has not given you a heart to know, eyes to see, and ears to hear, to this day.*

Jn 8:31,32,43 – *Jesus therefore said to those Jews who had believed him, "If you remain in my word, then you are truly my disciples. | You will know the truth, and the truth will make you free. | Why don't you understand my speech? Because you can't hear my word."*

16:28,29 – And Pilate [...] went out again to the Jews and said to them, "I find not one fault in him." But they were insisting, saying, "He stirs up the people, teaching throughout all of Judea, and has started *in* Galilee *before coming* as far as here."

Clearly, Pilate has discounted the accusations that Jesus considered himself a Jewish king and was fomenting political unrest. Redoubling their efforts, the chief priests now say that Jesus has been stirring up the people as far away as Galilee.

16:31-34 PILATE SENDS JESUS TO BE QUESTIONED BY HEROD

Herod might well have been in Jerusalem for the Passover, so Luke's account is not implausible, though it finds no echo in the other Gospels. Herod questions him at length, but Jesus remains resolutely silent, as he did the day before with the high priest.

16:33 – And the chief priests and the scribes had stood by, accusing him vehemently.

Ps 38:19,20 – *But my enemies are vigorous and many. Those who hate me without reason are numerous. | They who also render evil for good are adversaries to me, because I follow what is good.*

16:35-40 THE CHIEF PRIESTS OBJECT TO JESUS BEING RELEASED

The chief priests' calumnies were well-intentioned, but they have failed to persuade either Pilate or Herod to condemn Jesus to death as they'd hoped. They now put their cards on the table and make it very clear to Pilate that Jesus must die for reasons that are inherent to Judaism.

16:39 – But the Jews answered him, saying, "We have a law, and according to the law, he ought to die […]"

Ex 20:7 – *"You shall not take the name of Yahweh your God in vain […]"*

Le 24:16 – *"He who blasphemes Yahweh's name, he shall surely be put to death. […]"*

De 18:20 – *"But the prophet who speaks a word presumptuously in my name, which I have not commanded him to speak, or who speaks in the name of other gods, that same prophet shall die."*

The chief priests object to Jesus being released   16

35 Now Pilate, having called together the chief priests and the rulers and the people,[t]

36 said to them, "You brought this man to me, as *the cause of* the people turning away; and behold, having examined him before you, I have found not one fault in this man, against whom you make accusation.[u]

37 "But neither *did* Herod, for he sent him *back* up to us; and behold, nothing worthy of death is done by him.[v]

38 "Therefore, having chastised him, I will release him."[w]

39 But the Jews answered him, saying, "We have a law, and according to the law, he ought to die,[x] since he made himself a son of God."[y]

40 Therefore Pilate said to them, "Take him yourselves, and judge him according to your law." But they said to him, "It is not permitted to us to put anyone to death."[z]

41 And as he was sitting upon the tribunal, his wife sent *word* to him, saying, "*Let there be* nothing *between* you and that righteous *man*, for today I suffered many *things* in a dream on account of him."[a]

42 Therefore, when Pilate heard this word, he was

t Lu 23:13
u Le 22:20
   Lu 23:14
v Lu 23:15
w Lu 23:16
x Ex 20:7
   Le 24:16
   De 17:12
   De 18:20
y Ge 17:10-13
   Ex 4:22
   Le 12:3
   Ps 82:6
   Lu 2:21-24
   Jn 19:7
z Nu 19:11-13
   Jn 18:28
   Jn 18:31
a Mt 27:19

16   Pilate again questions Jesus

b Jn 19:8
c Ps 39:9
   Jn 19:9
d Jn 19:10
e Ps 22:28
   Ps 47:2,7,8
f Mt 26:39
   Mr 14:36
   Lu 22:42
   Jn 19:11
g Jn 19:12
h Jn 19:13
i Mt 27:12
   Mr 15:3

rather frightened,[b]

43   and he again went into the Praetorium, and said to Jesus, "Where are you from?" But Jesus did not give him an answer.[c]

44   Then Pilate said to him, "You do not speak to me? Do you not know that I have authority to release you, and I have authority to crucify you?"[d]

45   But Jesus answered him, saying, "You would not have any authority over me, except it be given to you from above.[e] On account of this, the *one* having handed me over to you has great sin."[f]

46   From this point, Pilate was seeking to release him. But the Jews were shouting, "If you release this *man*, you are no friend of Caesar! Everyone making himself the king speaks against Caesar!"[g]

47   Therefore Pilate, having heard these words, led Jesus out and sat down upon the tribunal, at a place called the [11]Lithostrotos, but in Hebrew, Gabbath.[h]

48   And in his being accused by the chief priests and the elders, he answered not one *thing*.[i]

49   And Pilate questioned him again, saying, "Do you not answer? Not one *thing*? See how many *things*

---

11 Lit., *strewn with stone*; or, *mosaic pavement*

16:39 – " […] since he made himself a son of God."[115]

Ge 17:10-13 – *"This is my covenant, which you shall keep, between me and you and your offspring after you. Every male among you shall be circumcised. | You shall be circumcised in the flesh of your foreskin. It will be a token of the covenant between me and you. | He who is eight days old will be circumcised among you, every male throughout your generations […]. | […] My covenant will be in your flesh for an everlasting covenant."*

Ex 4:22 – *" […] Israel is my son, my firstborn."*

Lu 2:21-24 – *When eight days were fulfilled for the circumcision of the child, his name was called Jesus […]. | […]*

Jesus is a son of Yнwн, and has been made so through his circumcision in fulfillment of the commandment.

16:40 – Therefore Pilate said to them, "Take him yourselves, and judge him according to your law." But they said to him, "It is not permitted to us to put anyone to death."

Since it seems likely that the Sanhedrin would not have refrained from carrying out the death sentence it had passed[116] unless the priests were in point of fact prevented from doing so by Roman dictate,[117] we may deduce that it must have indeed been the case at that time that the Jews were not permitted to put anyone to death.

16:41-45 PILATE AGAIN QUESTIONS JESUS

16:43-45 – […] But Jesus did not give him an answer. Then Pilate said to him, "You do not speak to me? Do you not know that I have authority to release you, and I have authority to crucify you?" But Jesus answered him, saying, "You would not have any authority over me, except it be given to you from above. On account of this, the *one* having handed me over to you has great sin."

Ps 39:9 – *I was mute. I didn't open my mouth, because you did it.*

I'll read that 'you' as being YHWH.

Mr 14:36 – *He said, "Abba, Father, all things are possible to you. Please remove this cup from me. However, not what I desire, but what you desire."*

With his prayer, Jesus made the God of Israel answerable for all that will happen to him. It is YHWH who, by the hand of Judas, delivers Jesus to the chief priests as a sacrificial lamb; in like manner, it is also YHWH who gives Pilate authority over Jesus, to raise him up as a sacrifice on the cross.

16:46-50 JESUS MAKES NO FURTHER ANSWER

Once again, the Jews do all they can to force Pilate's hand, this time by clamouring that he will be no friend of Caesar if he releases Jesus.

16:49 – And Pilate questioned him again, saying, "Do you not answer? Not one *thing*? See how many *things* they accuse you of!"

Isa 53:7 – *He was oppressed, yet when he was afflicted he didn't open his mouth. As a lamb that is led to the slaughter, and as a sheep that before its shearers is silent, so he didn't open his mouth.*

16:50 – But Jesus made no further answer, wherefore Pilate was amazed.

Jesus' silence must have mystified Pilate. Faced with such libel, why on earth would the man not say even one word in his own defense?

Ps 38:13-15 – *But I, as a deaf man, don't hear. I am as a mute man who doesn't open his mouth. | Yes, I am as a man who doesn't hear, in whose mouth are no reproofs. | For in you, Yahweh, do I hope. You will answer, Lord my God.*

The crowd calls on Pilate to release Barabbas   16

they accuse you of!"[j]

50 But Jesus made no further answer,[k] wherefore Pilate was amazed.[l]

51 Now at the feast, the governor was accustomed to release one prisoner to the crowd, whomever they wished.[m]

52 And they had at that time a notable prisoner called Jesus Barabbas.[n]

53 They being therefore gathered together, Pilate said to them, "Whom do you want me to release to you? Jesus Barabbas, or Jesus, whom you call the king of the Jews?"[o]

54 Therefore they were shouting again, saying "Not this *man*, but Barabbas!" Now Barabbas was a robber,[p] imprisoned with the fellow insurgents who had committed murder in the insurrection.[q]

55 And having gone up, the crowd began to petition *him to do* according to how he did for them.[r]

56 But Pilate answered them, saying, "Do you want me to release to you the king of the Jews?"[s]

57 But the chief priests stirred up the crowd, that he might rather release Barabbas to them.[t]

58 And again, Pilate called to them, *for he was*

j Isa 53:7
   Mr 15:4
   Mt 27:13
k Ps 38:13-15
l Mt 27:14
   Mr 15:5
m Mt 27:15
   Mr 15:6
n Mt 27:16
o Mt 27:17
   Mr 15:12
p Jn 18:40
q Mr 15:7
r Mr 15:8
s Mr 15:9
t Mt 27:20
   Mr 15:11

16   Pilate accedes to the crowd's demands

u *Mt 27:21*
    Mr 15:12
    Lu 23:20
v *Mt 27:22*
    Mr 15:13
    Lu 23:21
w *Mt 27:23*
    Mr 15:14
    Lu 23:22,23
x *Ps 26:5,6*
    Mt 27:24
y *Lu 23:24*
z *Jn 19:1*
a *Ge 22:11,12*
    Ps 79:11
    Mt 27:26
    Mr 15:15
    Lu 23:25

wishing to release Jesus.[u]

59 But they were shouting, saying, "Crucify! Crucify him!"[v]

60 And Pilate said to them, "For what? Did this *man* commit evil? I found in him no cause for death. Therefore, having punished him, I will release *him.*" But they were shouting all the more, "Crucify him!"[w]

61 But Pilate, having seen that it availed nothing, but rather that a riot was developing, having taken water, washed his hands in view of the crowd.[x]

62 And Pilate passed judgment, that their request be granted.[y]

63 Then he released Barabbas to them, but having scourged Jesus,[z] he handed him over so that he might be crucified.[a]

16:51-63 THE CROWD CALLS ON PILATE TO RELEASE BARABBAS

For reasons Pilate couldn't fathom, the Jews wanted this Jesus fellow crucified; more strangely still, the man himself raised no objection.

Though he may have anticipated that he risked seeing a riot break out should he oppose their demands, Pilate could have very well overruled the crowd and sent Barabbas off to Golgotha instead; certainly he had the authority, and he more often than not did as he liked.[122]

My guess, though, is that in the end, Pilate couldn't be bothered. What did he care? Likely weary of the Jews and their inscrutable superstitions, he chose to simply wash his hands of the matter and be done with it.[124]

16:63 – Then he released Barabbas to them, but having scourged Jesus, he handed him over so that he might be crucified.

Ge 22:11,12 – *Yahweh's angel called to him out of the sky, and said, "Abraham, Abraham!" He said, "Here I am." | He said, "Don't lay your hand on the boy or do anything to him. For now I know that you fear God, since you have not withheld your son, your only son, from me."*

Ps 79:11 – *Let the sighing of the prisoner come before you. According to the greatness of your power, preserve those who are sentenced to death.*

Well, we'll see if Yнwн intervenes according to the greatness of his power, as he did in the case of Isaac.

17

Jesus dies on the cross

17:1-4 JESUS IS MOCKED AND BEATEN BY PILATE'S SOLDIERS

17:3 – and having woven a crown out of thorns, they put *it* on his head, and a reed in his right hand; and falling on their knees before him, they mocked him, saying, "Hail, king of the Jews!"

    2Ki 11:12 – *Then he brought out the king's son, and put the crown on him, and gave him the covenant; and they made him king, and anointed him; and they clapped their hands, and said, "Long live the king!"*

    Ps 35:15-17 – *But in my adversity, they rejoiced, and gathered themselves together.* […] | *Like the profane mockers in feasts, they gnashed their teeth at me.* | *Lord, how long will you look on? Rescue my soul from their destruction, my precious life from the lions.*

17:4 – And having spat upon him, they took the reed and beat him on his head.

    2Sa 7:14 – *I will be his father, and he will be my son. If he commits iniquity, I will chasten him with the rod of men* […].

    Ps 39:10,11 – *"Remove your scourge away from me. I am overcome by the blow of your hand.* | *When you rebuke and correct man for iniquity, you consume his wealth like a moth. Surely every man is but a breath."*

    Isa 50:6 – *I gave my back to those who beat me, and my cheeks to those who plucked off the hair. I didn't hide my face from shame and spitting.*

    La 3:1 – *I am the man that has seen affliction by the rod of his wrath.*

CHAPTER 17

NOW the soldiers led him away within the courtyard, and they called together the entire cohort.[a]

2   And having stripped him, they put a crimson robe around him,[b]

3   and having woven a crown out of thorns, they put *it* on his head, and a reed in his right hand; and having fallen on their knees before him, they mocked him, saying,"Hail, king of the Jews!"[c]

4   And having spat upon him, they took the reed and beat him on his head.[d]

5   And when they had mocked him, they took the robe off him, and clothed him with his garments; and they led him away to crucify him.[e]

6   And they compelled one *who was* passing by — Simon of Cyrene, the father of Alexander and Rufus, *who was* coming from the country — that he might carry his cross.[f]

a Mt 27:27
   Mr 15:16
b Mt 27:28
   Mr 15:17
c 1Sa 10:24
   2Ki 11:12
   Ps 35:15-17
   Mt 27:29
   Mr 15:17-19
   Jn 19:2,3
d 2Sa 7:14
   Ps 39:10,11
   Pr 13:24
   Isa 50:6
   La 3:1
   Mt 27:30
   Mr 15:19
   Jn 19:3
e Mt 27:31
   Mr 15:20
f Mt 27:32
   Mr 15:21
   Lu 23:26

17 Jesus is crucified

g Pr 24:11
   Mt 27:33
   Mr 15:22
   Lu 23:33
   Jn 19:17
h Pr 31:6,7
i Mt 27:34
   Mr 15:23
j Ge 22:9
   Ex 12:3,6,7
   De 16:2
   Ps 38:2
   Isa 53:5
k Ps 22:18
   Mt 27:35
   Mr 15:24
   Lu 23:34
   Jn 19:23,24
l Zec 13:7
   Mr 15:25
m De 18:15
   Job 31:35
   Jer 23:5
   Mt 27:37
   Mr 15:26
   Lu 23:38
   Jn 1:49
   Jn 19:19
n Lu 23:38
   Jn 19:20
o Jn 19:21
p Jn 19:22

7   And they brought him to Golgotha, a place which is called *the* place of a skull.[g]

8   And they gave him wine laced with myrrh,[h] but he did not take it.[i]

9   And crucifying him,[j] they also divided his garments, casting lots for them, who should take what.[k]

10   And it was the [1]third hour, and they crucified him.[l]

11   Moreover, Pilate wrote an inscription *with the charge* and put it on the cross, and it was written *there,* "JESUS OF NAZARETH, THE KING OF THE JEWS."[m]

12   This inscription was therefore read by many of the Jews, for the place where Jesus was crucified was near to the city, and it was written in Hebrew, Latin *and* Greek.[n]

13   The chief priests of the Jews therefore said to Pilate, "Do not write, 'The King of the Jews', but 'Since he said, I am the King of the Jews.'"[o]

14   Pilate answered, "What I have written, I have written."[p]

---

1   I.e., 9 a.m.

17:5-10 JESUS IS LED AWAY TO BE CRUCIFIED

17:7 – And they brought him to Golgotha, a place which is called *the place of a skull.*

Pr 24:11 – *Rescue those who are being led away to death! Indeed, hold back those who are staggering to the slaughter!*

17:8 – And they gave him wine laced with myrrh,[125] but he did not take it.

Pr 31:6,7 – *Give strong drink to him who is ready to perish; and wine to the bitter in soul: | let him drink, and forget his poverty, and remember his misery no more.*

Jesus refuses the drink, which would have alleviated the ghastly pain he was about to face. I think he wanted to stay kosher, and keep his wits about him at all costs. Fulfilling his plan required presence of mind.

17:9 – And crucifying him [...]

Ge 22:9 – *They came to the place which God had told him of. Abraham built the altar there, and laid the wood in order, bound Isaac his son, and laid him on the altar, on the wood.*

De 16:2 – *You shall sacrifice the Passover to Yahweh your God, of the flock and the herd, in the place which Yahweh shall choose, to cause his name to dwell there.*

Ps 38:2 – *For your arrows have pierced me, your hand presses hard on me.*

Isa 53:5 – *But he was pierced for our transgressions. He was crushed for our iniquities. The punishment that brought our peace was on him; and by his wounds we are healed.*

17:9 – […] they also divided his garments, casting lots for them, who should take what.

Ps 22:18 – *They divide my garments among them. They cast lots for my clothing.*

This doesn't seem to be the sort of thing that could have been orchestrated in advance to fulfill yet more Scripture, yet it fits nicely. Mark may have made it up with that in mind, but who's to say it wasn't maybe just a serendipitous coincidence?

17:10 – And it was the third hour, and they crucified him.

Ze 13:7 – *"Awake, sword, against my shepherd, and against the man who is close to me," says Yahweh of Armies. "Strike the shepherd, and the sheep will be scattered; and I will turn my hand against the little ones."*

17:11-14 THE INSCRIPTION OF THE CHARGE

17:11 – Moreover, Pilate wrote an inscription *with the charge* and put it on the cross, and it was written *there*, "JESUS OF NAZARETH, THE KING OF THE JEWS."

Job 31:35 – *"Oh that I had one to hear me! Behold, here is my signature! Let the Almighty answer me! Let the accuser write my indictment!"*

It is the Latin form of this formula – IESUS NAZARENVS REX IVDAEORVM – that gives us the INRI abbreviation one sees so often in Christian art. The INBI acronym, also seen on occasion, stands for the Greek wording – *Iesous o Nazoraios o Basileus ton Ioudaion* – found in John 19:19.

17:13 – The chief priests of the Jews therefore said to Pilate, "Do not write, 'The King of the Jews', but 'Since he said, I am the King of the Jews.'"

The chief priests may have resorted to expediency to achieve their needs – whose moral basis, we do well to understand, answered to a much higher calling in their minds – but that was no reason to let Pilate get away with murder. They had told him that Jesus was *saying* he was the King of the Jews; they certainly hadn't brought Jesus to him *as* the King of the Jews.

Pilate, unsurprisingly, can't be bothered with such hair-splitting.

"What I have written, I have written."

17:15-21 JESUS IS REVILED

17:16 – And those passing by reviled him, shaking their heads and saying, […]

Ps 35:15,16 – *But in my adversity, they rejoiced, and gathered themselves together. The attackers gathered themselves together against me, and I didn't know it. They tore at me, and didn't cease. | Like the profane mockers in feasts, they gnashed their teeth at me.*

Ps 109:25 – *I have also become a reproach to them. When they see me, they shake their head.*

17:20 – "He trusted in God – let him deliver him now if he wants him […] "

Ge 22:7-13 – *[…] Abraham said, "God will provide himself the lamb for a burnt offering, my son." […] | Abraham lifted up his eyes, and looked, and saw that behind him was a ram caught in the thicket by his horns. Abraham went and took the ram, and offered him up for a burnt offering instead of his son.*

Ps 22:7,8 – *All those who see me mock me. They insult me with their lips. They shake their heads, saying, | "He trusts in Yahweh; let him deliver him. Let him rescue him, since he delights in him."*

Mr 14:36 – *He said, "Abba, Father, all things are possible to you. Please remove this cup from me. However, not what I desire, but what you desire."*

If YHWH does not want this sacrifice, then he will surely intervene, as he did when Isaac was on the verge of being slain by his father.

17:20 – " […] for he said, 'I am a son of God.'"

Le 25:55 – *"For to me the sons of Israel are slaves; they are my slaves whom I brought out of the land of Egypt. I am Yahweh your God."*

Mt 17:24-26 – *When they had come to Capernaum, those who collected the didrachma coins came to Peter, and said, "Doesn't your teacher pay the didrachma?" | He said, "Yes." When he came into the house, Jesus anticipated him, saying, "What do you think, Simon? From whom do the kings of the earth receive toll or tribute? From their children, or from strangers?" | Peter said to him, "From strangers." Jesus said to him, "Therefore the children are exempt."*

This is as good a place as any to point out that under the Romans, crucifixion was a punishment reserved for slaves.[126] Hence, no less than their obligation under the Law to pay the two-drachma temple tax (see above, THE TEMPLE TAX, page 176), that Jesus is crucified underscores the notion that the Jews are indeed, first and foremost, the slaves of their tribal god.[127]

17:22-24 THE WOMEN BESIDE THE CROSS

17:22 – But beside Jesus' cross stood his mother, […]

In John 19:25, it is stated that standing beside the cross is Jesus' mother, and his mother's sister, Mary of Clopas. We have no recorded instance of two sisters having the same given name, so the logical conclusion is that the woman identified as Jesus' mother is not his biological mother but rather some other woman, whom he considered to be his

15 And they crucified the two robbers with him,[q] one on the right, and one on his left.[r]

16 And those passing by reviled him, shaking their heads and saying,[s] "Aha! The *one* destroying the temple and raising it up in three days,[t]

17 save yourself, having come down from the cross!"[u]

18 And in like manner, the chief priests, mocking *him* among each other, with the scribes, said, "He saved others, *but* he is not able to save himself.[v]

19 "Let the King of Israel come down now from the cross, and we will believe!"[w]

20 "He trusted in God[x] – let him deliver him now if he wants him,[y] for he said, 'I am a son of God.'"[z]

21 And *with* the same *reproach*, the robbers, those having been crucified with him, reviled him *as well*.[a]

22 But beside Jesus' cross stood his mother,[b] and his mother's sister, Mary the [2]*mother* [3]of James the little and of Joses, and Mary the Magdalene.[c]

23 Therefore Jesus, having seen *his* mother, and the disciple standing by, whom he loved,[d] said to *his*

q Isa 53:12
r Mt 27:38
   Mr 15:27
   Lu 23:33
   Jn 19:18
s Ps 35:15,16
   Ps 109:25
   La 3:14,59-63
t Mt 27:39,40
   Mr 15:29
   Jn 2:19
u Mt 27:40
   Mr 15:30
v Mt 27:41
   Mr 15:31
   Lu 23:35
w Mt 27:42
   Mr 15:32
x Ps 22:7,8
   Ps 69:26
   Mt 26:39
   Mr 14:36
   Lu 22:42
y Ge 22:7-13
   Ps 3:2
z Le 25:55
   Mt 17:24-26
   Mt 27:43
a Isa 53:3
   Mt 27:44
   Mr 15:32
b Mt 12:48,49
   Mr 3:33,34
c Mr 15:40
   Jn 19:25
d Jn 13:23

---

2 The relationship is not clearly stated
3 According to the best ancient mss.; certain later mss. read, *of Clopas*

his mother. The margin verse therefore refers us to Mark, where Jesus, singling out one of his followers, clearly says, 'Behold my mother!'

Mr 3:33,34 – *He answered them, "Who are my mother and my brothers?" | Looking around at those who sat around him, he said, "Behold, my mother and my brothers!"*

We understand that his 'brothers' here are his disciples – an identification that is echoed in Matthew 28:10 – so it makes perfect sense that his 'mother' should be a woman who is present in the room as well.

17:22 – [...] and his mother's sister, Mary the *mother* of James the little and of Joses, and Mary the Magdalene.[128]

Mr 15:40 – *There were also women watching from afar, among whom were both Mary Magdalene, and Mary the mother of James the less and of Joses, and Salome.*

If we follow Mark, then, we may conjecture that the woman whom John designated as being Jesus' mother was none other than Salome.

Why would the author of John change the identity of Mary given in Mark 15:40 – where she is said to be the mother of James the less and of Joses – to that of Mary of Clopas?[129] Perhaps to increase the standing of Jesus' cousin Simeon,[130] who was the son of said Clopas and had been elected to become the second Bishop of Jerusalem (62-107 CE). When it came to credentials, having a mother (or grandmother) who stood at the foot of the cross would have been a surefire flock pleaser.

17:23 – Therefore Jesus, having seen *his* mother, and the disciple standing by, whom he loved, said to *his* mother, "Woman, behold your son!"

Salome is mentioned in the *Greek Gospel of the Egyptians*, where she says to Jesus, 'I have done well, then, in not bearing *children*.' We might wish to conjecture that Salome was an unmarried, childless woman for whom Jesus felt compassion. Being on poor terms with his own family (cf. Mr 3:21,31-34), he had perhaps 'adopted' Salome as a mother when he was staying in Capernaum, becoming like a son to her.

Now, barring a miraculous intervention by YHWH, Jesus knows that he will die on the cross and that his 'mother' will be henceforth alone in the world. He therefore commends the disciple whom he loves to her, as a son. (As the reader will recall, I advance that Judas was 'the disciple whom Jesus loved' – see above, JESUS HONORS JUDAS WITH THE MORSEL, page 279.)

17:25-29 JESUS DIES

17:25 – And it was now already about the sixth hour, and darkness came over all the land, until the ninth hour.

Job 30:22,23,26 – *You lift me up to the wind, and drive me with it. You dissolve me in the storm.* | *For I know that you will bring me to death, to the house appointed for all living.* | *When I looked for good, then evil came; when I waited for light, there came darkness.*

Am 8:9 – *"It will happen in that day," says the Lord Yahweh, "that I will cause the sun to go down at noon, and I will darken the earth in the clear day."*

The sky might have been filled with dust due to a seasonal east wind – known as a *ruḥa qadîm*, or *khamsin* – kicking up sand from the desert. It's the sort of thing that happens in the spring.

At any rate, the more Scriptures fulfilled, the merrier.

17:26 – But about the ninth hour, Jesus shouted with a loud voice […]

1Ki 18:27 – […] *"Cry aloud; for he is a god. Either he is deep in thought, or he has gone somewhere, or he is on a journey, or perhaps he sleeps and must be awakened."*

Hab 1:2 – *Yahweh, how long will I cry, and you will not hear? I cry out to you "Violence!" and will you not save?*

e *Jn 19:26*
f *Jn 19:27*
g *Job 30:22,23,26*
   Am 8:9
   Mt 27:45
   Mr 15:33
   Lu 23:44
h *1Ki 18:27*
   Hab 1:2
i *Ge 22:14*
   Ex 13:12-14
   De 12:31
   Job 10:7
   Job 19:6,7
   Job 30:20-23
   Ps 18:5,6
   Ps 22:1
   Ps 22:4,5,19
   Ps 28:1
   Ps 30:8,9
   Ps 69:16-18
   Ps 72:12-14
   Ps 88:1-18
   Ps 102:1,2,19,20
   Ps 106:37,38
   Ps 109:21,26,27
   Ps 116:3,4
   Ps 119:126
   Ps 143:1,7
   Isa 45:15
   Isa 53:10
   La 3:8,55,56
   Eze 28:15
   Mt 27:46
   Mr 15:34
j *Ps 69:3*
   Isa 41:17
   Jn 19:28
k *Ps 69:20,21*
   Mt 27:48
   Mr 15:36
   Jn 19:29
l *Ps 55:20*
   Ps 89:38,39
m *Job 30:23*
   Mt 27:50
   Mr 15:37
   Lu 23:46
   Jn 19:30

mother, "Woman, behold your son!"[e]

24 Then he said to the disciple, "Behold your mother!" And from that hour, the disciple was receiving her, among *his* own.[f]

25 And it was now already about the [4]sixth hour, and darkness came over all the land, until the [5]ninth hour.[g]

26 But about the [5]ninth hour, Jesus shouted with a loud voice,[h] "Eloi, eloi, lama sabachthani?" – which is translated, "My God, my God, why have You forsaken me?"[i]

27 After this, Jesus knowing that all things had now been accomplished, in order that the Scripture might be fulfilled, said, "I am thirsty."[j]

28 And immediately, one of them, having run and taken a sponge, and having filled *it* with sour wine and put *it* on a reed, gave *it* to him to drink.[k]

29 Therefore, when Jesus received the sour wine, he said, "It is finished."[l] And having bowed *his* head, he delivered up *his* spirit.[m]

30 Then the Jews, so that the bodies might not

---

4 I.e., noon
5 I.e., 3 p.m.

It is three o'clock in the afternoon, the moment at which the paschal lambs are being sacrificed in the temple.[131] To all evidence, Jesus has deliberately waited for this moment so that his death will be symbolically linked with the Passover, which signifies Israel's release from slavery as recounted in Exodus.

In my view, just as Israel went free from its bondage in Egypt, by his death Jesus hoped to free the Jews from their bondage to YHWH. That he and 'Moses' and 'Elijah' spoke of *'his exodus, which he was about to fulfill in Jerusalem'*, points to this interpretation.

17:26 – [...] "Eloi, eloi, lama sabachthani?" – which is translated, "MY GOD, MY GOD, WHY HAVE YOU FORSAKEN ME?"

Ge 22:14 – *Abraham called the name of that place Yahweh Will Provide. As it is said to this day, "On Yahweh's mountain, it will be provided."*

Job 10:7 – *Although you know that I am not wicked, there is no one who can deliver out of your hand.*

Ps 72:12-14 – *For he will deliver the needy when he cries; the poor, who has no helper. | [...] | He will redeem their soul from oppression and violence. Their blood will be precious in his sight.*

Ps 102:1,2,19,20 – *Hear my prayer, Yahweh! Let my cry come to you.| Don't hide your face from me in the day of my distress. [...] For he has looked down from the height of his sanctuary. From heaven, Yahweh saw the earth; | to hear the groans of the prisoner; to free those who are condemned to death.*

Ps 109:21,26,27 – *But deal with me, Yahweh the Lord, for your name's sake; because your loving kindness is good, deliver me. | Help me, Yahweh, my God. Save me according to your loving kindness; | that they may know that this is your hand; that you, Yahweh, have done it.*

Isa 53:10 – *Yet it pleased Yahweh to bruise him. He has caused him to suffer. When you make his soul an offering for sin, he will see his seed. [...]*[132]

Eze 28:15 – *You were perfect in your ways from the day that you were created, until unrighteousness was found in you.*

By this cry, Jesus points the finger at YHWH. It is by his silence,[133] and by his failure to intercede on Jesus' behalf, that the God of Israel clearly consents to the sacrificial death of his son on the cross – and in so doing, YHWH transgresses his own law, in which he condemns the sacrifice of sons and stipulates that they must be redeemed.

Jesus now knows that he has accomplished his mission. YHWH will not save him, and the prophecies of his downfall can now be fulfilled.

17:27 – After this, Jesus knowing that all things had now been accomplished, in order that the Scripture might be fulfilled, said, "I am thirsty."

Ps 69:3 – *I am weary with my crying. My throat is dry. My eyes fail, looking for my God.*

Isa 41:17 – *The poor and needy seek water, and there is none. Their tongue fails for thirst. I, Yahweh, will answer them. I, the God of Israel, will not forsake them.*

Even in the midst of his agony, Jesus has the presence of mind to evoke the Scriptures by saying that he is thirsty. It is an ultimate cry to YHWH, who has promised *"I, Yahweh, will answer them. I, the God of Israel, will not forsake them."*

Yet YHWH neither answers nor intervenes, and *In my thirst, they gave me vinegar to drink.* (Ps 69:21)

17:29 – Therefore, when Jesus received the sour wine, he said, "It is finished." […]

Ps 55:20 – *[…] He has violated his covenant.*

Ps 89:38,39 – *But you have rejected and spurned. You have been angry with your anointed. | You have renounced the covenant of your servant. You have defiled his crown in the dust.*

Truly, Yʜᴡʜ has violated his covenant by accepting the sacrifice of his innocent son.

17:29 – [...] And having bowed *his* head, he delivered up *his* spirit.

Job 30:23 – *For I know that you will bring me to death, to the house appointed for all living.*

I think it fair to surmise that Jesus deliberately yielded to death by allowing himself to hang freely from his arms and so die rapidly from asphyxiation.[134] In this way, he was able to time his death to coincide with the sacrificing of the paschal lambs in the temple court, and ensure that the Roman soldiers would have no reason to break his legs.

17:30-36 Tʜᴇ Jᴇᴡs ʀᴇǫᴜᴇsᴛ ᴛʜᴀᴛ ᴛʜᴇɪʀ ʟᴇɢs ʙᴇ ʙʀᴏᴋᴇɴ

17:30 – Then the Jews, so that the bodies might not remain upon the cross on the Sabbath – for the day *of* that Sabbath was *a* great *day* – requested of Pilate, that their legs might be broken, and *their bodies* taken away.

De 21:22,23 – *If a man has committed a sin worthy of death, and he is put to death, and you hang him on a tree; | his body shall not remain all night on the tree, but you shall surely bury him the same day; for he who is hanged is accursed of God [...].*

Le 23:6,7 – *"On the fifteenth day of the same month is the feast of unleavened bread to Yahweh. [...] | In the first day you shall have a holy convocation. You shall do no regular work."*

John says that this Sabbath was a 'great day', which implies that it fell that year on the 15ᵗʰ of Nisan, the first day of the Passover; this would make it especially important for the Jews that these crucified men be put out of their misery and taken down from their crosses. To have left them hanging about in agony as a major festival got underway would have been offensive to Yʜᴡʜ.

The Romans, of course, considered the gruesome sight a compelling deterrent to others and under normal circumstances would have left the men exposed for as long as they wished, even long after their deaths, to drive the repressive point home. That Pilate acquiesced to the Jews' request suggests that he was nevertheless willing to act with consideration for their concerns during major festivals such as Passover, when Jerusalem was full of pilgrims.

17:33 – However, one of the soldiers pierced his side with a spear [...]

La 3:13 – *He has caused the shafts of his quiver to enter into my kidneys.*

17:33 – [...] and blood came out immediately, and water.

Ge 9:6 – *Whoever sheds man's blood, his blood will be shed by man, for God made man in his own image.*

Nu 35:33 – *"So you shall not pollute the land in which you are; for blood pollutes the land. No atonement can be made for the land for the blood that is shed in it, but by the blood of him who shed it."*

De 19:10,13 – *This is so that innocent blood will not be shed in the middle of your land which Yahweh your God gives you for an inheritance, leaving blood guilt on you. | Your eye shall not pity him, but you shall purge the innocent blood from Israel, that it may go well with you.*

Ps 79:2,3 – *[...] | Their blood they have shed like water around Jerusalem. [...]*

In Jesus' case, it is the God of Israel himself who is guilty of spilling innocent blood, which has here poured out on the dusty ground.[135]

17:35 – For these things came to pass, in order that the Scripture might be fulfilled, "NOT ONE BONE OF IT WILL BE BROKEN."

Nu 9:12 – *"They shall leave none of it until the morning, nor break a bone of it. According to all the statute of the Passover they shall keep it."*

remain upon the cross on the Sabbath[n] – for the day of that Sabbath was *a great day*[o] – requested of Pilate, that their legs might be broken, and *their bodies* taken away.[p]

31 Therefore the soldiers came, and indeed, they broke the legs of the first, and of the other who had been crucified with him.[q]

32 But having come to Jesus, since they saw *that* he was already dead, they did not break his legs.[r]

33 However, one of the soldiers pierced his side with a spear,[s] and blood[t] came out immediately, and water.[u]

34 And he who has seen *this*[v] has borne witness, and his testimony is true; and that one knows, because he speaks truly, in order that you also might believe.[w]

35 For these things came to pass, in order that the Scripture might be fulfilled, "NOT ONE BONE OF IT WILL BE BROKEN."[x]

36 And again, another Scripture says, "THEY WILL LOOK ON THE ONE THEY HAVE PIERCED."[y]

37 And evening having now arrived, since it was the preparation *day*, that is, *the day* before the Sabbath,[z]

n De 21:22,23
o Le 23:6,7
p Jn 19:31
q Jn 19:32
r Jn 19:33
s La 3:13
t Ge 9:6
   Nu 35:33
   De 19:10,13
u Ps 79:2,3
   Jn 19:34
v Jn 19:26
w Jn 19:35
x Ex 12:46
   Nu 9:12
   Jn 19:36
y Ge 22:16
   Ex 34:20
   Zec 12:10
   Jn 19:37
z Mr 15:42
   Lu 23:54

Jesus' death points us to the Passover, so it was important that his legs not be broken, as befits a paschal sacrifice.

17:36 – And again, another Scripture says, "THEY WILL LOOK ON THE ONE THEY HAVE PIERCED."

Ge 22:16 – " […] *because you have done this thing, and have not withheld your son, your only son."*

Ex 34:20 – " […] *You shall redeem all the firstborn of your sons.* […] "

Zec 12:10 – *"I will pour on David's house, and on the inhabitants of Jerusalem, the spirit of grace and of supplication; and they will look to me whom they have pierced; and they shall mourn for him, as one mourns for his only son, and will grieve bitterly for him, as one grieves for his firstborn."*

Likewise, Jesus is understood to be a firstborn son, whom YHWH has thus sacrificed…in grievous violation of his covenant.

17:37-42 JOSEPH OF ARIMATHAEA PLACES JESUS' CORPSE IN AN UNUSED TOMB

17:38 – having come, Joseph of Arimathaea – an honorable councilor, and who was himself waiting for the kingdom of God – being bold, went in to Pilate and asked for Jesus' body.

Says Josephus, *'the Jews used to take so much care of the burial of men, that they took down those that were condemned and crucified, and buried them before the going down of the sun.'* [136]

If the centurion informed him that Jesus' legs had not been broken, Pilate may have been intrigued, even surprised, to learn that Jesus had succumbed so quickly. Accustomed to walking all over Galilee, Jesus was undoubteldy a fit man; despite the scourging he'd received, the indomitable human will to live confers unsuspected reserves of strength; under normal circumstances he should have had the wherewithal to survive at least several days on the cross.

Joseph of Arimathaea is said to be an honorable councilor, who was himself waiting for the kingdom of God. In view of what will happen to Jesus' body following the Sabbath, we might be justified in wondering whether Joseph was in cahoots with the contacts Jesus had met on the high mountain.

17:41 – And having bought a linen cloth, *and* having taken him down, he wrapped him in the linen cloth and laid him in a tomb, which was cut out of rock; and he rolled a stone across the door of the tomb.

De 21:23 – *His body shall not remain all night on the tree, but you shall surely bury him the same day. […]*

Isa 53:9 – *They made his grave with the wicked, and with a rich man in his death; although he had done no violence, nor was any deceit in his mouth.*

Interestingly, by handling Jesus' corpse, Joseph rendered himself ritually unclean for the Passover – cf. Numbers 19:11.

In John's account, Joseph is aided by a certain Nicodemus who brings along some 33 kilos of myrrh and aloes (which seems like an awful lot for one man to carry all by himself). Together, they are said to have wrapped Jesus' corpse in the linen cloth with the spices, *'as the custom of the Jews is to bury'*, and then transported him to the tomb. Given the weight added by the spices, I should think they would have needed help carrying the corpse.

Mark's account – *He bought a linen cloth, and taking him down, wound him in the linen cloth, and laid him in a tomb which had been cut out of a rock* – makes more sense, given the approaching Sabbath. With no mention of spices, Joseph sees to burying Jesus hastily.

Laying Jesus in a tomb, we should note, was not in keeping with the practices later spelled out in the Babylonian Talmud: 'AND THEY DID NOT BURY HIM [THE EXECUTED PERSON] IN HIS ANCESTRAL TOMB, BUT TWO BURIAL PLACES WERE PREPARED BY THE BETH DIN, ONE FOR

17   Joseph of Arimathaea places Jesus' corpse in a tomb

a   Mt 27:57
   Mr 15:43
   Lu 23:50-52
   Jn 19:38
b   Mr 15:44
c   Mt 27:58
   Mr 15:45
d   Mt 27:59
e   De 21:23
   Isa 53:9
f   Mt 27:60
   Mr 15:46
   Lu 23:53
g   Mt 27:61
   Mr 15:47
   Lu 23:55

38 having come, Joseph of Arimathaea – an honorable councilor, and who was himself waiting for the kingdom of God – being bold, went in to Pilate and asked for Jesus' body.[a]

39 But Pilate wondered if he were already dead. And having called to the centurion, he questioned him, if he had died some time ago.[b]

40 And having known *this* from the centurion, he gave the body to Joseph.[c]

41 And having bought a linen cloth, *and* having taken him down, he wrapped him in the linen cloth[d] and laid him in a tomb,[e] which was cut out of rock; and he rolled a stone across the door of the tomb.[f]

42 But Mary the Magdalene and Mary the [6]*mother* of Joses saw where he was laid.[g]

---

6   The relationship is not clearly stated

THOSE WHO WERE DECAPITATED OR STRANGLED, AND THE OTHER FOR THOSE WHO WERE STONED OR BURNED.'[137]

If these precepts were in force at the time, Jesus' corpse would have normally been consigned to a common grave, a burial that would be appropriate for one who had been sentenced to death for blasphemy. So it seems curious that Joseph of Arimathaea should see to placing the corpse in an unused tomb.[138] To my mind, it makes him party to the subsequent disappearance of Jesus' body. The tomb, as it were, was the designated drop box.

17:42 – But Mary the Magdalene and Mary the *mother* of Joses saw where he was laid.

This is of capital importance: having seen where Jesus' corpse has been entombed, the two Marys know where to come when the Sabbath is over. What the three Gospels do not tell us is whether Joseph of Arimathaea knew that the women were observing him in what he was doing, and whether their being witnesses would have troubled him.

18
The empty tomb

18:1-9 THE WOMEN COME TO THE TOMB

18:1 – And the Sabbath having passed, Mary the Magdalene, and Mary the *mother* of James, and Salome, bought spices in the marketplace, in order that, having come, they might anoint him.

The Sabbath ended on Saturday evening, when the sun went down. The women would have been able to go to the marketplace, which undoubtedly reopened for business once the Sabbath was over.

18:2 – And very early on the first *day* of the week, they came to the tomb, the sun having risen.

It is interesting to compare the four Gospels:

Mr 16:2 – *Very early on the first day of the week, they came to the tomb when the sun had risen.*

That obviously left open the possibility that someone had preceded the women to the tomb and removed Jesus' body. So Luke says,

Lu 24:1 – *But on the first day of the week, at early dawn, they and some others came to the tomb* […].

This early dawn arrival seemed to preclude body-snatchers. But Matthew was still uneasy. To counter the persistent rumors that someone had taken Jesus' body, he first relates that the chief priests had sent a guard to seal the stone and ensure the tomb was secure, and then says that the women arrived a bit earlier than that, *as* it began to dawn:

CHAPTER 18

AND the Sabbath having passed, Mary the Magdalene, and Mary the [1]*mother* of James, and Salome, bought spices in the marketplace, in order that, having come, they might anoint him.[a]

2   And very early on the first *day* of the week, they came to the tomb, the sun having risen.[b]

3   And they were saying to themselves, "Who will roll away the stone for us, out from the door of the tomb?"[c]

4   And having looked up, they saw that the stone had been rolled away, for it was exceedingly large.[d]

5   And it came to pass, as they were perplexed about this, that behold, two men[e] stood by them, in dazzling clothing.[f]

6   But having become terrified of them, and bowing *their* faces to the ground, they said to them,

a   Mr 16:1
b   Mr 16:2
    Lu 24:1
c   Mr 16:3
    Mr 16:4
d   Lu 24:2
e   Lu 9:30,31
f   Lu 24:4
    Jn 20:12

---

1 The relationship is not clearly stated

Mr 28:1 – *Now after the Sabbath, as it began to dawn on the first day of the week, Mary Magdalene and the other Mary came to see the tomb.*

Still not good enough, though, to quell ongoing doubts. So John has the women arrive even earlier than that:

Jn 20:1 – *Now on the first day of the week, Mary Magdalene went early, while it was still dark, to the tomb* […].

I think it unlikely that these women would have been out and about while it was still dark on this first day of the week, even if the Sabbath had ended at sunset the day before. Mark's version seems to me the most plausible.

18:5 – And it came to pass, as they were perplexed about this, that behold, two men stood by them, in dazzling clothing.

Lu 9:30,31 – *Behold, two men were talking with him, who were Moses and Elijah, | who appeared in glory, and spoke of his exodus which he was about to accomplish at Jerusalem.*

Lu 24:4 – *While they were greatly perplexed about this, behold, two men stood by them in dazzling clothing.*

Jn 20:12 – *And she saw two angels in white sitting, one at the head, and one at the feet, where the body of Jesus had lain.*

John says angels, but Luke says men – two men in dazzling clothing.

I think that having removed Jesus' body, these two snazzily dressed fellows have just come back to seal up the tomb when they find themselves unexpectedly face to face with Mary and the others. The women are understandably terrified. They don't know who these men are, nor why on earth they should be at the tomb.

18:6-8 – […] they said to them, "Why do you seek the living among the dead? Remember how he was speaking to you, being still in Galilee, saying, 'It is necessary *for* the son of man to be handed over into the hands of men, and to be crucified and to be raised up."

Necessary, because it is the only way to free the Jews from their god:

Le 25:55 – *"For to me the sons of Israel are slaves; they are my slaves whom I brought out of the land of Egypt. I am Yahweh your God."*

Ps 49:8 – *For the redemption of their life is costly, no payment is ever enough.*

Mr 10:45 – *"For the Son of Man also came not to be served, but to serve, and to give his life as a ransom for many."*

Jn 8:35,36 – *"A slave does not live in the house forever. A son remains forever. | If therefore the Son makes you free, you will be free indeed."*

Jn 11:50 – *"Nor do you consider that it is advantageous for us that one man should die for the people, and that the whole nation not perish."*

Granted, by having Caiaphas say that last bit, the author of John is deliberately putting the Jews in the hot seat, adding that *'he prophesied that Jesus would die for the nation.'* But in the context of *The Gospel of Jesus of Nazareth*, Caiaphas' remark happens to make perfect sense, because Jesus – one man, the son of man – *did* die to save the people…to save and free them from their tribal god.

We may note once again that while the slaves of YHWH will go free, Jesus, as 'the son', does not get to go free, but must remain in the house forever. This, his life, freely given, is the costly price that must be paid to redeem his friends.

18:10-13 THE TOMB IS EMPTY

18:10 – And having entered into the tomb [...]

In Mark, *'Mary Magdalene, and Mary the [mother] of James, and Salome'* are the first of Jesus' followers to actually enter into the empty tomb.

In Luke, *'they and some others [...] entered in'* – with 'they' referring to *'the women who had come with him out of Galilee'*. Only some verses later are the women identified as having been *'Mary Magdalene, Joanna, and Mary the [mother] of James and the others with them'*.

g Ge 1:2
   Ge 2:7
   Ec 12:7
   Lu 24:5
   Jn 3:6,8
h Eze 32:3
   Lu 24:6
i Le 25:55
   Ps 49:8
   Mr 10:45
   Lu 24:7
   Jn 8:35,36
   Jn 11:50
j Mt 16:21
   Mr 8:31
   Lu 9:22
   Lu 24:8
k Mr 14:51,52
l Mr 16:5
m Mt 12:11
n Mt 28:5,6
   Mr 16:6
o De 28:26
   Ps 89:12
   Isa 14:13
   Isa 57:7
   Eze 32:3-6
   Eze 39:17,19
   Mt 24:28
   Mt 26:32
   Mt 28:7
   Mt 28:16
   Mr 14:28
   Mr 16:7
   Lu 17:37
p Mr 16:8

"Why do you seek the living among the dead?[g]

7   "[2]Remember how he was speaking to you, being still in Galilee,[h]

8   saying, 'It is necessary *for* the son of man to be handed over into the hands of men, and to be crucified and [3]to be raised up.'"[i]

9   And they remembered his words.[j]

10   And having entered into the tomb, they saw a young man[k] sitting on the right, clothed with a white robe; and they were greatly astonished.[l]

11   But he said to them, "Do not be astonished. You are searching for Jesus of Nazareth, who has been crucified — he has been raised up,[m] *and* he is not here. Behold, the place where they laid him.[n]

12   "But go, say to his disciples, that he goes before you, into Galilee; you will see him there, as he said to you."[o]

13   And having gone out, they fled from the tomb, for trembling and bewilderment possessed them; and they said nothing to anyone, for they were terrified.[p]

14   And therefore they ran and came to the disciple

---

2 Certain later mss. add, *He is not here, but has been raised up*
3 Certain later mss. add, *the third day*

In Matthew, these same women are kept outside the tomb, where they talk with the angel who sits on the stone that has been rolled aside from the door; while in John, it is said that Mary came *'while it was still dark'* and, seeing *'the stone taken away from the tomb, [...] ran and came to Simon Peter, and to the other disciple whom Jesus loved, and said to them, "They have taken away the Lord out of the tomb, and we don't know where they have laid him!"'* – leaving how she could be so certain that the body itself was not still inside (in view of the darkness and with nothing to go on besides the stone having been rolled aside) unexplained.

We can only wonder why the women were gradually barred in the Gospels from having entered the tomb. But it is of note that although Mary Magdalene (accompanied, in Matthew, by *'the other Mary'*) is credited in three of the Gospels as having been the very first of Jesus' followers to have seen him in his resurrected form – a distinction that would seem to confer upon her a primary importance in the group, compared to all of the other disciples – neither Mary Magdalene nor these other women figure in the subsequent history of the Jesus-movement.

18:10 – [...] they saw a young man sitting on the right, clothed with a white robe [...]

Mr 14:51,52 – *A certain young man followed him, having a linen cloth thrown around himself, over his naked body. The young men grabbed him,* | *but he left the linen cloth, and fled from them naked.*

Sounds like Mark's young lad has had time to go back home and get himself a proper robe. Was this maybe Joseph of Arimathaea's son?

18:11 – But he said to them, "Do not be astonished. You are searching for Jesus of Nazareth, who has been crucified – he has been raised up, *and* he is not here. Behold, the place where they laid him."

The same Greek verb, *egeiró* – which is used in Matthew 28:6, Mark 16:6 and Luke 24:6 to say that Jesus has risen – is also found here:

Mt 12:11 – *He said to them, "What man is there among you, who has one sheep, and if this one falls into a pit on the Sabbath day, won't he grab on to it, and lift it out?"*

The verb *egeiró* can simply refer to the physical action of raising or lifting up. Here, like the sheep in the pit, Jesus' body has been raised up, or lifted out, from the tomb. That would be, after all, the *sine qua non* for conveying the corpse to a mountain in Galilee...

18:12 – "But go, say to his disciples, that he goes before you, into Galilee; you will see him there, as he said to you."

We do well to consider how this narrative evolves in the Synoptics:

In Mark 16:5-7, *'a young man [...] dressed in a white robe'* says to the women, *"Do not be amazed. You seek Jesus, the Nazarene, who has been crucified. He has risen. He is not here. Behold, the place where they laid him! | But go, tell his disciples and Peter, 'He goes before you into Galilee. There you will see him, as he said to you.'"*

In Luke 24:4-7 it is instead *'two men [...] in dazzling clothing'* who say, *"Why do you seek the living among the dead? | He is not here, but is risen. Remember what he told you when he was still in Galilee, | saying that the Son of Man must be delivered up into the hands of sinful men, and be crucified, and the third day rise again?"* (Interestingly, some ancient manuscripts omit the words *'He is not here, but is risen.'*)

Matthew 28:2-7, though, weighs in with a far grander finale. Kicking things off with an earthquake, the evangelist has an angel – who looks like lightning and is dressed white as snow – say to the women, *"Do not be afraid, for I know that you seek Jesus, who has been crucified. | He is not here, for he has risen, just like he said. Come, see the place where the Lord was lying. | Go quickly and tell his disciples, 'He has risen from the dead, and behold, he goes before you into Galilee; there you will see him.'*

What should strike us is that in all three, it is said that Jesus will go before them into Galilee, and that they will see him there. But in what follows, Jesus instead jumps the gun, showing himself to Mary Magdalene and the others while they are still in Jeurusalem, and to a certain Cleopas while he and a friend are on the road to Emmaus (as related in Luke 24:13-35; cf. Mark 16:12,13). Why, we should ask ourselves, did the promised program change? When the growing Jesus-movements gained control of Jesus' story, were these post-crucifixion appearances perhaps added to the original source material?

In any case, prior to his death, Jesus to all evidence told his disciples that after the Passover they should go to Galilee, to a particular mountain, and expect to see him there.

De 28:26 – *Your dead body will be food to all birds of the sky, and to the animals of the earth; and there will be no one to frighten them away.*

Eze 32:4-6 – *"I will leave you on the land, I will cast you out on the open field, and will cause all the birds of the sky to settle on you, and I will satisfy the animals of the whole earth with you. | I will lay your flesh on the mountains, and fill the valleys with your height. | […]"*

Eze 39:17,19 – *"You, son of man, thus says the Lord Yahweh: 'Speak to the birds of every sort, and to every animal of the field, "Assemble yourselves, and come; gather yourselves on every side to my sacrifice that I do sacrifice for you, even a great sacrifice on the mountains of Israel, that you may eat meat and drink blood. | […]"'"*

Mt 24:28 – *"For wherever the carcass is, there is where the vultures gather together."*

Mt 26:32 – *"But after I am raised up, I will go before you into Galilee."*

Mt 28:16 – *But the eleven disciples went into Galilee, to the mountain where Jesus had sent them.*

The disciples would have found Jesus' corpse on the the mountain that he had designated, exposed to YHWH's final injustice in 'fulfillment' of Ezekiel's prophesy.

18:14-18 THE WOMEN REPORT THE NEWS TO THE DISCIPLE WHOM JESUS LOVED

John's account is here modified, with the women informing *'the disciple whom Jesus loved'* that the tomb is empty, instead of Simon Peter. He will appear in a moment, in harmony with Luke's version of events.[139]

18:19-21 THE WOMEN REPORT THE NEWS TO THE DISCIPLES

18:19 – And having returned from the tomb, *the women* reported all these things to the eleven and to all the others.

The 'eleven' – this comes from Luke. One assumes that Judas is the odd-man out, but unlike Matthew, who says that Judas has gone and hanged himself (Mt 27:5), Luke does not explain why there are only eleven disciples at the role call – which is what allows me to propose that Judas was the first disciple to witness the empty tomb.

18:20,21 – But it was the Magdalene – Mary – and Joanna, and Mary the *mother* of James, and the others with them, who said these things to the disciples. And their statements appeared as nonsense in their sight, and they disbelieved them.

'What are you saying? That someone's stolen off with the master's corpse? You women are hysterical. Why on earth would anyone do that? For what reason? Utter nonsense!'

18:22 SIMON PETER SEES THAT THE TOMB IS EMPTY

For Luke, Simon Peter is among the eleven and now runs to the tomb to see for himself:

Lu 24:12 – *But Peter got up and ran to the tomb. Stooping and looking in, he saw the strips of linen lying by themselves, and he departed, wondering*

whom Jesus loved,[q] and said to him, "They have taken the master out of the tomb, and we do not know where they have laid him."[r]

15　Therefore, the disciple went forth, and came to the tomb.[s]

16　And he entered into the tomb, and he saw the linen cloths lying *there —*[t]

17　and the face cloth, which was upon his head, was not lying with the linen cloths, but in a place by itself, having been rolled up *separately —*[u]

18　and he saw and believed *them.*[v]

19　And having returned from the tomb, *the women* reported all these things to the eleven and to all the others.[w]

20　But it was the Magdalene — Mary — and Joanna,[x] and Mary the [4]*mother* of James, and the others with them, who said these things to the disciples.[y]

21　And their statements appeared as nonsense in their sight, and they disbelieved them.[z]

22　[5][But Simon, having risen up, ran to the tomb; and having leaned in to look, he saw only the linen

q　Jn 13:23
r　Jn 20:2
s　Jn 20:3
t　Jn 20:5,6
u　Jn 20:7
v　Jn 20:8
w　Mt 28:8
　　Mr 16:10
　　Lu 24:9
x　Lu 8:2,3
y　Lu 24:10
z　Mr 16:11
　　Lu 24:11

---

4 The relationship is not clearly stated
5 Verse 22 is not found in the best ancient mss.

a   Lu 4:13
    Lu 24:12
b   Ps 89:12
    Isa 57:7
    Eze 32:3-6
    Mt 28:16
    Mr 14:28
    Lu 17:37
c   De 8:19
    De 11:16
    De 30:17,18
d   *Mt 28:17*
    Mr 11:23
e   Mt 5:17,18
    Lu 18:31
f   De 33:2
    Ps 50:2
    Eze 1:26-28
    Hab 3:4
    Lu 10:18
e   Le 24:17
    De 19:13,21
    Isa 14:12
    Re 12:9
f   Ps 103:19
    Isa 66:1
g   Isa 2:2
    Isa 14:13
h   Ex 16:10
    Nu 10:34
    Job 22:14
    Ps 104:3
i   Isa 14:14
    Eze 28:2
j   Isa 14:15
    Eze 28:8
k   Ex 19:18
    Jg 5:5
    2Sa 22:8
    Ps 18:7
    Ps 60:1,2
    Ps 77:18
    Ps 99:1
    Isa 2:19,21
    Isa 13:13
    Jer 10:10
    Na 1:5
l   Isa 14:16,26
    Isa 23:11
    Hag 2:21,22

cloths. And he went away, wondering in himself at that which had happened.[a]]

23 But the [6]disciples went into Galilee, to the mountain which Jesus had designated to them.[b]

24 And having seen him, they worshipped;[c] but some doubted.[d]

25 Yet all these things have come to pass, so that the word of the prophets might be fulfilled —[e]

26 "HOW YOU HAVE FALLEN FROM HEAVEN, O SHINING ONE![f] HOW YOU HAVE BEEN CUT DOWN TO THE EARTH.[e]

27 "YOU SAID IN YOUR HEART, 'I SHALL ASCEND TO HEAVEN. I SHALL RAISE MY THRONE ABOVE THE STARS OF GOD,[f] AND I SHALL RESIDE UPON THE MOUNT OF ASSEMBLY, IN THE DISTANT NORTHERN PARTS.[g]

28 "'ABOVE THE CLOUDS SHALL I ASCEND,[h] AND I SHALL MAKE MYSELF RESEMBLE THE MOST HIGH.'[i]

29 "BUT YOU SHALL BE BROUGHT DOWN TO SHEOL, TO THE DARKEST DEPTH OF THE PIT.[j]

30 "AND THOSE WHO SEE YOU WILL STARE AT YOU IN WONDER, AND SAY, 'IS THIS THE MAN THAT

---

6 According to the best ancient mss.; certain late mss. add, *eleven*

what had happened.

Notice that in Luke, Peter does not actually enter the tomb, but – scaredy-cat – only stoops and looks in. In stark contrast, writing several decades later, John says that it was the *'disciple whom Jesus loved'* who only looked inside, and credits Peter instead with the preeminent role of being the first to bravely enter the empty tomb.

18:22 – […] And he went away, wondering in himself at that which had happened.

Lu 4:13 – *When the devil had completed every temptation, he departed from him until an opportune time.*

Christianity was born out of Jesus' empty tomb, and Simon Peter was its midwife. Wondering in himself what has happened, he will produce an answer that in my view was utterly inimical to Jesus' intentions.

I see Simon Peter as being the fertile, golden opportunity for which 'Satan' had been waiting. If you like, Jesus did indeed succeed in turning the tables on YHWH; the Jews who heeded Jesus' words and teachings would indeed go free, for they would be cut off from the Chosen People for apostasy. But with Jesus now dead, we might opine that the Jewish tribal god astutely found a way to snare a good many of them on the road to freedom, enslaving them once again. Christianity rightly looks to YHWH as its 'Father', for the Jesus-movement Christians never truly left the Jewish god's fold – and therein lies the tragic twist that Jesus could not preempt.

18:23,24 THE DISCIPLES GO TO THE MOUNTAIN IN GALILEE

18:23 – But the disciples went into Galilee […]

Acts 1:4-11 belies Matthew's account, for the disciples (minus Judas) are said to remain in Jerusalem, where they will stay until the Pente-cost;[140] the closest the apostles will get to a mountain is the Mount of

Olives, their prime vantage point for watching Jesus ascend as he gets lifted up to heaven.

Yet Jesus seems to have designated a mountain in Galilee where he wanted his disciples to go, and Matthew 28:16 says that *'the eleven disciples went into Galilee, to the mountain where Jesus had sent them.'* However, keeping in mind that the women reported the news of the empty tomb to 'the eleven' and to 'all the others', we might do well to suspect that there were other close followers besides the apostles who may have heeded Jesus' injunction. For this reason, I suggest here that the qualification 'eleven' was a later addition. In his version of events, Matthew of course has bumped Judas off, but my guess is that an earlier tradition held that a group of disciples – and why not Judas among them – went north to Galilee following the Passover.

18:23 – [...] to the mountain which Jesus had designated to them.

Ps 89:12 – *The north and the south, you have created them. Tabor and Hermon rejoice in your name.*

Isa 57:7 – *On a high and lofty mountain you have set your bed. You also went up there to offer sacrifice.*

Eze 32:3-6 – *Thus says the Lord Yahweh: "I will spread out my net on you with a company of many peoples; and they shall bring you up in my net. | [...] | I will lay your flesh on the mountains [...]."*

Mr 14:28 – *"However, after I am raised up, I will go before you into Galilee."*

Lu 17:37 – *They, answering, asked him, "Where, Lord?" He said to them, "Where the body is, there will the vultures also be gathered together."*

To which mountain? We have conjectured that the Transfiguration occurred on Mount Tabor, so here – to complete the pair mentioned in the psalm, and above all to reflect Isaiah and Ezekiel – we might surmise that Jesus sent his disciples all the way north to Mount Hermon. Full of pagan worship,[141] it would certainly be quite a place to expose a corpse, and the prophesies would implicate Yʜwʜ as the perpetrator.

18:24 – And having seen him, they worshipped […].

In the context of *The Gospel of Jesus of Nazareth*, Jesus had told his disciples that they would see him again on top of a certain mountain. His accomplices would have collected his corpse from the tomb early Sunday morning and transported it north to Galilee, thus insuring that it arrived ahead of the disciples. They, in turn, when they came to the mountain, would have found their teacher's body exposed and likely half-eaten by birds and animals, again, in fulfillment of the Scriptures. Jesus may have instructed his disciples that they should bow down and 'worship' before the sight, so that yet another insult would be added to the already apostate injury of eating flesh and drinking blood.

De 11:16 – *Be careful, lest your heart be deceived, and you turn aside, and serve other gods, and worship them.*

De 30:17,18 – *But if your heart turns away, and you will not hear, but are drawn away, and worship other gods, and serve them; | I denounce to you today, that you will surely perish. […]*

I think it makes sense that Jesus had his corpse taken to Galilee by others. I suspect that his accomplices were not – or were no longer – strictly Jewish, and so, not being in need of liberation themselves, they would have been free to lend a hand. Further, Jesus could have anticipated that the empty tomb would make a startling impact on his followers; when they later found his body exposed on the mountain top, they might have remembered the words of Yʜwʜ: *"I will leave you on the land, I will cast you out on the open field, and will cause all the birds of the sky to settle on you, and I will satisfy the animals of the whole earth with you. | I will lay your flesh on the mountains, and fill the valleys with your height. | I will also water with your blood the land in which you swim, even to the mountains; and the watercourses shall be full of you."* (Eze 32:4-6)

18:24 – […] but some doubted.

Mr 11:23 – *"For most certainly I tell you, whoever may tell this mountain, 'Be taken up and cast into the sea,' and doesn't doubt in his heart, but believes that what he says is happening; he shall have whatever he says."*

Oh, ye of little faith… Yet their doubt makes sense. They've made the trek to the mountain in Galilee, arriving at the very earliest several days, and far more probably a week or two, after the Passover. They've arrived at the designated spot, and what have they found? The gruesome sight of a decomposing corpse that has been disfigured by wild animals and birds. Is this their teacher Jesus? They would of course have good reason to conclude that it was, in light of what he had told them beforehand, but a truly positive visual identification might have been iffy. And it is that doubt – plus the simple fact that the cataclysmic apocalypse that Jesus had foretold did not come to pass – that paved the way for some of his followers to concoct a happier ending: Jesus was resurrected :-)

18:25-33 CONCLUDING PROPHESIES

If Jesus believed in the prophesies of YHWH's wrath and retribution, he would have had every reason to expect that the end times – as detailed above in THE TRIBULATIONS TO COME, page 246 – would arrive soon after his death. Surely the God of Israel would not let such apostasy go unpunished. By the same token, the prophets had foretold that the one who had made himself resemble the Most High, but who was only a man, would be cast down. As we have seen in the prologue, it would seem that this was none other than YHWH, and it is my view that Jesus was aiming to bring about this denouement by his sacrifical death. If we return one last time to the prophets, we may reflect on how the words of Isaiah and Ezekiel may be understood as referring to YHWH.

18:25 – Yet all these things have come to pass, so that the word of the prophets might be fulfilled –

Mt 5:17,18 – *"Don't think that I came to destroy the law or the prophets. I did not come to destroy, but to fulfill. | For most certainly, I tell you, until heaven and earth pass away, not one iota or apostrophe shall in any way pass away from the law, until all things are accomplished."*

We do not read these words carefully enough. Jesus knows that the Scriptures are a closed system. You cannot free the people from their religion through reason, nor destroy nor overthrow the covenant from without. As such, *"until heaven and earth pass away"*, the Law is destined to remain…until certain conditions are met. It is only when *"all things are accomplished"* **within** that context, that the Scriptures, which contain in themselves the very seeds of YHWH's own destruction, will pass away. This is why Jesus was so intent on fulfilling the Law and the prophets though his life and death, for it was the fulfillment of all that was written that was the *sine qua non* for triggering this denouement.

18:26 – "HOW YOU HAVE FALLEN FROM HEAVEN, O SHINING ONE! […]"

Ps 50:2 – *Out of Zion, the perfection of beauty, God shines out.*

Eze 1:26-28 – *[…] | As the appearance of the rainbow that is in the cloud in the day of rain, so was the appearance of the brightness all around. This was the appearance of the likeness of Yahweh's glory. […]*

Lu 10:18 – *He said to them, "I saw Satan having fallen like lightning from heaven."*

18:26 – " […] HOW YOU HAVE BEEN CUT DOWN TO THE EARTH."

De 19:13 – *Your eye shall not pity him, but you shall purge the innocent blood from Israel, that it may go well with you.*

Re 12:9 – *The great dragon was thrown down, the old serpent, he who* is called the devil and Satan, the deceiver of the whole world. He was thrown down to the earth, and his angels were thrown down with him.

18:27 – "You said in your heart, 'I shall ascend to heaven. I shall raise my throne above the stars of God [...] '"

Ps 103:19 – *Yahweh has established his throne in the heavens. [...]*

Isa 66:1 – *Yahweh says, "Heaven is my throne, and the earth is my footstool. [...]"*

18:27 – "' [...] and I shall reside upon the mount of assembly, in the distant northern parts.'"

Isa 2:2 – *It shall happen in the latter days, that the mountain of Yahweh's house shall be established on the top of the mountains, and shall be raised above the hills; and all nations shall flow to it.*

Mount Hermon was likely considered to be the natural northern border of Israel and a mount of assembly for numerous gods.[142]

18:28 – "'Above the clouds shall I ascend [...] '"

Ps 104:3 – *[...] He makes the clouds his chariot. He walks on the wings of the wind.*

18:28 – "' [...] and I shall make myself resemble the Most High.'"

Eze 28:2 – *"Because your heart is lifted up, and you have said, 'I am a god, I sit in the seat of God, in the middle of the seas;' yet you are a man, and not God, though you set your heart as the heart of God."*

18:29 – "But you shall be brought down to Sheol, to the darkest depth of the pit."

Eze 28:8 – *They shall bring you down to the pit; and you shall die the death of those who are slain, in the heart of the seas.*

18:30 – "AND THOSE WHO SEE YOU WILL STARE AT YOU IN WON-DER, AND SAY, 'IS THIS THE MAN THAT MADE THE EARTH TO TREMBLE […] '"

Jg 5:5 – *The mountains quaked Yahweh's presence, even Sinai at the presence of Yahweh, the God of Israel.*

2Sa 22:8 – *Then the earth shook and trembled. The foundations of heaven quaked and were shaken, because he was angry.*

Jer 10:10 – *[…] At his wrath, the earth trembles, and the nations are not able to withstand his indignation.*

18:30 – "' […] THAT SHOOK THE KINGDOMS; '"

Isa 23:11 – *He has stretched out his hand over the sea. He has shaken the kingdoms. […]*

Hag 2:21,22 – *" […] 'I will shake the heavens and the earth. | I will overthrow the throne of kingdoms. I will destroy the strength of the kingdoms of the nations. […] '"*

18:31 – "'THAT MADE THE WORLD AS A WILDERNESS […] '"

Ps 107:33,34 – *He turns rivers into a desert, water springs into a thirsty ground, | and a fruitful land into a salt waste […].*

Isa 24:1-3 – *Behold, Yahweh makes the earth empty, makes it waste, turns it upside down, and scatters its inhabitants. | […]*

18:31 – "' […] DESTROYING ITS CITIES; […] '"

Le 26:31,33 – *"I will lay your cities waste, and will bring your sanctuaries to desolation. […] | […] I will draw out the sword after you. Your land will be a desolation, and your cities shall be a waste."*

Isa 64:10 – *Your holy cities have become a wilderness. Zion has become a wilderness, Jerusalem a desolation.*

18:31 – "' […] THAT BROUGHT THE LAND TO RUIN […] '"

Le 26:20,32 – *"Your strength will be spent in vain; for your land won't yield its increase, neither will the trees of the land yield their fruit. | I will bring the land into desolation; and your enemies that dwell therein will be astonished at it."*

Isa 1:7 – *Your country is desolate. Your cities are burned with fire. Strangers devour your land in your presence, and it is desolate, as overthrown by strangers.*

18:31 – "' […] AND HAS SLAIN HIS OWN PEOPLE?'"

Le 26:14-33 – *"[…] | I will bring a sword upon you that will execute the vengeance of the covenant. […] | You will eat the flesh of your sons, and you will eat the flesh of your daughters."*

De 64:10 – *For Yahweh your God among you is a jealous God; lest the anger of Yahweh your God be kindled against you, and he destroy you from off the face of the earth.*

Jer 15:1-3,6,7 – *"[…] | I will appoint over them four kinds," says Yahweh: "the sword to kill, and the dogs to tear, and the birds of the sky, and the animals of the earth, to devour and to destroy. | You have gone backward: therefore I have stretched out my hand against you, and destroyed you […]. | […] I have destroyed my people. […]"*

La 2:20,21 – *Look, Yahweh, and see to whom you have done thus! Shall the women eat their offspring, the children that are dandled in the hands? Shall the priest and the prophet be killed in the sanctuary of the Lord? | The youth and the old man lie on the ground in the streets. My virgins and my young men have fallen by the sword. You have killed them in the day of your anger. You have slaughtered, and not pitied.*

18:32 – "AND YOU SHALL BE CAST DOWN FROM THE MOUNTAIN OF GOD, AND DESTROYED; […] "

Ex 24:12-18 – […] | *Moses rose up with Joshua, his servant, and Moses went up onto God's Mountain.* | […]

Isa 33:1,8 – *Woe to you who destroy, but you weren't destroyed; and who betray, but nobody betrayed you!* | […] *The covenant is broken. He has despised the cities. He doesn't respect man.*

Isa 47:8-11 – *"Now therefore hear this, you who are given to pleasures, who sit securely, who say in your heart, 'I am, and there is no one else besides me.' […]* | *For you have trusted in your wickedness. You have said, 'No one sees me.' Your wisdom and your knowledge has perverted you. You have said in your heart, 'I am, and there is no one else besides me.'* | *Therefore disaster will come on you. […]"*

Jn 12:31 – *"Now is the judgment of this world. Now the prince of this world will be cast out."*

18:32 – "[…] YOU SHALL BE BROUGHT TO ASHES UPON THE EARTH, IN THE SIGHT OF ALL."

Eze 33:18 – *"When the righteous turns from his righteousness, and commits iniquity, he shall even die therein."*

Jn 16:11 – *"about judgment, because the prince of this world has been judged."*

18:33 – "AND THOSE WHO KNOW YOU WILL BE ASTONISHED, AND YOU SHALL BE NO MORE."

Ps 106:10 – *He saved them from the hand of him who hated them, and redeemed them from the hand of the enemy.*

Isa 9:13 – *Yet the people have not turned to him who struck them, neither have they sought Yahweh of Armies.*

Isa 10:20 – *It will come to pass in that day that the remnant of Israel, and those who have escaped from the house of Jacob will no more again lean on him who struck them* […].

Isa 63:19 – *We have become like those over whom you never ruled, like those who were not called by your name.*

Mr 10:45 – *"For the Son of Man also came not to be served, but to serve, and to give his life as a ransom for many."*

Jn 8:32 – *"You will know the truth, and the truth will make you free."*

Concluding prophesies 18

MADE THE EARTH TO TREMBLE,[k] THAT SHOOK THE KINGDOMS;[l]

31 THAT MADE THE WORLD AS A WILDERNESS,[m] DESTROYING ITS CITIES;[n] THAT BROUGHT THE LAND TO RUIN,[o] AND HAS SLAIN HIS OWN PEOPLE?'[p]

32 "AND YOU SHALL BE CAST DOWN FROM THE MOUNTAIN OF GOD,[q] AND DESTROYED;[r] YOU SHALL BE BROUGHT TO ASHES UPON THE EARTH, IN THE SIGHT OF ALL.[s]

33 "AND THOSE WHO KNOW YOU WILL BE ASTONISHED, AND YOU SHALL BE NO MORE."[t]

m Ps 107:33,34
Isa 10:23
Isa 24:1-3
Jer 4:26
Zep 1:2,3,18
n Le 26:31,33
Isa 14:17
Isa 64:10
Jer 9:11
Jer 21:2-10
Jer 25:27-29
Jer 44:2,6
La 4:11
Zep 3:6
o Le 26:20,32
De 32:22
Isa 1:7
Isa 13:9
Jer 7:20
Jer 44:22
Eze 15:8
Eze 33:28
p Le 26:14-33
De 6:15
De 7:6
De 28:15-68
Isa 10:21-23
Isa 14:17,20
Jer 12:7
Jer 14:11,12
Jer 15:1-3,6,7
Jer 24:10
La 2:20,21
La 3:43
Am 3:2
q Ex 24:12-18
Ps 48:1,2
r Isa 33:1,8
Isa 47:8-11
Eze 28:16
Jn 12:31
s Eze 28:18
Eze 33:18
Jn 16:11
t Ps 106:10
Isa 9:13
Isa 10:20
Isa 63:19
Eze 28:19
Mr 10:45
Jn 8:32

19
So what happened?

I think Jesus died fully believing that he was giving his life to ransom his fellow Jews from their bondage to YHWH. If he were seen to have accepted the sacrifice of his blameless Jewish son, then all would know that the God of Israel had transgressed his own Law. No less than the symbolic eating of his flesh and blood, by which Jesus had ensured that his disciples would be cut off and so freed, the spilling of innocent blood imputed to YHWH would abrogate the covenant. That, surely, was all that was needed to bring the end times nigh as foretold by the prophets. The story of Judaism would conclude with the end of YHWH – 'AND YOU SHALL BE NO MORE' – and the Jews would be free.

But while the prophesies promised one thing, what came to pass was quite another. What Jesus could not foresee was how things would play out following his death. In my view, he had arranged with others for his body to be taken to Galilee and exposed on a mountain to fulfill certain scriptures; his accomplices seem to have done just that. But Jesus anticipated YHWH's wrathful return, with all hell breaking loose, and this did not come to pass. Instead, there was an anticlimactic silence – and that seems to be the one thing Jesus did not expect. Having banked on big, earth-shattering events, he had left his disciples with no written clue as to how to beat the devil of their own quiet doubt.

Thus was the denouement that Jesus intended first overshadowed and then superseded by reports that he had been seen in resurrected form. Simon Peter was instrumental in bruiting that story. The inner circle of disciples all signed up for the faith. What's more, despite their earlier disapprobation (cf. Mark 3:21,31 and John 7:5), Jesus' mother Mary[143] and his brothers joined the nascent Jesus-movement too, then about 120 strong – see Acts 1:14,15. Indeed, Jesus' brother James, later surnamed 'the Just', was apparently one of the contenders for the succession – in Acts 21:18, he is named as receiving Paul.

But not everyone would join in. Judas of course did not (Matthew hangs him in Mt 27:5; Luke kills him off with Acts 1:18), but nor apparently did Mary Magdalene, who, though a prominent figure – she was present at the crucifixion and is credited by Matthew, Mark and John as having been the very first or among the first of Jesus' followers to see him in his resurrected form – is yet wholly absent from the rest of the canon; nor did Joanna, Salome, and Mary of James, all of whom were variously named along with Mary Magdalene as having been on hand for Jesus' death and burial, and even witnesses of his resurrection,[144] and yet who likewise make no further appearance by name in the Christian scriptures.

My conclusion? That among those disciples who had been close to Jesus during his lifetime – certain followers who perhaps had a truer understanding of his intent – there were some who preferred to thoroughly distance themselves from the wrongheaded interpretation that was being subsequently touted by Simon Peter and the other apostles, championed by men like Paul and Stephen (neither of whom had ever met Jesus, much less walked with him), and approved of by members of his immediate family, who – no more than Paul – had never followed Jesus during his lifetime.

By proselytising that Jesus had been resurrected, Peter, Paul & Co. not only put a whole new spin on his crucifixion, they whitewashed the fact that *Jesus had truly died*. Sadly enough, in so doing they utterly nullified the import of their teacher's sacrifice. After all, if Jesus gets to come back to life two days later, then what exactly did he give up? Not much. Sure, he suffered a few ghastly scourgings in the days leading up to his crucifixion, followed by that gruesome six hour ordeal on the cross – but hey, after that, he was home free. Death spared him any further agony. Come Sunday morning, say the Gospels, our Galilean hero was up and about and in fine form, chatting with the ladies and going on from there to eat fish & chips with his friends. In the end, it turned out that Jesus didn't really die after all. He didn't give up his life. In fact, he gained *eternal* life – he was going to live forever! In exchange for a guaranteed return like that, wouldn't you consider braving a few hours' worth of torture? Or lay down your life? Seriously. Why not, if you're going to get it right back in spades two days later. But if you don't actually lose your life in the end, in what way, then, is death a 'sacrifice'?

•

Regardless, belief in Jesus' resurrection became the springboard for all that would follow. It was the keystone of Christian faith:

1Co 15:12-14 – *Now if Christ is preached, that he has been raised from the dead, how do some among you say that there is no resurrection of the dead? | But if there is no resurrection of the dead, neither has Christ been raised. | If Christ has not been raised, then our preaching is in vain, and your faith also is in vain.*

The various Jesus-movement groups that arose may have differed in their dogma as to whether Jesus had returned in a 'spiritual' body or a 'natural' physical body, but on one thing they all agreed: Jesus had been resurrected to eternal life.

This upended everything. Talk about topsy-turvy – all of a sudden the Latin cross, as horrific an instrument of torture and death as had ever been devised, became a symbol of God's love:

Jn 3:14,16 – *"As Moses lifted up the serpent in the wilderness, even so must the Son of Man be lifted up. | For God so loved the world, that he gave his one and only Son, that whoever believes in him should not perish, but have* *eternal life."*

Y HWH was not condemned but rather *praised* for having sacrificed his 'only begotten son' on the cross. In a mind-boggling volte-face, the detestable heathen practice of human sacrifice, for which YHWH had so violently rebuked the Jews time and again, was now said to be the key to salvation. Without the shedding of Jesus' all too human blood, mankind could not be forgiven for its sins:

Mt 26:28 – *"For this is my blood of the new covenant, which is poured out for many for the remission of sins."*

The 'old' everlasting covenant was now replaced by a 'new' covenant. The practice of sacrificing animals in the temple to atone for sin, as originally decreed by YHWH – *"Every day you shall offer the bull of sin offering for atonement"* (Ex 29:36) – was replaced by Jesus' one-off sacrifice on the cross. Concomitant with that, the eating of blood, which in the past would have resulted in your being cut off from the Chosen People forever, was now *de rigueur* if you were to have life:

Jn 6:53,54 – *"Most certainly I tell you, unless you eat the flesh of the Son of Man and drink his blood, you don't have life in yourselves. | He who eats my flesh and drinks my blood has eternal life, and I will raise him up at the last day."*

In short, you had a whole New Testament.[145] But the reward for faith in Jesus and obedience to the word of YHWH was no longer a Promised Land. What you now got was Eternal Life, thanks to Jesus' resurrection:

Jn 3:36 – *"One who believes in the Son has eternal life, but one who disobeys the Son won't see life, but the wrath of God remains on him."*

Jn 14:23,24 – *Jesus answered him, "If a man loves me, he will keep my word. My Father will love him, and we will come to him, and make our home with him. | He who doesn't love me doesn't keep my words. The word which you hear isn't mine, but the Father's who sent me."*

Jn 10:27,28 – *"My sheep hear my voice, and I know them, and they fol-*

low me. | I give eternal life to them. They will never perish, and no one will snatch them out of my hand."

Jn 5:21 – *"For as the Father raises the dead and gives them life, even so the Son also gives life to whom he desires."*

Jn 11:25,26 – *Jesus said to her, "I am the resurrection and the life. He who believes in me will still live, even if he dies. | Whoever lives and believes in me will never die. Do you believe this?"*

Although widely rejected by the Jewish faithful,[146] and subjected to well-intentioned Roman efforts to contain it early on,[147] the creed that promised its followers eternal life nevertheless spread like crabgrass and soon overran the ancient world's established spiritual order.

Yet the religion that named Jesus 'Christ', 'Lord and Savior', 'Son of God'; that theologically elevated him to consubstantiality with the God Almighty 'Father'; that promised 'eternal life' to those who believed in Him and hellish 'perdition' to those who did not; that, seeing itself as the sole proprietor and divinely authorised retailer of Jesus' message, systematically fought and ruthlessly quashed all competing interpretations, branding them as heresy; that was named the official state religion of the Roman Empire by Flavius Theodosius in 380 CE; that grew and spread and rose to temporal power; that over the course of centuries splintered more than once along major ideological fault lines, giving rise to East and West, Catholic and Protestant; that like a Hydra went on to thrive still more as numerous new sects sprang up among the cracks; and that two millennia later is one of the world's preeminent purveyors of spiritual dogma, with an instantly recognizable trademark – that religion, in my reading of the Gospels, would have been anathema to Jesus of Nazareth himself.

•

For me, the key to understanding Jesus is to be found not in his supposed resurrection, but in his death.

Jesus gave his life, that others might go free.

The Gospels present Jesus as the Son of God, and this is correct: in the scriptural context of the Bible, Jesus is the firstborn son. He went to Jerusalem in the same way that Isaac did, to be sacrificed. He is the innocent son that YHWH is called on to redeem:

Ge 22:10-13 – *Abraham stretched out his hand, and took the knife to kill his son. | Yahweh's angel called to him out of the sky, and said, "Abraham, Abraham!" He said, "Here I am." | He said, "Don't lay your hand on the boy or do anything to him. For now I know that you fear God, since you have not withheld your son, your only son, from me." | Abraham lifted up his eyes, and looked, and saw that behind him was a ram caught in the thicket by his horns. Abraham went and took the ram, and offered him up for a burnt offering instead of his son.*

The sacrifice is offered…but God must intervene at the last moment, as he did with Isaac:

Mr 15:34 – *At the ninth hour Jesus cried with a loud voice, saying, "Eloi, Eloi, lama sabachthani?" which is, being interpreted, "My God, my God, why have you forsaken me?"*

In not saving Jesus from the cross, YHWH showed that he accepted the human sacrifice of his son.

But Jesus did not *'pour out his soul to death'* to atone, as Paul would have it (Ti 2:13,14 ; Heb 1:3, 9:11-28), for mankind's sin.

Mr 10:45 – *"For the Son of Man also came not to be served, but to serve, and to give his life as a ransom for many."*

Rather, on behalf of his Jewish fellows, Jesus gave his life as a ransom – in Greek *lutron*, which signifies, literally, the redemption price of a slave. But to ransom them from what?

Ex 6:6 – *"Therefore tell the children of Israel, 'I am Yahweh, and I will bring you out from under the burdens of the Egyptians, and I will rid you out of their bondage, and I will redeem you with an outstretched arm, and with great judgments.'"*

Ex 13:3 – *Moses said to the people, "Remember this day, in which you came out of Egypt, out of the house of bondage. [...]"*

As signified by the Passover, from slavery. This was clearly his intent. We see this when Jesus says to the Jews, *"You will know the truth, and the truth will make you free."* In the Greek, *eleutheroó* means 'to release from bondage'. This, precisely, is the meaning that his interlocutors understood, and they were nonplussed:

Jn 8:33 – *They answered him, "We are Abraham's offspring, and have never been in bondage to anyone. How do you say, 'You will be made free'?"*

The Jews were only slaves to the God of Israel, to whom they were bound by an everlasting covenant. If Jesus therefore sought to release them from bondage, then it was surely to free them from YHWH. It was to secure *freedom* for his followers that Jesus gave his life. And the last thing he would have wanted would be to see his friends enslaved once again – and in his own name, no less! – by a new religion.[148]

Yet that is what Christianity achieved...and one imagines YHWH above, smirking with delight.

Ps 2:4 – *He who sits in the heavens will laugh. The Lord will have them in derision.*

Pr 1:26 – *"I also will laugh at your disaster. I will mock when calamity overtakes you."*

Epilogue

Greater love has no one than this, that someone
lay down his life for his friends.

Jesus tried. In the end, it didn't work out the way he might have hoped…
but he did try. He laid down his life, that his friends might go free.

Unlike many other spiritual masters, Jesus did not compose a written
record of his teachings. He might have guessed that if he did, people
would only use it later on to lay down yet a new 'Law', thus spawning
for themselves once again all the ills of religion. Better by far, he may
have reasoned, to trust in God to enlighten them.

Besides, his teaching was so simple. Any child could learn it.

Love your enemies.

Be compassionate.

Judge not, so that you won't be judged.

Hardly enough to fill a page, much less a scroll or codex. Why bother
to write it down?

But Jesus did have one word for his followers, one commandment, a
fresh commandment. No need to set it in stone; it was easy to remember.
To be at peace with one another, to find in themselves the kingdom of
God, his followers need only heed this, and all would be well –

Love one another.

•

The Jesus that my interpretation portrays is a singular person. I will try to describe him using a few broad strokes…

To begin with, he was a free-thinking maverick.

Lu 12:57 – *"Why don't you judge for yourselves what is right?"*

Judge for yourselves? Surely that contradicts the Scriptures:

Isa 33:22 – *For Yahweh is our judge. Yahweh is our lawgiver.* [...]

Unlike John the Baptist, Jesus does not seem to have set any great store by YHWH and his word. You don't hear him teaching his disciples to uphold the Law. By his own conduct, he seems to challenge it at every turn: he breaks the Sabbath; he forgives the adulteress; he gives his listeners to understand that the temple sacrifices are of no import. When it comes to his healing activities, Jesus offers no prayer to YHWH; he is wholly independent of the God of Israel.

This does not mean, however, that for Jesus there is no god. He does recognize God…it's just that his god is a god that, in stark contrast to YHWH, gives unstintingly without any regard for one's conduct.

Mt 5:45 – *"*[...]* For he makes his sun to rise on the evil and the good, and sends rain on the just and the unjust."*

God does not judge. He just is.

What's more, to get what you need or want from God, it's not a question of fearing him and being obedient; you need only ask, seek, knock on any closed door.

Lu 11:9 – *"I say to you, ask, and it will be given you. Seek, and you will find. Knock, and it will be opened to you."*

To get his disciples to appreciate and understand how this works in practical terms, he sends them out without money or provisions.

Lu 22:35 – *He said to them, "When I sent you out without purse, and wallet, and shoes, did you lack anything?" They said, "Nothing."*

But the Jews are the bond-servants of YHWH, to whom they are bound by an everlasting covenant. They cannot be free in the kingdom of God so long as they are the slaves of their tribal god.

So Jesus determined to free the Jews from their slavery under YHWH. Having divined in the Scriptures that YHWH could be brought down if the prophesied conditions relating to his downfall were met, Jesus sought to insure that end by fulfilling to the letter all that was spelled out in the Scriptures. Crucially, to bring about the abrogation of the Mosaic covenant and the end of religious slavery for the Jews, it would be necessary for blood to be shed.

Le 17:11 – *"For the life of the flesh is in the blood; and I have given it to you on the altar to make atonement for your souls: for it is the blood that makes atonement by reason of the life."*

Ps 49:8 – *For the redemption of their life is costly, no payment is ever enough.*

Jesus would give his life to free his friends. He would die on the cross. In accepting the human sacrifice of his scriptural 'Son', YHWH would sin by transgressing his own Law. As sure as day follows night, he who judged others would find himself judged in turn, and YHWH's ouster would ensue as prophesied, inexorably. This, for Jesus, was sure to happen within the lifetime of his friends...and they would find themselves freed from the hold of their tribal god.

Mr 10:45 – *"For the Son of Man came not to be served, but to serve, and to give his life as a ransom for many."*

No other spiritual leader before or since has ever dared to lead his followers on such a courageous quest to secure for themselves freedom from a god's religious bondage. He may not have achieved the aim he intended – and his design may have been wrongly construed and wholly distorted by countless generations – but in the moral contest of Jesus versus YHWH, I say Jesus is the true victor.

Notes

1. (page 1) For a further discussion of this position, see my commentary, Jesus is tempted by Satan in the wilderness, beginning on page 36.

2. (page 4) As advanced for example by Geza Vermes – see chapter 7, *The Authentic Gospel of Jesus* (London, Penguin Books, 2003), pp. 234-236.

3. (page 4) No less than 70 times as "son of man", and 23 times in the emphatic "you son of man" form, 'both vocative uses of the term' which are 'rarely found in later Jewish literature.' There are only 14 other occurrences of this idiom in the Hebrew Scriptures: in imitation of Ezekiel's vocative use, it appears once in Daniel 8:17; in the 13 other instances, 'the phrase occurs only in poetic couplets, [and] *always* in the second line,' indicating 'the presence of a Hebrew poetic convention.' – Son of man, *The International Standard Bible Encyclopedia*, vol. IV (Grand Rapids, Wm. B. Eerdmans Publishing Co, 1988), p. 574.

4. (page 4) We find this stated once again in Ezekiel 43:6,7 – *I heard one speaking to me out of the house; and a man stood by me. | He said to me, "Son of man, this is the place of my throne, and the place of the soles of my feet, where I will dwell among the children of Israel forever."* That's Yhwh speaking.

5. (page 5) Capital letters in English can be awfully pesky and charged with meaning: consider the differences in nuance between 'the son of man', 'the son of Man', and 'the Son of Man'.

If Jesus is 'the son of man', then we infer that he is simply the mortal son of his human father, a mortal man – or, as I interpret his meaning, the mortal son of Yhwh, of whom Ezekiel says, *"yet you are man, and not God."*

If Jesus is 'the son of Man', then we infer that he is the mortal son of the prototypical man, Adam.

If Jesus is 'the Son of Man', then we infer that he is himself the prototypical Son of the prototypical man, Adam.

Would being the prototypical Son of the prototypical Man make Jesus a god? No. But it would make him a universal symbol.

Since the earliest Greek uncials cannot be said to intentionally capitalise the idiom, my choice has been to render it as 'the son of man'. But Jesus still becomes the universal symbol of YHWH's Son, due to the definitive article 'the', which is routinely employed in the Gospels.

6. (page 12) The Babylonian Talmud, *Tractate Sanhedrin*, chapter VII, folio 50a (footnote), edited by Rabbi Dr. Isidore Epstein (London, Soncino Press, 1935-1952). For a virgin, the customary betrothal period lasted twelve months: 'A VIR-GIN IS ALLOWED TWELVE MONTHS FROM THE [TIME HER INTENDED] HUSBAND CLAIMED HER (*after their betrothal*) [IN WHICH] TO PREPARE HER MARRIAGE OUTFIT (*jewels and similar ornaments*).' – *Ibid., Tractate Kethuboth*, chapter V, folio 57a.

While certainly useful for preparing her wedding outfit, the twelve month waiting period would have also served to guarantee that a woman had not gotten herself pregnant prior to her betrothal. Mary, however, was found to be pregnant before she and Joseph came together; we cannot know for sure whether she gave birth to Jesus before or after the *huppah* ceremony that would have finalised the marriage, but I question whether Joseph – who had given thought to divorcing his betrothed wife secretly – would have consented to go through with it if Mary had already given birth prior to the home taking. There seems to be support, therefore, for the conclusion that Mary had a sexual encounter with a man *after* she was already betrothed…and hence committed adultery.

Finally, Mary was said to be a virgin. Although I think it unlikely that she was a widow from a previously unconsummated marriage, we may note that the waiting period until the huppah ceremony would have been shortened to one month: 'FOR A WIDOW (*who is presumed to be in the possession of some trinkets and jewellery from her first marriage*) THIRTY DAYS [ARE ALLOWED].' – *Ibid.*

7. (page 16) On this score, John 8:48 – *Then the Jews answered him, "Don't we say well that you are a Samaritan, and have a demon?"* – has always struck me. Samaria was but a day's walk from Nazareth, so I have often wondered: did young Mary fall in love with an itinerant Samaritan? If so, the men in Jerusalem who queried him may have been stating, not that Jesus was a Samaritan by religious conviction, but that he was a Samaritan through his biological father.

However, my fanciful notion concerning the charge that Jesus was a Samaritan is nonetheless handily discounted by James Montgomery, who writes as follows: 'There appear to be but two references to that sect in the early non-canonical literature of the Jews. The one is *Ecclus.* 50, 25f: "With two races is my soul vexed; and the third is no nation: with the dwellers of Seir and Philistia, and with the foolish race that sojourns in Shechem." It is to be noticed that the tone of the writer is one of contempt towards the Samaritans. The identical contemptuous attitude appears in the apocryphal *Testament of Levi*, c. 7: "From this day will Shechem be called the City of Fools". This epithet of fool as applied to the northern sectarian is further witnessed to in the New Testament. In *Jn.* 8, 48 the Jews are represented as saying to Jesus: "Do we not well say, Thou art a Samaritan and hast a devil?" In what sense was Jesus called a Samaritan? The answer has not been satisfactorily given. Commentators variously hold that the epithet refers to Jesus' heresy, to his not being a genuine son of Abraham (cf. v. 39ff), or to his hostility to the Jews. But the context leads much rather to the inference that "Samaritan" means here "fool." This comes out clearly in the subsequent conversation, v. 51ff: "Verily, verily I say unto you, if a man keep my saying, he shall never see death. The Jews said to him, Now we know that thou hast a devil. Abraham is dead, and the prophets, and thou sayest," etc. That is, their argument lies against the utter absurdity of Jesus' words. There are thus three distinct references from as many quarters in which the epithet "fool" appears as a byword of common application to the Samaritans. The origin of the epithet is most probably the contempt felt by the Jews for the absurd pretensions of their rivals. That the term was an extreme one, but nevertheless was used by the Jews among themselves, is shown by *Mt.* 5, 22.' – James A. Montgomery, *The Samaritans* (The J.C. Winston Co., Philadelphia, 1907), pp. 154-155.

8. (page 18) Matthew and Luke insist that Mary was still a virgin when Jesus was born, likely taking their cue from the Septuagint's use in Isaiah 7:14 of *parthenos*, or 'physical virgin' – a Greek mistranslation of the original *'almah* or 'young woman' in the Hebrew Scriptures. See Robert Crotty, *Peter the Rock* (Melbourne, Spectrum Publications, 2015), p. 31.

9. (page 20) Jesus was not an orphan *per se*, but his father was gone, and the man who raised an orphan was looked upon as being the child's father: 'This teaches thee that whoever brings up an orphan in his home, Scripture ascribes it to him as though he had begotten him.' (The Babylonian Talmud, *op. cit.*, Tractate *Sanhedrin*, chapter II, folio 19b.) Hence, those who said *"Isn't this the carpenter's son?"* (Mt 13:55) or *"Isn't this Joseph's son?"* (Lu 4:22) were stating what was likely a commonly held view. Even so, the good people of Nazareth apparently knew that Jesus' biological father was someone else (Mr 6:3). That Mary had committed an act of adultery might be echoed by John 8:41 – *They said to him, "We were*

not born of sexual immorality."

10. (page 21) You'd have thought angels would have hoovered the Holy Prepuce up to heaven along with Jesus at the time of the Ascension, but it seems it stayed behind in Galilee. Indeed, a flaccid relic purported to be Jesus' foreskin was given to Pope Leo III as a Christmas present by Charlemagne, on the occasion of the latter's coronation as Emperor of the Romans on 25 December, 800 CE. Interestingly, in the centuries that followed, a dozen or more foreskins came to light and were housed in Catholic reliquaries across Europe. Were these subsequent claimants spurious snippets of flesh? Or were they, perhaps, all cut from the same cloth? After all, a man of Jesus' stature might have had a foreskin to match, with plenty to go around.

11. (page 24) Luke 2:49 is generally translated along the lines of *"Why were you looking for me? Didn't you know that I must be in my Father's house?"* Why, then, do I have Jesus say instead, "Did you not know that I should be among the *children* of my Father?"

The original Greek texts for Luke 2:49 actually read, *"Why were you searching for me? Did you not know that I should be among the _____ of my Father?"* That blank stands for the fact that there is no noun, only a dative neuter plural article. In Greek, when only an article is given, its referent is usually to be found nearby. So the question becomes, which nearby noun in Luke's passage best fits the context?

While *house* has been popularized by many translations – 'did you not know that I should be in the *house* of my Father?' – the word seems a poor choice for two reasons: it does not appear elsewhere in Luke's passage, and neither of the Greek words that would likely be used for house – *oikia* and *oikos* – are neuter.

In like manner, *business* – 'did you not know that I should be about the *business* of my Father?' – also seems inappropriate: out of half a dozen Greek words for 'business', there is only one word – *pragma* – which is neuter, and it too does not appear elsewhere in Luke's passage.

Temple, however, is a valid possibility, since the neuter noun *hieron* appears three verses earlier, in Luke 2:46, and it is an odd characteristic of Greek that a plural article can nevertheless stand for a noun in the singular. So we could read Luke 2:49 as saying, *"Did you not know that I should be in the temple of my Father?"*

But there is another neuter noun that is also worth considering: in Luke 2:48, Mary has just exclaimed, "Child!" *Teknon* is a neuter noun referring to a child of either sex. There are three reasons to favour *teknon* as Luke's dative neuter plural article's referent: in the text that precedes, this word is the nearest neuter noun; it gives a correct reading in the plural (whereas 'temples' does not, since YHWH had only one temple); and it can be seen to make sense in the context.

"Why were you searching for me? Did you not know that I should be among the children of my Father?" Who would these children be? The fatherless. Two reference verses given in the margin serve to convey this notion:

Ps 26:8 establishes that the temple is where YHWH resides: *Yahweh, I love the habitation of your house, the place where your glory dwells.*

Ps 68:5 declares: *A father of the fatherless, and a defender of the widows, is God in his holy habitation.*

As a young boy, Jesus might have found solace in seeing YHWH, said by the psalmist to be *'a father of the fatherless'*, as his true father. So in Luke's account, we would see Jesus as wishing to stay in Jerusalem, 'in his Father's house'.

Well, what do you know about that? Talk about coming full circle. Maybe the standard translation has it right, after all…

12. (page 24) Joseph was said to be a righteous man (Mt 1:19), which recalls Psalm 106:3 – *Blessed is one who does what is right at all times.* According to the Gemara, 'This refers to a man who brings up an orphan boy or orphan girl in his house and enables them to marry.' – The Babylonian Talmud, *op. cit., Tractate Kethuboth*, chapter IV, folio 50a.

13. (page 33) This according to the Synoptic Gospels. However, John 1:28 states that *'These things were done in Bethany beyond the Jordan, where John was baptizing.'* Scholars such as D.A. Carson place this Bethany in the territory of Batanea (Carson, *The Gospel according to John*, Pillar New Testament Commentary; Grand Rapids: Eerdmans, 1990, 146-7). Batanea was in the larger province of Gaulonitis, the present day Golan Heights, and was ruled by Philip the Tetrarch. That John came this far north is plausible, and certainly it would make it easier for Galileans like Andrew, Simon, Philip and Jesus to come hear his preaching.

14. (page 35) Indeed, the evangelist John is wont to libel Judas, as may be gleaned from comparing Matthew 26:8-10 and Mark 14:4-6 to John 12:4-7. Whereas his co-evangelists tell us that several disciples were offended to see the perfume used in spendthrift fashion, John lays the charge on Judas alone, contumeliously adding that *he was a thief, and having the money box, used to steal what was put into it.* For this reason, I think it likely that the evangelist would see to it that Judas' name be expunged in contexts where his presence might possibly be seen in a favourable light.

15. (page 35) The author of the Gospel according to John writes that Andrew 'led' his brother Simon to Jesus. This business of 'leading' people to 'Christ' became a holy mission among believers as the Jesus-movement expanded and established itself as a religion. It persists to this day.

16. (page 47) With Exodus 13:21 in mind – *Yahweh went before them by day in a pillar of cloud, to lead them on their way* – I wonder if the 'Follow me!' injunction became an inside joke with them. I can imagine Jesus laughing about this. 'Hey, guys, what do you think? Did our holy God say *"Follow me!"* as he led the Jews in circles round the desert? *"Follow me!"* Sure thing. But does the cloud know where he's going? I mean, getting from the Nile to Jerusalem by foot or camel is a trek that normally takes us only two or three weeks. So why on earth did it take our God forty whole years to lead his Chosen People to the Promised Land? *"Follow me, follow me!"* For crying out loud, Elohim, that wasn't some sort of 'test' for us – that was you not knowing which way you were going.'

17. (page 48) I find it curious that we never hear about Simon Peter's wife. Gallivanting about the Galilean countryside with Jesus is hardly conducive to a maintaining a happy home life, but Peter may have had his reasons for being out and about. He may likewise have been among the disciples who balked when Jesus declared that *"whoever divorces his wife, except for sexual immorality, and marries another, commits adultery."* (Mt 9:19) We'll return to this in chapter 10.

18. (page 51) That parents were responsible for their children's acts may be inferred from a view expressed by the *tanna* Eleazar b. Simeon in the second century CE – 'You are responsible for your son till he is thirteen; then say, "Blessed be He who has rid me of responsibility for this."' (Gen. R., 63.10)

19. (page 52) In the lists of apostles, Luke 6:15 cites 'Matthew' and Matthew 10:3 cites 'Matthew the tax gatherer'. Some have assumed that the Levi here mentioned and the Matthew given in the lists of disciples were one and the same, and have even gone so far as to call him 'Matthew-Levi' – a name not found in the Gospels. What makes more sense, though, is that Jesus called "Levi *the son* of Alphaeus" to be a follower, per Mark 2:14, but did not choose him to be one of the twelve apostles. Luke 6:15 says that "James *the son* of Alphaeus" was chosen; perhaps James (or Jacob) was Levi's brother.

20. (page 55) In the Synoptics, Jesus readily enjoys the company of tax-gatherers and sinners – cf. Mt 9:10,11, 11:19; Mr 2:15,16; Lu 5:30, 7:34, 15:1,2. In striking contrast, John's gospel does not make a point of portraying Jesus in this way.

21. (page 70) While Matthew frequently employs the designation 'Father who is in the heavens', Mark and Luke only use this formulation on a few rare occasions. The notion that the god in the sky, or 'sky father', is masculine – and not feminine – seems to have arisen in Proto-Indo-European times; it would have given rise to Zeus, the Greek god of the sky, and his Roman counterpart, Jupiter, whose name may be translated 'father Jove' (*The American Heritage Dictionary of the English Language*, 5th edition, 2015). It seems logical to conclude that Jesus' designation of a heavenly god as 'Father' derives from his Mediterranean cultural heritage.

Since Jesus is speaking about sunshine and rain in Matthew 5:45, it is natural that he should refer to a heavenly 'father' in the sky. But he does so again a dozen verses later: *"Pray like this: 'Our Father in heaven, may your name be kept holy. | Give us today our daily bread.'"* (Mt 6:9,11)

Why does Jesus tell his disciples to pray to a god in heaven for bread? Is it because YHWH rained down manna from the sky to feed the Jews as they trekked around in the wilderness for forty years? A poor choice, in my opinion: that 'Father in heaven' is hardly reputable as a baker. His ersatz bread may have filled hungry Hebrew tummies, but the Jews soon got tired of living on manna alone (Numbers 11:6). Doesn't sound like the bread was up to scratch. Maybe Jesus should have referred his disciples instead to a good, down-to-earth female god, one who could have supplied them with daily bread made with real grain – for example, Demeter, the Greek goddess of the harvest.

The Mediterranean's polytheistic religions struck a healthy balance between male and female gods; in comparison, the monotheistic Abrahamic religions seem decidedly off-kilter, with their masculine 'God in the heavens' deity having no female consort or counterpart. In the Greek pantheon, Zeus had Hera; for the Romans, Jupiter had Juno. If we look further afield, we find that Hinduism's three Trimurti gods each have a female consort – Saraswati for Brahma, Lakshmi for Vishnu, Parvati for Shiva – and in Shinto, we have the pairing of Izanagi and Izanami. So why does the Jewish god YHWH have no wife? It's unhealthy for the guy. Then again, maybe he's a closet homosexual – hence those nasty, repressive laws he lays down, like *"If a man lies with a male, as with a woman, both of them have committed an abomination: they shall surely be put to death; their blood shall be upon them."* (Le 20:13) Either way, an unhealthy state of human affairs is engendered: women are told what they can and cannot do; Jewish men chauvinistically pray, *'Blessed are you, Lord our God, Ruler of the Universe, who has not made me a woman'*; homosexuality is demonized. You sure wouldn't find a skewed state of affairs like that up on Mount Olympus – Hera, a fully independent goddess in her own right, takes no orders from her husband. What's more, Tiresias, who testified from his own experience that *"Of ten parts, a man enjoys one only"*, confirmed Zeus' opinion that women enjoy sexual intercourse more than men – hardly a reason to crow a daily cock-a-doodle-do about being made a man and not a woman. As for homosexual encounters, Zeus very happily bedded Ganymede.

Of the three Abrahamic religions, Christianity makes a weird stab at rectifying the imbalance of having a solitary male god at the celestial helm by elevating Jesus' mother Mary up to heaven with the Assumption; but once there, even though she bore him a son, she doesn't get to be YHWH's wife; instead, she's set aside as a holy virgin. This puts sex completely out of the picture, with the doctrine of the Immaculate Conception only serving to exclude it further. The cult of Mary clearly reflects a deep human need for a female deity, but the sexually truncated Virgin Mary is an unhealthy role model for both women and men. All told, the Christian pantheon ends up being a decidedly anomalous group: the heavenly Father, YHWH, though a stickler for morality, has committed adultery with a betrothed woman – immorality that is whitewashed for both of them. The Father has no regular consort, nor does he sleep around. He's a male god, but he has no sexual nature apart from his one-off indiscretion with Mary (what, did he feel a need to prove himself?) Then you have the Son of that illicit tryst, Jesus. He too is without any sexuality – no wife, and no reported adventures with his numerous female followers; homosexual leanings possibly suspected, but hard evidence lacking. The Holy Spirit, third member of the clan, is patently asexual – in Greek, *pneuma* is a neuter noun. Finally, you have the immaculate Virgin Mary, a perpetual virgin who, despite having birthed five sons and several daughters, seems to have never engaged, not even once, in normal, human sexual congress – she's up there in heaven, too, a blue-robed queen of sorts, but with no clear Biblical mandate of her own, apart from being the virgin Mother of God. In other words, a Christian looking to heaven will hardly find there a suitable role model for his or her own conduct on earth as a healthy man or woman.

With the 'Father who is in the heavens' formula for God being found almost exclusively in the Gospel according to Matthew, I am inclined to think that Jesus did not himself view God in this way. His patriarchal Mediterranean culture may have inclined him to refer to God as 'Father', but if pressed on the issue, I'd like to think that Jesus would have pantheistically replied that God was simply everywhere, and in everyone, along the lines of *"the kingdom of God is within you."* This would put God above dualities such as male-female in the same way that Jesus' remark about how *"he makes his sun to rise on the evil and the good, and sends rain on the just and the unjust"* places God above the duality of good-evil.

22. (page 73) *Aphiémi* is generally translated as 'forgive' in the following Gospel verses: Mt 6:14 ; Mt 9:2,5,6 ; Mt 12:31,32 ; Mt 18:21,27,32,35 ; Mr 2:5,7,9,10 ; Mr 3:28 ; Mr 4:12 ; Mr 11:25,26 ; Lu 5:20,21,23,24 ; Lu 7:47,48,49 ; Lu 11:4 ; Lu 12:10 ; Lu 17:4 ; Lu 23:34 ; Jn 20:23.

A second word, *charizomai*, is also so translated, but seems a far less likely choice, since it appears in the Gospels only three times, in Luke, where it is twice rendered – in Luke 7:42 and 7:43 – as 'forgive'.

23. (page 97) Byron R. McCane argues that the disciple in question was in fact requesting permission to assist in the 'secondary burial' of his dead father – see McCane (1990), *"Let the Dead Bury Their Own Dead"; Secondary Burial and Matt 8:21–22.* (Harvard Theological Review, 83, pp 31-43). It is a very nicely constructed justification for what otherwise appears to be an unfathomable insensitivity on Jesus' part. However, to achieve his aim, McCane dispenses perforce with the context, in which it is the level of devotion that is expected – one of total commitment to following Jesus – that is being addressed.

24. (page 105) We could see this as being a natural denouement for any system devised by humans, including religions, if Mark Twain is right in saying that "Every civilization carries the seeds of its own destruction, and the same cycle shows in them all."

25. (page 106) See Geza Vermes, *The Changing Faces of Jesus* (Viking Compass, 2001), pp 246-263, under the headings *Popular religion in the age of Jesus* and *Models of charismatic holy men in the age of Jesus.*

While prayer may not have been a prominent and requisite feature of all healings, it is nevertheless mentioned in many instances. Among the examples given by Vermes, we find that Abraham prayed for the Pharaoh when he laid his hands on his head, and that Hanina ben Dosa – whose 'prayer was seen not simply as an intercession to God, but as directly efficient' – prayed that the son of Rabban Yohanan ben Zakkai might live and that the fever might leave the son of Rabban Gamaliel; also, that 'the Hasid was famous for his prayer, which was believed to be all-powerful, capable of performing miracles […].'

To these we may add the example of Elisha, who prayed when he revived the Shunammite's dead son – *He went in therefore, and shut the door on them both, and prayed to Yahweh.* (2Ki 4:33)

26. (page 106) The following are the relevant passages:
Mr 14:23 – *After he had sent the multitudes away, he went up into the mountain by himself to pray. When evening had come, he was there alone.*

Mr 1:35 – *Early in the morning, while it was still dark, he rose up and went out, and departed into a deserted place, and prayed there.*

Mr 6:46 – *After he had taken leave of them, he went up the mountain to pray.*

Mr 14:32 – *They came to a place which was named Gethsemane. He said to his disciples, "Sit here, while I pray."* (Also Mt 26:36 and Lu 22:41)

Lu 6:12 – *In these days, he went out to the mountain to pray, and he continued all night in prayer to God.*

Lu 9:18 – *As he was praying alone, the disciples were with him, and he asked them, "Who do the multitudes say that I am?"*

Lu 9:28 – *About eight days after these sayings, he took with him Peter, John, and James, and went up onto the mountain to pray.*

Lu 11:1 – *When he finished praying in a certain place, one of his disciples said to him, "Lord, teach us to pray, just as John also taught his disciples."*

27. (page 115) Tim Hegg presents an admirable analysis of the problems posed by Mark 7:19 and its textual variants in his paper titled *Mark 7:19b – A Short Technical Note* (TorahResource, May 2005).

I agree with his conclusions about the verse and its translation *per se*. Nevertheless, since Jesus, in my view, intended to abrogate the Law, I can only conclude that he would have considered Moses' dietary restrictions to be irrelevant. By stating that nothing that goes into the mouth can defile a man, I read him as tacitly giving his listeners to understand that any and all foods – kosher and non kosher – are fine. It does not matter what you eat. What comes out the other end, be it Gentile or Jewish, is poop, pure and simple.

28. (page 122) The passage's chiastic structure may be outlined as follows:

A   But he said to them, "When you pray, say, '**Our Father**, who *is* in heaven, **give us today our daily bread**.'"

    B   And he said to them, "Who among you will have a friend, and will go to him at midnight, and say to him, 'Friend, lend me **three loaves of bread**, for a friend of mine has come to me on a journey, and I have nothing to set before him.' And he, answering from within, will say, 'Do not cause me trouble! The door has already been shut, and my children are in bed with me. I cannot get up to give you *anything*.' I say to you, even if he will not get up and give him *anything* on account of being his friend, yet because of his shameless importunity, having *been* woken, he will give him as much as he needs."

> C "I even say to you, ask, and it will be given to you; seek, and you will find; knock, and it will be opened to you."
>
> C¹ "For everyone who asks, receives; and everyone who seeks, finds; and to everyone who knocks, it will be opened."
>
> B¹ "But which of you who is a father, to a son who will ask for a loaf of **bread**, will give him a stone? Or indeed a **fish**, and instead of a fish, will give him a serpent? Or if he should ask for an **egg**, will give him a scorpion?"
>
> A¹ "Therefore, if you, being evil, know *how* to give good gifts to your children, how much more will **your Father**, who *is* in the heavens, **give good *gifts* to those who ask Him?**"

The bread, fish and egg sayings found in Matthew 7:9-10 and Luke 11:11-12 are thought to derive from the Sayings Gospel Q. It would seem the authors of Matthew and Luke have been deliberately selective in drawing from Q: how might we account for Luke citing only the fish and egg sayings, Matthew citing only the bread and fish sayings, and Matthew suppressing the story of the pesky friend in dire need of three loaves at midnight?

I propose that the author of Luke omits Q's verse about bread and stone for narrative reasons. The serpent and the scorpion are living terrors that grab the reader's imagination; the inanimate stone is not. Preferring dramatic flourish to chiastic symmetry, the author may have decided that a dull stone was not only ill-assorted with a scary serpent and a stinging scorpion, but it added dead weight to the lengthy narrative. Stones he can do without.

As for Matthew, the author's handling of the source text has utterly disrupted the chiastic structure: the Lord's Prayer (A) appears in Matthew 6:9-13; he's omitted the story (B) about the three loaves altogether; and the sayings (C, B1, A1) appear fully 27 verses later, in Matthew 7:7-11.

In the first place, why omit the story? Consider the teaching put forth in Matthew 6:31-34 – *"Therefore do not be anxious, saying, 'What will we eat?', 'What will we drink?' or, 'With what will we be clothed?'* | […] *For your heavenly Father knows that you need all these things.* | *But seek first God's Kingdom, and his righteousness; and all these things will be given to you as well.* | *Therefore do not be anxious for tomorrow, for tomorrow will be anxious for itself. Each day's own evil is sufficient."* This laissez-faire approach to sustenance is at odds with Jesus' importunate seeker of bread, and the author of Matthew may have felt that the story of the latter ran counter to what he judged to be a more 'spiritual' teaching.

With regard to his decision to pass over the saying about the egg and the scorpion, the author's choice seems motivated in this case not by Luke's concern for dramatic tension, but by interest as to what's on the menu: choosing items that fit with the miraculous feedings of 5000 and 4000, the author of Matthew keeps the sayings that speak of bread and fish. Eggs he can do without.

29. (page 130) Beyond their simple irritation with Jesus acting like a know-it-all do-gooder, I wonder if the people of Nazareth may have been offended by what he said because they deduced from it that, in proclaiming their release from bondage, he was in fact speaking rebellion against YHWH:

De 13:1,3,5 – *If a prophet or a dreamer of dreams arises among you, and he gives you a sign or a wonder | you shall not listen to the words of that prophet, or to that dreamer of dreams* […] *| That prophet, or that dreamer of dreams* […] *has spoken rebellion against Yahweh your God, who brought you out of the land of Egypt, and redeemed you out of the house of bondage, to draw you aside out of the way which Yahweh your God commanded you to walk in.* […]

30. (page 133) Flavius Josephus, *Antiquities of the Jews*, Book xviii, chapter 5, 2 (translation by William Whiston).

31. (page 137) There are only three stories in the Gospels that contain significant numerical symbolism – the feeding of the 5000 (Mark 6:35-44, with parallels in Matthew, Luke and John); the feeding of the 4000 (Mark 8:1-9, with a parallel in Matthew); and the miraculous catch of 153 fish (John 21:1-11).[32]

I have yet to read a convincing argument for the significance of the numerical size of the crowds. As for the intended symbolism linked to the loaves and fishes, our best guesses – e.g., that the two fish represent Pisces, and, by extension, Virgo, its complementary opposite in the sky; that the five loaves represent either the Pentateuch or the five observable planets (Mercury, Venus, Mars, Jupiter and Saturn); that the seven loaves represent those five planets plus the moon and the sun, and hence the seven days of the week; that the twelve baskets represent the twelve tribes of Israel, or the twelve signs of the zodiac; that the 153 fish amount to a gematria that identifies 'the beloved disciple' as being 'the Magdalene' – are all plausible indeed, but since we lack genuine initiation into Gnostic mysteries, we can never be sure if they are right.

32. (note 31) There is also numerical symbolism in the parable of the sower, which ends thus: *"Others fell into the good ground, and yielded fruit, growing up and increasing. Some produced thirty times, some sixty times, and some one hundred times as much."* (Mr 4:8) But it is a parable, not an event that is reported.

33. (page 138) On this occasion in Matthew and Mark, Jesus says to the disciples, "Be of good cheer. I AM, fear not." In John, he simply says, "I AM, fear not."

The original Greek in all three Gospels reads *egó eimi*. This formulation seems to deliberately point to the 'I AM' of Exodus 3:14 – a notion that finds support in the reaction of both the Sanhedrin (Mr 14:63,64) and the guard sent by the chief priests (Jn 18:6) to Jesus' statement, *'Egó eimi'* in Mark 14:62 and John 18:5 – so it is notable that Jesus' disciples do not react here in any particular way to the evocation of the Sacred Name. Indeed, their failure to react is all the more striking at this stage in the chronology, for the incident precedes two watershed events – Simon Peter's naming of Jesus as the Messiah, and the Transfiguration, where Jesus is singled out as YHWH's beloved son – that would have arguably prepared the disciples in some way for this 'I AM' that comes out of the blue, and which in the Jewish context could only have been heard as a blasphemy of the Name. Yet the disciples express neither awe nor consternation – not even Simon Peter, who had no qualms about rebuking his teacher for breaches of form (cf. Mr 8:32).

I therefore think it highly unlikely that Jesus actually said 'I AM' on this occasion, when he called to his disciples from the shore; consequently, his words 'I am' are not rendered in small capitals in the text. But this is an exception. In all other instances, *The Gospel of Jesus of Nazareth* employs small capitals to indicate those passages in the Gospels where the original Greek reads *egó eimi*, apparently to signify YHWH's name as given in Exodus 3:14 – *God said to Moses, "I AM WHO I AM," and he said, "You shall tell the children of Israel this: 'I AM has sent me to you.'"*

34. (page 141) Matthew 16:2,3 reads – *But he answered them, "When it is evening, you say, 'It will be fair weather, for the sky is red.' | In the morning, 'It will be foul weather today, for the sky is red and threatening.'"*

The phenomenon is widely known: *'Red sky at morning, sailor takes warning; red sky at night, sailor's delight.'* The sky is red in both instances, yet we read the sign as presaging foul weather in one, fair in the other. This is the point that Jesus is making: in terms of predicting the weather, the Pharisees are able to correctly interpret signs that would confound the uninitiated. However, this nugget of red sky meteorological wisdom was apparently unfamiliar to the evangelist or a later copyist, who must have asked himself, *"How could a sky that is identical in both cases portend two such divergent outcomes?"* Having never been introduced to the intricacies of celestial red sky forecasting, he couldn't make sense of it. So he very helpfully added a word: *'for the sky is red and **threatening**.'*

There! Now it made sense.

But, sadly, the point that Jesus wished to make was now hopelessly clouded.

35. (page 148) If we follow Matthew, we learn that *Simon Peter answered, "You are the Christ, the Son of the living God."* | *Then he commanded the disciples that they should tell no one that he was Jesus the Christ.* (Mt 16:16,20)

Simon Peter and the others, we may regret to learn, blithely disregarded their beloved teacher's admonition.

Act 5:27-42 – *When they had brought them, they set them before the council. The high priest questioned them,* | *saying, "Didn't we strictly command you not to teach in this name? [...] "* | *But Peter and the apostles answered, [...]* | *"The God of our fathers raised up Jesus, whom you killed, hanging him on a tree.* | *God exalted him with his right hand to be a Prince and a Savior, to give repentance to Israel, and remission of sins."* | *[...]* | *Every day, in the temple and at home, they never stopped teaching and preaching Jesus, the Christ.*

As noted in Acts, Peter and his fellow disciples were speaking 'in the name of Jesus' and 'preaching Jesus, the Christ.' That corresponds perfectly with what Jesus tried to warn them about, false prophets who would rise up and *"lead many astray."*

36. (page 150) Should we make anything of the fact that it was *'on the third day'* that Abraham *'lifted up'* his eyes?

37. (page 150) In his *Antiquities of the Jews*, Josephus relates a few incidents that can attest to that, with examples that precede Jesus' time by less than 200 years:

'But the best men [...] every day underwent great miseries and bitter torments; for they were whipped with rods, and their bodies were torn to pieces, and were crucified, while they were still alive, and breathed.' – *Op.cit.*, Book XII, chapter 5.

'And when [Alexander Jannaeus] had taken the city, and gotten the men into his power, he brought them to Jerusalem, and did one of the most barbarous actions in the world to them; for as he was feasting with his concubines, in the sight of all the city, he ordered about eight hundred of them to be crucified; and while they were living, he ordered the throats of their children and wives to be cut before their eyes.' – *Ibid.*, Book XIII, chapter 14.

'Upon this, Varus sent a part of his army into the country, to seek out those that had been the authors of the revolt; and when they were discovered, he punished some of them that were most guilty, and some he dismissed: now the number of those that were crucified on this account were two thousand.' – *Ibid.*, Book XVII, chapter 10.

'And besides this, the sons of Judas of Galilee were now slain; I mean of that Judas who caused the people to revolt, when Cyrenius came to take an account of the estates of the Jews [...]. The names of those sons were James and Simon, whom Alexander commanded to be crucified.' – *Ibid.*, Book xx chapter 5.

38. (page 150) No wonder, then, that Judas is said to have gone *'away and hanged himself.'* (Mt 27:5)

39. (page 151) The Babylonian Talmud, *op. cit.*, *Tractate Sanhedrin*, chapter vi, folio 45b.

40. (page 151) *Ibid.*, folio 46a.

41. (page 158) As we have seen, Simon Peter rebuked Jesus for saying that he would be put to death at the hands of the chief priests; presently, he will also cheerfully affirm that his teacher pays the two-drachma temple tax. I see both positions as being consistent with a traditionalist Jewish outlook.

As for James and John, their eagerness to repay the inhospitable village with fire and brimstone suggests that they adhered to the widespread Jewish contempt for Samaritans.

Lu 9:54 – *When his disciples, James and John, saw this, they said, "Lord, do you want us to command fire to come down from the sky, and destroy them, just as Elijah did?"*

Jewish to the core, they evoke Elijah as an example.

Incidentally, this might be another reason why Jesus would call these two the 'sons of thunder'.

Ex 9:23 – *Moses stretched out his rod toward the heavens, and Yahweh sent thunder, hail, and lightning flashed down to the earth. Yahweh rained hail on the land of Egypt.*

Isa 29:6 – *She will be visited by Yahweh of Armies with thunder, with earthquake, with great noise, with whirlwind and storm, and with the flame of a devouring fire.*

42. (page 158) Matthew and Mark both refer to a 'high mountain'. In contrast, Luke only says that Jesus goes with his three disciples up 'the mountain to pray'. The simpler designation might imply his usual haunt (see page 120), but my guess is that Luke, wanting to head his readers off at the pass from drawing pagan conclusions, thought it best to downplay the 'high' mountain bit.

43. (page 160) From where they sat on their heavenly perch – with their angel's-eye view of all that the Chosen People had had to put up with in terms of judgment and punishment since arriving from Egypt – Moses and Elijah may have come to the conclusion that YHWH's covenant was for the birds.

44. (page 161) It's fun to conjecture whether the angels in the wilderness, the men who met with Jesus on the high mountain, and the men who appeared to Mary at the tomb are two and the same:

Mr 1:13 – *He was there in the wilderness forty days tempted by Satan. He was with the wild animals; and the angels were serving him.*

Lu 9:30,31 – *Behold, two men were talking with him, who were Moses and Elijah, | who appeared in glory* […].

Lu 24:4 – *While they were greatly perplexed about this, behold, two men stood by them in dazzling clothing.*

Jn 20:12 – *And she saw two angels in white sitting, one at the head, and one at the feet, where the body of Jesus had lain.*

45. (page 161) Readers might object that this is not so, for an angel of YHWH appeared to Moses in the burning bush:

Ex 3:2 – *Yahweh's angel appeared to him in a flame of fire out of the middle of a bush. He looked, and behold, the bush burned with fire, and the bush was not consumed.*

But I have to wonder – on that occasion, was it perhaps only the flame that was incandescent?

46. (page 162) If so, then perhaps the young man who was at the tomb was also an initiate:

Mr 16:5 – *Entering into the tomb, they saw a young man sitting on the right side, dressed in a white robe, and they were amazed.*

47. (page 162) At any rate, perhaps as a mark of respect or fellowship, Jesus had himself dressed for the occasion:

Mt 17:2 – […] *His face shone like the sun, and his garments became as white as the light.*

Mr 9:3 – *His clothing became glistening, exceedingly white, like snow, such as no launderer on earth can whiten them.*

Lu 9:29 – *As he was praying,* […] *his clothing became white and dazzling.*

48. (page 163) See 2 Chronicles 3:1. The Second Temple was destroyed in 70 CE. Some six centuries later, the Umayyad caliph Abd al-Malik built the Dome of the Rock to enshrine the Foundation Stone, sacred to Islam, and held by Jews to be the altar where Isaac was laid out by his father Abraham for sacrifice to YHWH.

49. (page 166) Who's to say? Maybe Moses and Elijah had connections with Mount Hermon – see below, THE DISCIPLES GO TO THE MOUNTAIN IN GALILEE, page 357.

50. (page 170) The Babylonian Talmud, *op. cit.*, *Tractate Sanhedrin*, chapter VII, folio 53a.

51. (page 170) 'For obviously the offence of an *arusah*, who is still in her father's house and thereby profanes him, is greater than that of a *nesu'ah*; and therefore we may assume that her punishment is correspondingly greater. This conclusion is further supported by the fact that a *nesu'ah*, if an Israelite's daughter, is punished by strangulation, the most lenient of all death penalties, whilst an *arusah* is punished by stoning, the most severe.' – The Babylonian Talmud, *op. cit.*, *Tractate Sanhedrin*, chapter VII, folio 50a.

52. (page 170) The Babylonian Talmud, *op. cit.*, *Tractate Sanhedrin*, chapter VII, folio 52b. In other words, you can shtup with a married goy girl as much as you like without risk of being strangled by an angry Jewish crowd for having committed adultery. Whether her goy husband will be as forbearing is anybody's guess.

53. (page 173) I know… for the Christian faithful, Jesus was the Son of God: holiness incarnate, perfect in every way, untainted by original sin and utterly devoid of carnal desire. Of course, that might be true. Then again, who's to say? It might also be true that Jesus himself committed adultery at one point with one of his many female followers.

Readers will note that in John 8:11, the *pericope adulterae* ends with Jesus saying, *"Neither do I condemn you. Go, and sin no more."* It is my opinion that the latter part of that statement is untenable – can Jesus reasonably say *'Neither do I condemn you'* and then follow with *'Sin no more'*? Surely to say 'sin no more' conveys that in his view she has sinned, which is a judgment in itself; yet four verses later, Jesus is quoted in John as saying *"I judge no one."* For this reason, I omit the 'sin no more' remark and have Jesus say instead 'Go in peace.' In the freewheeling context of *The Gospel of Jesus of Nazareth*, we would naturally understand that Jesus saying 'Go in peace' to an adulteress would have rubbed more than one Church Father the wrong way – and invariably led to the neat expungement of the words 'in peace' when the notorious *pericope adulterae* finally made it into the Christian scriptures.

At any rate, in the manuscripts that have come down to us, the Greek just reads 'Go!', in the imperative. I think some moralistic scribe felt obliged to add, *'And sin no more!'* (That the wording has been worked on by others may be gleaned from the fact that certain texts read, *'And from now on, sin no more!'*)

54. (page 175) *On the Sacred Disease*, written ca 400 BCE, authorship uncertain but belonging to his corpus.

55. (page 180) I have wondered if the explanation for this verse might not be found in a play on words, with the Aramaic word for 'fish' or 'mouth' or 'stater' evoking the Aramaic or Greek or Hebrew word for 'custom' or 'tribute' or 'shekel'. Alternately, perhaps mention of the stater in the fish's mouth was added to the story at a later date, with the original verse only reading, *"But so that we might not offend them, having gone to the sea, cast in a hook, and take the first fish having come up; and having taken that, give that to them for me and you."* What if Jesus was actually proposing to pay the tax with a fish? Is there perhaps a link to be made here between this fish and some Mediterranean tradition or cult?

56. (page 180) Nevertheless, while he may have found himself the butt of a joke and empty-handed this time around, the next time Simon Peter went fishing things would turn out very differently – see John 21:1-11.

57. (page 180) Which is hardly consistent with Jesus' usual indifference to 'offending' others, or causing them to 'stumble':

Mt 11:6 – *"Blessed is he who finds no occasion for stumbling in me."*

Mt 13:57 – *They were offended by him. But Jesus said to them, "A prophet is not without honor, except in his own country, and in his own house."*

Mt 15:2-14 – *Then the disciples came, and said to him, "Do you know that the Pharisees were offended, when they heard this saying?" | But he answered, […] | " […] They are blind guides of the blind. If the blind guide the blind, both will fall into a pit."*

Mt 26:31 – *Then Jesus said to them, "All of you will be made to stumble because of me tonight […]"*

Nor does he ever pull punches when lambasting Pharisees and lawyers – cf. Luke 11:39-52. So I don't think Jesus worried too much about causing offense.

58. (page 182) In the Jesus-movement that followed, and more broadly in all the centuries since, these words seem to have fallen on deaf Christian ears.

59. (page 185) My reason for suspecting this is that Simon neglected to give Jesus water with which to wash his feet (Lu 7:44), though it was customary: 'Since the Israelites, like all other Oriental peoples, wore sandals instead of shoes, and as they usually went barefoot in the house, frequent washing of the feet was a necessity. Hence among the Israelites it was the first duty of the host to give his guest water for the washing of his feet (Gen. XVIII. 4, XIX. 2, xxiv. 32, XLIII. 24; Judges XIX. 21); to omit this was a sign of marked unfriendliness.' – 'FEET, WASH-

ING OF', *Jewish Encyclopedia*, 1906.

Since it is hard to imagine a Pharisee expressly inviting Jesus to dinner and then being such a rudely inconsiderate host when his guest arrives, this breach of etiquette sounds to me more like the behavior of someone who is on decidedly familiar terms with Jesus – such as his disciple Simon Peter.

60. (page 187) If we consider Numbers 19:22 – *"Whatever the unclean person touches shall be unclean; and the soul that touches it shall be unclean until evening"* – it may be that Simon, knowing the woman to be a prostitute, considered that Jesus would be rendered 'unclean' by her touch.

61. (page 188) Josephus reports that it was Herodias who took it upon herself *'to confound the laws of our country, and divorced herself from her husband while he was alive'* – see his *Antiquities of the Jews*, Book XVIII, chapter 5, 4 (translation by William Whiston).

62. (page 188) Viewed in that light, Jesus definitely ran the risk of provoking Herodias' ire by saying that *"If a woman herself divorces her husband, and marries another, she commits adultery."* (Mark 10:12)

63. (page 193) As explained in note 7 above, I think we might reasonably wonder if Mary had gotten herself pregnant by a Samaritan lover. Impetuous young love notwithstanding, Mary and her beau could never have overcome the unyielding animosity that existed between their two disparate branches of Judaism: the star-crossed couple would have been forbidden to marry by their respective clans. Jesus may have rejected marriage for being an instrument of society's *status quo*.

64. (page 193) There is no evidence that Jesus was ever married; then again, there is no evidence that he wasn't, either. As for the many female followers – including Mary Magdalene – who were apparently accompanying Jesus and even 'serving' him and the twelve from their private means or possessions, we learn from Luke 8:1-3 that at least one, Joanna, was married.

65. (page 194) 'WHILST A MINOR IS EXEMPT, SINCE HE DOES NOT COME WITHIN THE SCOPE OF THE COMMANDMENTS.' – The Babylonian Talmud, *op. cit.*, *Tractate Sanhedrin*, chapter VIII, folio 68b.

It's probably too lovey-dovey for most readers' tastes, but also I like to think that children are 'the kingdom of God' because they have not yet begun to judge and condemn; they have not yet been infected with the notion of sin and so inoculated against spontaneous fun. They welcome each day with fresh wonder and joy; they live in the moment and follow their whims.

Then again, if you prefer, we might consider Sophocles, who, writing some four centuries earlier, set childhood apart from all that follows:

> *The simple playtime of our youth behind,*
> *What woe is absent, what fierce agony?*
> *Strife, and the bloody test*
> *Of battle, envy and hatred – and at length*
> *Unloved, unkind,*
> *Unfriended age, worst ill of all, and last,*
> *Consumes our strength.*

> – Sophocles, *Oedipus at Colonus*, in *The Theban Plays*, translated by
> E.F. Watling (London, Penguin Books, 1947) p. 109.

Perhaps the simple playtime of youth was a kingdom of God for Jesus.

66. (page 194) That children are not held accountable for their vows is found in the Mishnah, *Tractate Niddah*, chapter v, folio 45b. That they are not responsible for their sins obtains from Jewish tradition that can at least be dated to the second century CE – e.g., Eleazar b. Simeon's statement that 'You are responsible for your son till he is thirteen; then say, "Blessed be He who has rid me of responsibility for this."' (Gen. R., 63.10)

67. (page 215) Geza Vermes has this to say about Matthew's addition of a colt: 'In order to associate the event with a messianic prophecy, Matthew rewrote Mark, and introduced a she-ass as well as her colt. His story is laboured and artificial. The quotation 'Tell the daughter of Zion, Behold, your king is coming to you, humble, and mounted on an *ass*, and on *a colt, the foal of an ass*' (Matt. 21:5) does not come directly from the Hebrew Bible or from the Greek Septuagint, but results from a combination of Isaiah 62:11 with an otherwise unknown form of Zechariah 9:9. Matthew's understanding of the text is idiosyncratic. He deliberately overlooks that in the poetry of Zechariah 'a colt, the foal of an ass' is a mere literary parallelism. The prophet envisaged a single donkey and not a mother together with her young. Nevertheless the Greek Matthew (21:7) speaks of *two* animals: the garments were placed on '*them*', and in some curious way Jesus was sitting on them (two donkeys)! No native Semitic speaker would have made such a mistake.' – Geza Vermes, *The Authentic Gospel of Jesus* (London, Penguin Books, 2003), pp. 21-22.

68. (page 215) The Synoptic Gospels all state that the crowds spread their cloaks on the road. If we link this to 2 Kings 9:13, we may suppose that for the Jews, the gesture was associated with the proclamation of a newly anointed king: *Then they*

hurried, and each man took his cloak, and put it under him on the top of the stairs, and blew the trumpet, saying, "Jehu is king."

Luke only mentions the cloaks, but Matthew and Mark both assert that the crowds cut branches from trees as well:

Mt 21:8 – *A very great multitude spread their clothes on the road. Others cut branches from the trees, and spread them on the road.*

Mr 11:8 – *Many spread their garments on the way, and others were cutting down branches from the trees, and spreading them on the road.*

Thus, the popular notion of a crowd waving palm fronds only derives from John's account – which, incidentally, has no cloaks at all:

Jn 12:12,13 – *On the next day a great multitude had come to the feast. When they heard that Jesus was coming to Jerusalem, | they took the branches of the palm trees, and went out to meet him, and cried out, "Hosanna! Blessed is he who comes in the name of the Lord, the King of Israel!"*

Palm trees are not native to Jerusalem, so if the crowds were waving palm branches, one supposes they must have brought them in beforehand from somewhere else – perhaps Jericho, which was known as 'the city of palm trees' (De 34:3). This is something they might have done in the fall: of the three pilgrimage festivals celebrated in Jerusalem, the Feast of Booths, or Tabernacles, called for the use of palm branches:

Le 23:40 – *"You shall take on the first day the fruit of goodly trees, branches of palm trees, and boughs of thick trees, and willows of the brook; and you shall rejoice before Yahweh your God seven days."*

However, since palm fronds play no role in Pesach, or Passover – and since the Feast of Tabernacles wouldn't be celebrated for another six months – I rather doubt the crowds would have come to Jerusalem in the spring bearing palm branches.

69. (page 219) Again, it is a premise of *The Gospel of Jesus of Nazareth* that YHWH, inherently divided against himself, brings about his own downfall, a denouement that Jesus was seeking to initiate with his sacrificial death.

70. (page 226) John's gospel would seem to support this notion:

Jn 18:31 – *Pilate therefore said to them, "Take him yourselves, and judge him according to your law."*

Likewise, in his *Antiquities of the Jews*, Josephus conveys that the Roman rulers were inclined to respect and safeguard the Jews in their religious practices and in their temple, so as to maintain peace within the empire.

For example, Josephus tells us that in an edict issued on behalf of the Jews of Alexandria, Tiberius Claudius Caesar ordered that they *'be not deprived of their rights and privileges, on account of the madness of Caius; but that those rights and privileges, which they formerly enjoyed, be preserved to them, and that they may continue in their own customs.'* This was extended in a second decree *'to the Jews which are in all the Roman Empire'* : *'It will therefore be fit to permit the Jews, who are in all the world under us, to keep their ancient customs, without being hindred so to do.'* (Book XIX, chapter 5, 3) In his letter to the Alexandrians, Claudius himself wrote, *'I conjure you that, on the one hand, the Alexandrians show themselves forebearing and kindly towards the Jews who for many years have dwelt in the same city, and dishonor none of the rites observed by them in the worship of their god, but allow them to observe their customs as in the time of the Deified Augustus, which customs I also, after hearing both sides, have sanctioned.'* – 'Letter of the Emperor Claudius to the Alexandrians', P. London 1912, CPJ I 151. Claudius' 41 CE letter postdates Jesus' time by up to a decade, but it tells us that the Jews of Alexandria had enjoyed religious freedoms since the time of Caesar Augustus. One supposes that such freedoms would have been enjoyed by Jews throughout the Roman Empire.

Josephus subsequently relates that Publius Petronius lambasted *'the magistrates of Doris'* for allowing a statue of Caesar to be set up in *'a synogogue of the Jews.'* Reminding them that *'every one should have the power over the places belonging peculiarly to themselves, according to the determination of Cæsar; [...] which gives the Jews leave to make use of their own customs, as also gives order, that they enjoy equally the rights of citizens with the Greeks themselves,'* Petronius exorted them to *'take care that no handle be hence taken for raising a sedition or quarrel among them, [...] that the nation of the Jews may have no occasion given them of getting together, under the pretence of avenging themselves, and become tumultuous. [...] The Jews ought not to be deprived of those rights which Augustus hath granted them. I therefore charge you, that you do not, for the time to come, seek for any occasion of sedition or disturbance, but that every one be allowed to follow their own religious customs.'* (Book XIX, chapter 6, 3)

In Book XX of his *Antiquities of the Jews*, Josephus relates how Nero upheld the right of the Jews to keep a wall that they had erected to block Agrippa's view of the temple:

About the same time king Agrippa built himself a very large dining-room in the royal palace at Jerusalem, near to the portico. Now this palace had been erected of old by the children of Asamoneus, and was situate upon an elevation, and afforded a most delightful prospect to those that had a mind to take a view of the city, which prospect was desired by the king; and there he could lie down, and eat, and thence observe what was done in the temple: which thing, when the chief men of Jerusalem saw, they were very much displeased at it; for it was not agreeable to the institutions of our country or law, that what was done in the temple should be viewed by others, especially what belonged to the sacrifices. They therefore erected a wall upon the upper-most building which belonged to the inner-court of the temple towards the west, which wall, when it was built, did not only intercept the prospect of the dining-room in the palace, but also of the western cloisters that belonged to the outer-court of the temple also, where it was that the Romans kept guards for the temple at the festivals. At these doings both king Agrippa, and principally Festus the procurator, were much displeased; and Festus ordered them to pull the wall down again: but the Jews petitioned him to give them leave to send an embassage about this matter to Nero; for they said they could not endure to live if any part of the temple should be demolished: and when Festus had given them leave so to do, they sent ten of their principal men to Nero, as also Ismael the high-priest, and Helcias the keeper of the sacred treasure. And when Nero had heard what they had to say, he not only forgave them what they had already done, but also gave them leave to let the wall they had built stand. – Flavius Josephus, *Antiquities of the Jews*, Book xx, chapter 8, 11 (translation by William Whiston).

71. (page 229) Jesus could have taken the quite defendable position that paying tribute to Caesar was not unlike Zedekiah having to submit to the king of Babylon (a punishment that was decreed by YHWH – cf. Jer 27:1-15), or Zedekiah's brother Jehoiakim having to pay tribute to Pharaoh Neco (cf. 2Ki 23:34,35).[72]

72. (note 71) The young Egyptian pharaoh, incidentally, was apparently a protégé of YHWH:

2Ch 35:20-22 – *After all this, when Josiah had prepared the temple, Neco king of Egypt went up to fight against Carchemish by the Euphrates, and Josiah went out against him. | But he sent ambassadors to him, saying, "What have I to do with you, you king of Judah? I come not against you today, but against the house with which I have war. God has commanded me to make haste. Beware that it is God who is with me, that he not destroy you." | Nevertheless Josiah would not turn his face from him, but disguised himself, that he might fight with him, and didn't listen to the words of Neco from the mouth of God, and came to fight in the valley of Megiddo.*

Who could blame Josiah for not heeding Neco's threat? What, is a Jewish king supposed to take a pagan's word? If YHWH had wanted his servant Josiah to let the Egyptian pharaoh pass through the Promised Land unchallenged, surely he'd have told him so through proper channels – a **Jewish** prophet! Besides, Josiah was praised for being good – *He did that which was right in Yahweh's eyes, and walked in the ways of David his father, and didn't turn aside to the right hand or to the left.* This was the guy who'd purged Judah of idolatrous worship (2Ch 34:2-7), rebuilt the temple (2Ch 34:8-13), renewed the covenant with YHWH (2Ch 34:14-18,29-32), and celebrated a Passover to beat all Passovers (2Ch 35:1-19).

2Ch 34:33 – *Josiah took away all the abominations out of all the countries that belonged to the children of Israel, and made all who were found in Israel to serve, even to serve Yahweh their God. All his days they didn't depart from following Yahweh, the God of their fathers.*

In fact, it was for all that that YHWH had promised him a peaceful end through Huldah the prophetess:

2Ch 34:23-28 – *"Yahweh, the God of Israel says: 'Tell the man who sent you to me, | "Yahweh says, 'Behold, I will bring evil on this place, and on its inhabitants, even all the curses that are written in the book which they have read before the king of Judah. | Because they have forsaken me, and have burned incense to other gods, that they might provoke me to anger with all the works of their hands; therefore my wrath is poured out on this place, and it will not be quenched.'"' | But to the king of Judah, who sent you to inquire of Yahweh, you shall tell him this, 'Yahweh, the God of Israel says: "About the words which you have heard, | because your heart was tender, and you humbled yourself before God, when you heard his words against this place, and against its inhabitants, and have humbled yourself before me, and have torn your clothes, and wept before me, I also have heard you," says Yahweh. | "Behold, I will gather you to your fathers, and you will be gathered to your grave in peace. Your eyes won't see all the evil that I will bring on this place and on its inhabitants."'"*

Giving up idolatry and rebuilding the temple and observing the covenant and faithfully serving their tribal god according to all the words that were written in his Law may not have done the Jews as a whole a whole lot of good – YHWH still said he would pour out his wrath on them in the decades to come – but for their good king Josiah it would be different: he'd go to his grave in peace.

So when Pharaoh Neco came a-calling, Josiah must have thought the Egyptian a pagan liar when he said, *"God has commanded me to make haste. Beware that it is God who is with me, that he not destroy you."*

'Neco, my boy,' Josiah may have said quite coolly, feeling himself invincible, 'you're forgetting Moses and what happened to your forebear. My god YHWH is the God of Israel, not pagans like you.'

2Ch 35:23,24 – *The archers shot at king Josiah; and the king said to his servants, "Take me away, because I am seriously wounded!" | So his servants took him out of the chariot, and put him in the second chariot that he had, and brought him to Jerusalem; and he died, and was buried in the tombs of his fathers. All Judah and Jerusalem mourned for Josiah.*

Can you beat that? Josiah must have felt sorely betrayed. 'Hey, YHWH! Since when is going to one's grave under a hailstorm of arrows "going in peace"?'

73. (page 229) Well, in those days, the Tyrian shekel would have had to do, but I don't suppose YHWH was picky, so long as he collected his due.

74. (page 238) Again, it is my view that Jesus understood 'God' as being utterly distinct from YHWH, and that God's kingdom is not an earthly nor even a heavenly 'kingdom', but a state of spiritual awakening and self-awareness.

75. (page 246) To come in someone's name is to assert that what you are saying is commanded by that person or god – cf. De 18:18-20, 1Sa 25:5.

76. (page 248) Matthew 24:5 makes even less sense if one believes that Jesus was himself the messiah: if the imposters come in his name, how can they claim in the *messiah*'s name that *they* are in fact the messiah?

77. (page 257) 'PASSOVER SACRIFICE', *Jewish Encyclopedia*, 1906.

78. (page 258) Contradicting John, the Synoptics imply that Jesus celebrated the Passover Seder with his disciples. Some scholars account for this by arguing that Jesus celebrated the meal according to the Essene calendar – cf. for example Annie Jaubert in *The Date of the Last Supper* (New York, Alba House, 1965). I do not hold with such views.

79. (page 259) When all is said and done, it's to wonder why YHWH kept the Jews to be his people at all. Bringing them out of Egypt, he'd found out what they were like. Anyone could see they weren't going to be good slaves: *Yahweh said to Moses, "I have seen these people, and behold, they are a stiff-necked people."* (Ex 32:9)

80. (page 259) The practice of anointing a corpse is mentioned in the Mishnah – 'ALL THE REQUIREMENTS OF THE DEAD MAY BE DONE; HE MAY BE ANOINTED WITH OIL AND WASHED' (*Tractate Shabbath*, chapter XXIII, folio 151a – The Babylonian Talmud, *op. cit.*) – and in the Gospels: Mark 16:1; Luke 23:55,56; John 12:7, 19:39,40.

81. (page 260) It was also common practice, in general, to apply oil to the head: 'As a means of soothing the skin in the fierce heat of the Palestinian climate, oil seems to have been applied to the exposed parts of the body, especially to the face (Ps. CIV. 15); that this was a part of the daily toilet may be inferred from Matt. VI. 17.' – 'ANOINTING', *Jewish Encyclopedia*, 1906.

Further, the Talmud stipulates that when it comes to applying oil, one must anoint the head first: 'When one anoints with oil, […] one who desires to anoint his whole body must anoint his head first, because it is the king of all the limbs (*i.e., the most important*).' – *Tractate Shabbath*, chapter vi, folio 61a – The Babylonian Talmud, *op. cit.*

82. (page 266) What, you want examples? Oh, ye of little faith! Well, all right, but just a few:

Mt 4:1 – *Then Jesus was led up by the Spirit into the wilderness* […]

Mt 5:1 – *Seeing the multitudes, he went up onto the mountain.* […]

Mt 8:1 – *When he came down from the mountain* […]

Mt 8:5 – *When he came into Capernaum* […]

Mt 8:28 – *When he came to the other side, into the country of the Gergesenes* […]

Mt 9:1 – *He entered into a boat, and crossed over, and came into his own city.*

Mt 11:1 – *When Jesus had finished directing his twelve disciples, he departed from there to teach and preach in their cities.*

Mt 13:1 – *On that day Jesus went out of the house, and sat by the seaside.*

Mt 13:36 – *Then Jesus sent the multitudes away, and went into the house.* […]

Mt 13:53,54 – *When Jesus had finished these parables, he departed from there.* | *Coming into his own country, he taught them in their synagogue* […]

Mt 15:21 – *Jesus went out from there,* […] *into the region of Tyre and Sidon.*

Mt 15:29 – *Jesus departed there, and came near to the sea of Galilee; and he went up into the mountain, and sat there.*

Mt 21:17 – *He left them, and went out of the city to Bethany* […]

Mt 21:18 – *Now in the morning, as he returned to the city* […]

Mt 26:30 – *When they had sung a hymn, they went out to the Mount of Olives.*

Mr 1:35 – *Early in the morning, while it was still dark, he rose up and went out, and departed into a deserted place* […]

Mr 2:13 – *He went out again by the seaside.* […]

Mr 6:1 – *He went out from there. He came into his own country* […].

Mr 11:11 – *Jesus entered into the temple in Jerusalem. When he had looked around at everything, it being now evening, he went out to Bethany with the twelve.*

Mr 11:12 – *The next day, when they had come out from Bethany, he was hungry.*

Mr 11:15 – *They came to Jerusalem, and Jesus entered into the temple* […]

Mr 11:19 – *When evening came, he went out of the city.*

Mr 11:27 – *They came again to Jerusalem* […]

Mr 14:26 – *When they had sung a hymn, they went out to the Mount of Olives.*

Lu 4:1 – *Jesus, full of the Holy Spirit, returned from the Jordan, and was led by the Spirit into the wilderness*

Lu 4:31 – *He came down to Capernaum, a city of Galilee.* […]

Lu 7:1– *After he had finished speaking* [...], *he entered into Capernaum.*

Lu 22:39 – *He came out, and went, as his custom was, to the Mount of Olives.* [...]

Jn 2:12 – *After this, he went down to Capernaum* [...]

Jn 3:22 – *After these things, Jesus came with his disciples into the land of Judea.* [...]

Jn 4:43 – *After the two days he went out from there and went into Galilee.*

Jn 5:1 – *After these things* [...] *Jesus went up to Jerusalem.*

Jn 6:1 – *After these things, Jesus went away to the other side of the sea* [...]

Jn 8:1 – *But Jesus went to the Mount of Olives.*

Jn 10:1 – *He went away again beyond the Jordan* [...]

Jn 12:1 – *Then six days before the Passover, Jesus came to Bethany* [...]

Jn 18:1 – *When Jesus had spoken these words, he went out with his disciples over the brook Kidron, where there was a garden, into which he and his disciples entered.*

That's not a complete list, by any means, but you get the idea.

83. (page 267) Cf. Genesis 18:4, 19:2, 24:32, 43:24; Judges 19:21; Luke 7:44. See also note 59, above.

84. (page 267) The Pharisee may have been expecting Jesus to wash not only his hands and forearms, but to bathe himself entirely before eating:

Mr :7:3,4 – *For the Pharisees and all the Jews, don't eat unless they wash their hands and forearms, holding to the tradition of the elders.* | *They don't eat when they come from the marketplace unless they bathe themselves.* [...]

85. (page 267) Given the numbers of pilgrims present in Jerusalem on such occasions, we may consider it likely that there were long queues at the mikvehs, meaning that people would see to taking their ritual bath even many days in advance of a festival. The key would be to observe the immersion and then to scrupulously safeguard one's ritual purity in the days leading up to the festival (otherwise, it was back to the mikveh and the long queues). This is why the priests refuse to enter the Praetorium in John 18:28 – *They themselves didn't enter into the Praetorium, that they might not be defiled, but might eat the Passover.*

Some think Jesus and his disciples might have possibly taken their ritual bath in the grotto that was discovered in Bethany and explored in the early 1950's – cf. Bargil Pixner, *With Jesus in Jerusalem* (Rosh Pina, Corazin Publishing, 1996), pp. 85-87.

86. (page 269) 'FEET, WASHING OF', *Jewish Encyclopedia*, 1906.

We also find a woman in the Bible who takes this a step further:

1Sa 25:40-42 – *When David's servants had come to Abigail at Carmel, they spoke to her, saying, "David has sent us to you, to take you to him as wife."* | *She arose, and* *bowed herself with her face to the earth, and said, "Behold, your servant is a servant to wash the feet of the servants of my lord." | Abigail hurried, and arose, and rode on a donkey, with five ladies of hers who followed her; and she went after the messengers of David, and became his wife.*

Abigail's offer was a bit over the top. Most women would have only concerned themselves with feet belonging to their husbands.

87. (page 269) At least, as seemed natural to the Greek historian Plutarch, who relates that "[...] Flavonius, seeing that Pompey, having no servants to attend him, was beginning to take off his own shoes, ran up to him, took off his shoes for him, and helped him to anoint himself. And from that time on he continued to wait on him and do for him all the things that servants do, **even down to washing his feet and preparing his meals**. Indeed anyone who saw this generous service, so simple and unaffected, might well have quoted the line: 'How every action of a noble mind is fair!'" – Plutarch, *Pompey*, in *Fall of the Roman Republic: Six Lives by Plutarch*, translated by Rex Warner (Middlesex, Penguin Books, 1958) p. 209.

88. (page 272) Though symbolized by bread and wine, let us make no mistake: this *is* anthropophagy, pure and simple. Symbols have all the force of reality. Indeed, the Roman Catholic Church's teaching on transubstantiation confirms this view.

89. (page 274) *Vine's Complete Expository Dictionary of Old and New Testament Words* (1940).

90. (page 278) Aeschylus presents this view when he has the chorus sing:

> *For fear, enforcing goodness,*
> *Must somewhere reign enthroned,*
> *And watch men's ways, and teach them,*
> *Through self-inflicted sorrow,*
> *That sin is not condoned.*
> *What man, no longer nursing*
> *Fear at his heart – what city,*
> *Once fear is cast away,*
> *Will bow the knee to Justice*
> *As in an earlier day?*
>
> > – Aeschylus, *The Eumenides*, in *The Oresteian Trilogy*, translated by
> > Philip Vellacott (Middlesex, Penguin Books, 1959) p. 165.

91. (page 279) It is odd that Christians should vilify Judas for this. Had Jesus not been handed over, had Jesus not stood trial and been condemned to death, he

would never have been crucified – and if Jesus had not been crucified, Christianity would not exist. Surely Christians should venerate Judas as the *Patron Saint of Complicity with God's Great Plan*.

92. (page 283) I have wondered whether Judas might have originally hailed from one of the cities of the Decapolis, and not from Galilee like his fellow disciples. The Greek Ἰσκαριώθ used in Mark sounds similiar to the Hebrew *miq-qiryoth*, which means 'from the cites' (cf. Nu 21:28, where *miq-qiryat*, in the singular, means 'from the city'). Given that *Ir* also means 'city' in Hebrew, and that the 'sc' in Iscariot can be a 'q', *Judas Iscariot* may derive from the Hebrew and mean 'Judas *of one* city from the cities' – in other words, one of the cities of the Decapolis.*

As mentioned earlier, it is my view that Judas originally met Jesus on the banks of the Jordan, where many Judeans came to hear John the Baptist. If Judas were the one disciple to hail from somewhere other than Galilee, I think he would be seen and probably treated as an outsider by his fellow apostles. It would also make him Jesus' ideal confidant, for he would be less likely to share secrets with those who saw him as being different.

93. (page 284) 'To be denied burial was the most humiliating indignity that could be offered to the deceased, for it meant "to become food for beasts of prey" (Deut. xxviii. 26; I Kings xiii. 22, xiv. 11, xxi. 24; II Kings ix. 34-37; Jer. vii. 33; viii. 1, 2; ix. 21 [22]; xiv. 16; Ezek. xxix. 5; Ps. lxxix. 2, 3). The law, therefore, requires even the criminal to be buried who has been put to death (Deut. xxi. 23).' – 'Burial', *Jewish Encyclopedia*, 1906.

That not being properly buried was deemed an indignity in the ancient world is also made clear by Sophocles' play *Antigone*.

Interestingly, crucifixion implied being denied burial: 'The body remained on the cross, food for birds of prey until it rotted, or was cast before wild beasts.' – 'Crucifixion', *Jewish Encyclopedia*, 1906.

94. (page 291) We see the importance of this elsewhere in the Mediterranean in such works as Sophocles' play *Oedipus at Colonus*, when the chorus instructs Oedipus on how to pour his offering with the decorated chalices – *"Three times you must pour – emptying them with the last."*

Likewise, as Isabelle Torrance observes, 'Auspicious prayer was tripartite in structure, consisting of invocation, argument, and request.' – *Aeschylus: Seven*

---

* In researching support for this conjecture, I am indebted to Robert Crotty for his help with the Hebrew and Greek. It was he who proposed that putting *I* or *Ir* together with *scarioth* could be 'one city from the Cities'.

Against Thebes (London, Bloomsbury Academic, 2007), p. 57.

By the same token, an insult thrice repeated could have disastrous conse-quences: 'Like Peter, who denied Christ three times, Laius had defied Apollo three times, returning to the oracle each time in hope of a different answer to his query (746). His ultimate disregard for Apollo's warning caused his sin to remain into the third generation (744-5), which recalls the Old Testament [*sic*] God of Exodus 20.5-6, who visits the sins of the fathers upon the children of the third and fourth generations.' – *Ibid.*, p. 56.

95. (page 291) Consider, though, what Jesus teaches his disciples elsewhere about prayer: *"When you pray, you shall not be as the hypocrites, for they love to stand and pray […] that they may be seen by men. […] | But you, when you pray, enter into your inner room, and having shut your door, pray to your Father who is in secret, and your Father who sees in secret will reward you openly. | In praying, don't use vain repeti-tions, as the Gentiles do; for they think that they will be heard for their much speaking."* (Mt 6:5-7) Yet here he prays openly, that he may be seen by his disciples, and he repeats his prayer three times, which surely amounts to the 'vain repetition' that he pokes fun at – *"they think that they will be heard for their much speaking."*

Thus, in praying publicly and with what he would consider 'unnecessary' rep-etition on this one occasion, Jesus clearly has a purpose – to fulfill the prevailing standards of prayer as they were widely understood, so that his followers could be sure that he had observed proper prayer protocol; and to make his disciples witnesses, so that they will fully comprehend Yнwн's crucial responsibility in the events that will follow.

96. (page 292) I feel this readily explains why the other disciples were not made privy to Judas' mission. For the impression to stick, it was necessary that they be kept in the dark.

I suppose we could roughly equate Judas' role with that of a projectionist in a cinema. He gets to see the same film as those in the audience, but he knows better than they the mechanism that is at work behind the scenes.

97. (page 295) Of course, John, who relates this I AM episode, does not follow it up with a trial before the Sanhedrin, so his reasons for doing so are necessarily different.

98. (page 295) However, it is structurally handy in the context of *The Gospel of Jesus of Nazareth* that Jesus here says the Sacred Name twice, for he will now say it one more time before the Sanhedrin and bring the total to three. As we have seen, three is the sum that cinches a deal.

99. (page 304) *Journal de la vie*, n° 126 (Paris, 1973) p. 8.

100. (page 304) As previously noted, I am well aware that the Mishnah cannot be used to support arguments with regard to the Sanhedrin in Jerusalem. My remarks in the pages that follow about the composition of the court and its conduct are therefore purely conjectural, and are to be liberally sprinkled with grains of salt from the Dead Sea.

101. (page 304) *Tractate Sanhedrin*, chapter IV, folio 32a, and chapter I, folio 2a, respectively – The Babylonian Talmud, *op. cit.* I will leave the reader to guess which freely chosen war – of liberation? – Jesus might have been thinking of. (Cf. Luke 21:9,10,20.)

102. (page 305) As follows:
   Mt 26:3,4 – *Then the chief priests, the scribes, and the elders of the people were gathered together in the court of the high priest, who was called Caiaphas. | They took counsel together that they might take Jesus by deceit, and kill him.*
   Mr 11:18 – *The chief priests and the scribes heard it, and sought how they might destroy him.* [...]
   Mr 14:55 – *Now the chief priests and the whole council sought witnesses against Jesus to put him to death* [...].
   Lu 19:47 – *He was teaching daily in the temple, but the chief priests and the scribes and the leading men among the people sought to destroy him.*
   Lu 22:2 – *The chief priests and the scribes sought how they might put him to death, for they feared the people.*

103. (page 306) I know what you're thinking, but there is no evidence that the two others who were crucified with Jesus were these two false witnesses. Sorry.

104. (page 306) In the Gospel accounts, no charge is upheld. In contrast, the *Tractate Sanhedrin* speaks of a Jesus who was found guilty of being a false prophet: "On the eve of the Passover Yeshu (*manuscript M. adds 'the Nasarean'*) was hanged. For forty days before the execution took place, a herald went forth and cried, 'He is going forth to be stoned because he has practised sorcery and enticed Israel to apostasy. Any one who can say anything in his favour, let him come forward and plead on his behalf.' But since nothing was brought forward in his favour he was hanged on the eve of the Passover (*a Florentine manuscript adds: 'and the eve of the Sabbath'*)! – Ulla retorted: 'Do you suppose that he was one for whom a defence could be made? Was he not a Mesith [enticer], concerning whom Scripture says, Neither shalt thou spare, neither shalt thou conceal him?

(*Deut. XIII, 9*) With Yeshu however it was different, for he was connected with the government [or royalty, i.e., influential].'" – The Babylonian Talmud, *op. cit.*, *Tractate Sanhedrin*, chapter VI, folio 43a.

With its tale of a certain Jesus having been afforded every fair chance for a re-trial, the passage could appear as having been wholly fabricated in view of fend-ing off Christian attacks. Well, perhaps…but with due regard for the rabbis who contributed to the Gemara, I am circumspect. Of course, the two additions – the one specifying that it was Jesus *'the Nasarean'*, and the other, that he was hanged on *'the eve of the Sabbath'* – do answer to that charge, since they clearly serve to reinforce the idea that the passage refers to Jesus of Nazareth, who was indeed 'hanged' on the eve of the Sabbath; but if we take out the additions, nothing says that the Yeshu in question was Jesus of Nazareth. He could well have been a di-fferent Jesus, one who was tried and found guilty of apostasy and sentenced to death.

We may note that the passage misrepresents the lawful procedures that might be presumed to have applied at the time of Jesus' trial, for the Mishnah nowhere requires that a herald go about making announcements for a full forty days prior to an execution. Another interesting thing about the passage is that we may de-duce from it that death sentences could indeed be legally carried out on the eve of the Passover, and even on the eve of a Sabbath (according to that Florentine manuscript) – for if such were not the case under Jewish law, the Sanhedrin would not have been presented as having done just that.

105. (page 308) His wasn't the only god's name with this sort of caveat: "The Romans have a goddess whom they call 'the Good Goddess', the same one as the Greeks call 'the Woman's Goddess' […]; the Greeks say that she is that one of the mothers of Dionysus whose name must not be spoken." – Plutarch, *Caesar*, in *Fall of the Roman Republic: Six Lives by Plutarch*, translated by Rex Warner (Middlesex, Penguin Books, 1958) p. 224.

106. (page 308) Originally, simply pronouncing the Name was not considered blasphemous; rather, what counted for blasphemy was 'to curse or revile the same. The later law, however, took the word "nokeb" in the sense of "pronounc-ing" and declared that the Ineffable Name must have been pronounced before the offender could be subjected to the punishment provided by the Law. […] The Mishnah, however, laying stress on the term "nokeb," declares that the blasphem-er is not guilty unless he pronounce the name of God (Mishnah Sanh. VII. 5). […] As long as the Jewish courts exercised criminal jurisdiction, the death penalty was inflicted only upon the blasphemer who used the Ineffable Name […]. According

to Talmudic tradition, the Sacred Name was in early times known to all; but later its use was restricted (Kid. 71a).' – 'BLASPHEMY', *Jewish Encyclopedia*, 1906.

So the correct pronunciation of the Sacred Name was apparently known beyond the strict confines of the Holy of Holies.

107. (page 308) Reference to the tearing of robes is found in the *Tractate Sanhedrin*, folio 56a. It is of interest to note that 'The Talmud bases the custom of rending the garments in such cases upon the Biblical precedent in II Kings XVIII. 37), where Eliakim and others rent their garments when they heard the blasphemy of Rab-shakeh […]. According to R. Hiyya , the rending of garments was no longer required after the fall of the Temple ("He who hears blasphemy nowadays is not obliged to rend his garments, because otherwise his garments would be nothing but tatters,"); for the criminal jurisdiction of the Jewish courts had ceased, and the fear of death no longer deterred the blasphemers. The later law, however, restored the practise of rending the garments.' – 'BLASPHEMY', *Jewish Encyclopedia*, 1906.

108. (page 308) Such testimony would have led to torn robes as well: 'Even in taking testimony during the trial of a blasphemer, the witnesses who heard the blasphemy were not permitted to repeat the very words, but an arbitrary phrase was adopted to indicate the blasphemy. Thus, R. Joshua ben Karhah said: "Throughout the examination of the witnesses, 'Yosé' should be used for YHWH, and they should say, 'Yosé shall strike Yosé,' to indicate the blasphemy" (Mishnah Sanh. VII. 5). At the conclusion of the trial sentence of death could not be passed by such testimony only, and it thus became necessary for one of the witnesses to use once the very words which they had heard. The court directed all persons not immediately concerned in the trial to be removed, and the chief witness was then addressed thus: "State literally what you heard"; and when he repeated the blasphemous words the judges stood up and rent their garments, that being the common sign of mourning. And the rents were not sewed up again, indicating the profound degree of the mourning. After the first witness had thus testified, the second and the following witnesses were not called on to repeat the identical words; but were obliged to say, "I also heard it thus" (Mishnah Sanh. *ib.*).' – 'BLASPHEMY', *Jewish Encyclopedia*, 1906.

109. (page 310) See the excerpt from the *Tractate Sanhedrin*, chapter IV, folio 32a, quoted on page 311, JESUS IS CONDEMNED TO DEATH.

110. (page 311) 'THE BLASPHEMER IS PUNISHED ONLY IF HE UTTERS [THE

DIVINE] NAME.' – The Babylonian Talmud, *op. cit.*, *Tractate Sanhedrin*, chapter VII, folio 55b.

'THE FOLLOWING ARE STONED: HE WHO COMMITS INCEST WITH HIS MOTHER, HIS FATHER'S WIFE, OR HIS DAUGHTER-IN-LAW; HE WHO SEXUALLY ABUSES A MALE OR BEAST; A BLASPHEMER; AN IDOLATER; HE WHO GIVES OF HIS SEED TO MOLECH; A NECROMANCER OR A WIZARD; ONE WHO DESECRATES THE SABBATH; HE WHO CURSES HIS FATHER OR MOTHER; HE WHO COMMITS ADULTERY WITH A BETROTHED MAIDEN; HE WHO INCITES [INDIVIDUALS TO IDOLATRY]; HE WHO SEDUCES [A WHOLE TOWN TO IDOLATRY]; A SORCERER; AND A WAYWARD AND REBELLIOUS SON.' – *Ibid.*, folio 53a.

Although it didn't come up in his trial, Jesus could have been perhaps condemned as well for desecrating the Sabbath (cf. Luke 6:1-5), but not for being a wayward and rebellious son (cf. Mark 3:21,31-34), for a wayward and rebellious son is only liable 'FROM THE TIME THAT HE PRODUCES TWO HAIRS UNTIL HE GROWS A BEARD RIGHT ROUND (BY WHICH IS MEANT THE HAIR OF THE GENITALS, NOT THAT OF THE FACE, BUT THAT THE SAGES SPOKE IN POLITE TERMS)' – *Ibid.*, chapter VIII, folio 68b. Hence, the charge of being 'a wayward and rebellious son' can only be made with regard to a boy, not a man: 'The term "man" is used of one who has reached the age of thirteen, and one cannot be declared rebellious once he has reached that age.' – *Ibid.*, footnote, chapter VI, folio 46a.

111. (page 311) *Ibid.*, chapter IV, folio 32a.

112. (page 311) *Ibid.*, chapter VI, folio 42b.
Per the Mishnah, for blasphemy the Sanhedrin would have sentenced Jesus to death by stoning (see above, note 110), not by crucifixion, which was not among the four authorised methods of execution: stoning, burning, slaying (by the sword), and strangulation (cf. *Tractate Sanhedrin*, chapter VII, folio 49b). That they did not proceed with his lapidation suggests that they did not have the freedom to carry out capital punishment under Roman rule – see below, note 117.

113. (page 311) This is not the wording from Matthew 27:4 – which runs, *"I have sinned in that I betrayed innocent blood"* – but rather from Matthew 27:24, where Pilate supposedly washes his hands in front of the crowd and says, *"I am guiltless of the blood of this man – you will see."*

114. (page 314) In like manner, Rabbi Shila did not hesitate to misrepresent a man's crime to the governing authorities, so that they would condemn him to death – see below, notes 117 to 121.

115. (page 321) The sentence would have been the same even if Jesus had not been a Jew: " [...] *The foreigner as well as the native-born, when he blasphemes the Name, shall be put to death."* (Le 24:16)

116. (page 321) Their own laws would have certainly mandated that the Sanhedrin carry out the sentence itself. If their procedures resembled those related in the Mishnah that was compiled by Judah ha-Nasi, then the course of events would have been as follows: "WHEN THE TRIAL IS ENDED (*and the accused is found guilty*), HE [THE CONDEMNED] IS LED FORTH TO BE STONED (*if he be so sentenced*). THE PLACE OF STONING WAS WITHOUT THE COURT, EVEN AS IT IS WRITTEN, BRING FORTH HIM THAT HATH CURSED. A MAN WAS STATIONED AT THE DOOR OF THE COURT WITH THE SIGNALLING FLAG IN HIS HAND, AND A HORSE-MAN WAS STATIONED AT THE DISTANCE YET WITH SIGHT OF HIM (*the signal man*), AND THEN IF ONE (*of the judges*) SAYS, 'I HAVE SOMETHING [FURTHER] TO STATE IN HIS FAVOUR,' HE [THE SIGNALLER] WAVES THE FLAG, AND THE HORSE-MAN RUNS AND STOPS THEM (*from carrying out the sentence until the court has gone into the details to see whether there is any substance in the new statement offered*). AND EVEN IF HE HIMSELF SAYS, 'I HAVE SOMETHING TO PLEAD IN MY OWN FAVOUR,' HE IS BROUGHT BACK, EVEN FOUR OR FIVE TIMES, PROVIDING, HOWEVER, THAT THERE IS SUBSTANCE IN HIS ASSERTION." In like manner, it is stated that "IF THEN THEY FIND HIM INNOCENT, THEY DISCHARGE HIM; BUT IF NOT, HE GOES FORTH TO BE STONED, AND A HERALD PRECEDES HIM [CRYING]: SO AND SO, THE SON OF SO AND SO, IS GOING FORTH TO BE STONED BECAUSE HE COMMITTED SUCH AND SUCH AN OFFENCE, AND SO AND SO ARE HIS WITNESSES. WHOEVER KNOWS ANYTHING IN HIS FAVOUR, LET HIM COME AND STATE IT." If they get as far as the place of execution, then "WHEN HE IS ABOUT TEN CUBITS AWAY FROM THE PLACE OF STONING, THEY SAY TO HIM, 'CONFESS' (*this and any other sins you may have committed*), FOR SUCH IS THE PRACTICE OF ALL WHO ARE EXECUTED, THAT THEY [FIRST] CONFESS, FOR HE WHO CONFESSES HAS A PORTION IN THE WORLD TO COME." "WHEN HE IS ABOUT FOUR CUBITS DISTANT FROM THE PLACE OF STONING, HE IS STRIPPED OF HIS GARMENTS (*in order to hasten his death and lessen the pain*)." – The Babylonian Talmud, *op. cit., Tractate Sanhedrin*, chapter VI, folios 42b, 43a, 43b and 44b.

117. (page 321) That it was at this time unlawful for the Jews to carry out a death sentence on their own initiative is indirectly supported by Agrippa's reaction to Ananus' stoning of James: 'Josephus tells how Festus, the procurator of Judaea, died in office and was succeeded by Albinus. The interregnum provided Ananus, the Sadducean High Priest appointed by Herod Agrippa II, an opportunity to

rid himself of James. James was brought before the Sanhedrin and sentenced to death. The sentence was immediately carried out. Ananus was deposed by Agrippa for this unlawful action.' – Robert Crotty, *op. cit.*, p. 42.

While Stephen's execution by stoning could be said to contradict this, it is of note that in the account of his trial given in Acts 7, the Sanhedrin does not follow proper judicial procedure when it comes to judgment and sentencing. Hence, it would seem that the stony outcome was due to an angry mob either acting on impulse with a total disregard for both Jewish and Roman law, or, instead, with tacit approval for their actions from those in power: 'The Jewish authorities were probably authorised by their Roman superiors to carry out such an execution and the Romans would have been quite pleased to see a disturber of the peace dispatched.' (*Ibid.*, p. 44.)

It seems worthwhile to mention that of further interst in this regard is a case involving Rabbi Shila, a third century CE Talmudic authority, who "administered lashes to a man who had intercourse with an Egyptian (var. lec. *Gentile*) woman. The man went and informed against him to the Government, saying: There is a man among the Jews who passes judgment without the permission of the Government. An official was sent to [summon] him. When he came he was asked: Why did you flog that man? He replied: Because he had intercourse with a she-ass. They said to him: Have you witnesses? He replied: I have. Elijah thereupon came in the form of a man and gave evidence. They said to him: If that is the case he ought to be put to death! He replied: **Since we have been exiled from our land, we have no authority to put to death**; you do with him what you please." [118]

The punishment for bestiality was death – cf. Ex 22:19, Le 20:15,16 – and the Mishna states 'HE WHO COMMITS SODOMY WITH A MALE OR A BEAST, AND A WOMAN THAT COMMITS BESTIALITY ARE STONED.' [119] Rabbi Shila's reply therefore indicates that had they had the authority to do so, the Jews would have executed the man. [120]

Granted, this happened a few centuries later, and in Babylonia, not Roman-occupied Judea. Still, the Romans would have had good reason to forbid Jews from carrying out death sentences on fellow Jews if only to preclude them from dealing harshly with delators, who would have been beneficial to Roman interests but held in contempt – and possibly punished with death – by their Jewish compatriots. [121]

118. (notes 117, 120, 121) The Babylonian Talmud, *op. cit.*, *Tractate Berakoth*, chapter IX, folio 58a.

119. (note 117) *Ibid., Tractate Sanhedrin*, chapter VII, folio 54a.

120. (note 117) You might object, 'Wait a minute...Rabbi Shila lied. The man slept with an Egyptian woman – he didn't commit bestiality!' Indeed. But Rabbi Shila's story goes on: "While they were considering his case, R. Shila exclaimed, Thine, Oh Lord, is the greatness and the power. What are you saying? they asked him. He replied: What I am saying is this: Blessed is the All-Merciful Who has made the earthly royalty on the model of the heavenly, and has invested you with dominion, and made you lovers of justice. They said to him: Are you so solicitous for the honour of the Government? They handed him a staff and said to him: You may act as judge. When he went out that man said to him: Does the All-Merciful perform miracles for liars? He replied: Wretch! Are they not called asses? For it is written: Whose flesh is as the flesh of asses." [118] That was a reference to Ezekiel 23:20 – *She lusted after their paramours, whose flesh is as the flesh of donkeys, and whose issue is like the issue of horses* – so Rabbi Shila didn't consider himself a liar.

121. (note 117) Jewish *moserim* have been tried and executed down through the centuries. 'According to Talmudic law, the delator was punished with death; and although in general the jurisdiction of the Jewish courts in criminal cases ceased with the destruction of the Jewish commonwealth, in the case of informers the penalty remained in force, those convicted being punished the more severely because they deliberately increased the danger which constantly threatened the people.' – 'MOSER', *Jewish Encyclopedia*, 1906.

We find this in the story about Rabbi Shila: to punish the man who had informed against him, he accused him of having slept with an ass so that the government could only conclude, "If that is the case he ought to be put to death!" When they then armed Rabbi Shila with a staff and a mandate to act as judge himself, he did not hesitate: "He noticed that the man was about to inform them that he had called them asses. He said: This man is a persecutor, and the Torah has said: If a man comes to kill you, rise early and kill him first. (*This lesson is derived by the Rabbis from Ex. XXII, 2 which declares it legitimate to kill a burglar who is prepared to commit murder.*) So he struck him with the staff and killed him." [118]

See also D. Kaufmann, *Jewish Informers in the Middle Ages*, The Jewish Quarterly Review, Vol. 8, No. 2, Jan., 1896 (University of Pennsylvania Press, Philadelphia), pp. 217-228.

But enough digression! Let's get back to the text. We were on page 321, before we got sidetracked by the question of Roman dictates...

122. (page 325) Pilate, according to Philo, was 'a man of a very inflexible disposition, and very merciless as well as very obstinate […] in respect of his corruption, and his acts of insolence, and his rapine, and his habit of insulting people, and his cruelty, and his continual murders of people untried and uncondemned, and his never ending, and gratuitous, and most grievous inhumanity.' (*On The Embassy of Gaius*, Book XXXVIII, 299-305) That said, who's to say he might not have learned to temper his insensitivity for the feelings of his subjects, following the protests that erupted when he permitted his soldiers to introduce their standards into Jerusalem by night: 'On the next day Pilate sat upon his tribunal, in the open market-place, and called to him the multitude […]. Hereupon Pilate was greatly surprised by their prodigious superstition, and gave order that the ensigns should be presently carried out of Jerusalem.' (*Wars* 2.9.2-3) Having thus experienced firsthand how far the Jews were willing to go when provoked in their 'prodigious superstition',[123] Pilate could have easily guessed that he would be facing yet another riot in this instance. He may have considered Jesus innocent of any crime that would have called for him to be crucified under Roman law, but he surely had no compelling reason to oppose his being put to death, if that is what his Jewish subjects demanded with regard to their own.

123. (note 122) 'After five days of discussion he ordered his soldiers to surround the petitioners and to put them to death unless they ceased to trouble him. He yielded only when he saw that the Jews would rather die than bear this affront.' – 'PILATE, PONTIUS', *Jewish Encyclopedia*, 1906.

His awareness, at least, would have been likewise reinforced by the protests that once again arose when he allowed gilt shields to be hung in Herod's palace in honor of Tiberius (although this incident may have occurred later).

124. (page 325) Pilate's act of washing his hands is of interest. Given Philo's description of the man, it is hard to imagine him feeling any compunction about seeing the innocent Jesus go off to his death; so if he did deliberately perform this act in the sight of the Jewish crowds, it may be that he did so in mockery.

I doubt whether Pilate would have been familiar with Deuteronomy 21:7-9, but the passage in John does bring it to mind: *All the elders of that city, who are nearest to the slain man, shall wash their hands over the heifer whose neck was broken in the valley. | They shall answer and say, "Our hands have not shed this blood, neither have our eyes seen it. | Forgive, Yahweh, your people Israel, whom you have redeemed, and don't allow innocent blood among your people Israel." The blood shall be forgiven them.* This reference may have been the author's intention.

125. (page 329) There is mention of this practice in the Babylonian Talmud: 'Again, what of R. Hiyya b. Ashi's dictum in R. Hisda's name; When one is led out to execution, he is given a goblet of wine containing a grain of frankincense, in order to benumb his senses, for it is written, Give strong drink unto him that is ready to perish, and wine unto the bitter in soul. And it has also been taught; The noble women in Jerusalem used to donate and bring it.' – The Babylonian Talmud, *op. cit., Tractate Sanhedrin*, chapter VI, folio 43a.

126. (page 332) 'The Roman penal code recognized this cruel penalty from remote times (Aurelius Victor Cæsar, 41). It may have developed out of the primitive custom of "hanging" ("arbori suspendere") on the "arbor infelix," which was dedicated to the gods of the nether world. Seneca ("Epistola," 101) still calls the cross "infelix lignum." Trees were often used for crucifying convicts (Tertullian, "Apologia," VIII. 16). **Originally only slaves were crucified;** hence "death on the cross" and "supplicium servile" were used indiscriminately (Tacitus, "Historia," IV. 3, 11). **Later, provincial freedmen of obscure station ("humiles") were added to the class liable to this sentence.** Roman citizens were exempt under all circumstances (Cicero, "Verr." i. 7; III. 2, 24, 26; IV. 10 *et seq.*). The following crimes entailed this penalty: piracy, highway robbery, assassination, forgery, false testimony, mutiny, high treason, rebellion (see Pauly-Wissowa, "Real-Encyc." *s.v.* "Crux"; Josephus, "B. J." v. 11, § 1). Soldiers that deserted to the enemy and **slaves who denounced their masters ("delatio domini") were also punished by death on the cross.'** – 'CRUCIFIXION', *Jewish Encyclopedia*, 1906.

In like manner, Cicero wrote that crucifixion was 'the most miserable and most painful punishment appropriate to slaves alone.' – *Against Verres*, 2.5.169, in *The Orations of Marcus Tullius Cicero*, translated by C. D. Yonge (London, George Bell & Sons, 1903).

127. (page 332) As we have just remarked in note 126, 'slaves who denounced their masters ("delatio domini") were also punished by death on the cross.' This offers an interesting parallel in the context of *The Gospel of Jesus of Nazareth*, which presents Jesus as a 'slave' who denounces his master.

128. (page 334) Matthew 27:56 also singles out three women as being present and looking on from a distance: 1) Mary Magdalene; 2) Mary the mother of James and Joseph; and 3) *'the mother of the sons of Zebedee.'*

Matthew is the only evangelist to speak of James and John's mother. She appears on one other occasion, in Matthew 20:20, in a role that seems designed to save face for her two sons: whereas Mark states that the two brothers had presumptuously asked Jesus to accord them seats of honor (Mark 10:35-41), Matthew lets their mother take the rap.

In this instance, naming James and John's mother as being present at the foot of the cross would have nicely served to increase the two disciples' standing in the eyes of the early Church.

I do not hold with the view that links the mother of James and John in Matthew 27:56 to the Salome who appears in Mark 15:40.

129. (page 334) We may note that Mary's relationship to Clopas is not clearly stated in the John 19:25. The logic of Greek would have it that she be 'the *mother* of' (or possibly 'the *sister* of') whomever is named, since the word 'mother' has twice preceded the article 'the' only a few words before (and the word 'sister' once); so it is a curious assumption indeed that most Bibles make when they say that Mary is the 'wife' of Clopas.

130. (page 334) According to Eusebius of Caesarea, Simeon 'was a cousin, as they say, of the Saviour. For Hegesippus records that Clopas was a brother of Joseph.' – *Church History*, Book III, chapter 11.

131. (page 337) Actually, it was probably two o'clock: 'The animal was slain on the eve of the Passover, on the afternoon of the 14th of Nisan, after the Tamid sacrifice had been killed, *i.e.*, at three o'clock, or, in case the eve of the Passover fell on Friday, at two.' – 'PASSOVER SACRIFICE', *Jewish Encyclopedia*, 1906.

But we've no need to quibble – the evangelist was likely preoccupied with the niceties of style... *third, sixth, ninth*.

132. (page 337) Again, this refers us to the Parable of the Sower – *"Listen! Behold, the farmer went out to sow…"* (Mark 4:3-9).

133. (page 338) That silence expresses acceptance in the ancient world may be attested by the words of Orestes, when he says to Tyndareos, *"In the gods' name – and I know it's not the time, when I am justifying murder, to call on gods – yet, suppose, now, I had approved my mother's act by silence […] ?"* – Euripides, *Orestes*, in *Orestes and Other Plays*, translated by Philip Vellacott (London, Penguin Books, 1972) p. 320.

134. (page 339) Victims of crucifixion generally survived several days and sometimes even longer than a week before their strength failed them; when they could no longer partially support themselves with their legs, and were left to hang only from their arms, a slow suffocation would set in.

Gerald Messadié offers a compelling description of the effects of crucifixion:

> Il était conçu pour maintenir la victime au bord de la suffocation, capable de respirer en s'appuyant à la fois sur ses pieds, pour autant qu'elle pût endurer la tension causée par le clou qui les traversait, et sur un billot triangulaire qui soutenait les fesses, la *sedula*. En effet, la position les bras en extension empêchait le libre jeu des muscles thoraciques et contraignait le crucifié à la respiration superficielle, pénible pour le cœur; en fait, elle se ramène à un halètement. Entre autre effets, la respiration superficielle prolongée entraîne une acidose qui délabre les tissus et réduit la résistance du supplicié proportionnellement à sa constitution, et cela d'autant plus qu'elle s'accompagne d'anoxémie, c'est-à-dire de diminution de la quantité d'oxygène contenue dans le sang. La situation pouvait s'aggraver d'une accumulation de liquide pleural dans la partie inférieure de la plèvre, c'est-à-dire d'une pleurésie.
>
> En tout état de cause, la tétanisation des muscles du thorax, l'acidose, l'anoxémie et la pleurésie éventuelle n'entraînaient pas une mort rapide. Douris, historien, gouverneur de Samos, cité par Hengel, rapporte que les dix chefs de la ville crucifiés par Périclès survécurent dix jours sur le croix; il ne fut mis fin à leur supplice que par fracture du crâne à coups de massue. Les Romains, eux, mettaient fin à la vie du supplicié, si la nature n'y avait pas déjà pourvu par une défaillance d'organe, en brisant ses tibias. Incapable dès lors de se soulever sur ses jambes, ni même par extension du thorax, la *sedula* étant inclinée, le supplicié était entièrement pendu à la croix par ses bras. La tétanisation des muscles thoraciques s'accélérait alors jusqu'à entraîner l'asphyxie terminale.
>
> – Gerald Messadié, *L'homme qui devint Dieu – Les Sources*, (Paris, Editions Robert Laffont, 1989) p. 84.

135. (page 340) I am reminded of Aeschylus, whose Apollo says, '*But when blood of man sinks in the thirsty dust, the life once lost can live no more. For death alone my father has ordained no healing spell; all other things his effortless and sovereign power casts down or raises up at will.*' – Aeschylus, *The Eumenides*, in *The Oresteian Trilogy*, *op. cit.*, p. 169.

136. (page 342) Flavius Josephus, *War of the Jews*, Book IV, chapter 5, 2 (translation by William Whiston).

137. (page 345) The Babylonian Talmud, *op. cit.*, *Tractate Sanhedrin*, chapter VI, folio 46a.

138. (page 345) Only Matthew relates that it was Joseph's own tomb. Mark's account, the earliest written, does not specify that it was a new tomb where no one had ever been buried before.

139. (page 354) As Robert Crotty has ably set out (*op. cit.*, chapter 3, *The Church Story – 'Peter'*), one of the primary aims of the Synoptic Gospels – and in a more conflicted way, John's gospel – was to firmly establish Peter as Jesus' personally chosen successor. Yet there were other contenders in the various early Jesus-movements – James the Just; John; the Hellenists (led by Stephen); Apollos; Paul (who was in competition with Peter); and groups such as the Gnostics and the 'circumcision faction'. It therefore seems to me that the author of John's gospel has written Simon Peter into an earlier story: the *'disciple whom Jesus loved'* is duly acknowledged to be the first to reach the empty tomb, but the privilege of being the first disciple to enter is accorded to his rival runner. That definitely puts Peter in the superior position. Only after Peter has entered and duly witnessed the empty tomb does the first disciple get to enter in and 'believe'.

140. (page 357) Significantly, Shavuot celebrates the giving of the Law on Mount Sinai…so here we go again, with a new religion spawned on the occasion of the Pentecost, i.e. Shavuot.

141. (page 358) Mount Hermon was teeming with pagan worship: dozens of shrines adorned its slopes, and at its summit a temple was apparently dedicated to *'the greatest and holy god'*, according to a stele discovered by Sir Charles Warren in 1869 and today kept in the British Museum – see Julien Aliquot, *Sanctuaries and villages on Mt Hermon during the Roman period*, in *The variety of local religious life in the Near East in the Hellenistic and Roman period*, ed. Ted Kaizer (Leiden, Brill, 2008), p. 82.

Writing in the early 4th century CE, Eusebius had this to say about Hermon: *'Mountain of the Amorrites [which is reported] the Phoenicians called Sanior and the Amorrites called it "This Sanir." They say it is the mountain even now called Mt. Hermon which is revered as a shrine by the gentiles (on its summit is a wonderful temple where the people worship) opposite (near) Paneas and Lebanon.'* – Eusebius of Caesarea, *Onomasticon*, translation by C. Umhau Wolf.

142. (page 362) See Julien Aliquot, *op. cit.*

143. (page 369) As a grieving mother, Mary may have desperately wanted to

believe in what Simon Peter and the others were claiming, namely that Jesus had been resurrected and was alive once again. Their version of events would have offered hope that the crucifixion and death of her firstborn son was but a ghastly nightmare that had somehow been miraculously undone.

144. (page 369) The accounts vary.

In Matthew 28, *'Mary Magdalene and the other Mary came to see the tomb'*, with 'the other Mary' presumably being the *'Mary the mother of James and Joseph'* mentioned earlier in Matthew 27:56. At the tomb, they are greeted by an angel, who scares the bejesus out of them:

Mt 28:8-10 – *They departed quickly from the tomb with fear and great joy, and ran to bring his disciples word. | As they went to tell his disciples, behold, Jesus met them, saying, "Rejoice!" They came and took hold of his feet, and worshiped him. | Then Jesus said to them, "Don't be afraid. Go tell my brothers that they should go into Galilee, and there they will see me."*

So in Matthew, Jesus appears to Mary Magdalene and Mary the mother of James and Joseph.

In Mark 16 – in a passage that however does not appear in the earliest manuscripts – Jesus is said to appear to Mary Magdalene (Mr 16:9).

In John 20, Jesus appears to Mary Magdalene (Jn 20:11-18).

Finally, in Luke 24, we are given to understand that *'the women, who had come with him out of Galilee,'* went to the tomb on the first day of the week and there ran into *'two men'* in *'dazzling clothing'*. Mary Magdalene, Joanna, and Mary the (mother) of James are part of this group, of which there were other women as well. But in marked contrast to his confrères Matthew, Mark and John, the evangelist Luke does not report that any of these women saw the resurrected Jesus.

145. (page 371) And with it, a revised power structure at the top:

Mt 28:19 – *"Go, and make disciples of all nations, baptizing them in the name of the Father and of the Son and of the Holy Spirit."*

Like a Roman triumvirate, the God of Israel was now in league with his resurrected son Jesus and that shadowy, behind-the-scenes puller of strings, the Holy Spirit. Together, they were 'God'. And each separately was 'God', too. See Tertullian, *Against Praxeas*, for a 3rd century defense of such monotheistic polytheism.

146. (page 372) *How many Jews became Christians in the first century? The failure of the Christian mission to the Jews*, by David C Sim, in HTS Vol. 61, n° 1&2, (2005).

147. (page 372) The Roman view of Christianity is neatly summed up by Tacitus: *[Nero] punished with every refinement the notoriously depraved Christians (as*

they were popularly called). Their originator, Christ, had been executed in Tiberius'
reign by the governor of Judaea, Pontius Pilatus. But in spite of this temporary setback
the deadly superstition had broken out afresh, not only in Judaea (where the mischief
had started) but even in Rome. All degraded and shameful practices collect and flourish
in the capital. – Tacitus, *The Annals of Imperial Rome*, translated by Michael Grant
(Middlesex, Penguin Books, 1956; Revised Edition 1985) p. 365.

148. (page 374) In their epistles, Paul and others speak of being a 'slave of Christ'
– cf. Romans 1:1, Galatians 1:10, Jude 1:1, James 1:1, and 2 Peter 1:1, which all
employ the Greek word *doulos*, a 'slave'.

Here we do well to point out that it seems reasonable to surmise that Jesus
was in almost all instances and situations addressed as *Rabbi*. In the Gospels, this
Hebrew word was more often than not translated into Greek as *Didaskale*, or
'Teacher'. We may contrast this with *Kyrie*, or 'Lord',* a form of address which,
as may be gleaned from Seutonius, evoked in the ancient world the master/slave
relationship: *"He always felt horrified and insulted when called 'My Lord', a form of*
address used by slaves to their owners." – Seutonius, *Augustus*, in *The Twelve Caesars*,
translated by Robert Graves (Baltimore, Penguin Books, 1957) §53, p. 80.

In his biography of Tiberius, the historian likewise relates that *"if anyone, either*
in conversation or a speech, spoke of him in too fulsome terms, Tiberius would interrupt
and sternly correct the phrase.[†] *Once, when addressed as 'My Lord and Master', he gave*
warning that no such insult must ever again be thrown at him." – Seutonius, *Tiberius*,
in *The Twelve Caesars, op. cit.*, §27, p. 124.

Given that in the earliest of the four Gospels the use of *Kyrie* ('Lord') to refer to
Jesus is limited to but three instances – Mark 5:19, 7:28, and 11:3 (omitting Mark
16:19 and 16:20, which belong to a passage that is absent from the oldest manuscripts) – we might conjecture that Jesus never once heard himself addressed in
this manner...and would have rebuked anyone who spoke to him thus.

In Matthew's Gospel, the term 'Lord' is employed quite a bit more freely, but
it is Luke and John who really go to town with it: Jesus is overwhelmingly called
Kyrie, establishing an equivalence between YHWH and his Son that casts the die
for Christians to become the slaves of their 'Lord and Savior, Jesus Christ'.

---

* In English, both *Didaskale* and *Kyrie* are also sometimes translated as 'Master', a translational
overlap that obfuscates the marked difference in meaning between the two words: though both
may be said to lord it over their charges, a schoolmaster and a slave master are not the same.

† This calls to mind the way Jesus responded to the man who addressed him as 'Good Teacher':
Jesus said to him, "Why do you call me good? No one is good except one – God." (Mark 10:18)

BIBLICAL QUOTATIONS
AND 'ANCIENT' MANUSCRIPTS

Biblical quotations in this work are taken from the *World English Bible*, a Public Domain translation of the Hebrew and Christian scriptures. Readers are advised that in a few instances, I have availed myself of the provision that words may be changed so long as the meaning of the text is not altered.

In *The Gospel of Jesus of Nazareth*, footnotes make reference to various 'manuscripts', both 'ancient' and 'later', from which the texts supposedly derive. The reader is to understand that this is purely fictive – no such manuscripts exist. My purpose has been to conjecture antecedent readings that would help to clarify those that have come down to us and to explain certain incongruities that are to be found in the authentic Gospel texts. We would imagine that these 'earlier' manuscripts were perhaps written by those unnamed persons who apparently assisted Jesus in his design, and who may have had ties with the 'Moses' and 'Elijah' of Mark 9:4; the household that provided the donkey in Mark 11:2; the man carrying the pitcher of water in Mark 14:13; the 'certain young man' of Mark 14:51 who seems to have been on hand later at the empty tomb in Mark 16:5; and Joseph of Arimathaea, who took charge of Jesus' corpse in Mark 15:46. At any rate, whoever wrote the texts would have been fully conversant with the Scriptures and the intent behind Jesus' teachings and sacrifice. If such persons did exist, we might indeed wonder if they had perhaps contributed to the very conception of Jesus' mission *'to give his life as a ransom for many.'*

ABBREVIATIONS

Italicized reference verses point to parallel passages in the canonical Gospels.
Non-italicized reference verses indicate passages that serve to define and support
the premises advanced by the author's interpretation of the scriptures.

Am	Amos	Joe	Joel
Ca	Song of Solomon	Jon	Jonah
	(Canticles)	Jos	Joshua
1Ch	1 Chronicles	1Ki	1 Kings
2Ch	2 Chronicles	2Ki	2 Kings
Da	Daniel	La	Lamentations
De	Deuteronomy	Le	Leviticus
Ec	Ecclesiastes	Mal	Malachi
Es	Esther	Mic	Micah
Ex	Exodus	Na	Nahum
Eze	Ezekiel	Ne	Nehemiah
Ezr	Ezra	Nu	Numbers
Ge	Genesis	Ob	Obadiah
Hab	Habakkuk	Pr	Proverbs
Hag	Haggai	Ps	Psalms
Ho	Hosea	Ru	Ruth
Isa	Isaiah	1Sa	1 Samuel
Jer	Jeremiah	2Sa	2 Samuel
Jg	Judges	Zec	Zechariah
Job	Job	Zep	Zephaniah

Act	Acts	Mr	Mark
Col	Colossians	Mt	Matthew
1Co	1 Corinthians	1Pe	1 Peter
2Co	2 Corinthians	2Pe	2 Peter
Eph	Ephesians	Phe	Philemon
Gal	Galatians	Phi	Philippians
Heb	Hebrews	Re	Revelation
Ja	James	Ro	Romans
Jn	John	1Th	1 Thessalonians
1Jn	1 John	2Th	2 Thessalonians
2Jn	2 John	1Tm	1 Timothy
3Jn	3 John	2Tm	2 Timothy
Ju	Jude	Ti	Titus
Lu	Luke		

*Over the years, I have been inspired and guided by many teachers,
but I would like to express my deep gratitude to three in particular –*

> *To Larry Lutchmansingh, who taught me how to think…*

> *To Geza Vermes, who awakened in me a keen delight in
> the original Scriptures…*

> *And to Robert Crotty, who nourished my understanding.*

A·B·C· EDITIONS
17840 • LA BREE • FRANCE

REMERCIEMENTS A
FRANCINE FEVRE • ROBERT CROTTY

IMPRIME DANS LE ROYAUME-UNI PAR
INGRAM LIGHTNING SOURCE
CHAPTER HOUSE • PITFIELD • KILN FARM
MILTON KEYNES • MK11 3LW

EDITION ACHEVEE LE 19 SEPTEMBRE 2018
ISBN 978-2-9546352-7-9
PRIX PUBLIC EN FRANCE • 20,00
DEPOT LEGAL OCTOBRE 2018

www.ingramcontent.com/pod-product-compliance
Lightning Source LLC
Chambersburg PA
CBHW050853150626
46549CB00013B/1430